Romanticism

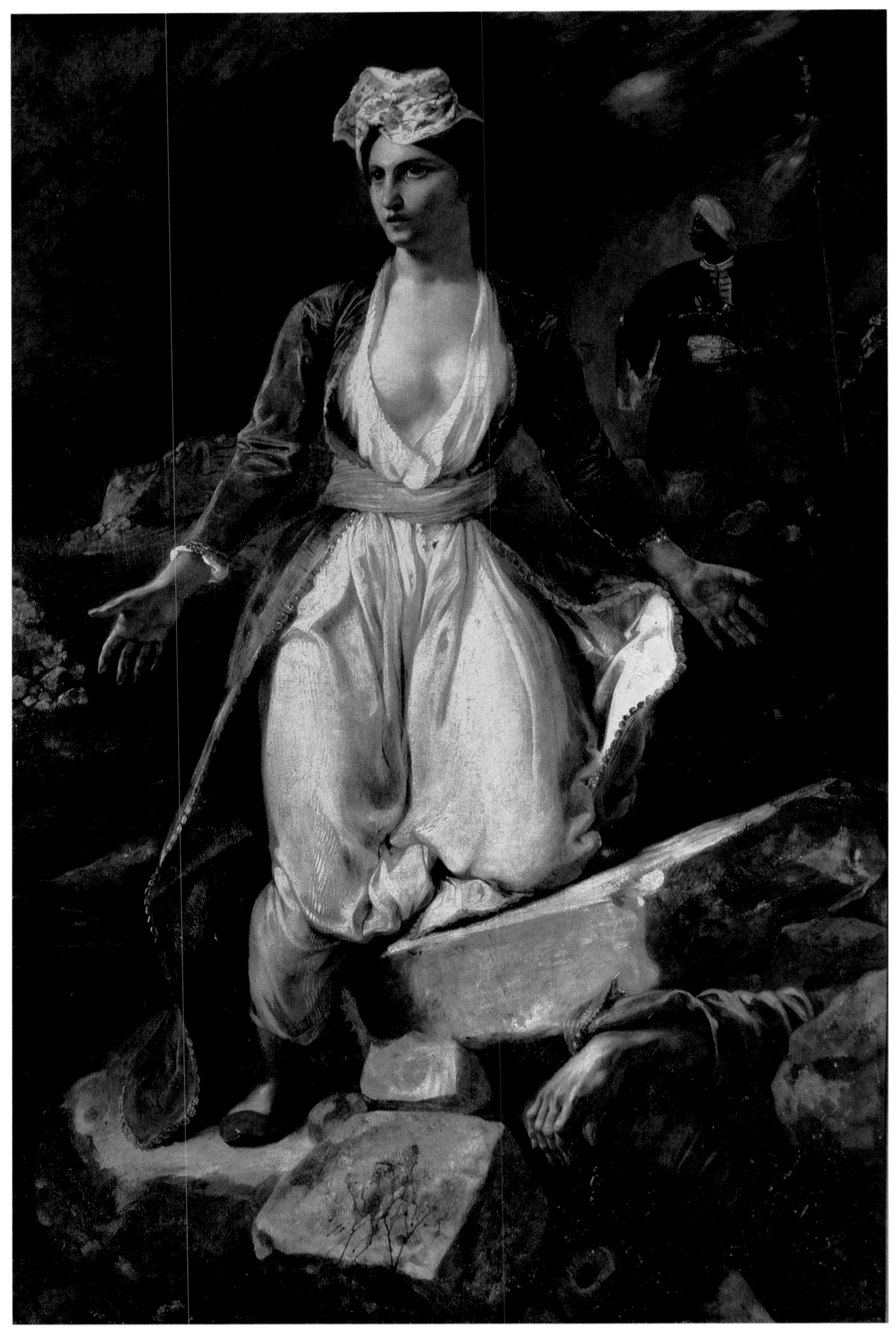

JOSEPH WRIGHT OF DERBY

HENRY FUSELI

FRANCISCO GOYA

JACQUES-LOUIS DAVID

WILLIAM BLAKE

ANNE-LOUIS GIRODET-TRIOSON

CASPAR DAVID FRIEDRICH

JOSEPH MALLORD WILLIAM TURNER

JOHN CONSTABLE

PHILIPP OTTO RUNGE

ILARIA CISERI

Romanticism

1780-1860: THE BIRTH OF A NEW SENSIBILITY

JEAN-AUGUSTE-DOMINIQUE INGRES

FRIEDRICH OVERBECK

THÉODORE GÉRICAULT

FRANCESCO HAYEZ

EUGÈNE DELACROIX

THOMAS COLE

DANTE GABRIEL ROSSETTI

JOHN EVERETT MILLAIS

BARNES & NOBLE BOOKS
NEW YORK

Captions for the preceding pages

Pages 2-3: Caspar David Friedrich, *Moon Rising Over the Sea* (detail), 1820; Nationalgalerie, Berlin
Pages 4-5: Anne-Louis Girodet-Trioson, *The Revolt at Cairo* (detail), 1810; Musée National des Châteaux de Versailles et de Trianon, Versailles
Pages 6–7: Jean-Auguste-Dominique Ingres, *Angelica and Ruggero* (detail), 1819; Musée du Louvre, Paris
Page 8: Eugène Delacroix, *Greece on the Ruins of Missolonghi* (detail), 1826; Musée des Beaux-Arts, Bordeaux

Note to the reader

In each chapter introduction, the page references to illustrations (given in parentheses) refer to works that do not appear in the chapter itself.

ART DIRECTOR
Giorgio Seppi

SENIOR EDITOR
Tatjana Pauli

MANAGING EDITOR
Veronica Buzzano

PAGE LAYOUT
Elàstico, Milan

PICTURE RESEARCH
Valentina Minucciani and Cristina Proserpio

ENGLISH TRANSLATION
Jay Hyams

TYPESETTING
Michael Shaw

This edition published by Barnes & Noble, Inc. by arrangement with Mondadori

2004 Barnes & Noble Books

M 10 9 8 7 6 5 4 3 2 1

ISBN 0-7607-5941-3

Printed and bound in Spain by Artes Gráficas Toledo, SA

Contents

12 Introduction

22 Neoclassicism and pre-Romanticism

40 The myth of Napoleon

58 Portraits: aristocratic ideals and middle-class models

80 Myths and ancient history

102 Historical revival and the fascination of the Middle Ages

118 Contemporary history

138 Daily life and Biedermeier

156 Nazarenes, Purists, and Pre-Raphaelites

176 Images of the sacred

194 The appeal of the Orient and of the exotic

214 The New World

228 Fables and sentimental tales

246 From visionary-fantasy painting to the exploration of the psyche

264 The sublime

284 The presentation of the landscape

300 Exhibitions, museums, and the ateliers of artists

314 Steam, electricity, and the arrival of the camera

326 Novels and literature

346 Melodrama

358 Toward realism

376 1780–1859: Events, artists, works

378 References

379 *Biographies*

394 *Bibliography*

395 *Index of names and places*

399 *Photographic references*

Introduction

"To say Romanticism is to say modern art—that is, intimacy, spirituality, color, aspiration toward the infinite, expressed with all the means available to the arts." With these words Charles Baudelaire, in 1846, summarized the essence of the major cultural movement that took hold of Europe at the beginning of the nineteenth century and remained an element in its history for several decades. A phenomenon of revolutionary import to all sectors of art, from painting to music to the theater, Romanticism had deep roots extending to the very heart of the century of Enlightenment. The major aspects of Romanticism were originally formulated by the members of the German literary movement that flourished between roughly 1770 and 1780 and came to be known as *Sturm und Drang* ("storm and stress"). Taken from the title of a play by Friedrich Maximilian von Klinger, the movement's name reflected the rebellious aspects of its ideological program, based on rejection of the dominant Enlightenment culture, on the exultation of subjective feelings as an uncontrollable force, and on individuality taken as the necessary condition for the creation of any work. This did not represent a sudden break with the accepted standards but was instead the further elaboration of the cult of sentiment and of the great myth of nature presented by the Swiss-French philosopher Jean-Jacques Rousseau at the middle of the eighteenth century and embraced by the German philosopher and dramatist Gotthold Ephraim Lessing. The Sturm und Drang group, initially composed of Johann Gottfried von Herder, Friedrich Gottlieb Klopstock, and Johann Georg Hamann, later came to include other intellectuals, including Johann Wolfgang von Goethe and Friedrich von Schiller. One of the movement's most innovative ideals was the concept of the artistic genius, irrational and creative, no longer disciplined by reason, as during the Enlightenment, but instead animated by an interior will capable of breaking all bonds of laws and conventions and drawing inspiration from subjective realms, thus heeding divine inspiration, intuition, and passion. In substance, this formed the basic profile of the figure of the Titan in revolt, the superman who measures himself against God. Most of all, a new concept of art had come into being, one that understood art as absolute creative freedom, that rejected the limitations imposed by rules and traditions, and that claimed the right of individual fantasy to express itself using its own language—a concept that would come to be identified with the very nature of Romantic art. Although the members of the Sturm und Drang movement opened the way to a new vision of life, including the overflowing of passions and the spontaneity of the individual, they could not be defined as Romantics, most of all because of the opinions they held in the artistic field. Their models of beauty were still based on the classical canons of art, the works of antiquity or those made by modern artists who conformed with the classical criteria of perfection and harmony.

Thomas Lawrence, *Lord Granville Leveson-Gower, First Earl Granville*, 1804, oil on canvas, 238.8 x 144.8 cm; Yale Center for British Art, New Haven

The opposition to classicism that is a fundamental aspect of Romanticism was also originally elaborated in Germany, by the intellectuals who contributed to the magazine *Athenaeum*, founded in 1798 by the brothers August and Friedrich Schlegel. Along with Ludwig Tieck, Friedrich Schelling, and Novalis (pseudonym of Friedrich von Hardenberg), they formed the so-called Jena group, named for the city in which the Schlegels lived, making their home the headquarters of the first Romantics. They were soon joined by other friends, drawn together by their new concept of literature and art. This concept, putting aside Greek and Roman models—and precisely in the very years that saw the triumph of the neoclassical aesthetic—was to be founded on the expression of the irrational and on mysticism, on the sense of the infinite and the immense, on the relationship between interior sentiment and nature. Such affirmations found an immediate echo in a story with an historical character, *Outpourings from the Heart of an Art-Loving Monk*, written by the German poet Wilhelm Heinrich Wackenroder and published in 1797, which expressed a mystical concept of art understood as a gift of God conceding to men the great power of

Caspar David Friedrich, *Morning in the Riesengebirge*, 1811, oil on canvas, 108 x 170 cm; Nationalgalerie, Berlin

creativity. The character of the story's protagonist represented a topos of Romantic culture, that of the intellectual isolated from society but able to interpret the "religion of art." Wackenroder's work inaugurated the genre of the *Künstlerroman*, the novel centered on the figure of an artist; other examples immediately appeared, including *Frans Sternbalds Wanderungen* ("The Wanderings of Frans Sternbald") by Ludwig Tieck (1798) and *Heinrich von Ofterdingen* by Novalis (1801).

Even before the exciting exploits of the Sturm und Drang writers, works like *The Philosophical Enquiry into the Origin of Our Ideas of the Sublime and Beautiful*, published in 1756 by the Anglo-Irish political writer and statesman Edmund Burke, had contributed to attracting the most restless minds to a Romantic vision of nature that resulted in the painting of the sublime and in the mysticism of the landscape carried forward by Caspar David Friedrich. Presenting the theory that the sense of the sublime was a reaction of the soul to the violent manifestations of nature that terrify humans with cataclysms or disconcerting visions, Burke put himself in opposition to the classical concept of nature as a harmony that inspires serenity, as proposed during this same period by Johann Joachim Wincklemann with regard to ancient Greece. Burke's book circulated rapidly throughout Europe, translated in various languages. By the middle of the eighteenth century Britain was experiencing the beginning of the Gothic revival, with its interest in the mysterious aspects of life, thus anticipating a trend later continued in Romantic art. In 1762, not long after Burke's essay, the Scottish author James Macpherson published *The Songs of Ossian*, soon followed by the publication of *The Castle of Otranto* (1765) by Horace Walpole, forerunner of the Gothic romance, the type of novel set in haunted castles with the kind of dark, shadowy atmospheres that Burke referred to as sublime. In 1750, Walpole had begun constructing a home at Twickenham, the celebrated Strawberry Hill, an eccentric Gothic building in the London countryside. Those who followed his example included, near the end of the century, the English author William Beckford. To provide an adequate home for his extraordinary collection of thousands of books and works of art (today divided between the Victoria and Albert Museum and London's National Gallery), he decided to have built nothing less than an enormous Gothic abbey, Fonthill Abbey, with an 84-meter-high tower and doors almost 12 meters high, which he had a dwarf open to give his guests the illusion of even greater height.

Far from weakening during the Romantic age, the fascination of the Middle Ages grew sharper, particularly since that part of the distant past

Pierre Révoil, *A Tournament in the 14th Century*, 1812, oil on canvas, 133 x 174 cm; Musée des Beaux-Arts, Lyons

Karl Friedrich Schinkel, *Cathedral*, 19th century; Kunstsammlungen, Weimar

could be drawn on to provide historical roots to those countries, such as Germany and Italy, that had experienced the foreign invasion of Napoleonic troops and now sought their own national identity. The evocation of the Middle Ages assumed different aspects in art, at times providing an aesthetic to follow, at other times providing only the content, not the form. Certain artists attempted the visual restitution of that world, as in the Gothic cathedrals painted in extreme detail by the German architect Karl Friedrich Schinkel or in the evocative Musée des Antiquités et Monuments Français set up by Alexandre Lenoir in Paris in 1796 and closed in 1816. The Middle Ages also show up in theatrical forms, from operas, which were increasingly based on themes taken from historical dramas, to the sumptuous costume balls at which princes and courtiers dressed up in the costumes of their ancestors.

In painting, two very different currents in terms of background took the subject of medieval life as their objective: the Troubadours and the Nazarenes. The first was a style of history painting that arose between the two centuries in the area between Paris and Lyons and was begun by two young students of Jacques-Louis David, Fleury Richard and Pierre Révoil, who sought to reproduce medieval artistic techniques in paintings of historical episodes or ancient customs (hence the reference to medieval troubadours). Their paintings have an anecdotal flavor and are characterized by the subtle and elaborate reproduction of every detail, as in *A Tournament in the 14th Century*, exhibited by Révoil at the Salon of 1814.

The second current was German in origin and was animated by a more marked nationalism. It had nothing to do with the nostalgic, sentimental approach of the Troubadours and sought to reawaken in the German public ideals of simplicity and national pride through images drawn, in terms of style and content, from the fourteenth century. In Rome, where they had gone in 1810 along with their followers, Franz Pforr and Friederich Overbeck came to be called Nazarenes because of their long-haired, unkempt appearance.

For many decades the Middle Ages furnished subjects for so-called historical Romanticism, painting that turned to examples of past national glories to inspire faith that equally positive events were to come. This point of view became particularly strong in Italy, where the academy artists competed in the production of such works, which were also directly requested by the revolutionary leader Giuseppe Mazzini. This was the social setting behind *The Kiss*, painted by Francesco Hayez in 1859, the year of Italy's second war of independence. The amorous embrace presented in this worked delivered an implicit political message, alluding to the departure for the front of volunteers.

By the end of the eighteenth century the past and antiquity were being interpreted in an anticlassical way by such painters as the Dane Nicolai Abraham Abildgaard and the Swiss-born Englishman Henry Fuseli, both of whom were drawn to the disturbing and irrational aspects of life, those areas ruled by obscure forces like nightmares and the phantoms of the unconscious. A Romantic myth soon took form around Fuseli himself, a result of the wild nature of his figures, the "satanic" power of his creativity, the fantastic and hallucinating world in which his paintings were immersed. His works mark the beginning of a style of painting that, drawing inspiration from the magical figures created by Shakespeare (such as his *Titania Finds the Magic Ring on the Beach*), delved into the world of the fabulous, making use of the Romantic fondness for tales of fairies, sprites, and elves while also turning to visionary themes, those composed of the seductive mixture of the fearsome and the erotic, with an obsession with the unconscious and nocturnal apparitions.

The night was a favorite theme of Romantic creativity, sometimes inhabited by phantoms and creations of visionary minds, sometimes chosen as the setting for amorous encounters or scenes of harmony with the mystery of nature, as in the masterpieces of Caspar David Friedrich. The theme soon spread from painting to music, becoming a genre unto itself in piano compositions with a dreamy melodic line: the *nocturne*, introduced by the Irish composer and pianist John Field and brought to its highest levels by Frédéric Chopin. The *Hymns to the Night* by Novalis date to 1797, the same year in which William Blake finished a colossal series of more than five hundred watercolors made to illustrate Edward Young's long didactic poem *The Complaint, or Night Thoughts on Life, Death, and Immortality* (1742–45), the work with which Young had inaugurated sepulchral literature. The visionary and fantastic side of pre-Romantic art—represented by Fuseli, William Blake, and John Martin—constitutes one of the most fascinating periods of European painting between the two centuries, both for the strong visual involvement of the works and for the thematic connections that emerge from them. Drawing on literary subjects from every epoch, from the Bible to Shakespeare, Dante, and Milton, this genre created the basis for the cult of imagination that was to have a dominant role in the Romantic sensibility. In August of 1799 Blake wrote a friend, "This world is a world of imagination and vision. I see everything I paint in this world, but everybody does not see alike." At a distance of exactly seventy years, Eugène Delacroix noted in his diary that "even in the face of nature, it is our imagination that creates the painting." The imagination of the artist was thus the instrument that revealed the spiritual reality enclosed within the sensible world. It was a sort of mediator between man and nature, a sensibility with which Caspar David Friedrich agreed, believing, as he wrote in 1830, that the painter should place himself in a state of particular concentration: "Close your bodily eye so that you may see your picture first with the spiritual eye."

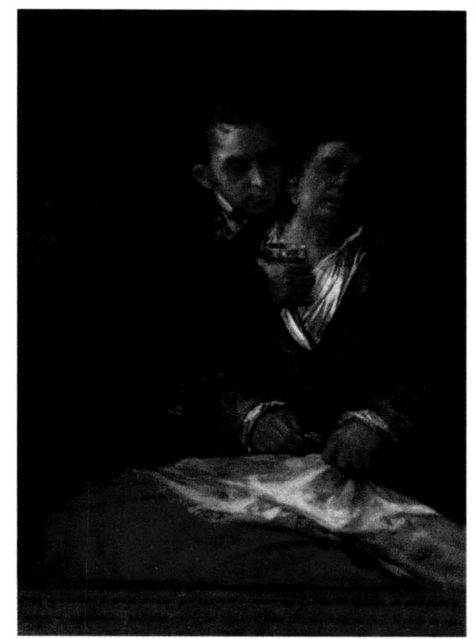

Francisco Goya, *Self-Portrait with Dr. Arrieta*, 1820, oil on canvas, 117 x 79 cm; Minneapolis Institute of Arts, Minneapolis

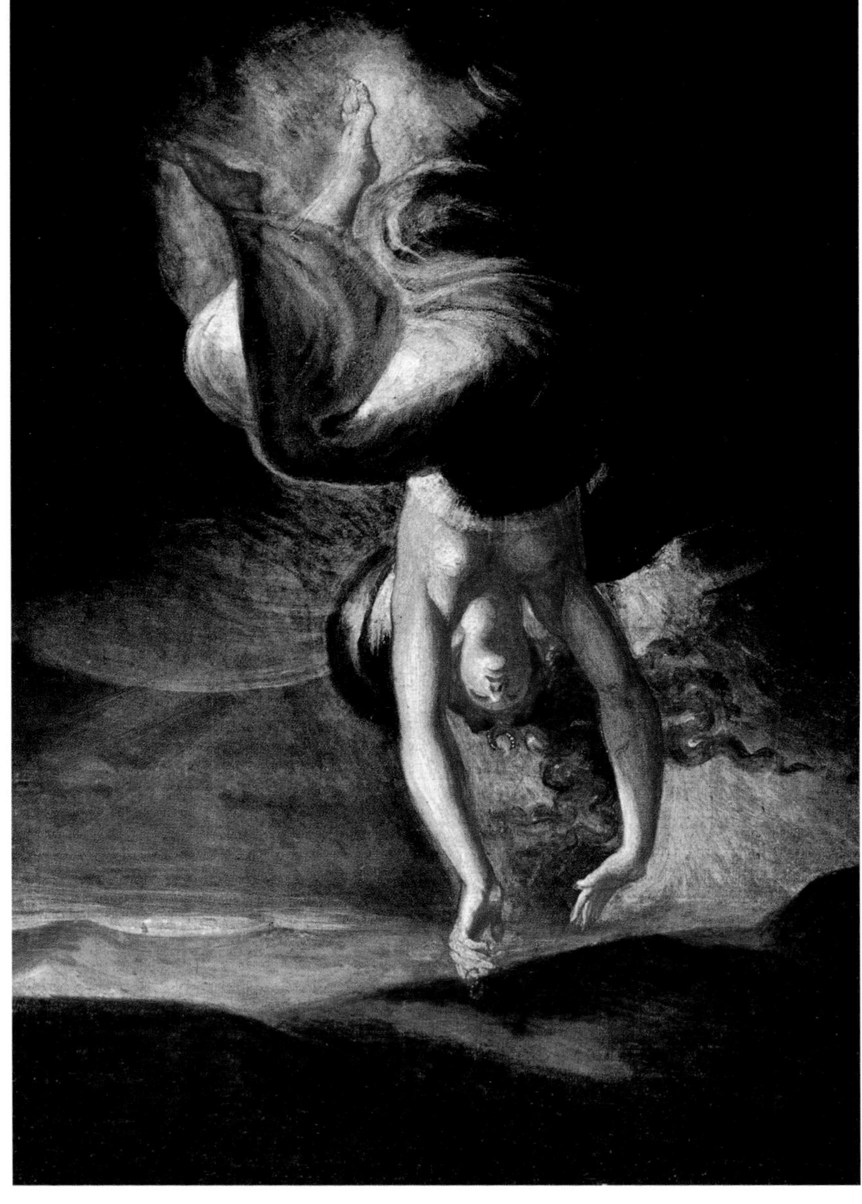

Henry Fuseli, *Titania Finds the Magic Ring on the Beach*, 1805, oil on canvas, 61 x 45 cm; Kunsthaus, Zurich

The imagination, negation of Enlightenment rationality, became the symbol of the obscure and unexplored potentialities of the mind, of a vast unknown world that became a field of continuous research for the Romantics: from the unknown paths of the psyche in its most dramatic aspects to the most exalted results of the creative genius, from madness to the triumph of the individual, all the many shadings that came to involve such visionary artists as Blake and Fuseli in England, Francisco Goya in Spain, and Théodore Géricault in France. Géricault portrays his figures with a disconcerting realism that he sometimes takes to the border of physiognomic deformity. This exploration of human character led to the age of the great caricaturists, among them Carl Jakob Lindstroem, Louis-Léopold Boilly, and Honoré Daumier.

The names Goya and Géricault call to mind another fundamental area of Romantic art, history painting. Throughout Europe, the first half of the nineteenth century was a period marked by frequent political changes and realignments. The rapid rise of Napoleon involved military invasions and campaigns extending all the way to Russia, but the

Congress of Vienna that marked the end of his career did not bring an end to such internal disturbances, which were often the results of economic crises caused by the wars. In addition to this there was the Greek struggle for independence in the years between 1821 and 1828, which also came to involve the leading European powers, as well as the revolutionary movements that broke out in France in 1830 and in most European nations in the dramatic year 1848.

European painters had a vast repertory of historical subjects to which they could turn to celebrate the government of the moment or patriotic pride, but this period also saw a progressive expansion of the themes available to art, which were extended to include various kinds of contemporary events that until then had never been considered suitable material for history painting. As early as the second decade of the century, artists began creating works based on new sources of reflection, making new images that the public was not used to seeing in art and that presented in some cases the antiheroic side of war, casting light on human suffering in and of itself. An epochal moment in art was reached with Goya's *Disasters of War* series of etchings, made between 1810 and 1820, which narrate with stark objectivity the violence and the crimes of the French invaders and the suffering of the Spanish people,

Carl Jakob Lindstroem, *The French Landscapist*, 1830, watercolor, pen, and black ink on paper, 19.3 x 25.8 cm; Nationalmuseum, Stockholm

including the ferocious repression illustrated in the famous paintings dedicated to May 2 and 3, 1808. There were also artists like Géricault, who turned to an event from contemporary history—the sinking of the frigate *Medusa* in the Atlantic in July 1816—and dared to lift the desperate struggle of the survivors to stay alive to the same level as a historical battle of the past. Not long after, Delacroix created a personal homage to the massacre of Chios, a slaughter inflicted by Turks on the Greek people, under the horrified eyes of Europe.

That painting was among the much discussed protagonists at the Paris Salon of 1824, an event of extraordinary importance that was decisive in the definitive affirmation of Romanticism on the European scene. Many masterpieces were displayed on that occasion: the *Slaughter of the Innocents* by Léon Cogniet, the *Joan of Arc in Prison* by Paul Delaroche, and the *Hay Wain* and other landscapes by John Constable, who was showing his work to the Parisian public for the first time and was meeting with enormous favor. The high point of the Salon, however, was the comparison of *The Vow of Louis XIII* by Jean-Auguste-Dominique Ingres with the *Scenes from the Massacre at Chios* by Delacroix. It was a sort of clash of Titans, the first representing the classical tradition—based on design—and the other the Romantic innovation—based on color and expressive vitality—and it came to be seen as a face-to-face struggle between the two epochs. In the end both artists exited victors. Ingres was then forty-four years old, and this triumph came very much unexpectedly; he had left Florence and set off for Paris and the Salon with only a few belongings, expecting to return soon. Delacroix had just passed twenty-six, and his canvas was challenged for its chromatic excesses and formal liberties at the same time that it was being hailed as the manifesto of Romanticism. From then on the artists' two styles became emblematic of two opposing schools. Their different stances were still very much alive by the time of the Universal Exposition of 1855, at which time Ingristes and "colorists," the latter being the followers of Delacroix, continued to be divided, each camp assaulting the other with cartoons in newspapers and with heated debates in magazines, carrying on the discussions around the tables of cafés even as the new air of realism was blowing in the wind around them.

Three years later, at the Salon of 1827, Ingres reclaimed his primacy in stately refinement with *The Apotheosis of Homer*, and Delacroix again caused scandal with *The Death of Sardanapalus*, a sensual and violent work, loaded with exotic suggestions, that was embraced by the more avant-garde members of the public. In that same year Victor Hugo, in the preface to his *Cromwell*, an historical drama set in England, laid out the Romantic manifesto in terms of the theater, extolling expressive variety in contrast to the sterile codifications of classical drama and recognizing the value of the ugly and the grotesque since they were capable of awakening emotions that differed from the simple admiration dictated by beauty.

In these years the Romantic rebellion reached the more tranquil hillsides of Italian painting and was embraced by Francesco Hayez, Massimo D'Azeglio, and Giovanni Carnevali. The presence of so many foreign artists and art students in Rome facilitated contacts among

Joseph Mallord William Turner, *Rome from the Vatican: Raffaelle Accompanied by La Fornarina Preparing His Pictures for the Decoration of the Loggia*, 1820, oil on canvas, 177 x 335 cm; Tate Gallery, London

artists and the circulation of new ideas. It was in Rome that Ingres painted his *Valpinçon Bather*, *Oedipus and the Sphinx*, and the *Sleeper*, made for Caroline Murat in 1808 and lost to history in the fall of the Murat regime in 1815. There were also the dozens of artists year by year who studied within the walls of the French Academy and the Villa Medici and those who rented rooms and mansards in order to be able to study the masterpieces in local collections as well as the Italian landscape. (A typical art-student's room in the Villa Medici appears in Cogniet's *First Letter from Home*.) In 1810, still bursting with the proclamations of Friedrich Schlegel and his followers, the Nazarenes arrived in Rome from Austria and Germany, and two decades later the theories of Purismo ("Purism") took form in Rome, later renewed by Luigi Mussini following his contact with Ingres. Among the crowd of foreigners who spent time in Rome was Joseph Mallord William Turner, who beginning in 1815 traveled across half of Europe, visiting France, Germany, and Switzerland; he set off again from Italy in 1820, the year of the centenary of the death of Raphael, which he celebrated in a painting he then completed and exhibited at the Royal Academy, *Rome from the Vatican: Raffaelle Accompanied by La Fornarina Preparing His Pictures for the Decoration of the Loggia*. This canvas was in reality an homage to Italy, to its monuments of every century, to its azure blue sky. The vibrant *Regulus*, which presents the port of Carthage as seen through the eyes of the Roman general Atilius Regulus, dates to Turner's second trip to the Italian peninsula, in 1828; it weaves ancient history, the landscape, and the theme of heroism, all presented with Turner's penetrating atmospheric effects.

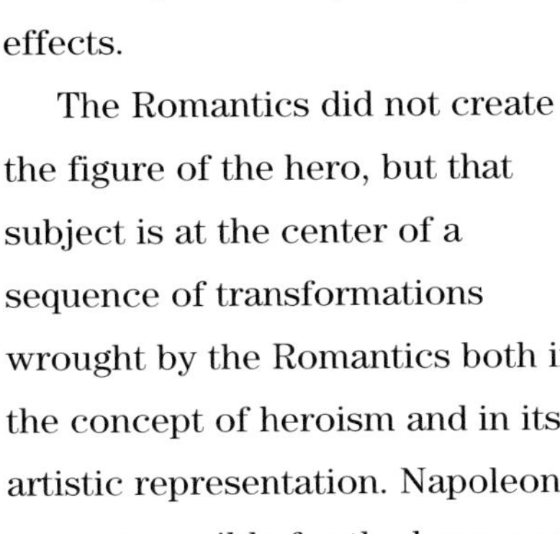

Joseph Mallord William Turner, *Regulus*, 1828 (and 1837), oil on canvas, 113.5 x 146.1 cm; Tate Gallery, London

The Romantics did not create the figure of the hero, but that subject is at the center of a sequence of transformations wrought by the Romantics both in the concept of heroism and in its artistic representation. Napoleon was responsible for the large-scale

Eugène Delacroix, *Chopin*, 1838, oil on canvas, 45 x 38 cm; Musée du Louvre, Paris

presentation of the image of heroism, making it a symbol of self-celebration and spreading it by way of a highly efficient policy of propaganda, which separated and united past and future, entrusting the construction of the Napoleonic myth both to classical art, led by Jacques-Louis David, and to the first manifestations of a new art present in the paintings of his students, such as Antoine-Jean Gros, Pierre Narcisse Guérin, and Anne-Louis Girodet-Trioson. Napoleon made use of official art, which fed the opinions of the public at large, astonishing viewers with evocations of imperial pomp and the regime's classical style. Overlooking the less glorious aspects of reality, he had David portray him astride a spirited war horse during the crossing of the Alps in 1800, and he had Antonio Canova present him in marble statues and busts that likened him to a hero of antiquity. Hundreds of copies were made of such paintings and sculptures, and these were then located in appropriate sites throughout much of Europe.

The emperor used the new iconography to promote the exaltation of virtues and to present scenes with great emotional impact. So it is that in the great canvases by Gros or Guérin it is not only military heroism that emerges but also the values of Christian piety or even the healing powers once believed to be possessed by sovereigns. Personally given to the sentimental and the fantastic, Napoleon was very fond of certain aspects of pre-Romantic culture, such as the theories of Rousseau and the poems of Ossian, commissioning various paintings that present that legendary poet.

One of the first indications of the new concept of the hero appears in a painting by Gros from 1810 in which he reveals his opening to change in a work that fits the encomiastic cycles requested by Bonaparte. This is *Napoleon on the Battlefield at Eylau*, in which the emperor is presented like a stately equestrian statue at the center of the canvas, but the foreground includes a moving vision of the wounded and dead victims of war, a vision that later—in the periodical *L'Artiste* of 1831—was recognized as the departure point for the Romantic school. Only a short time later Géricault overturned the classical concept of the hero in *The Wounded Cuirassier*, which lays bare the reality of an individual in the face of death. At the same time, the hymn of the Byronic hero was being sung on other, more literary, artistic fronts. Solitary and proud, dedicated to sacrifice in the name of noble ideals more than to military exploits, this hero was a rebellious spirit struggling with a society that is indifferent to the needs of the soul, a poet of aesthetics and of melancholy, the melancholy known as the *mal du siècle*. George Gordon Byron was himself the example *par excellence* of this style of life, lived with aristocratic disdain for the tedium of middle-class mentality but also with impulsive action when the right thing to do meant setting off for Greece to battle the barbarous Turks. The artist who most came to identify himself with this Romantic attitude was Eugène Delacroix. A great admirer of Byron, he often turned to his poems for the subjects of his paintings, from the *Death of Sardanapalus* to the *Combat of the Giaour and the Pasha*. He was drawn to the themes of these works for their blending of Orientalism, desperate passions, and the cult of sensuality. Delacroix always struggled to make painting express the personal and the irrational, abilities he recognized only in music, most of all that of Frédéric Chopin, one of the few contemporary artists he admired without reservation. Delacroix made a portrait of the great musician in 1838 in which Chopin appeared together with the writer George Sand at the time of the beginning of their relationship. Although that work is lost it is known in part from an unfinished preparatory version preserved in the Louvre.

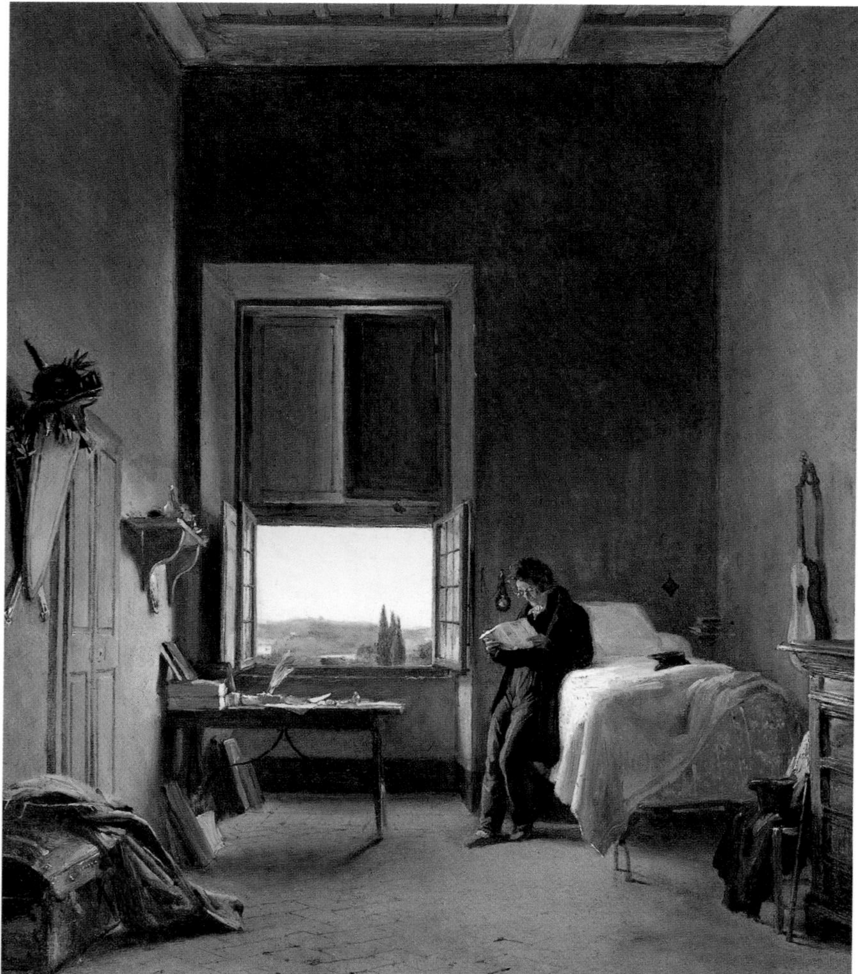

Léon Cogniet, *First Letter from Home*, 1818, oil on canvas, 58 x 51 cm; Museum of Art, Cleveland

The figures of Byron and Delacroix are closely related to the subject of Romantic Orientalism, of which both were protagonists. The sudden enormous passion for Egypt and the Middle East in general, which rapidly flared to Europe-wide dimensions, dates to Napoleon's military campaign in Egypt. Fruit of the cultural propaganda related to the expedition to Egypt and Syria in 1798 and to the large-scale expeditions of scholars and archaeologists, the taste for Egyptian art rapidly extended to every type of ornament, such that images of sphinxes, elephants, and obelisks showed up everywhere, on the furnishings in city and country homes, on the porcelain table services produced by the Sèvres factory, on the furniture made of precious woods used in Napoleonic courts, on monuments in the squares of Paris. During the three years of French domination, an army of nearly two hundred persons, including botanists, geographers, archaeologists, and scholars of every type, including artists, threw itself into the study of the history of Egyptian civilization. Most of this information was later collected in the monumental *Description de l'Egypte*, published between 1809 and 1828 by the Institut d'Egypte, founded by Napoleon. With the beginning of the nineteenth century various conflicts kept Europe's attention directed to the Middle East, and the vision of the Middle Eastern countries, beginning with their geographical position, was soon made into a great exotic myth. A great many artists contributed to the formation of a true artistic genre, Orientalism. At first it involved scenes immersed in the Romantic fusion of dreamy atmospheres and subtle eroticism; it later evolved into the meticulous transcription of those distant civilizations, reaching an almost documentary style with a realist imprint. Each artist, guided by temperament and style, arrived at a subjective interpretation of the exotic. Far from abandoning himself to the fiery vision of Delacroix, Ingres created a series of odalisques with a highly sophisticated sensuality, sometimes distinguished by erudite citations, such as the turban from *La Fornarina* by Raphael that appears on the head of the *Grande Odalisque*, sometimes inserted in a lush harem, sometimes alone, such as the youthful *Valpinçon Bather*.

Other painters, such as Alexandre-Gabriel Decamps, Horace Vernet, Delacroix, and the Italian Ippolito Caffi, took the all-important trip to the Orient, bringing back impressions that deeply affected their painting. Eugène Fromentin made many trips to Algeria and wrote a book on the subject, *Une Année dans le Sahel* (1858), in which he commented on the forms of Romantic Orientalism adopted by his colleagues. In Italy, Orientalism appeared most of all in history painting and religious works, providing realistic models for the dress and settings of biblical themes, as in works by Cherubino Cornienti and Francesco Hayez.

The artistic passion for the exotic did not consume itself exclusively in the atmospheres of harems or in sunny Bedouin encampments. Artists were commissioned to make portraits of exotic animals bought for the menageries of European princes (such as the *Nubian Giraffe* that belonged to King George IV and was painted in London by Jacques-Laurent Agasse), and Orientalism appears in room furnishings, including rare plants and Oriental-style decorations. The fascination of distant worlds drove some Romantics to cross even more distant borders, traveling to the Far East and the last areas of the world discovered by explorers or crossing the ocean to the New World.

The arrival of Romantic ideals in North America, and most of all the formation of schools of painting closely related to those in Europe during the first half of the nineteenth century, indicates that Romanticism was a worldwide phenomena. Writers like François-René de Chateaubriand wrote dramatic tales about the mistreatment of Native Americans; one of these, *Atala* (1801), became well known from the canvas that Girodet made in 1808 for Louis François Bertin, the powerful politician whose portrait Ingres made in 1832 (Musée du Louvre, Paris). In the United States, painting began to find its identity precisely at the time that the Romantic sensibility was taking hold in France and England. The Hudson River School, led by Thomas Cole, was the first major school of American painting; its members explored aspects of the landscape, from the worship of nature to the sense of the sublime to the cult of the affinity between the individual and the wilderness.

In Europe landscape painting, perhaps more than any other genre,

Jean-Auguste-Dominique Ingres, *Valpinçon Bather*, 1808, oil on canvas, 146 x 97 cm; Musée du Louvre, Paris

Jean-François Millet, *The Angelus*, 1858, oil on canvas, 55 x 66 cm; Musée d'Orsay, Paris

served as the interpreter of all the directions taken by Romantic thought, with its contrasts and innovations, eventually achieving a kind of union with nascent realism. The marine paintings by Joseph Vernet present pre-Romantic scenes, views that are also "picturesque," scenes of the wild and melancholy aspects of nature that awaken a singular state of mind, defined by the term *Romantic*. (That word, which is the root of *Romanticism*, began with the *romance*, the medieval tale of chivalry, but by the seventeenth century it had acquired the sense of being fictional, not true, outside the limits of ordinary life and thus also picturesque, evocative, becoming a synonym for the sentimental or fantastic.) The sublime became the symbol itself of Romantic art thanks to Caspar David Friedrich, who succeeded in visualizing the profound link between the immensity of space and the sense of the divine, between limitless vastness and the power of uncontaminated nature, as in *Morning in the Riesengebirge*, a view from the heights of Silesia pervaded by a sense of the infinite and by the profound sacredness of nature. The cult of nature was also presented with great but different sensibilities by the group of French artists united around Théodore Rousseau in the 1830s that came to be known as the Barbizon School, from the name of the locality near the forest of Fontainebleau where the *barbizonniers* met to paint *en plein air*, "in the open air." United by the desire to portray nature with fidelity, each saw in nature the elements that were most in keeping with his temperament. Their names were Charles-François Daubigny, Constant Troyon, and Camille Corot, the father of a new way of seeing the landscape that flowed directly into realism and would later be a reference point for the young Impressionists. In 1849 they were joined by Jean-François Millet, whose interest soon turned to rural life and the figures of peasants at work in the fields, which reminded him of his childhood. *The Angelus* is in fact an autobiographical memory of the painter, who provided an explanation of the painting: "While at work in the fields, whenever my grandmother heard the tolling of the bell she always made us pause in our labors to say the Angelus for the poor dead." The dramatic luminosity and sense of peace in the scene reflect the calm, inspirational vision of the traditions of the peasant world that Millet further developed in the 1860s. Like him were such artists as Constant Troyon, Jules Breton, and Rosa Bonheur, all followers of a naturalism that saw the life of the fields as the final refuge from modern cities.

Meanwhile, beginning in the 1840s, the highly original artist Gustave Courbet, despite a myriad of obstacles, promoted a new and exclusive way of conceiving painting as "an essentially concrete art that can consist only in the representation of real and existing things": realism. Across the top of his letter paper he often wrote: "Courbet, without ideals and without religion." It was the end of Romanticism.

Gustave Courbet, *Self-Portrait with a Black Dog*, 1844, oil on canvas, 46 x 56 cm; Musée du Petit Palais, Paris

Opposite: Francesco Hayez, *The Kiss* (detail), 1859, oil on canvas, 112 x 88 cm; Pinacoteca di Brera, Milan

The second half of the eighteenth century, usually identified as the age of Enlightenment, with the triumph of reason over sentiment, was a period of cultural turmoil, with changes that saw the formation of the basic elements of Romantic thought. In terms of the arts, during the neoclassical period tendencies of taste and style that anticipated in a surprising way the most radical principles of the next century began to take shape, for which reason the period can be called pre-Romantic. In particular, during the last thirty years of the century, the principal manifestations of an artistic sensibility that would be emblematic of Romanticism came into being. This can be seen in landscape painting, in portraiture, in the passionate embrace of the Gothic revival in Britain, in the increasing displeasure found across Europe over the encroachments of industrialization, and finally in the new viewpoint taken on history. The Grand Tour, the long trip to the European continent, but most of all

Johann Heinrich Wüest, *Rhone Glacier*, circa 1795, oil on canvas, 126 x 100 cm; Kunsthaus, Zurich

combine two of the concepts most in vogue at that moment, the picturesque and the sublime. Both concepts are related to the theories of philosophers and intellectuals: Edmund Burke with the *Philosophical Enquiry into the Origin of Our Ideas of the Sublime and Beautiful* (1756), Immanuel Kant with his formulations on the sublime in the *Critique of Practical Reason* (1790), and Uvedale Price with his theory of the picturesque that referred in a specific way to Britain. There were immediate applications of the poetics of the sublime in France from painters like Joseph Vernet, whose *Storm* of 1780 seems to illustrate the scene of a shipwreck described by the landscape painter Pierre-Henri de Valenciennes in his treatise *Advice to a Student on Painting, and Particularly on Landscape* (1800), in which he suggests conveying the violence of the wind with the image of people hugging to rocks or with objects tossed on the waves, while "those on the coast seek to save the shipwrecked,

Neoclassicism and

Italy, that Britons and other foreigners felt obliged to take at least once offers meaningful elements in terms of the history of Romanticism. During his stay in Naples in 1787, Johann Wolfgang von Goethe recalled an excursion up the slopes of Mount Vesuvius in the company of his friend the painter Wilhelm Tischbein, in the course of which the two were surprised by an eruption of lapilli and ash. The view of the volcano in activity—and such activity was recorded with particular frequency during the 1770s and 1780s—was one of the favorite attractions for foreign travelers in Italy, and as a result views of Vesuvius in eruption multiplied on the art market. Pierre-Jacques Volaire became a true specialist in the genre, which happened to

Joseph Vernet, *Storm*, 1780, oil on canvas, 42 x 33 cm; Musée des Beaux-Arts, Troyes

throwing them ropes or diving into the sea to go to them, and these should truly strike the sensibility with their movements and attitudes." Toward the end of the century other artists took up the theme in Germany, among them Johann Heinrich Wüest with his *Rhone Glacier*. A bizarre visualization of the sublime was created by Philippe Jacques de Loutherbourg, a French painter and stage designer called to London in 1771 by the actor David Garrick, for whom he worked at the Drury Lane Theatre, where he became famous for the invention, in 1781, of the Eidophusikon, or "spectacle of nature," a kind of miniature theater about four meters square that could create an impression of motion and could simulate weather, with dynamic images of flashing storms, light effects for thunder and lightning, wind and sea storms, all with such accurate effects that Sir Joshua Reynolds, president of the Royal Academy of London, advised his students to go see this machine as an excellent example of the artificial sublime. De Loutherbourg was also among the first artists to illustrate the disturbing presence of factories in the rural landscape. The advance of industry was perceived as dangerous to the pristine state of nature, capable of ruining natural rhythms, disturbing the peace of the night, changing forever the architectural profile of the countryside, as seen in his *View of Coalbrookdale by Night*. The theme of the nocturne was also the vehicle for pictorial language connected to the revelation of emotions and passions, those aspects of the unconscious that entrust their manifestations to sleep. More than a few artists felt the need to express this Romantic sensibility even in the climate still dominated by the more refined neoclassic style. Anne-Louis Girodet-Trioson can be taken as representative of this pre-Romantic current, so dramatic and full of passion are such works as *The Sleep of Endymion*, the portrait of the young *Romainville Trioson*, with its moving intensity, and *Ossian* same years that Girodet painted his *Endymion*. The approach to politics and with it history were in fact undergoing change. Comparison of *The Death of General Warren at the Battle of Bunker's Hill*, painted in 1786 by John Trumbull, with a similar subject, *The Death of General Wolfe* (see page 218), made by

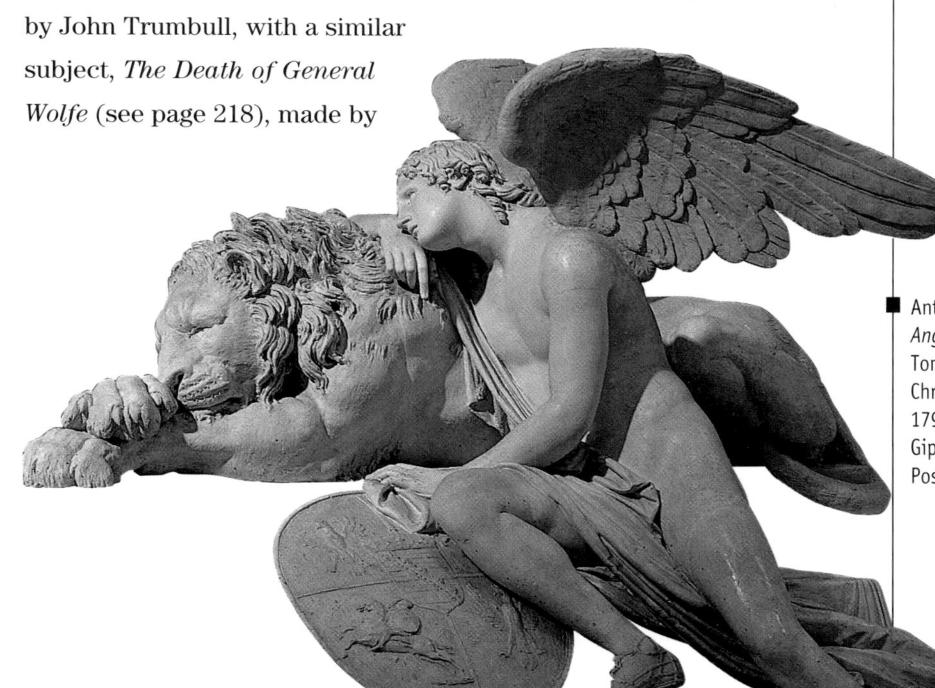

Antonio Canova, *Angel*, detail from the Tomb of Maria Christina of Austria, 1799–1800; Gipsoteca Canoviana, Possagno

pre-Romanticism

Receiving the Generals of the Republic, which he painted for Napoleon. While belonging to different genres, all three canvases provide a measurement of the enormous change that was about to take place on the French and European scene. Girodet was a student of Jacques-Louis David. Although considered the peerless leader of official painting, even David was not immune to pre-Romantic stimuli, at least at the beginning of his career, as in his youthful portrait of Count Stanislaw Potocki, and he was also involved in masterpieces of unquestionable modernity, such as the *Death of Marat*, which he painted during the

Anne-Louis Girodet-Trioson, *Romainville Trioson*, 1800, oil on canvas, 73 x 59 cm; Musée du Louvre, Paris

Benjamin West in 1770, reveals a drama of pre-Romantic imprint destined to rapidly increase. Under a different profile, not stylistic but involving the artist's attitude toward the past, the reflection on history was also evolving. It was during the 1770s that Henry Fuseli made his symbolic image of the relationship between artists and Rome, *The Artist in Despair over the Magnitude of Antique Fragments*, which provides a measurement of the layer of sacredness then being applied to the ruins of antiquity. The painting also expresses the sense of the inadequacy of the present when compared to the grandiose past, which the artist experienced with a sort of emotional frustration, convinced that it would be impossible to equal it. Step by step the sense of a distant and dead antiquity was being animated by a new sentimental warmth that was reflected both in the gaze of the painters who went to Rome to portray the ruins of monuments and in the sculpture of Antonio Canova, which began to express deeply felt passions and affections, as in the beautiful *Penitent Magdalene* of 1796 (see page 176) or the languid *Angel* from the tomb of Maria Christina of Austria (1799–1800), a work that marked the passage to the new century.

PIERRE-JACQUES VOLAIRE
Mount Vesuvius in Moonlight
1774, oil on canvas
248 x 378 cm
Ministère de la Culture, Paris

Until the second half of the eighteenth century, Naples was one of the obligatory stops for those European travelers able to permit themselves the luxury of the Grand Tour. Aside from the ruins of ancient monuments and the beauty of the sea, Mount Vesuvius in eruption constituted one of the main attractions, an image that fit with the contemporary concepts of the picturesque and the sublime, looked upon with admiration by intellectuals and artists at the end of century. A grand but also terrible manifestation of nature ("Whatever is in any sort terrible . . . is a source of the Sublime," wrote Edmund Burke in 1756), the activity of Vesuvius, which erupted several times during the 1770s, was seen as a sensational event on both the visual and emotional planes, most of all when seen at night. Such is the moment that Volaire portrayed in numerous canvases, with pale moonlight reflected on the sea beside a sky enflamed by lapilli and incandescent magma.

Philippe Jacques de Loutherbourg
View of Coalbrookdale by Night
1801, oil on canvas
67.9 x 106.6 cm
Science Museum, London

The initial phase of Romanticism saw the development of a point of view that called attention to the dramatic contrast between the natural landscape, still intact in its idyllic atmosphere, and the changes wrought to it by the first industrial installations, which caused environmental and social squalor in many of the suburbs of larger cities. De Loutherbourg, a French painter and stage designer who moved to London to work in the Drury Lane Theatre, was among the first artists to illustrate the industrial growth in England. His sense of the spectacular nature of such early industrial sites is made clear in this canvas, in which the fiery glow from the kilns of Coalbrookdale brightens the night, revealing the profiles of the local structures, the smoke stacks, and, in the foreground, the workers' difficult labors.

Charles Wild
Fonthill Abbey
circa 1799, watercolor
29.3 x 23.5 cm
Victoria and Albert
Museum, London

Only the north wing of the building remains today, but it has an appealing history that is representative of the Gothic revival that so engaged Romantic intellectuals and their precursors. It was built in Wiltshire by the architect James Wyatt for William Beckford (1760–1844), an eccentric writer of Gothic stories, a brilliant man, wealthy collector, and musician with a scandalous reputation. Around 1796 Beckford designed this enormous abbey in the Gothic style, intending to make it his residence. Anxious for it to be completed in a short time he used less solid building materials and did not have a sufficient basement built, which led to the building's collapse, in particular its 84-meter-high octagonal tower, which had to be rebuilt six times. By the time Beckford put it on sale, in 1823, he had made Fonthill Abbey into a symbol of neo-Gothic eccentricity.

Henry Fuseli
The Artist in Despair over the Magnitude of Antique Fragments
1778–80, pencil and watercolor on paper
42 x 35.2 cm
Kunsthaus, Zurich

By the time he made this celebrated drawing, Fuseli had already spent several years in Rome. Unlike those artists who, following in the footsteps of Winckelmann, were fascinated by the "quiet grandeur" and noble magnificence of classical antiquity, Fuseli was involved at an emotional level by Rome's art and ruins, such as the left foot and right hand of the Colossus of Constantine, the gigantic fragments of which are shown here. The perception of a distant past that was lost, in ruin, and unrepeatable awakened a sort of dismay in the artist, which he communicates to the spectator, accentuating the contrast in size between the figure and the two colossal remains. This attitude of despair and commotion places Fuseli in a perspective far distant from the neoclassical approach of Piranesi, for Fuseli sought a kind of spiritual interpenetration with the ancient, a spirit that is markedly pre-Romantic.

Gottlieb Schick
The Hereditary Prince of Saxe-Gotha-Altenburg, Future Frederick IV
1806, oil on canvas
200.5 x 158 cm
Sammlung Herzoglicher Kunstbesitz Schloss Callenberg, Coburg

This portrait is an example of the many paintings that, since the eighteenth century, travelers had commissioned as testimony and souvenirs of their stays in Italy or Europe during a Grand Tour. As with most souvenir portraits, the patron had himself presented against a background of Roman monuments, some of them highly recognizable, such as the Colosseum and the church of Santa Francesca Romana, others perhaps less well known, such as the temple of Saturn, two columns of which appear at the upper right, and the relief with the *Goddess of Rome Afflicted* at below right. The young Prince Frederick of Saxony visited Rome for the first time between 1805 and 1806; while there he met many artists, including the German Gottlieb Schick, and created a lively salon in his residence in Via del Corso, popular with the Roman nobility and foreign visitors.

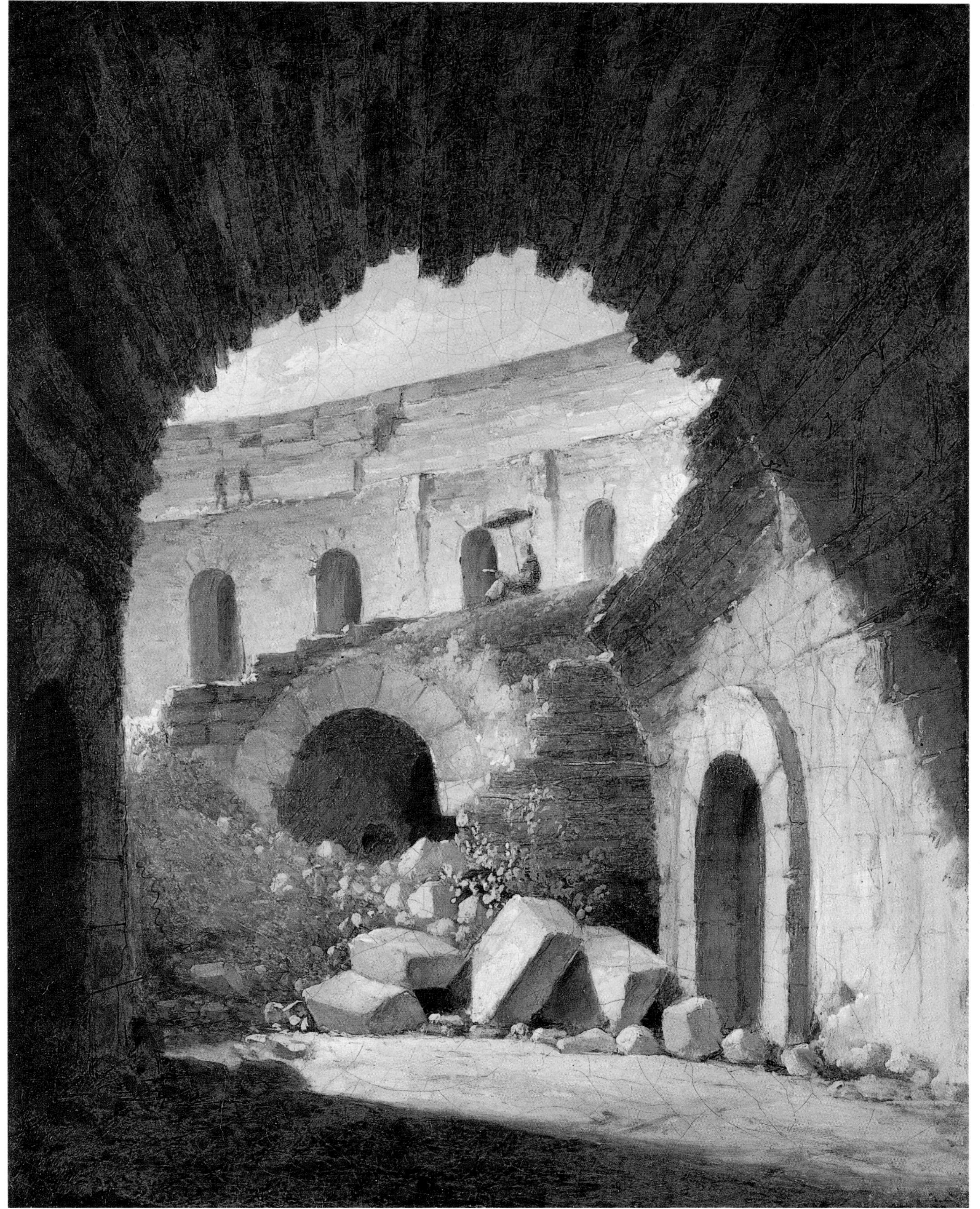

François-Marius Granet
A Painter at Work in the Colosseum
1802, oil on paper applied to canvas
28.5 x 22.5 cm
Private collection

The Colosseum was a traditional subject in neoclassical views of ancient ruins, but it began to assume different tones with painters like Granet. He went there not to examine cold relics of antiquity but for the sensation of being enfolded in a moving atmosphere, evocative of life. When he arrived in Rome in 1802, the young student of Jacques-Louis David noted in his journal that he had chosen the famous amphitheater as the site for his first life studies. He was drawn to the ruins not only for the stones, so laden with history, but also for the wild plants, the acanthus and yellow carnations, which he presents in this small painting. The artist happily at work beneath his parasol does not communicate a sense of solitude but seems to be in complete harmony with his surroundings. In fact, everything in this view reveals a new sensibility, a way of perceiving the past that makes Granet recognizable as a Romantic.

Hubert Robert
The Bastille in the First Days of Its Demolition
1789, oil on canvas
77 x 114 cm
Musée Carnavalet, Paris

In the repertory of Hubert Robert, a landscape painter who specialized in architectural scenes and the representation of ruins, real or imaginary, this canvas occupies a place to itself and is of great historical importance. Abandoning the traditional eighteenth-century picturesque style, Robert seeks to document the spectacular scene of the fire at the Bastille during the crucial days of the Revolution, an event that occurred on July 20, 1789, as indicated by writing at the lower right. Wrapped in smoke and partially illuminated by flames, the building occupies the foreground of the painting without leaving much visible room around it, in that way assuming an even greater sense of importance. The artist does not present the swarming assault of the revolutionaries, but the gradual and tangible collapse of a symbol of the past, successfully imbuing the scene with an almost epic sense.

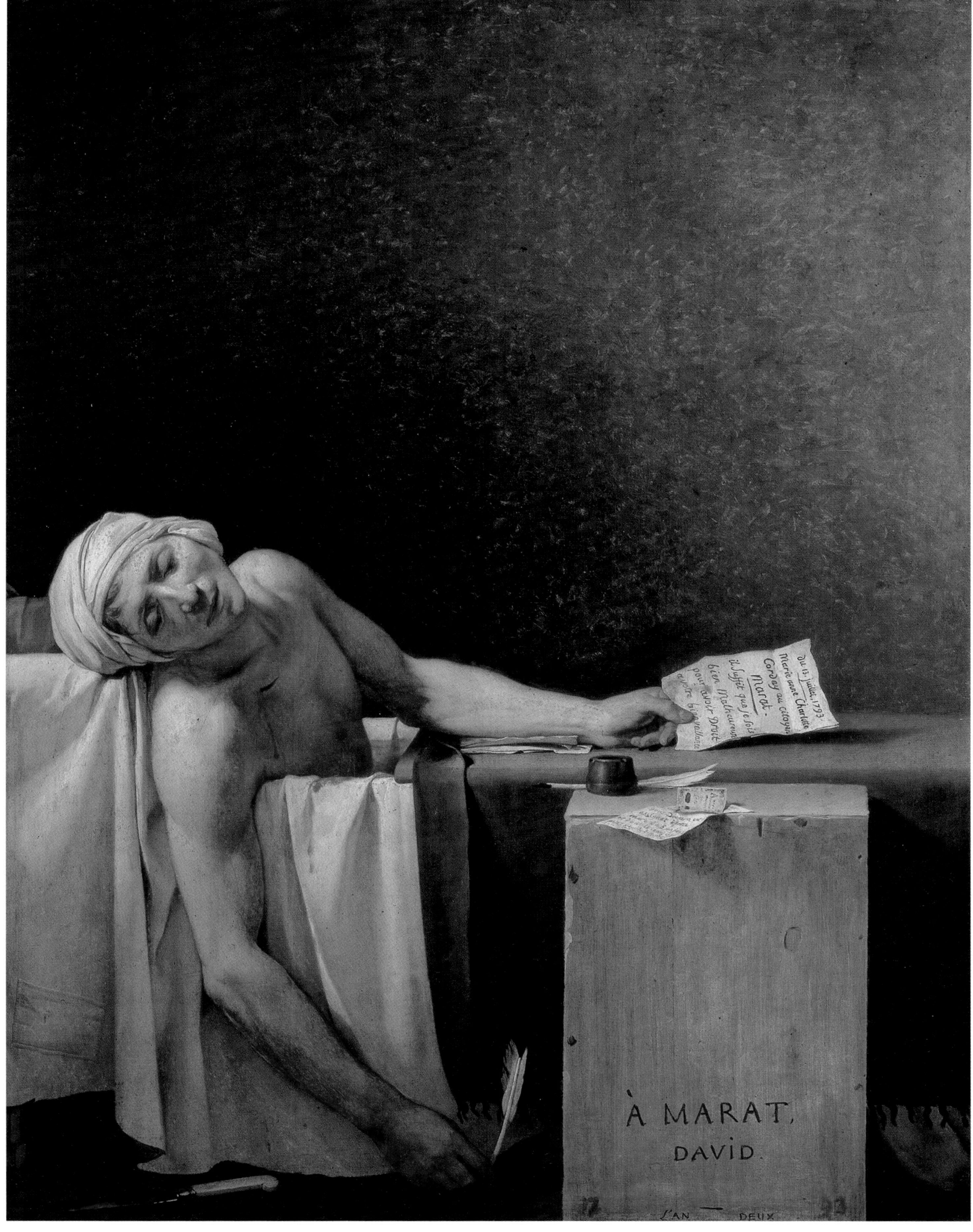

Jacques-Louis David
The Death of Marat
1793, oil on canvas
165 x 128 cm
Musées Royaux des Beaux-Arts, Brussels

On July 13, 1793, with the excuse of having a petition to present him—the piece of paper in Marat's left hand—the Girondist Charlotte Corday killed one of the great heroes of the French Revolution. David, who had been a friend of Jean-Paul Marat, immortalized the event with a painting laid out following the rational values of classicism, using all the details essential to recreate the tragic event: the bath with the lifeless corpse, the sheet, the bloody knife, the inkstand, the pens, the writing stand improvised from a box; the document that served as the tool of the betrayal. Despite the lack of emphasis or emotional involvement, the painter created a highly dramatic image that invites the viewer to meditate on the cruelty of the murder, with the dead man's pose giving the image the sense of a martyrdom. David's final homage to his friend is the dedicatory writing on the side of the wooden box: "To Marat, David, Year Two."

Anne-Louis Girodet-Trioson
The Sleep of Endymion
1793, oil on canvas
197 x 260 cm
Musée du Louvre, Paris

The beautiful Greek shepherd Endymion was the beloved of Selene, goddess of the moon, who gave him eternal sleep in order to kiss him every night. Here, Cupid moves aside branches so that the rays of the moon can caress the youth's body. A popular subject in ancient iconography, the figure of Endymion inspired writers and artists of the modern age, such as Girodet, who presented him in a languid and sensual pose made even more appealing by the suggestive effects of moonlight. In this canvas the painter, a student of David, shows that he had moved away from the classicism of his master, opening himself to the taste for highly evocative paintings full of the mystery and power of emotion, thus in 1791 creating a work with a strongly Romantic sensibility.

Anne-Louis Girodet-Trioson
Ossian Receiving the Generals of the Republic
1802, oil on canvas
192 x 182 cm
Musée National de la Malmaison, Paris

Made for the Salon Doré of Malmaison—the favorite residence of Napoleon's first wife, Josephine de Beauharnais—this canvas presents Valhalla, the afterlife for heroes in Germanic mythology, where Ossian is shown welcoming many of the generals fallen in Napoleonic campaigns. The mythical Gaelic cantor Ossian, supposed author of epic poems, was considered the Nordic equivalent of Homer. He was also one of Napoleon's favorite personages. In this extraordinary composition Girodet seems to announce, in 1802, the complete break with the neoclassical canons of order and harmonic balance: the scene is totally immersed in a fantastic and supernatural vision, with the almost swirling and incessant convergence of ghosts, evanescent shades, of warriors of the past and recent heroes, such as the French generals Desaix and Kléber, recognizable at the center.

Jacques-Louis David
Count Stanislaw Potocki
1781, oil on canvas
304 x 218 cm
Muzeum Narodowe, Warsaw

Observing this appealing portrait, animated by an expressive vitality that seems to find echo in the impatience of the horse, a critic wondered how different David's painting would have been had he adhered to the youthful temperament manifested here in all its exuberance instead of letting himself fall under the sway of classical theories. A little over thirty when he was asked to make this portrait of the brilliant Polish aristocrat visiting Italy during a Grand Tour, David was nearing the end of his period of studies in Rome. In five years he had been able to visit Naples and other centers on the peninsula with their works of art, making copies of masterpieces by Raphael that would later mark a change in his career, and also copying paintings by Rubens and Van Dyck, whose styles emerge here, releasing a pictorial energy of strongly pre-Romantic sensibility.

Thomas Lawrence
Elizabeth Hervey Foster, Duchess of Devonshire
1805, oil on canvas
250 x 144 cm
National Gallery of Ireland, Dublin

Official painter to the English aristocracy, Sir Lawrence distinguished himself during the neoclassical period for his ability to capture something of the inner character of the people he portrayed. In this canvas he presents the future duchess of Devonshire, Elizabeth Hervey Foster, dressed as the Tiburtine sibyl; the noblewoman stands out against an enigmatic and not well defined landscape, immersed in an evocative light in keeping with the figure's prophetic role. The expression on her face seems to travel outward, to lose itself in an intense reflection that ends in an abstraction from the present. In this painting, which was begun in 1801 and completed four years later, the artist shows a modern sensibility in bringing to light the interpenetration between individual and landscape, rendered with a vibrant style, no longer restrained by neoclassical formulas.

Tommaso Minardi
Self-Portrait
1807, oil on canvas
37 x 33 cm
Galleria degli Uffizi, Florence

Painted at the age of twenty, this self-portrait by Minardi anticipates in an emblematic way the Romantic ideal of the bohemian artist. The young artist is presented in a casual, informal pose, absorbed in his melancholy thoughts. The space in which he is located is of great interest and also quite unusual in terms of the aesthetic criteria in the painting of the time. It is a mansard being used as a studio that reveals, in the mattress on the floor and the few elements of furnishing located amid the general disorder, the unregulated and penniless life of the young artist. The two skulls, one to each side of the painter, add a note of erudition since they are antique symbols of meditation on life and its rapid passing. A few years later Minardi set aside this more intimately Romantic vision of art, directing himself toward a pictorial sensibility that led him to be one of the primary exponents of the Purismo movement.

Luigi Sabatelli
Radamistus Killing Zenobia
1803, oil on canvas
Museo Civico, Pistoia

Made for the Pistoian Tommaso Puccini, this painting presents an episode from the *Annals of Imperial Rome* by Tacitus that Handel had made into a musical drama, *Radamistus*, in 1720. Protagonist in a complicated tale of wars and amorous passions, Radamistus, son of Pharasmanes, king of Thrace, flees with his faithful wife Zenobia, who at the advance of enemies asks her husband to kill her; slightly wounded, she saves herself by diving into the River Aras. Sabatelli synthesizes the episode in a simple composition that isolates the pair in highly dramatic light, thus revealing the strongly pre-Romantic sensibility the artist had assimilated during his stay in Rome in the preceding decade, which had been enriched by contact with such northern European artists as Fuseli and Abildgaard.

John Trumbull
The Death of General Warren at the Battle of Bunker's Hill
1786, oil on canvas
63.5 x 86.4 cm
Trumbull Collection, Yale University Art Gallery, New Haven

The Battle of Bunker Hill took place to the north of Boston on June 17, 1775, and was one of the outstanding events of the American Revolution. Trumbull witnessed the encounter on the hill from across Boston Harbor; here he records on canvas the last moments in the life of Major-General Joseph Warren. Wounded by the British, he collapses into the arms of a soldier, while in a noble gesture British Major John Small prevents a grenadier from bayoneting him. The composition is animated by strong dynamism, with the mass of the soldiers forming parallel diagonal lines, flags fluttering in the fray, and the rising cloud of smoke. The natural gestures of the figures, no longer in keeping with the rhetorical canons of neoclassical art, dramatically express the artist's patriotic involvement in the historical event and also reveal his decidedly pre-Romantic sensibility.

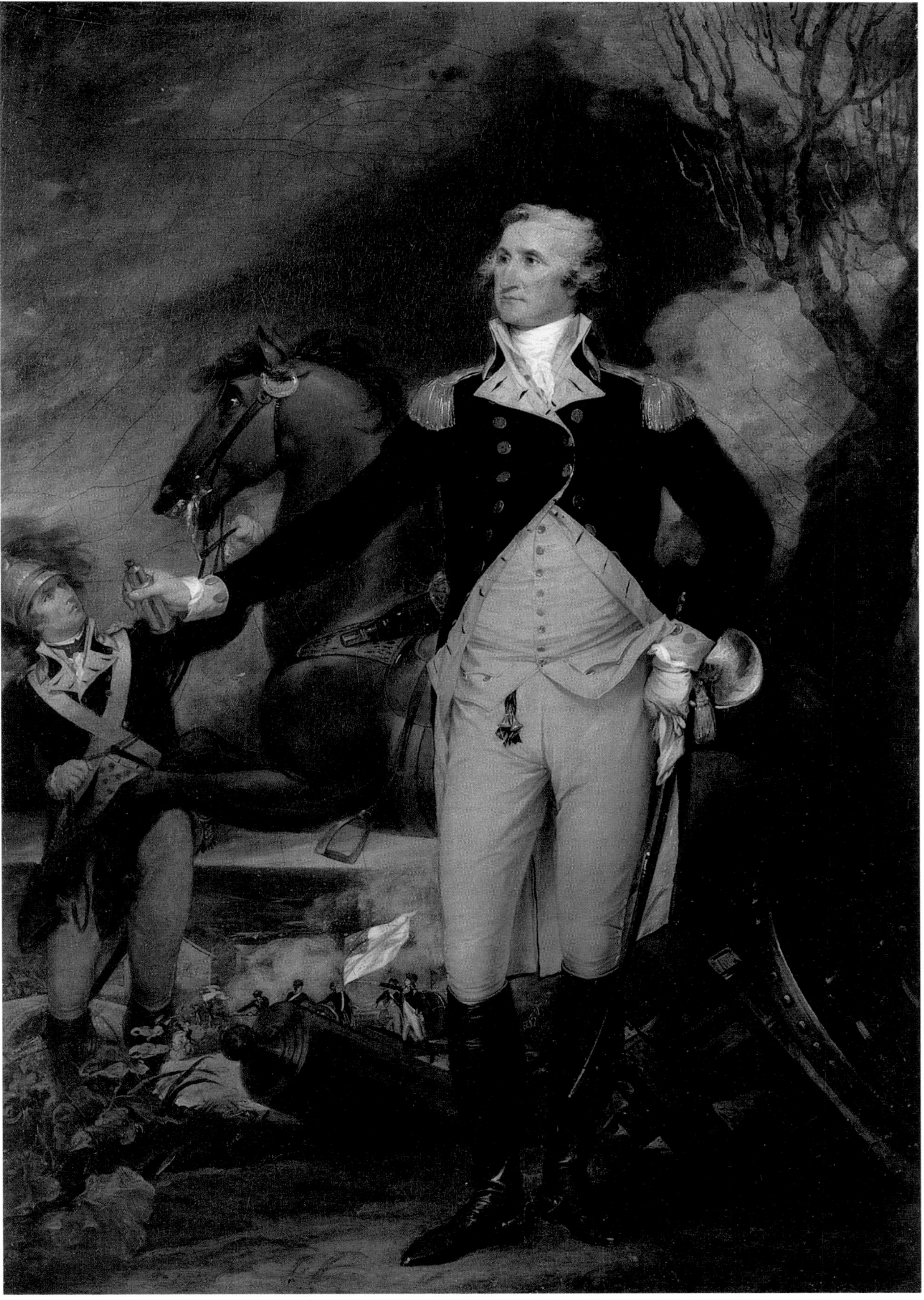

JOHN TRUMBULL
George Washington before the Battle of Trenton
circa 1793,
oil on canvas
67.3 x 45 cm
Metropolitan Museum of Art, New York

Artist and patriot, John Trumbull was born in Connecticut and served in various capacities during the Revolution, becoming aide-de-camp to George Washington. In this portrait he presents the general before the famous Battle of Trenton, the American victory over Britain's Hessian troops under Colonel Rall that was fought on December 26, 1776. The determination of the American troops and their artillery fire disrupted their enemy, who, rapidly surrounded, were forced to surrender. Trumbull shows those weapons in this painting in memory of Washington's first great military victory; he presents the general in a victorious pose, allusive to his imminent triumph, but presents in the dark and stormy sky the uneasy atmosphere and emotional tension that pervaded the field a few hours before the battle.

The myth of

Alfred de Musset began his *La Confession d'un enfant du siècle* (1836): "During the Imperial wars . . . there was one man alive in Europe . . . the rest were simply trying to fill their lungs with the air he breathed. Every year France made him a present of three hundred thousand young men; it was the tribute paid to Caesar, and if he did not have this troop behind him he could not try his luck. It was the escort he needed in order to cover the globe and to finish up in the obscure valley of a desert island, under a weeping willow." It is an image of Napoleon far distant from the myth he had created for himself. Born at Ajaccio on Corsica on August 15, 1769, Napoleon Bonaparte died at Longwood, on the island of Saint Helena, on May 5, 1821. His career had been rapid and thunderous, and he had been heedless of early defeats in his headlong rush to accomplish ambitious projects. In 1793, at the age of twenty-four, he had obtained the rank of general and was given command of the artillery in Italy; he was a friend of Robespierre and of the powerful Barras, who in 1795 introduced him to the influential Josephine de Beauharnais, whom he married on March 9 of the following year. In 1796 he achieved his first major military successes, with the defeat of Piedmont and Austria in the course of a series of successful battles (Montenotte, Lodi, Arcole, Rivoli). On his return to France following the expedition to Egypt in 1798, the general reconquered power, becoming first consul in 1799, and in 1800 the military campaign in Italy ended with the victory at Marengo after crossing the Alps at the Great St. Bernard Pass. From then on the self-celebrative policies of Napoleon, involving carefully planned propaganda, assumed large-scale dimensions. The painting commissioned from Gros to immortalize the victory at Arcole was immediately spread through engravings by Giuseppe Longhi; numerous ephemeral monuments were erected in the Cisalpine Republic and in the Kingdom of Italy on the occasion of celebrations in honor of Napoleon or those that reflected the calendar of the French national holidays. Named first consul for life in 1802, on December 2, 1804, Bonaparte was consecrated in stately fashion by Pope Pius VII emperor of the French; not long after that, in May 1805, he was crowned king of Italy in the cathedral of Milan. The series of military victories in northern Europe continued without interruption until October 21, 1805, when Admiral Horatio Nelson defeated the French fleet in the Battle of Trafalgar, giving his life in this great triumph for Great Britain. The next decade, which saw many events and ended with Napoleon's final defeat at Waterloo in 1815, was marked by important moments in Napoleon's personal life: his divorce from Josephine; his second marriage, to Marie Louise, daughter of the emperor of Austria, in 1810; and the birth of his son the next year. The period also experienced the further short-lived expansion of the empire. The dense twenty years that saw the ascent, domination, and decline of Napoleon were affected on the artistic plane by the taste he imposed on Europe. The recourse to the iconography of ancient imperial Rome, emblematically allusive to the greatness and power of the present empire, extended to every form of ornamental production. Related to it was the strong "Egyptian" component that associated the image of Bonaparte with that mysterious and rich land that he had not succeeded in conquering militarily in 1798 but that he was conquering instead with expeditions of archaeologists, researchers, and designers, who were bringing to light its most recondite secrets. With the intention of giving

Sèvres porcelain vase, 1813, with decoration by A. Béranger, *Arrival at the Louvre of the Works of Art Acquired by Napoleon during the Campaign in Italy*; Musée National de la Céramique, Sèvres

Francesco Hayez, *The Return to Rome of Her Stolen Works of Art*, 1817, fresco; Museo Chiaramonti, Vatican

Napoleon

the Louvre the greatest collection of masterpieces in the world, after changing the name of the institution to the Musée Napoléon, he ordered his experts to select the most beautiful or precious works of art from the principal museums in conquered countries, beginning with those of Italy and Spain, and bring them to Paris. A vase made of Sèvres porcelain in 1813 was decorated by Béranger with a representation of the parade in Paris on July 27, 1798, to celebrate the arrival of the paintings and sculptures stolen from Italy: among the works that can be recognized are the Apollo Belvedere, the *Laocoön*, and the Medici Venus, transported on rudimentary wooden carts. Many canvases and paintings on panels were also removed from palaces and galleries. With the fall of Napoleon, the Congress of Vienna ruled that France must return the works; thus the masterpieces made the return trip, as presented by Francesco Hayez in *The Return to Rome of Her Stolen Works of Art*, a fresco in the Vatican. An excellent strategist, Napoleon skillfully directed the diffusion of his image, paying attention to the smallest detail. Dozens of portraits were made that celebrated his effigy in many cities of the empire, expressing his impressive person and the determination of his character, aspects he was more concerned with than the reproduction of his actual features, unwilling as he was to stand still and pose in front of a painter. Each one of his triumphs was documented in paintings, sometimes with canvases of exceptional size. Many were created with the intention of forming a gallery of the emperor's glorious deeds that was to be accompanied by a series of portraits of the French marshals and would be placed in the Tuileries. A team of artists was at his service to help carry out this large propaganda campaign. In terms of style these artists were quite eclectic, for they were representative of the gradual passage from classicism to Romanticism that took place during Napoleon's reign. The leader of his group was Jacques-Louis David, *premier peintre de l'empereur* since 1804, followed by his leading students: Girodet, Guérin, and most of all the Romantic Gros. There was also Ingres, who portrayed Napoleon as first consul and then as Zeus on the imperial throne. David had the honor of painting what are perhaps the most famous paintings, including the colossal imperial *Coronation* in Notre-Dame and *Napoleon Crossing the St. Bernard Pass*. A crucial moment in his military ascent, Napoleon had crossed the Alps in the snow on a mule led by a local guide following the rear guard of his troops; and so it is that he appears, realistic and at the same time dignified, in the painting made in 1848 by Paul Delaroche. But Napoleon wanted to hand on to the world a far different version and had David present him at the triumphant head of his army, "calm on a fiery steed," with an inscription that linked him to two other great leaders of history, Hannibal and Charlemagne. Napoleon was able to entrust the divinization of his image and those of his family members to sculptors of the level of Canova and Thorvaldsen, but as the end neared the mechanism of propaganda ground to a halt. At the same time, however, other images rose in value: the duke of Wellington, hero of Waterloo, paid the astronomical price of twelve hundred guineas for the *Chelsea Pensioners Reading the Waterloo Dispatch*, painted by David Wilkie in 1818–22, by which time Napoleon had been safely relegated to Saint Helena.

David Wilkie, *Chelsea Pensioners Reading the Waterloo Dispatch*, 1818-22, oil on panel, 97 x 158 cm; Wellington Museum (Apsley House), London

Bertel Thorvaldsen, *Apotheosis of Napoleon*, 1820, marble; Thorvaldsens Museum, Copenhagen

Jacques-Louis David
Napoleon Crossing the St. Bernard Pass
1800, oil on canvas
272 x 241.3 cm
Musée National de la Malmaison, Paris

Napoleon's crossing of the St. Bernard Pass began the military campaign that led to his conquest of Italy in 1800. This painting, celebrating the general in a heroic, monumental pose, immediately helped spread his fame. To make the point clear, David includes Napoleon's name carved in the rock in the foreground beside those of Hannibal and Charlemagne, great heroes who had also crossed the Alps.

Sèvres Porcelain
Vase with reproduction of "Napoleon Crossing the St. Bernard Pass" by J.-L. David
1813, porcelain
height 108 cm
Musée du Louvre, Paris

Made by the most prestigious French porcelain factory, this vase was given by Napoleon to his mother in 1811, on the occasion of the baptism of the "king of Rome," his firstborn child. It reproduces his triumphant image, painted thirteen years earlier by David, which became an important element in the emperor's propagandistic iconography of power.

Antoine-Jean Gros
Bonaparte on the Bridge at Arcole
1796, oil on canvas
130 x 94 cm
Musée National des Châteaux de Versailles et de Trianon, Versailles

The battle fought between November 15 and 17, 1796, between French and Austrian troops near Arcole in the province of Verona was one of the outstanding moments of Napoleon's first Italian campaign and marked the beginning of his rapid political ascent. In Milan, not long after the battle, the general commissioned this painting from Gros with the precise intention of spreading his victorious image. He is shown in the pivotal moment in which, grabbing hold of the flag, he moved toward the bridge that separated the two armies, thus inspiring his troops to attack. The elegant uniform, seemingly better suited to a parade than to war, and the triumphant pose give the image an almost universal character and make the figure's heroism unmistakable.

ANDREA APPIANI
Napoleon, King of Italy
1805, oil on canvas
100 x 75 cm
Kunsthistorisches Museum, Vienna

In 1805 Appiani was named *premier peintre* to the king of Italy and was thus personally involved in the large-scale program celebrating Napoleon, including the *Fasti di Napoleone*, thirty-five monochrome canvases painted for Milan's Palazzo Reale, as well as numerous portraits. This portrait, today in Vienna, is among the most fascinating, not only because of the enamellike rendering of the elaborate uniform, but most of all because of the modernity with which the artist confronts the genre of the official portrait. The emperor is presented at half-bust, a form that was gradually replacing the full-figure image in the pre-Romantic period because it made it possible to concentrate on the psychological aspects of the individual. Thus Appiani presents the impressive fascination of the emperor but at the same time makes clear the power of his character, his determination as a man to succeed in his grandiose schemes of conquest.

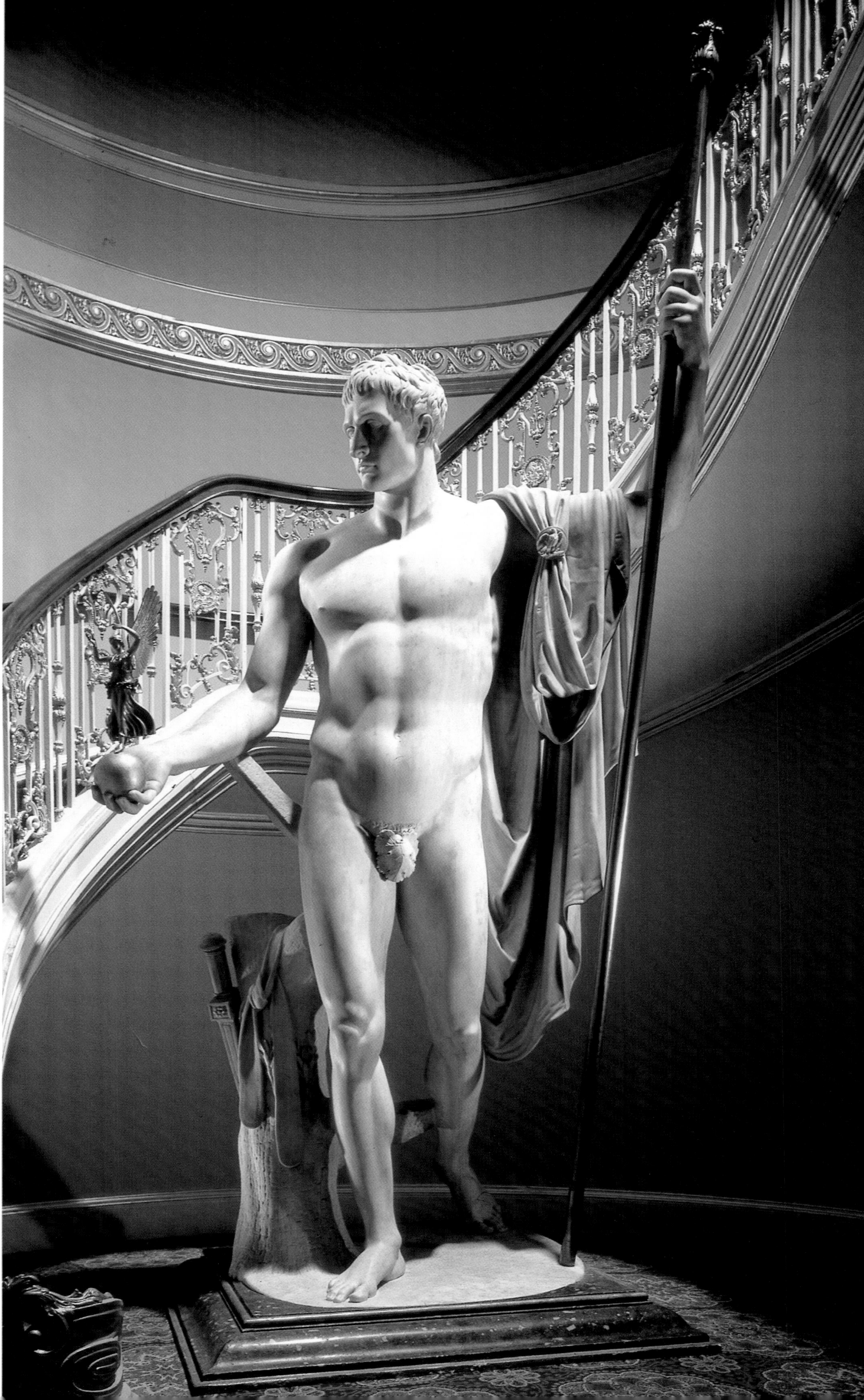

Antonio Canova
Napoleon as Mars the Pacifier
1806, marble
height 340 cm
Wellington Museum (Apsley House), London

Made between 1803 and 1806 this statue was designed to exalt Napoleon in the same way the sculptors of antiquity exalted Roman emperors, by putting a head of the emperor atop the kind of idealized body associated with the divine. Thus Canova sculpted a nude male figure bearing a staff and a globe surmounted by a statue of Victory, attributes that make the figure identifiable as Mars, god of war and pacifier, while the face displays the features of Bonaparte, who in those very years had become emperor of the French and king of Italy. Canova also portrayed Napoleon's sisters as divinities (most famously Pauline as *Venus Victorious* in the Borghese Gallery, Rome) as well as his second wife, the empress Marie Louise (as *Concordia*, Galleria Nazionale, Parma).

JEAN-AUGUSTE-DOMINIQUE INGRES
Napoleon as First Consul
1804, oil on canvas, 247 x 147 cm
Musée des Beaux-Arts, Liège

Ingres was twenty-four when he made this painting. It was not easy to make a portrait of Napoleon since he could not bear to stand still and hold a pose, so Ingres had to make rapid sketches to capture his features. The young artist, summoned together with Jean-Baptiste Greuze, had little time and only a single occasion to delineate that face. Nominated first consul after the *coup d'état* of 1799 and then made consul for life in 1802, Bonaparte wears the red velvet uniform with gold embroidery that distinguished consular office. Ingres reproduces the uniform in every detail, even pausing on the details of the furnishings and the page with the writing "*Faub*[ourg] *d'Amercoeur rebati*." The canvas had been commissioned by the city of Liège in memory of the reconstruction of its suburb of Amercoeur—visible outside the window—financed by Napoleon after the Austrian bombardments of 1794.

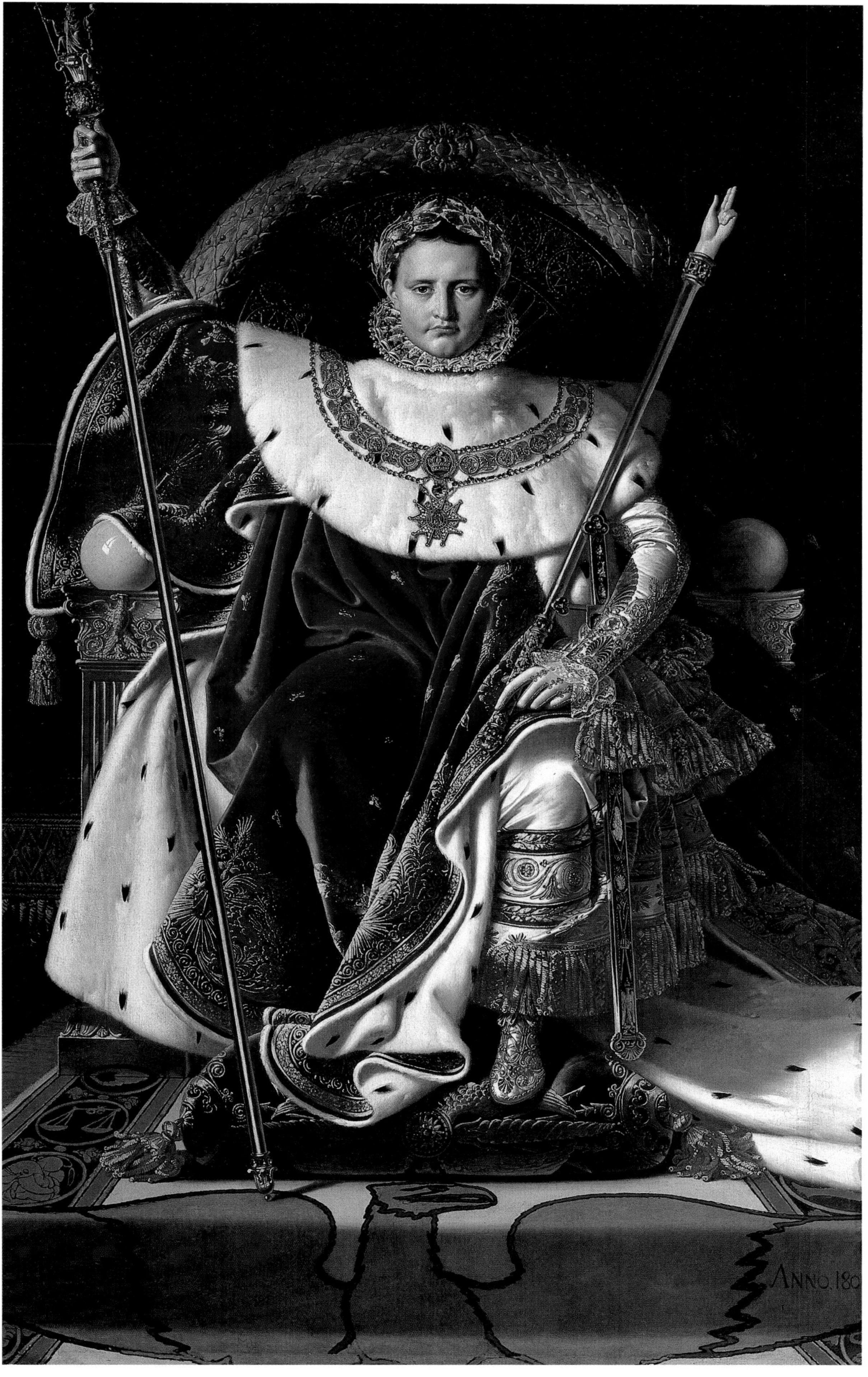

Jean-Auguste-Dominique Ingres
Napoleon I on the Imperial Throne
1806, oil on canvas
259 x 162 cm
Musée de l'Armée, Paris

The Paris Salon of 1806 was quite a fiasco for Ingres, since this and another four of his paintings met with severe scorn from critics. He was faulted for the face of the emperor, which critics claimed bore little resemblance to reality, but the artist knew that such accuracy was of far less importance to the emperor than the projection of a powerful image. So it is that Ingres presented him with the colossal solemnity of an enthroned divinity; he is presented in a majestic frontal pose, just as the ancients sculpted their gods or as the painters of the Renaissance painted the Blessing Father. Aside from the imperial scepter that he holds with his right hand, Napoleon had himself portrayed with the royal insignia that had been preserved in Saint-Denis since the Revolution: the finely engraved sword and the so-called hand of justice in ivory and precious stones, the antique scepter of the king of France that was believed to have belonged to Charlemagne. It is interesting to note that the tondo in the carpet at below left reproduces the *Madonna of the Chair* by Raphael.

Jacques-Louis David
Coronation of Napoleon in Notre-Dame
1807, oil on canvas
621 x 979 cm
Musée du Louvre, Paris

Napoleon himself commissioned this colossal canvas to commemorate his ascent to the imperial throne. The ceremony took place in Paris in the ancient cathedral of Notre-Dame on December 2, 1804. The artist represented the moment in which Napoleon, having already crowned himself emperor, was about to crown his wife, Josephine, kneeling before him, while the pope, seated at the center of the choir, gave his blessing. It took David nearly two years to complete the work, which presents a grandiose group portrait, including more than one hundred figures of the court and even himself, seated on the second tier of the gallery, busy making sketches in an album. The spectacular nature of the event revolves

around the rows of dignitaries and members of Napoleon's family. The first, in keeping with protocol, are dressed in the ancient style of ceremonial dress that dates back to the period of Henry IV; the others wear clothes in keeping with the most up-to-date Empire-style fashions. All of the people are presented in such accurate portraits that they can be recognized. To the far right, wearing the large red mantle, is the powerful and corpulent Charles de Talleyrand; farther up, to the left of the altar, is a group of ambassadors that includes the American John Armstrong; to the left, holding up the end of the empress's ceremonial robe, are the countess de la Rochefoucauld and madame de la Valette; farther to the left stand Napoleon's sisters Caroline, Pauline, and Elisa, while his mother, Madame Mère (Letizia Ramolino), looks down on the scene proudly from a seat in the transept.

Antoine-Jean Gros
Napoleon Visits the Plague Victims of Jaffa on March 11, 1799
1804, oil on canvas
523 x 715 cm
Musée du Louvre, Paris

This highly dramatic scene anticipates several elements typical of later Romantic painting. The bodies of the plague victims are rendered with a pathetic realism, in natural poses that emphasize their suffering, while Napoleon is given a heroic dimension that does not allude to military glory but exalts his human and almost divine side, since his gesture of touching the victim reflects the healing touch of ancient sovereigns.

Pietro Benvenuti
The Oath of the Saxons
1812, oil on canvas
380 x 480 cm
Galleria d'Arte Moderna di Palazzo Pitti, Florence

Defeated at Jena in 1806, Saxon officers pledge fidelity to Napoleon. The dark sky is barely illuminated by the moon, while the faces and suffering bodies of the defeated, along with the victorious French, are illuminated by an almost dazzling light located behind Napoleon. Among the French are Joachim Murat, with the white plume, and, in the turban to the right, the Mameluke Roustam, the emperor's personal bodyguard.

Antoine-Jean Gros
Napoleon on the Battlefield at Eylau
1808, oil on canvas
533 x 800 cm
Musée du Louvre, Paris

On February 8, 1807, Napoleon defeated the Russian army near the city of Eylau. In memory of that victory Gros did not want to create a conventional battle image, preferring instead to describe the moment following the encounter and its dramatic human consequences. The emperor is shown on horseback surrounded by his marshals, his triumph suggested by the black smoke in the distance that still rises from the fields and by the ranks of soldiers. The snow-covered bodies of dead soldiers in the foreground tell of the horror of war, as do the wounded who drag themselves near the victors to beg for compassion. Napoleon passes through this scene magnanimously, his gesture almost like that of a blessing, conceding pity and religious comfort, as can be deduced from the crucifixes being offered to the dying, visible in the corner at below left.

Pierre Narcisse Guérin
Bonaparte Pardoning the Rebels at Cairo
1808, oil on canvas
365 x 500 cm
Musée National des Châteaux de Versailles et de Trianon, Versailles

Napoleon had shown clemency toward the Mamelukes who rebelled against his rule at Cairo in 1798, but in reality the pardon had arrived only after the leaders responsible for the insurrection had been killed. Guérin creates a work with a celebratory role, adopting an unusual layout that is made subtle through the play of light. Rather than locate Napoleon in the foreground he places him a little back, thus making room for the group of pardoned rebels who, standing out in their exotic and colorful garb, support the notion that their well-being is the result of actions of the general himself.

Pietro Benvenuti
Elisa Baciocchi and Her Court
1813, oil on canvas
325 x 485 cm
Musée National des Châteaux de Versailles et de Trianon, Versailles

Elisa Baciocchi, made grand duchess of Tuscany in 1809 by her brother Napoleon, appears here in Florence's Pitti Palace, that city's royal palace, surrounded by the prestigious team of artists of whom she was an active patron in the five years that preceded the Restoration. Among the highly recognizable artists are Antonio Canova, shown presenting Elisa's husband, Félix-Pascal Baciocchi, with a marble portrait bust of her, made in Florence in the spring of 1812 and today at Versailles, and, seated behind the bust in front of a canvas, François-Xavier Fabre, a student of David, who occupied the post of court painter and is making a portrait of the grand duchess, whose crown has already been painted on the canvas. Behind the easel is Benvenuti himself, intent on drawing Elisa's profile on a sheet of paper. Elisa appears yet again in the small colored-wax portrait exhibited to the left rear by the sculptor Emilio Santarelli.

JEAN-PIERRE FRANQUE
Allegory of the Condition of France before the Return from Egypt
1810, oil on canvas
261 x 326 cm
Musée du Louvre, Paris

Jean-Pierre Franque (1774–1860) is not a well-known painter: we know he was a student of David and that he belonged to the group of the so-called primitives, artists who were the first to rebel against the style of David and propose a return to a simple art, inspired by that of the ancients or the early Renaissance. This painting, however, reveals a quite different sensibility, projected toward a vision with a dreamy, unreal intonation. In a spectacular scene, a source of almost blinding light reaches from the distant background to illuminate the group of allegorical figures turned toward Napoleon; his profile is effectively placed against the light to capture the emotion that grips him in the presence of this vision, while the pyramid in the distance makes reference to the Egyptian campaign that he led as first consul.

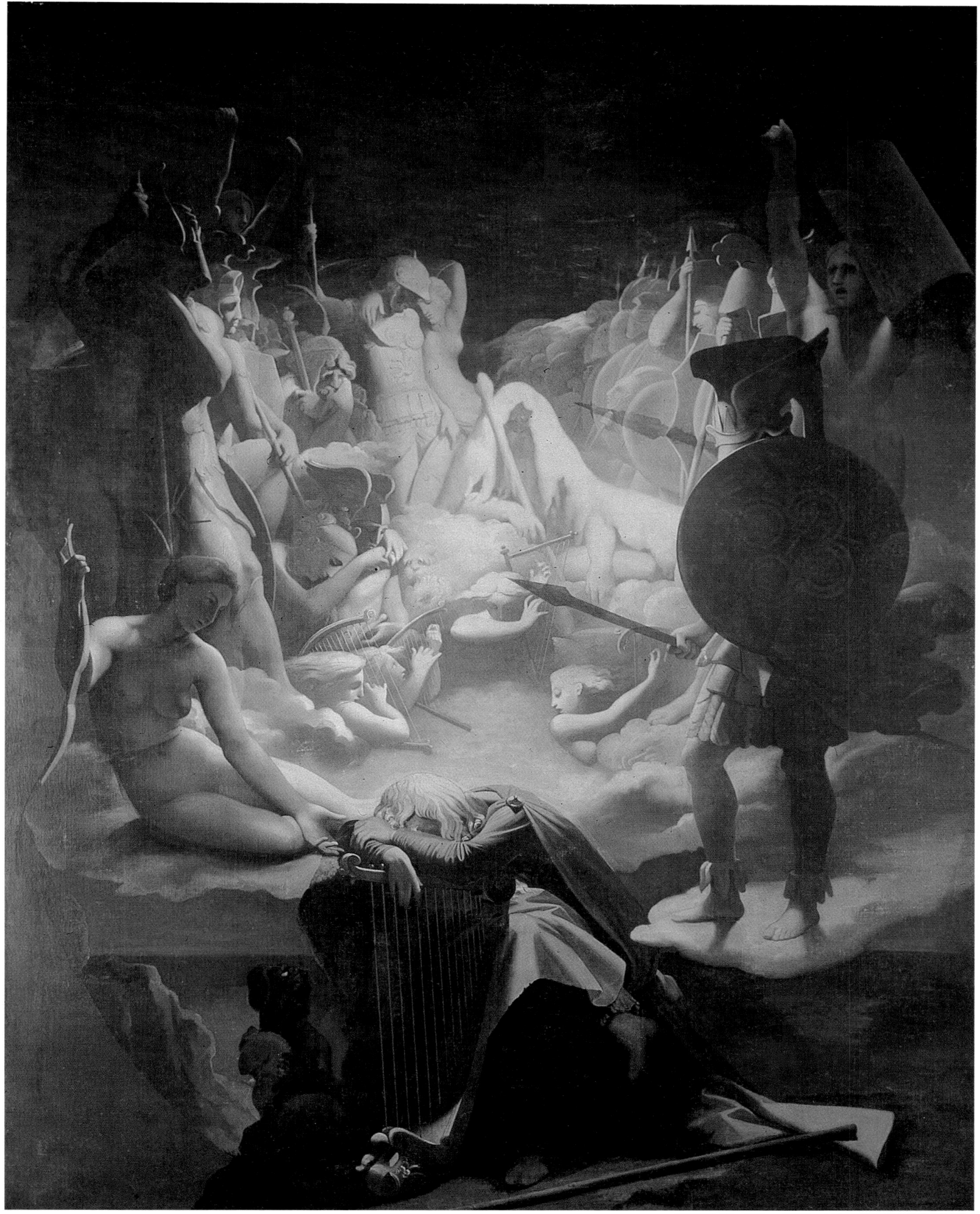

Jean-Auguste-Dominique Ingres
The Dream of Ossian
1813, oil on canvas
348 x 275 cm
Musée Ingres, Montauban

Napoleon had Ingres make this canvas as a ceiling decoration for his bedroom in the Quirinal Palace in Rome. The emperor was among those most responsible for spreading the popularity in France of the poems of Ossian, the legendary Gaelic bard made famous by the Scottish poet James Macpherson in a series of books beginning in 1760. Ossian was soon being compared to Homer, and in fact he appears in the foreground of this image accompanied by many of the attributes that for centuries had been used for the image of Homer, including the lyre, cloak, and long white hair. In the background Ingres presents an unusual opening to the visionary style of Romanticism, in this case achieved through the evocative effect of a supernatural glow that illuminates the figures, making them almost evanescent.

Eugène Isabey
Transfer of the Ashes of Napoleon I to "La Belle Poule," October 15, 1840
1842, oil on canvas
238 x 369 cm
Musée National des Châteaux de Versailles et de Trianon, Versailles

In 1840, King Louis Philippe decreed the transfer of the ashes of Napoleon from Saint Helena to the church of the Invalides in Paris. Eugène Isabey, an artist who specialized in marine scenes, preserved the memory in this highly effective image. Since he had not himself witnessed the event, he interviewed people who had taken part in the expedition. The canvas shows the emotional moment in which the emperor's remains were transferred aboard the French frigate *La Belle Poule*, on which they were then carried back to France. Highlighted by black-and-white drapery, the coffin appears suspended between the sky and the sea, assuming a sort of sacredness that Isabey emphasized in the suggestive atmospheric rendering. The scene is framed by the dark sea and dark sky, clouds of smoke from the three hundred cannons fired in salvos still hanging in the air, lines of rigging and cables in an almost obsessive abundance, along with the pennons on the ships and the sloops.

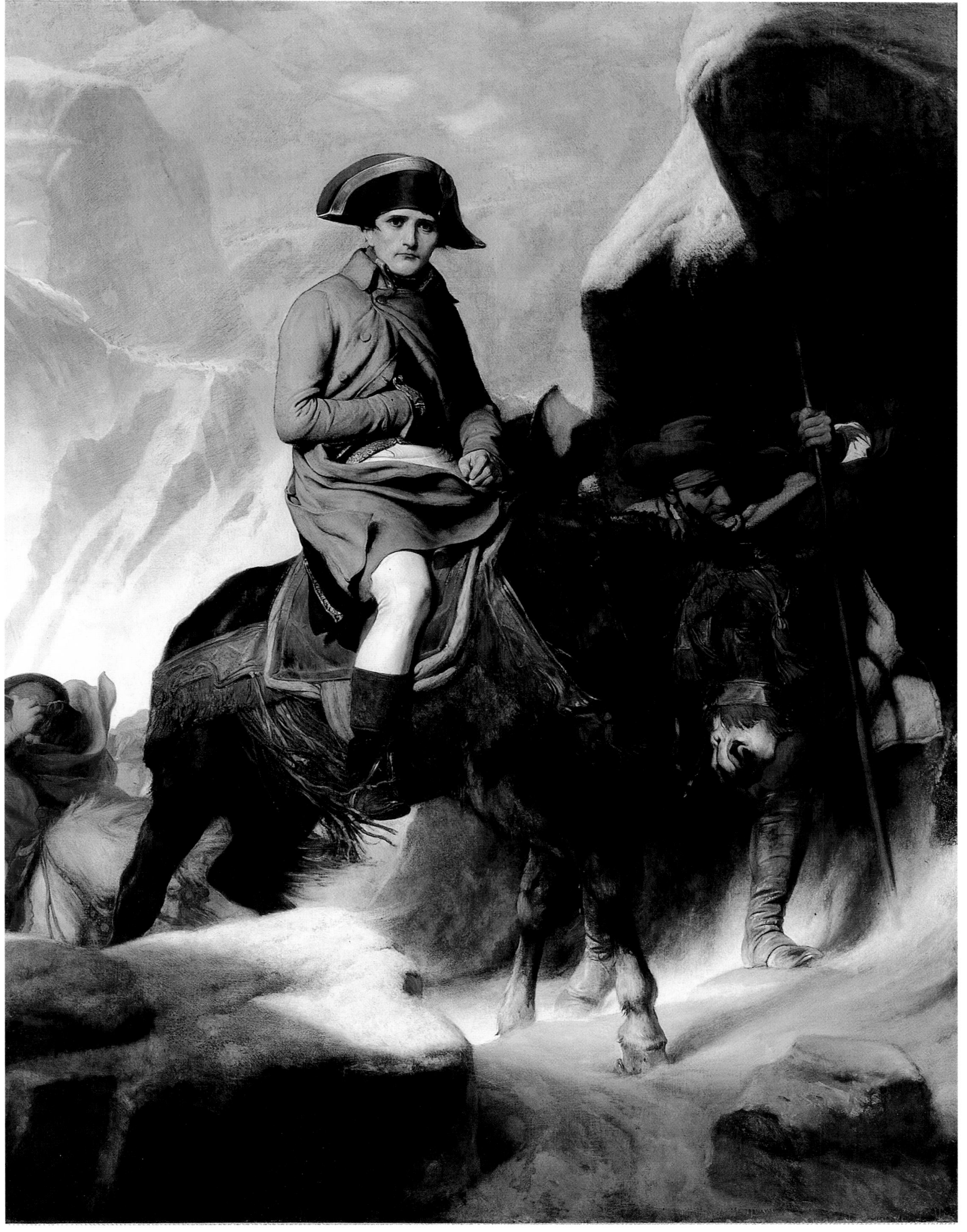

PAUL DELAROCHE
Napoleon Crossing the Alps
1848, oil on canvas
289 x 222 cm
Musée du Louvre,
Paris

Many years after the death of Napoleon, in 1848, a politically crucial year for Europe and for France, Delaroche made a work conceived following a new viewpoint, no longer concentrating on the heroism of the figure but applying instead a form of historical revisionism. The crossing of the Alps undertaken by Napoleon and his troops here finds an interpretation enormously different from the triumphant tones expressed by David in 1800. Without malicious intentions, but seeking to examine the human side of the event, the canvas presents Napoleon on a mule being led with difficulty by a guide who moves ahead slowly in the snow. The general looks tired but determined, seated in the pose by which he will always be identified, one hand inserted in the chest of his coat, emphasizing the contrast between official display and the hard realities of war.

Since the Renaissance, portraiture had enjoyed great popularity, and with the opening of the market to an increasingly large public of patrons, the genre came to enjoy even greater fortune during the first decades of the nineteenth century. The typological variety of portraiture was already quite broad. There were the traditional full-figure or half-bust formulas, whether in official or more natural poses; there were idealized or allegorical portraits; individual or group portraits; and there were self-portraits. For a certain period the portrait souvenir, an inheritance from the late eighteenth century related to the custom of the Grand Tour, was very much in vogue. The tourist would have himself portrayed against a background of a city visited on the tour, most often Rome. The profound social upheavals brought about by the French Revolution opened the way for the middle-class portrait, which arrived in time to support a style that had been taking shape during the previous decades, that of images of self-confident ease, such as *Reverend Robert Walker Skating on Duddingston Loch*, painted by Henry Raeburn

Jean-Auguste-Dominique Ingres, *The Comtesse d'Haussonville,* 1845, oil on canvas, 132 x 92 cm; Frick Collection, New York

the Salon of 1824: "The school of David can paint only bodies; it is decidedly incapable of painting souls." The implicit accusation of the great master brings into focus the discrepancy between two different conceptions of the portrait, which continued to coexist for many decades, even past the middle of the century. There was the more courtly trend of the sophisticated production of Ingres, who carried on the aristocratic style of David, and there was the trend that preferred, as Baudelaire said in exalting the painting of Delacroix, "the energetic temperament that is the fatality of

Portraits: and middle-

in 1784. Not only England but also France saw the gradual rise in popularity of the portrait with a landscape background, a formula that made possible the visual expression of the relationship between individual and natural setting that was so dear to the Romantic viewpoint. To that was added, during the years of the empire, a fondness for the psychological investigation already perceptible in the portrait of Empress Josephine made at the dawn of the century by Pierre-Paul Prud'hon. Romanticism made a cult of such introspective studies, as indicated by Géricault's paintings of the faces of the insane (see page 253) or the opinion expressed by Stendhal in his comment on

Henry Raeburn, *Reverend Robert Walker Skating on Duddingston Loch,* 1784, oil on canvas, 76.2 x 63.5 cm; National Gallery of Scotland, Edinburgh

the genius." In terms of the Salon, the Ingres trend was long the winning one. The portraits he painted in the name of the perfection of the line were greatly desired by high society, also because he imbued such compositions with details of sophisticated feminine seduction or he amplified the available space with reflections in a mirror, as in *The Comtesse d'Haussonville* or *Madame Moitesser*. The famous *Monsieur Bertin* (1832; Musée du Louvre, Paris) is a portrait without background. But in the sitter's extemporaneous pose and eloquent gaze Ingres summarized the triumph of the liberal middle class of the 1830s. Francisco Goya played on the subtle combination of psychology and social role, producing such masterpieces as the portrait of Ferdinand Guillemardet, which was exhibited in 1799 at the Academy of San Fernando together with the series of *Witches* painted for the duchess of Osuna. In the pre-Romantic age the concept of ideal beauty, which had been a cornerstone of neoclassical aesthetics, leading artists to ennoble the natural appearance of the person being portrayed, correcting defects, was gradually moderated, leaving room for a more objective observation of features. Another trend began to make itself felt in portraits from the age of Napoleon. In making portraits of that ruler painters put more emphasis on expressing the great man's character than on achieving an accurate reproduction of his features, beginning a process of humanizing sovereigns that was continued by Romantic artists, sometimes with truly fascinating results. There is, for example, the pompous but terribly realistic portrait of the Emperor Ferdinand I of Austria made by Hayez in 1840 or the canvas made three years later by Franz Xaver Winterhalter, in which the young Queen

aristocratic ideals class models

Victoria wanted to be shown in her simple femininity. Another English masterpiece is the portrait of King George IV made by Thomas Lawrence in 1821. Official and majestic, at the same time it puts the accent on the extravagant character of the sovereign, further demonstrating how, beginning with Joshua Reynolds, English portraiture had anticipated the exaltation of personality. A separate chapter is constituted by portraiture strictly tied to specific movements within painting, such as Purismo, the Nazarenes, or the English Pre-Raphaelites, each of which at various interpretative levels used stylistic models from a distant past to create images outside time, including portraits of contemporaries in which the relationship with modern reality has been altered or eliminated. Such is the portrait of Costanza Monti Perticari (see page 164), conceived by Filippo Agricola as a work by Raphael, or the portrait of Franz Pforr (see page 158), whom Friedrich Overbeck transformed into a young German of the 1400s. In Italy Francesco Hayez drew his inspiration from Renaissance portraits but achieved quite different results; taking from the great Venetian tradition the values of the inner nature, of the enigmatic silence of figures, he captured the subtle psychological shadings in the expressions of his sitters, often aristocrats, high-ranking members of the political and cultural life of Italy, or their children, such as the intense *Giulio Vigoni as a Child.* The equilibrium between officialness and sentiment that triumphs in his portraits eventually brought him victory in his competition with Giuseppe Molteni, who was more given to satisfying the vanity of the bel monde of Milan. Just as politicians, entrepreneurs, and members of the economically ascendant middle class became increasingly assiduous patrons of self-celebrative portraits, many Romantic intellectuals too wanted to see their personalities exalted. Thus we have the portrait of Franz Liszt made by Henry Lehmann in 1840 (Musée Carnavalet, Paris) and the portrait of Charles Baudelaire made by Émile Deroy in 1844 (Musée National des Châteaux de Versailles et de Trianon, Versailles). The first of these was criticized for exaggerating the sense of the figure's inner turmoil; the second reproduced the poet's almost satanic vein with such psychological penetration that the work disturbed the jury and was not admitted to the Salon.

Francesco Hayez, *Giulio Vigoni as a Child,* 1842, oil on canvas, 110 x 85 cm; Villa Mylius Vigoni, Loveno (Como)

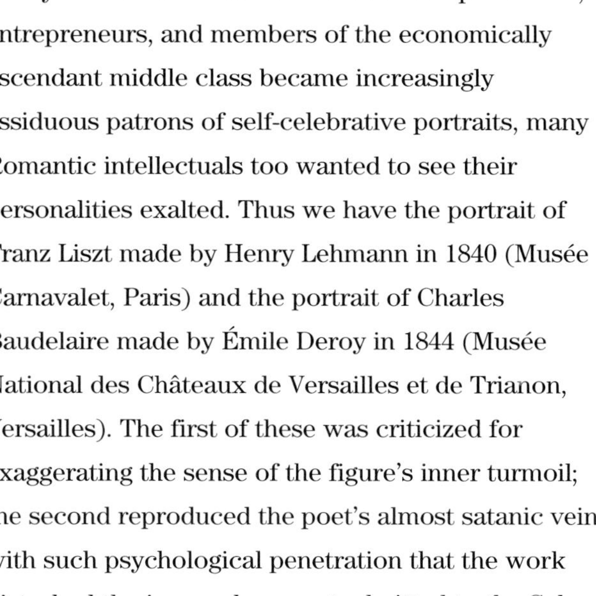

Francisco Goya, *Ferdinand Guillemardet,* 1797, oil on canvas, 186 x 124 cm; Musée du Louvre, Paris

Anne-Louis Girodet-Trioson
Jean-Baptiste Belley, Deputy for Santo Domingo
1797, oil on canvas
159 x 113 cm
Musée National des Châteaux de Versailles et de Trianon, Versailles

Jean-Baptiste Belley, born a slave, had been sent as representative of the colony of Santo Domingo to the French Republican Convention; in 1794 he had led a successful campaign to abolish slavery in the colonies and had succeeded in guaranteeing the rights of citizenship to the black population. Girodet portrayed him leaning on the pedestal of a bust of the philosopher Guillaume Raynal (1713–1796), who had only recently died and who in 1770 had laid the basis for the condemnation of slavery. The figure of the deputy stands out with beautiful chromatic clarity against the enameled background of the landscape and the marble of the sculpture; contrasting the refinement of the clothes and the casual attitude of the pose, the artist achieves a fascinating effect of naturalness, reinforcing the portrait's political message.

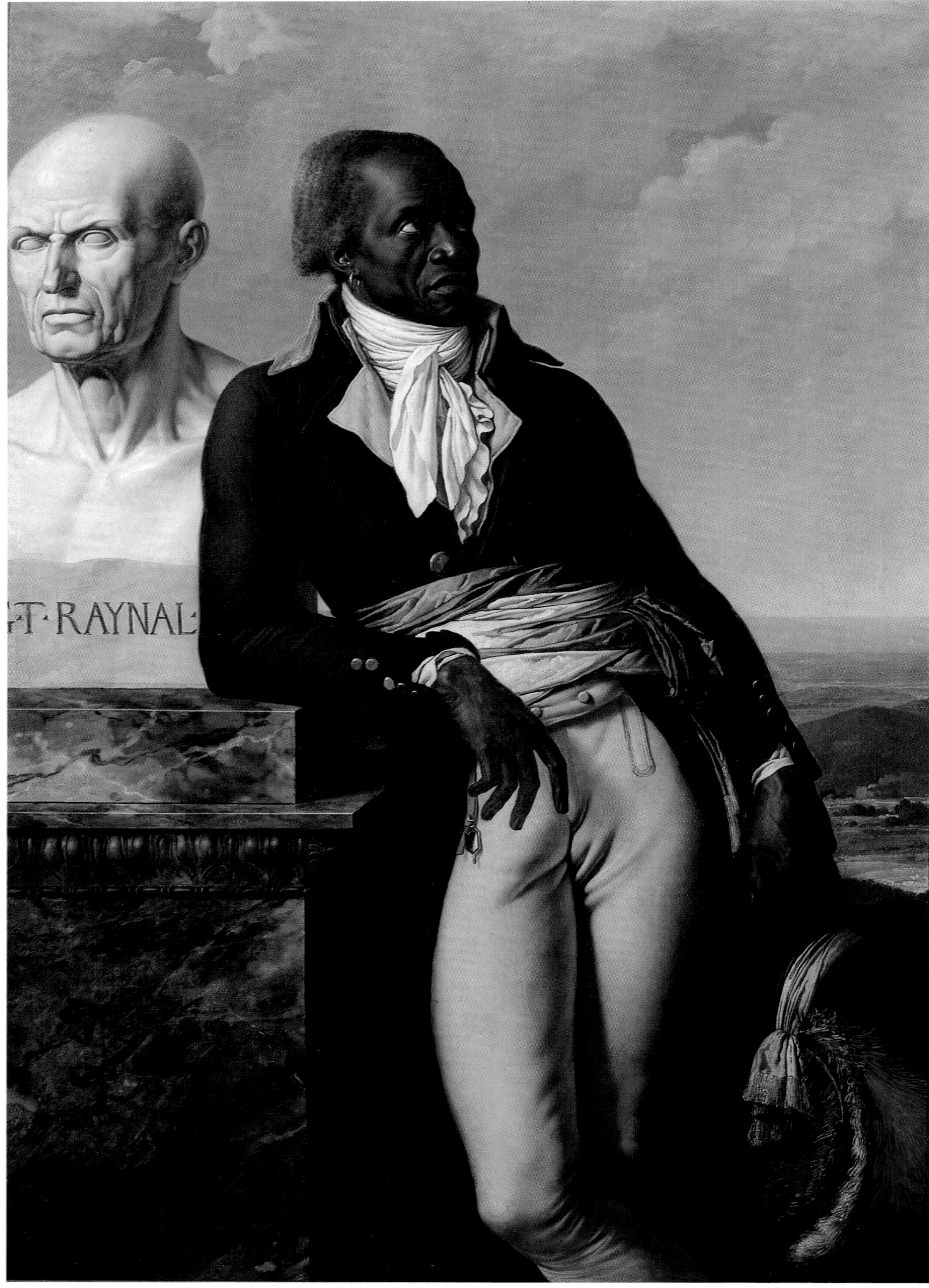

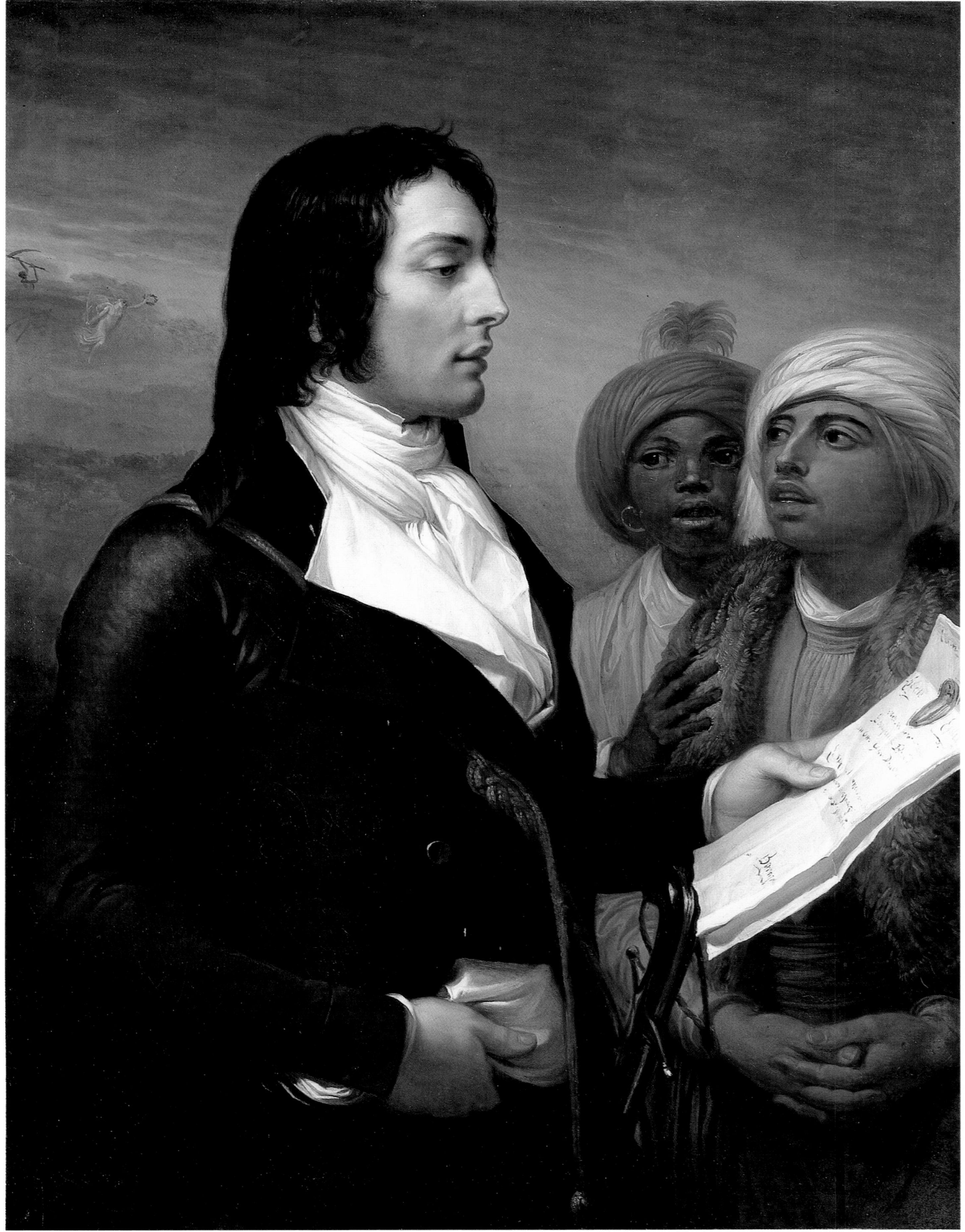

Andrea Appiani
General Desaix
1801, oil on canvas
115 x 88 cm
Musée National des Châteaux de Versailles et de Trianon, Versailles

Louis-Charles-Antoine Desaix (1768–1800), a general in the Revolutionary Wars, had performed a fundamental role in the conquest of the Upper Nile Valley in Egypt, where he had been named "the just governor" because of his humane treatment of the Egyptians. His strategic skills had been of determinant importance in Napoleon's success in Italy; in 1800 it had been Desaix's surprise attack on the Austrians that had won the battle of Marengo, in which he lost his life. Bonaparte commissioned Appiani to make this portrait of the young general that same year. The work is among the most appealing of the artist's production; the delicate allegorical insert with the figures of Time and, right behind her, Death in the sky to the left are the only allusions to the officer's premature death. The two turbaned figures evoke the military glories of Desaix, who appears absorbed, indifferent to the document he holds in his hands and delineated in the full fascination of his success.

PIERRE-PAUL PRUD'HON
The Empress Josephine
1805, oil on canvas
244 x 179 cm
Musée du Louvre, Paris

Originally from Martinique, Josèphe Rose Tascher de La Pagerie was born in 1763; widow of General de Beauharnais, she married Napoleon Bonaparte in 1796 and at the period of this painting had only recently been made empress. Prud'hon portrayed her in a languid, dreamy attitude following the English style. Although a painter of neoclassical training, he imbues the scene with a clearly Romantic sensibility, harmonizing the delicate, shadowy atmosphere of the setting—the park of Malmaison—with the absorbed and slightly melancholy expression of Josephine. The figure's sinuous elegance is enriched by the vaporous sense of the typically Empire-style dress; the long red shawl was an accessory very much in vogue among the French aristocracy of the time. Josephine failed to produce an heir to the empire, and in 1809 Napoleon had their marriage annulled (after which she lived in retirement at Malmaison).

François Gérard
The Marchesa Visconti
1810, oil on canvas
224 x 144 cm
Musée du Louvre, Paris

An artist born into the French aristocracy, Gérard made more than two hundred portraits of the leading lights of his time. Even the young subject of this canvas, wife of the ambassador of the Cisalpine Republic to France, reflects the notoriety of his clientele. The artist portrays her in an almost stormy atmosphere, against the background of a darkening sky that preludes rain, her dress moved by the wind as she leans against the ruins of a wall draped with vine shoots. With her stylish dress, the marchesa seems both elegant and seductive, but at the same time she is animated by an intense expression of sentiment, vaguely melancholic.

Anne-Louis Girodet-Trioson
Satirical Portrait of Mademoiselle Lange as Danaë
1799, oil on canvas
65 x 54 cm
Minneapolis Institute of Arts, Minneapolis

This portrait was made as a small vendetta, after Mademoiselle Lange, a stage actress, forced the painter to withdraw an earlier version from the Salon, holding that it did not do justice to her beauty. Girodet complied, but two weeks later brought back the canvas, enriched with delicious elements alluding to the actress's not always moral behavior. The young woman is presented as Danaë, who was impregnated by Zeus in the form of a golden shower; Girodet turns the shower into coins and presents Lange, known for her wealthy lovers, in the act of collecting them. At her feet is a scroll identified as the *Asinaria* by Plautus, a comic drama in which a courtesan bestows her favors on a father and son at the same time. Even more biting to contemporaries was the inclusion of the turkey with the peacock-feather tail and ring on its foot, in the face of which contemporaries saw an uncanny resemblance to the actress's husband.

Anne-Louis Girodet-Trioson
Jacques Cathelineau, Vendéan General
1816, oil on canvas
266 x 141 cm
Musée d'Art et d'Histoire, Cholet

Jacques Cathelineau (1759–1793) was one of the leaders of the Vendéan insurrection, which in March 1793 took over various towns to the south of the Loire. After being made general of the Catholic and royal army, the young man successfully led the conquest of Nantes but fell mortally wounded shortly after its capture. Girodet presents him without emphasizing his glory, wrapped in a silk-lined cloak and in a simple pose, his sword lowered, pistol stuck in his sash. Cathelineau, of peasant origin, is not presented with the rhetoric of a military victory. He points toward the battle behind him while looking into the distance, but in the opposite direction, almost to signify his coming detachment from earthly things. His sad and intense expression is echoed by the dark storminess of the sky and by the cross visible to the left.

GIUSEPPE TOMINZ
Self-Portrait with Brother Francesco
circa 1820,
oil on canvas
168 x 139 cm
Musei Provinciali, Gorizia

Born in Gorizia in 1790, Giuseppe Tominz was about thirty when he painted this self-portrait, in which he presents himself together with his brother Francesco, perhaps on the eve of a separation. In fact the two men look in different directions, and the way they are dressed emphasizes their differing aspirations. Francesco's fondness for elegant clothes and his passion for hunting are made clear, reinforced by the two beautiful hunting dogs and the statue of Diana to the right. The palette and brushes identify the artist, who is dressed in an ancient-style outfit, evocative of the atmosphere of Rome, where he had spent an important period of study. Also alluding to Rome is the base of the giant column behind the two brothers, wrapped in a heavy cloth, balanced on the right by the city of Gorizia, illuminated by a mellow, serene light. It is a sentimental, familiar insert that reveals signs of Romantic intonations in Tominz.

Giuseppe Molteni
Carlo Vassalli
1830, oil on canvas
250 x 178 cm
Museo del Risorgimento, Milan

For many decades Molteni competed with Francesco Hayez on the art scene in Lombardy, but without ever reaching the other artist's level. He was an active portraitist of the Milanese *bel monde,* as indicated by this canvas, in which he captured the casual elegance of Carlo Vassalli, groom to Caroline of Brunswick.

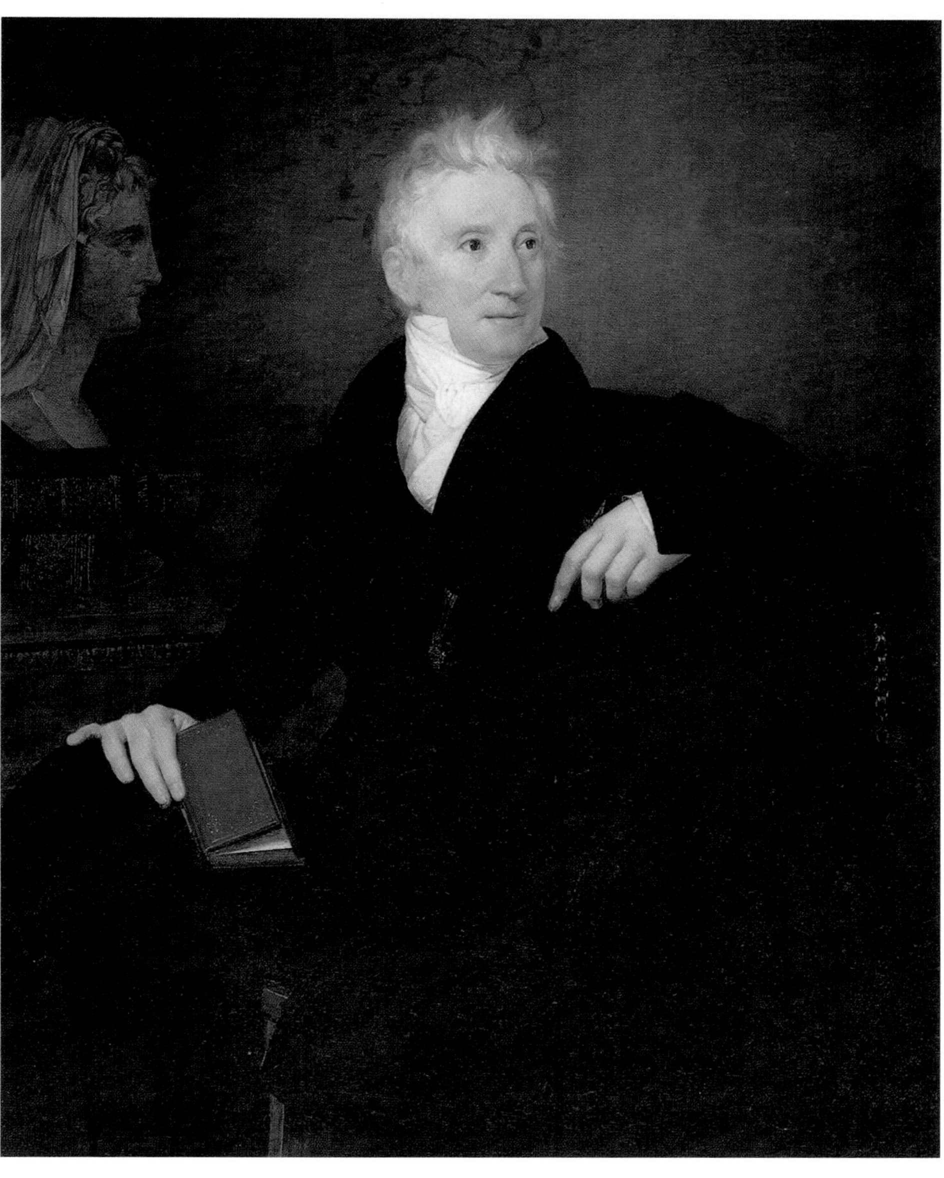

Ludovico Lipparini
Leopoldo Cicognara
1825, oil on canvas
118 x 93 cm
Galleria d'Arte Moderna di Ca' Pesaro, Venice

Cicognara was made president of Venice's Academy of Fine Arts in 1807; he was a close friend of Hayez and, in particular, of Canova, which explains the inclusion to the left of the *Bust of Beatrice*, given him by the sculptor in 1818. The two volumes on the table are works by Winckelmann and D'Agincourt, supporters of the theories of ancient art proposed by Cicognara in his *History of Italian Sculpture* (1813–18).

Thomas Lawrence
King George IV
1821, oil on canvas
289.6 x 200.7 cm
Royal Collection,
Windsor

George IV ascended the throne on January 29, 1820, at the age of fifty-eight. A singular personality, somewhat eccentric, he had secretly married a Roman Catholic in 1785, a marriage that was held illegal; as king he did not cease to conduct a dissolute life, full of adventurous loves until his political marriage to Caroline of Brunswick in 1795. Sternly conservative politically, George IV permitted himself every type of personal luxury. He was known to his subjects not only for his large collection of masterpieces, with which he filled his London residences, but also for his rich and extravagant wardrobe. In this portrait he appears in majestic official dress, but despite the monumentality of the pose, Lawrence succeeds in subtly catching the mental vivacity of the ruler, concentrating more on the angle of his head and the ruffled hair than on the expression of his face, which is full of lively, vital energy.

Jacques-Louis David
Juliette de Villeneuve
1824, oil on canvas
198 x 123 cm
Musée du Louvre, Paris

Dating to the year of the epochal Salon that saw the definitive affirmation of Romantic painting in France, this portrait strikes a balance between the more traditional artistic style and the innovations of the period. The layout is sober and orderly, with a precise attention to the setting that surrounds the woman and defines her social level: the beautiful harp, the Empire-style armchair, the stylish hat hanging from the music stand, which confers a joyful note to the painting and is echoed by the bright colors of the silk shawl. But David also permits himself to overcome the old canons; no longer holding it necessary to adapt the face of the woman to the aesthetic demands of the past, he presents her as she is. Even the way the rug is slightly disarranged by the feet of the stand contributes to the sense of immediacy.

Francesco Hayez
The Emperor Ferdinand I of Austria
1840, oil on canvas
121 x 90.5 cm
Museo del Risorgimento, Milan

With surprising audacity and psychological penetration of a rare expressive power, Hayez here presents a work that is completely detached from the official canons of celebratory portraiture. The emperor, who came to Milan in 1838 for his coronation in the cathedral with the Iron Crown, is not presented with the solemnity of his position—confirmed by the royal uniform—but is shown instead in his true character, the result of an introspective analysis that makes an almost cruel assessment of his personality. The somewhat absent expression, the distracted gesture with which the monarch holds the scepter, and his disregard for the crown, which seems about to slip off the cushion, concur in presenting a pitiless image of the man in a work that is the opposite of a standard portrait of a ruler. Hayez presents a clumsy emperor, indifferent to the affairs of government, as even Prince Metternich, his chancellor, did not hesitate to admit.

Karl Pavlovich Briullov
Amazon
1832, oil on canvas
291.5 x 206 cm
Tretyakov Gallery, Moscow

Painted during Briullov's first stay in Italy, between 1822 and 1834, with time spent in Milan, Naples, and most of all Rome, this painting reveals the thoroughly Romantic approach of his painting. The work presents an image of daily life located in the aristocratic atmosphere of the time, in which refined and precious details are presented with spontaneity and domestic warmth. The portrait is also tied to the artist's personal life, since it presents Giovannina and Amacilia Pacini, the two adopted daughters of Countess Yulia Samoilova, a rich Russian noblewoman whom Briullov met in Rome and who became the great love of his life.

HORACE VERNET
Thorvaldsen Sculpts the Bust of Vernet
1833, oil on canvas
99.8 x 75.2 cm
Thorvaldsens Museum, Copenhagen

The combination of portraits gives this painting a singular character. It is testimony to the friendship between the two artists, who were among the most notable foreigners in Rome during the 1830s. The celebrated Danish sculptor Bertel Thorvaldsen, who in fact spent most of his life in Rome, is here presented, scalpel in hand, beside the bust he had made of Horace Vernet (Musée Calvet, Avignon) the year before. The painter, commissioned by the Fine Arts Association of Copenhagen to make a portrait of Thorvaldsen, thus made a kind of double portrait that bears witness to the mutual respect that united the two artists. The sculptor is presented with exceptional pictorial emphasis, the pallor of his work clothes illuminating the entire portrait; Vernet succeeds in transferring his friend's forceful personality to the canvas: brilliant and decisive, with a serious but lively expression, he is also slightly disheveled, as is expected of all artists.

THOMAS PHILLIPS
Lord Byron in Albanian Costume
1835, oil on canvas
76.5 x 63.9 cm
National Portrait Gallery, London

The myth of Lord George Gordon Byron (1788–1824) began taking shape while the poet was still alive, and many portraits of him were made after his premature death in Greece (perhaps from meningitis), where he had gone to fight in the war of liberation against the Turks. This painting is a replica of a portrait that was probably made in 1813; Byron, on the request of his publisher John Murray, posed for Phillips dressed in Albanian clothes that he had bought during a trip to Epirus in 1809 and that are still preserved at Bowood in Wiltshire. The costume reflects his great passion for the East, which even before his involvement in the cause of Greek independence had led him to write poems set in exotic locales, works that became sources of inspiration for many Romantic painters.

EDWIN HENRY LANDSEER
Eos
1841, oil on canvas
111.8 x 142.9 cm
Royal Collection, Windsor

Queen Victoria had this unusual portrait made as a Christmas present for her husband, Prince Albert, in 1841. Eos, a beautiful female greyhound, was the prince consort's favorite dog. He had brought her with him from Germany in 1840 when he came to London to marry Victoria. The animal appears in other paintings by Landseer, such as *Windsor Castle in Modern Times* (see page 138). The artist, who specialized in animal portraits, here presents a composition that is evocative of the aristocratic climate

to which the dog belonged. Seen in profile, with his silver collar, Eos is posed in front of an elegant *table habilée* covered in red drapery on which rests the prince's walking cane, its ivory handle carved in the shape of a hunting dog, an item typical of the style of the period but still in use at the beginning of the twentieth century. To the left is an elegant foot rest whose style further emphasizes Albert's passion for hunting; resting atop it, as though idly tossed there, are his top hat and gloves, details that suggest the dog may be waiting to take a walk with her master. Eos died on July 31, 1843, and this portrait was used as the basis for a bronze statue for her tomb in Home Park, Windsor.

FRANCESCO HAYEZ
Venus Playing with Two Doves (Portrait of Carlotta Chabert)
1830, oil on canvas
183 x 137 cm
Cassa di Risparmio di Trento e Rovereto, Trent

Commissioned by Count Girolamo Malfatti, this work was made during Hayez's visit to Trent, where he was commissioned to make a portrait of the ballerina Carlotta Chabert, lover of the Trent nobleman. Exhibited at the Brera in 1830, the painting caused heated discussion between Romantics, who supported Hayez, and classicists, still strongly anchored to tradition. Hayez drew inspiration from the classical model of the Callipygian Venus (Museo Archeologico Nazionale, Naples), adapting it, on the example of the great Titian, to the features of the model chosen by his patron. The melding of a ballerina and a goddess was seen as scandalous by those who, in defense of the classical concept of beauty, thought the image of Venus had been desecrated by the superimposition of the portrait of the controversial ballerina on an aesthetic model.

Franz Xaver Winterhalter
Queen Victoria
1843, oil on canvas
65.4 x 53.3 cm
Royal Collection, Windsor

Thoroughly unusual as the portrait of a queen, this canvas was commissioned by Victoria herself as a birthday present for Prince Albert, to whom she had by then been married for three years.
She wanted to be portrayed in private clothes, with her hair falling loosely to her shoulders, without any reference to her royal position. The artist succeeded perfectly in meeting her request, presenting the sovereign in her youthful freshness and simple femininity in a dreamy pose that the prince consort found enormously pleasing. On August 26, 1843, Victoria noted in her diary the joy of having given her husband the "secret picture" and that it had made him happy.

THÉODORE CHASSÉRIAU
Two Sisters
1843, oil on canvas
180 x 135 cm
Musée du Louvre, Paris

Having entered the atelier of Ingres when he was only twelve years old, Chassériau became Ingres's favorite student because of his exceptional precociousness. When Chassériau made this double portrait he was already turning to the appealing repertory of Delacroix, but perhaps in no other work of his did he more clearly apply the teachings of his master. The two girls stand out sharply and brightly against the background, their figures emerging from the arrangement of enameled colors that gives their bodies distinct, three-dimensional solidity. Their faces are almost the same, but differ with the subtle acuteness with which Chassériau defined their characters, bringing to light the very different expressions of their personalities.

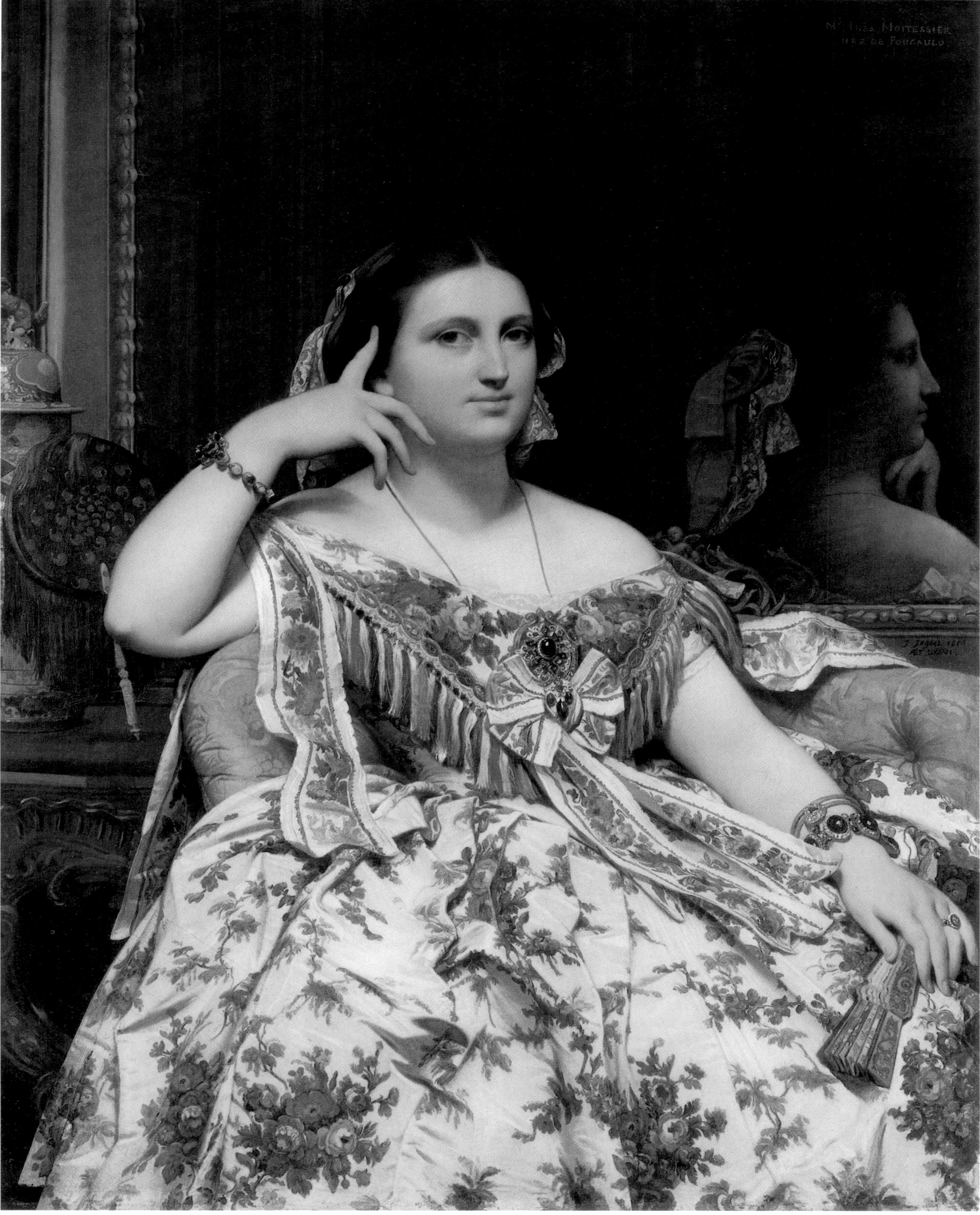

Jean-Auguste-Dominique Ingres
Madame Moitessier Seated
1856, oil on canvas
120 x 92.1 cm
National Gallery, London

Born in 1821, Marie-Clotilde-Ines de Foucauld was twenty-one when she married the rich banker Sigisbert Moitessier; in 1844 the banker asked Ingres to make a portrait of his young wife. At first reluctant, the painter accepted after being struck by the fascination of Ines. Even so, the painting remained unfinished for a long time, being finally completed only in 1856. The work offers an emblematic example of Ingres' portraiture and the refined manner that earned him a reputation as the "painter of motionless beauty." With her enigmatic expression, the woman is presented in all her gaudy elegance, with jewels, the *cachepeigne* made visible by the position of the mirror, the peacock-feather fan behind her. But it is the magnificence of the dress with its rose bouquets that becomes the protagonist of the work, transformed by Ingres into an image of wonderful painterly virtuosity.

Myths and

Following his triumph at the Salon of 1824, Ingres was commissioned to make *The Apotheosis of Homer* for the ceiling of one of the rooms with which Charles X planned to extend the exhibition space of the Louvre. The artist presented the great poet enthroned in front of a Greek temple, surrounded by artists, writers, poets, philosophers, and sculptors, both ancient and modern, who render him homage in a composition of perfect harmony. At the Salon of 1827 the painting competed with another milestone of Romantic painting, on a canvas of equal size and also dedicated to a subject from the ancient world—reworked by Lord Byron—*The Death of Sardanapalus* by Delacroix (see page 198). The works were representatives of the two artistic currents of the time, which were completely divergent but were also of fundamental importance to the culture of the period. One was founded on the perfection of the line, on elegance, on compositional balance; the other burst out of the expressive exuberance that gave voice to the sensuality of Romanticism. The nineteenth century inherited from the artistic repertory of neoclassicism a wealth of subjects connected to mythology and to the history of the ancient world, and within the academic sphere the copying of works from the ancient world was still considered an important training exercise even though it led to a restricted design vocabulary. The end-of-year works made by the students—such as the *Shepherds of Arcadia* by Filippo Marsigli or the *Figure Study: Polites, Son of Priam, Observes the Movements of the Greeks* by Hippolyte Flandrin—were almost always studies of figures drawn from mythology or ancient history, in part because any nude figure had to have an explanation and moral justification drawn from those areas. Since the eighteenth century Homer had been the poet *par excellence*, in comparison to whom even Dante and Shakespeare maintained their ranking only with difficulty; the culture of Romanticism absorbed all the myth that had been woven around the figure of Homer and also around that of his Western counterpart, the legendary Gaelic bard Ossian. Other poets of antiquity were embraced by the Romantics because of the passion expressed in their works, such as Sappho, whose legendary suicide crowned a biographical tale that thrilled many moderns. Many heroes and heroines were found among the great host of characters in ancient literature whose exploits offered precedents to such Romantic themes as titanism, unrestrained emotions, and the total abandonment to strong emotions. The figure of Ajax of Oileus came to represent the defiance of man in the face of divine omnipotence and was thus also symbolic of rebellion against tyrants—which resounded toward the middle of the century in the *Spartacus* by the sculptor Vincenzo Vela. There was also Leander, enamored of Hero, who swam the Hellespont every night to see her, an almost inconceivable feat that Lord Byron wanted to undertake personally in 1809. In 1824 Delacroix got the idea for a painting that he was to make many years later, in 1838, *Medea about to Kill Her Children;* according to legend, when Jason abandoned her for another woman, Medea unleashed her terrible wrath by giving poisoned clothes to her rival and then by murdering the two children she had had with Jason. Rather than present the bloody act itself, the artist presents the state of mind that gripped the heroine before committing the infanticide. To emphasize the dramatic and furious expression on her face he cast it

Jean-Auguste-Dominique Ingres, *The Apotheosis of Homer,* 1827, oil on canvas, 386 x 512 cm; Musée du Louvre, Paris

Félix-Joseph Barrias, *Gallic Soldier and His Daughter Imprisoned in Rome,* 1847, oil on canvas, 236 x 171.5 cm; Musée Rolin, Autun

beneath a dark shadow. Painters like Félix-Joseph Barrias turned to the ancient history of France. In his *Gallic Soldier and His Daughter Imprisoned in Rome* (1847), he used an academic and almost theatrical tone to celebrate a representative of the ancestors of the French, a people around whom Chateaubriand had woven a heroic aura. The ancient myths and history of England had one of their most genial and fecund interpreters in William Turner. He drew on that repertory to celebrate tragic love stories, such as *The Parting of Hero and Leander*, to make enduring images of the victories of humans over adversity, such as *Ulysses Deriding Polyphemus*, and to present eloquent comparisons of past and current history. Such is the intent of *Snow Storm: Hannibal and His Army Crossing the Alps* (see page 278) and *The Decline of the Carthaginian Empire*, works that suggested symbolic mirrors of the ruthless ambition of Napoleon and his later political collapse. Ancient civilizations were often the subject of Romantic reflections on modern history; the Russian Karl Pavlovich Briullov drew on antiquity for *The Last Day of Pompeii*, an allusion to the final moments in a cycle of civilization that had reached great heights. In America Thomas Cole made similar reflections. In a cycle of five canvases entitled *The Course of Empire* (New-York Historical Society, New York) he described in allegorical form the evolution of society from its wilderness state to civilization to the corruption and vice that lead to its final collapse. Ancient myth came to be elaborated throughout Europe and in America from different points of view. During the first decades the academic approach still dominated in Italy, although this did not rule out important works from Francesco Hayez and Pelagio Palagi. In Germany Karl Friedrich Schinkel explored ancient Greece from a viewpoint stylistically different from that of neoclassicism, directed more at seeing antiquity as a model for functional forms, most of all in architectural terms. His *Glimpse of Greece in the Golden Age*, today known through a copy made by Wilhelm Ahlborn, reveals a stylistic arrangement that was to be further developed in the 1840s by a group of young French artists, Jean-Léon Gérôme, Henri-Pierre Picou, Jean-Louis Hamon, and François Jalabert. Dubbed the Néo-Grecs ("neo-Greeks") by the critic Théophile Gautier because they presented classical antiquity in a manner different from that of David, they worked out a type of elegant painting, realistic in detail, evoking a world that was distant in terms of its contents but with a strong visual impact. At the opposite end were the dramatic views of antiquity made by the artists who contributed to ending the Romantic age with an affectation of aestheticism expressed in spectacular forms. As early as 1847 the virtuosity of Thomas Couture immersed *The Romans in the Decadence of Their Empire* in a climate abounding with sensuality and audacious realistic inserts; the second half of the nineteenth century opened with the young Gustave Moreau, who in *The Suitors*, begun in 1852, anticipated in an almost visionary expression the symbolism of the end of the century of which he was to be the outstanding representative.

Eugène Delacroix, *Medea about to Kill Her Children*, 1838, oil on canvas, 260 x 165 cm; Musée des Beaux-Arts, Lille

ancient history

Filippo Marsigli, *The Shepherds of Arcadia*, 1830, oil on canvas, 230 x 313 cm; Museo Nazionale di Capodimonte, Naples

Antoine-Jean Gros
Sappho at Leucates
1801, oil on canvas
122 x 100 cm
Musée Baron Gérard, Bayeux

According to ancient legend, the sixth-century B.C. Greek lyric poet Sappho committed suicide for the love of the youth Phaon by throwing herself from the cliff at Leucates. In this painting from 1801 Gros presents the episode in tones that are already amply Romantic, marked by the beautiful transparency of the veils and the light of the moon.

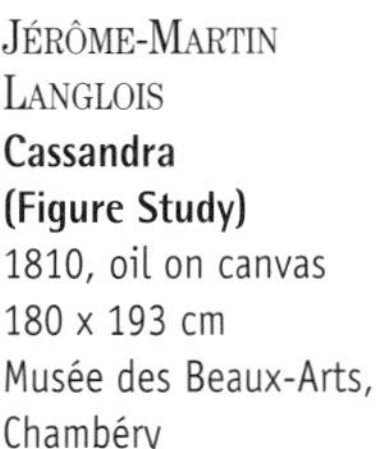

Jérôme-Martin Langlois
Cassandra (Figure Study)
1810, oil on canvas
180 x 193 cm
Musée des Beaux-Arts, Chambéry

Cassandra, tied to the altar of Athena by the Greek Ajax Oileus, awaits her fate from the goddess, while in the background the destruction of Troy and the slaughter of its people—which she had predicted without being believed—are taking place. The spectacular and surprising contrast between shadows and light assumes expressive importance of an almost visionary kind.

Merry-Joseph Blondel
The Death of Hyacinth
1810, oil on canvas
230 x 151 cm
Musée Baron Martin, Gray

Ovid relates how Hyacinth was mortally wounded while competing with Apollo in the throwing of the discus; from his blood that fell to the ground was born the flower that today still bears his name. The French painter Blondel, neoclassical by training, here presents the theme of Apollo's sorrow over the death of the beloved Hyacinth, following formulas still closely tied to the schemes imposed by the academy. The expression of desperation is controlled, limited to the god's gesture of placing his hand on his forehead, while the lifeless body of the youth, who seems to fall back into a deep sleep, has no sense of the horror of death. Only his limp neck suggests a sense of tragedy, conferring drama on this study of the human figure that, in keeping with academic parameters, included the application of idealized forms to the nude.

Joseph Mallord William Turner
The Decline of the Carthaginian Empire
1817, oil on canvas, 170 x 238.5 cm
Tate Gallery, London

Created as the pendant to *Dido Building Carthage* (National Gallery, London), this painting presents a pictorial theme that had been in vogue since the end of the eighteenth century, that of the rise and fall of empires. In 1817, the theme could not avoid making clear allusions to the political situation of the time, with a not accidental reference to victorious Britain following France's defeat at Waterloo. The subject had been the material of allegory in preceding centuries, as in the case of Claude Lorrain, to whom Turner makes explicit reference, evoking that painter's pictorial style and compositional structure. In fact, Turner is known to have thought of giving this painting to the National Gallery in London on the condition that it be displayed alongside the canvases by the famous French artist.

Joseph Mallord William Turner
Ulysses Deriding Polyphemus
1829, oil on canvas
132.5 x 203.2 cm
National Gallery, London

Ulysses pulls his ship away from the cave of the cyclops Polyphemus, indicated by Turner as the imprecise reddish glow at the left; the blinded monster lies on the rocks above, grasping his head in his heads. As the hero's ship approaches the rest of the fleet, water nymphs rush toward him like a phosphorescent wave, and the carriage of Apollo brings dawn to the new day, which spreads across the sky with a golden light. Ulysses was always ready to defy the laws of nature, and Turner here applies his singular style to a celebration of one of the Greek hero's victorious exploits. Turner takes things a step further in this canvas, for in emulation of the Greek hero, he in turn defies the conventions of his time, adopting a painting style that scandalized the more conservative public, since it replaced the traditional chiaroscuro with an almost uncontrolled use of color.

François Gérard
Hylas and the Nymph
1825, oil on canvas
173 x 203 cm
Musée Baron Gérard, Bayeux

Gérard presents a mythological story that enjoyed great popularity in European art over a long period: the beautiful youth Hylas, member of the expedition of the Argonauts and sent by his companions in search of water, finds a spring but is grabbed by water nymphs enchanted by his beauty who drag him off to their realm. The artist makes a small variation in the original version by limiting the scene to only one nymph, thus freeing up the space of the composition in which he gives preference to the decorative aspects, in keeping with the destination of the work, which he made for the Galerie de Diane in the Tuileries. So it is that the more ornamental details of the canvas emerge with clarity, presented in minute detail and thus much in harmony with the graceful tone of the narration, which transforms the myth into a pleasant sentimental tale.

Fyodor Bruni
Bacchante Giving Cupid a Drink
1828, oil on canvas
91 x 67 cm
Russian State Museum,
St. Petersburg

The Russian painter, who had been born in Italy but lived in Russia during his infancy, made this painting during his first stay in Rome, where he spent a good part of his career. He treats the subject with a liberty that indicates the surpassing of classical canons for the presentation of mythological themes. In its treatment of drapery and in the figure of the bacchante, the work reveals the influence of sixteenth-century Venetian painting, which Bruni had the opportunity to study during his trip to the major Italian cities. The mild sensuality of the young woman—thought to be a portrait of Angelica Serni, whom Bruni married in 1835—was enough to cause censure when Bruni proposed displaying the painting at a show in the Piazza del Campidoglio, since the show was scheduled to take place during Lent.

Pelagio Palagi
The Huntress Diana
1828–30,
oil on canvas
217 x 143 cm
Galleria d'Arte
Moderna, Bologna

This image of Diana, goddess of the moon and the hunt, was almost certainly commissioned by Count Girolamo Malfatti as a pendant to the *Venus Playing with Two Doves* painted in 1830 by Hayez (see page 76). It seems probable that the model for this work was again Carlotta Chabert, the young ballerina who was also the count's lover. The figure of the goddess, identified by her usual attributes—the quiver, bow, and dog—seems to suggest a naturalness that goes beyond the canons of traditional personifications of the goddess, and her face, which has a strength of character suggestive of portraiture, seems in fact to resemble Chabert.

Francesco Sabatelli
Ajax of Oileus
1829, oil on canvas
210 x 148 cm
Galleria d'Arte Moderna di Palazzo Pitti, Florence

An uncommon figure in the pictorial repertory, the Greek warrior Ajax of Oileus led the forces from Locris in the Trojan War. He committed the sacrilege of violating Cassandra at the altar of Athena, and the goddess forced him to be shipwrecked on his way home. Just as he was about to save himself, holding tight to land, he offended the gods by boasting of how he had escaped death against their will, at which Poseidon punished him by making him fall back into the sea. The canvas presents the hero's supreme effort to resist divine fury; the terrible expression on his face and the muscular tension of his body are visual embodiments of the Romantic concept of titanism, which exalts the affirmation of man in the struggle against the forces of nature and tyranny, the defiance of the individual in the face of fate.

Hippolyte Flandrin
Figure Study: Polites, Son of Priam, Observes the Movements of the Greeks
1834, oil on canvas
205 x 148 cm
Musée d'Art Moderne, Saint-Étienne

The painting that the students of the French Academy in Rome were required to present as a sample of their work after their first year called for an individual figure study. The subject Flandrin chose is mentioned in the second book of the *Iliad*: at the approach of the Greeks, Polites, youngest of the sons of Priam, decides to courageously remain on guard at the walls of Troy to observe the enemy's movements. As presented by Flandrin, the youth makes no reference to the Homeric episode beyond the sandals and the altar he sits on (in the text it is the tomb of Aisyetes); nothing else directly recalls the ancient world. The artist took a Homeric subject as the pretext for making a study of a model of evocative intensity, the portrait of a boy whose gaze is lost in infinity, in intimate colloquy with the sea that extends to the horizon.

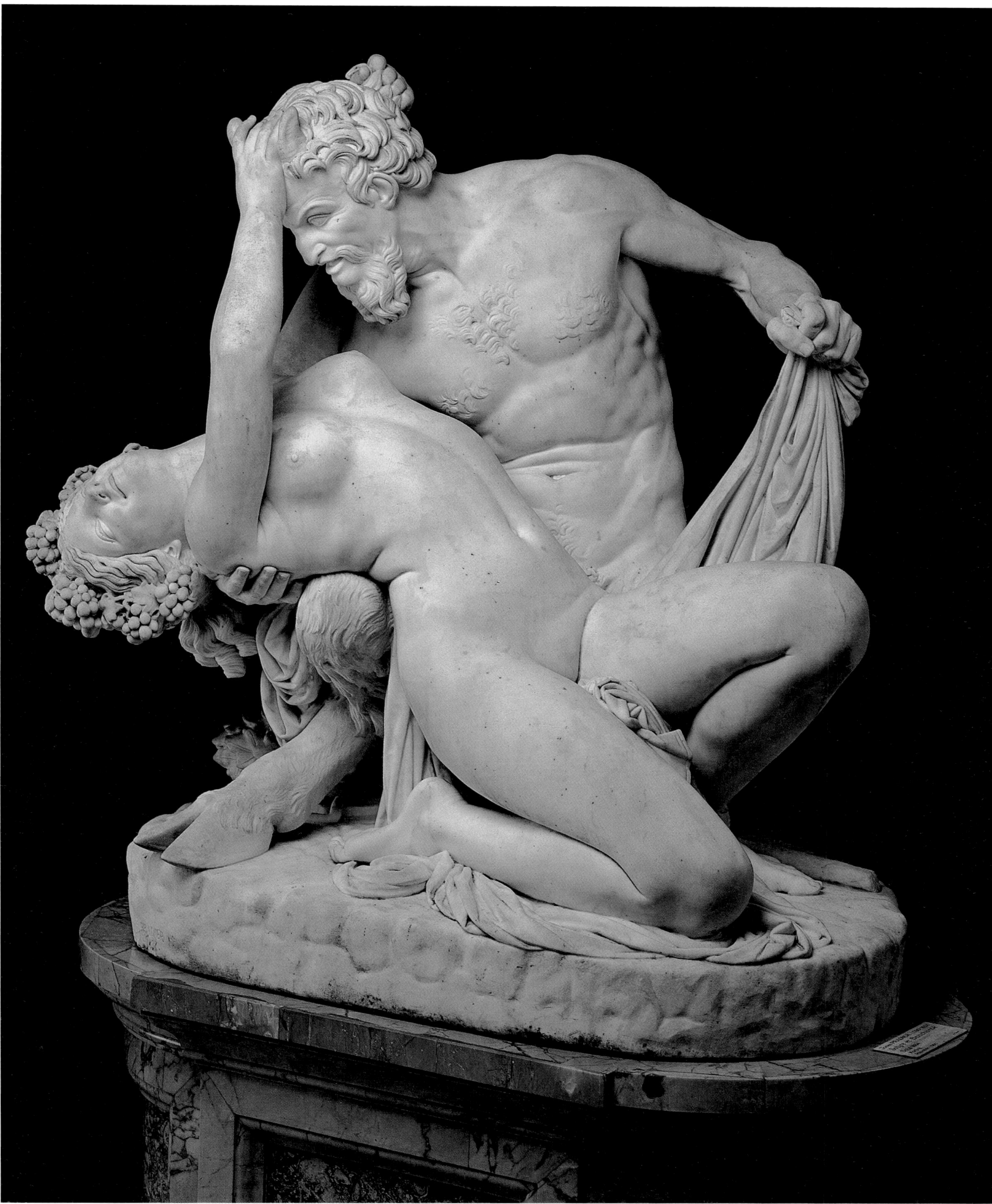

JAMES PRADIER
Satyr and Bacchante
1834, marble
height 120 cm
Musée du Louvre,
Paris

Critics screamed scandal when Pradier displayed the model of this sculpture at the Salon of 1834. His interpretation of the mythical scene went far beyond the canons applied to the presentation of such subjects; in particular, it brought to the foreground the sheer sensuality of the embrace of the satyr and the bacchante and did so with a realism that at the time was not permitted in the presentation of the nude. The work was also the subject of gossip, since the resemblance of the two figures to Pradier himself and to his lover, Juliette Drouet, was abundantly clear.

Joseph Mallord William Turner
The Parting of Hero and Leander
1836, oil on canvas
146 x 236.2 cm
National Gallery, London

The fifth-century B.C. Greek poet Musaeus relates the legend of the young Leander, who at night crossed the Hellespont to meet his beloved, Hero, a priestess of Aphrodite at Sestus, until one day he drowned, overcome at sea by a storm. Hearing the terrible news, Hero killed herself, throwing herself from a tower. Turner presents the two youths still alive, on the edge of the water, at the moment of parting: the apparently calm sea reflects the moon, but the scene is pervaded by a sense of desolation and foreboding, including evanescent figures to the right. The two figures who turn toward the couple from the terrace are Cynthia, who holds a "warning beam," and "Love," bearing the torch of Hymen, as would have been understood by viewers since, as was the custom, verses were printed beside the painting when it was displayed at the Royal Academy.

Jean-Léon Gérôme
The Cockfight
1846, oil on canvas
143 x 204 cm
Musée d'Orsay, Paris

Twenty-two when he painted this canvas, Gérôme had shown much promise as a student in Delaroche's atelier and had accompanied that master on a trip to study in Rome; he had then slipped into the shadows, unable to make his mark. It was with this painting, exhibited at the Salon of 1847, that he finally achieved success. Critics, in particular Théophile Gautier, embraced the work as an example of the necessary "return to order" that was to purify French painting of the excesses into which it was falling. Gérôme found himself as the leader of the group of French artists known as the Néo-Grecs, known for their renderings of antiquity, thus beginning a singular period in French art.

Wilhelm Ahlborn
Glimpse of Greece in the Golden Age
(copy of Karl Friedrich Schinkel)
1836, oil on canvas
94 x 235 cm
Nationalgalerie, Berlin

This canvas is a copy of a painting that Karl Friedrich Schinkel made between 1824 and 1825; the work is of particular value today since the original has been lost. Schinkel made the original as a gift to the city of Berlin on the occasion of the engagement of Princess Louise of Prussia, youngest daughter of the king, to Prince Frederick of Holland. A copy of the work was made for the hereditary prince in 1826, and ten years later Ahlborn made this copy, the only one of the three versions to survive World War II. Schinkel was an architect as well as a painter, and his canvas synthesized in allegorical form his ambitious plan for a Berlin raised to the artistic level

of ancient Athens, an ideal city well organized on the functional plane. In a letter to Goethe of 1826, Bettina von Arnim enthusiastically described the painting by her friend Schinkel in which she saw the reconstruction of a world ruled by the harmony to which every individual is drawn by nature to aspire. The composition is broken down on two levels of observation: the first is located more or less at the height of the workers on the temple in construction, busy dragging a just-finished bas-relief into place; to the right, near the already completed columns, a tent is being raised under which a tympanum is being put in place. Off in the background, beyond this vision of serene daily labor, spreads the new Athens, perfectly laid out with all the classical buildings that mark the achievement of a great civilization.

JEAN-LÉON GÉRÔME
Anacreon, Bacchus, and Amor
1848, oil on canvas
134 x 203 cm
Musée des Augustins, Toulouse

The Greek lyric poet Anacreon, who lived between the sixth and fifth centuries B.C., often celebrated wine and love in his hedonistic verses. For this reason Gérôme presents him flanked by Amor and a baby Bacchus, while a procession of young dancers moves past behind them. The limpid, cadenced scene is balanced between the dynamism of the main figures and the group behind them and the static sense of the young girl playing pipes to the left, seated amid the trunks of trees. The transparent, enameled colors reveal the imprint of the school of Delaroche, with whom Gérôme studied, and there is an echo of the artistic theories of Ingres, but the measured elegance of the gestures and the lines attempts to give the work an ancient feeling, the emblem of the Néo-Grecs, of whom Gérôme was by then the leader.

Vincenzo Vela
Spartacus
1847–50, marble
height 208 cm
Museo Vela,
Ligornetto

Firsthand participant in the 1848 uprisings against the Austrians, Vincenzo Vela chose Spartacus, the symbolic figure of the rebellious slave, to proclaim the Italian people's wish to be freed of the oppression of the foreign invader. He began work on the statue in 1847 and finished it after taking part in the battles in Milan known as the Five Days. The expression on the figure's face, while somewhat melodramatic, is an effective expression of the anger and interior dynamism of a man fighting for his freedom. This work marks the first time that Italian sculpture opened to emotion and could call itself fully Romantic. Vela, who in the 1880s became an artistic spokesman of social conflicts, here made a powerful political allegory that, with its explosion of moral energy that was revolutionary for its time, excited the public at the Brera in Milan.

Karl Pavlovich Briullov
The Last Day of Pompeii
1833, oil on canvas
456.5 x 657 cm
Russian State Museum, St. Petersburg

Briullov visited the excavations at Pompeii in 1827 and came away deeply moved by the image of a city being brought to light almost intact and also by the sense of the terrible cataclysm that had so suddenly ended the city's existence. In this monumental composition he sought to recreate the terrified flight of the inhabitants from Pompeii when, on August 24, A.D. 79, the eruption of Mount Vesuvius swept away humans and palaces. The fiery sky, fearful faces, and expressive power of the gestures and poses met with immediate and unanimous praise both in Rome and in all the other cities where it was exhibited. But the meaning of the scene goes beyond the terror, alluding to the collapse of the classical civilization of which Rome was the tangible testimony. Briullov's fame spread immediately throughout Italy and beyond; in Russia, the young Gogol made out in this painting the coming "resurrection" of Russian painting.

THOMAS COUTURE
Romans in the Decadence of Their Empire
1847, oil on canvas
466 x 775 cm
Musée d'Orsay, Paris

Applauded at the Paris Salon in 1847, this painting made Couture's fame. The spectacular banquet, inspired by Juvenal's sixth *Satire*, is conceived not so much as an historical reconstruction as a sort of colossal allegory of vices: figures in lascivious poses interpret the moral decadence of the late Roman empire, although probably not without allusions to the costumes and habits of the Parisian court of Louis Philippe. The painting offers an example of the eclectic style that, toward the middle of the century, characterized the closing phase of Romanticism. Couture cites the scenographic layouts of such great masters as Veronese and Poussin, but also inserts anticipations of realist painting in images whose audacity was the cause for scandal, all the while creating a work immersed in an abundant virtuosity reminiscent of the style of Delacroix.

THÉODORE CHASSÉRIAU
The Tepidarium of Pompeii
1853, oil on canvas
171 x 258 cm
Musée d'Orsay, Paris

Inspired by one of the large rooms of the Roman baths excavated at Pompeii, the so-called bath of Venus Genitrix, this painting presents an alluring view of daily life in ancient Rome. In this work Chassériau reconciles the contrasting points of view of the period's two rival French schools, that of Ingres, according to which design was more important than color, and that of Delacroix, which maintained the contrary. The sense of calm, the idealized poses of the young females, and the Ingres-like drapery do not prevent Chassériau from achieving effects of sensual languor, supported by the use of evocative warm tonalities, creating an atmosphere more properly Oriental. These tonalities date to Chassériau's 1846 trip to Algeria, an experience he found overwhelming.

Gustave Moreau
The Suitors
1852–53,
oil on canvas
343 x 385 cm
Musée Gustave Moreau, Paris

In the background to the right Ulysses stands in the doorway, drawing back the string of his bow. He will soon begin settling the score with the suitors who have invaded his palace and besieged his wife, Penelope. The scene is surprisingly fascinating and offers an example of the aestheticism that took over the last phase of Romanticism, eventually blending unbridled sensuality, pompous excess, evocations of the Orient, and classical antiquity. This large canvas is the youthful work of Gustave Moreau, admirer of Delacroix, Chassériau, and Couture, and also of the antique sumptuousness of Poussin. Although an early work, it already reveals the artist's inclination to rework classical themes in the strongly expressive, almost visionary way that would lead him, near the end of the century, to become one of the leading interpreters of symbolism.

Historical revival and the

In 1795 the Musée des Antiquités et Monuments Français opened in Paris. It had taken Alexandre Lenoir three years to set it up in the former convent of the Petits Augustins. Painter and antiquarian, Lenoir had taken to heart the destruction of the sculptures, tombs, and decorations in churches that was part of the devastating fury of the revolutionaries and that had been followed in 1791 by the state seizure of the works of art belonging to the Church. Stored and then organized following precise criteria in the various spaces of the Augustinian buildings, the monuments were presented to the public with the intention of reconstructing in the memory of the French people a sense of the past that had been so brutally contested and swept away by the Revolution. By throwing light on sentimental events Lenoir hoped to awaken a sense of inner commotion, a melancholy longing for history and its protagonists. He decorated the rooms in a style suitable to the monuments on display, and at the center of each hall he placed large tombs of rulers or other memorable personages, such as the medieval lovers Heloïse and Abelard, whose voices—or so indicated the museum guide—might still be heard echoing off those ancient stones. One of those sepulchers, the tomb of Valentina of Milan, is connected to the birth of an important painting movement in France. Its members came to be called Troubadours, using the name related to medieval poetry in allusion to their preference for chivalrous subjects. Halfway between genre painting and history painting, the works of the Troubadours inaugurated the so-called historical anecdote genre, characterized by subjects that narrated legends of love, entertaining exploits, or moral examples, painted with the exquisite detail of medieval miniatures on small-size canvases. The manifesto of this new genre was *Valentina of Milan Mourning the Death of Her Husband*, presented at the Salon of 1802 by Fleury Richard, founding member of the young Troubadours and like all of them trained in the atelier of Jacques-Louis David. The artist made the canvas after being deeply moved at seeing the monument in the museum and having meditated on the young woman's unhappy life. The work has an interesting history. After nearly a century of oblivion it appeared on the art market in 1997 and became part of the Hermitage collection in 1999. It had been in Russia since the middle of the nineteenth century; earlier it had been the property of Josephine de Beauharnais, who acquired it in 1805 from its original owner. The empress had been among the passionate collectors of works in the Troubadour style; in this she was doubtless following a personal taste, but she also received the support of her husband, who was eager to awaken national pride in the French people. Presenting himself as the spiritual and political heir to Charlemagne, Napoleon had a deep interest in making the French proud of their past and its heroic figures. By way of such paintings artists like Richard, Pierre Révoil, Jean-Antoine Laurent, and François-Marius Granet brought to life Gothic atmospheres equal to those created by Lenoir in his

Paul Delaroche, *The State Barge of Cardinal Richelieu on the Rhone*, 1829, oil on canvas, 56.4 x 97.5 cm; Wallace Collection, London

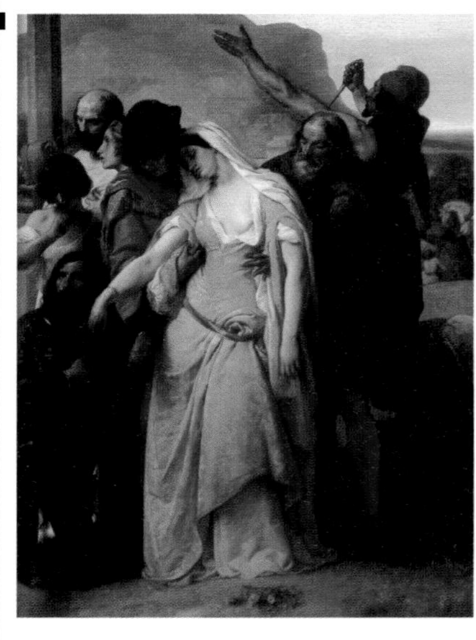

Francesco Hayez, *The Sicilian Vespers*, detail, 1846, oil on canvas, 300 x 225 cm; Galleria Nazionale d'Arte Moderna, Rome

museum and, giving faces to actual figures from the past, invited the public, as Dominique-Vivant Denon remarked, to learn about their private lives. In all of this France was joining—and adding new appeal to—a style that dated back to the eighteenth century and was related to the Gothic revival, which had been affirmed in England by the novels of Horace Walpole, most especially *The Castle of Otranto* (1765), and with the eccentric construction of castles and abbeys, most famously Strawberry Hill and Fonthill Abbey (see page 26). In Germany the rediscovery of the medieval had been consecrated by pre-Romantic philosophers and poets, from Johann Gottfried Herder, whose philosophy of history gave unexpected attention to the importance of national contexts, to young Johann Wolfgang von Goethe, who in 1772 dedicated an essay on German architecture to the builder of Strasbourg cathedral, to the theories of the poet Novalis, who in 1799 related the lost unity among the medieval nations to changes in Christianity. This concept was reworked in a radical way by the Nazarenes (see page 156) and with different accents by other German artists. In Germany, the Gothic revival performed the function of iconographic filter of the nationalistic sentiments awakened during the period of the French occupation and expressed, for example,

the glories of France: five halls were dedicated to the Crusades, a subject dear to the Romantic heart that had already been dealt with by such artists as the German Karl Lessing, who made a painting on that subject

Karl Friedrich Schinkel, *Gothic Church on a Rock by the Sea*, 1815, oil on canvas, 72 x 98 cm; Staatliche Museen Preussischer Kulturbesitz, Gemäldegalerie, Berlin

fascination of the Middle Ages

by Caspar David Friedrich in his *Tomb of Ulrich von Hutten* or, less explicitly, by Karl Friedrich Schinkel, whose paintings of evocative Gothic cathedrals immersed in dreamy landscapes expressed the yearning for the king's return to the throne of Prussia after Napoleon's fall. So it is that in his *Medieval City on a River* a procession escorts a prince toward the cathedral while the rainbow announces the return of harmony. Many times during this period European rulers made the reappropriation of a national past the basis of a political strategy. France's Louis XVIII sought to affirm the legitimacy of his power by commissioning, beginning in 1816, a series of major portraits of his sovereign ancestors as well as history paintings, and before being put on display in the royal palaces these works were exhibited at the Salon. The policy was continued under Charles X and Louis Philippe, who beginning in 1833 sought to transform the château of Versailles into a museum dedicated to

in 1835 that is imbued with a moving sense of humanity. A highly popular subject, the Crusades had been introduced in Italy ten years earlier by Massimo D'Azeglio with *The Death of Montmorency* (see page 334), a work that confronts the relationship among historical romance, painting, and the Gothic revival, which had taken hold of every aspect of European culture and had been exported across the Atlantic by Thomas Cole, who made evocative "Gothic fantasies" in America. In Italy, the efforts of intellectuals and politicians worked in favor of convincing reconstructions of historical events that served as incitements designed to awaken patriotic pride. The royal court in Great Britain sought to surround itself with historical evocations, both for the fascination of chivalric subjects and because they served to celebrate the royal dynasty itself. Among the most popular events were the costume balls given at court in which the rulers and their guests were transformed for one night into their famous ancestors.

Karl Friedrich Lessing, *The Return from the Crusades*, 1835, oil on canvas, 66 x 64 cm; Landesmuseum, Bonn

FLEURY RICHARD
Valentina of Milan Mourning the Death of Her Husband, the Duke of Orléans, Slain in 1407 by John the Fearless, Duke of Burgundy
1802, oil on canvas
55.1 x 43.2 cm
Hermitage, St. Petersburg

In this work of 1802, Fleury Richard, member of the Troubadours group of painters, already reveals his deeply Romantic sensibility. Entrusting the history of the subject to the work's title, the painting concentrates in a surprising way on the state of mind of Valentina Visconti, inconsolable widow presented in her anguished solitude. She sits beside a window whose panes bear the heraldic arms of the two families (the lilies of Orléans and the blue snake of the Visconti). Even her dog seems to share her sorrow. Richard had been drawn to this sad event after visiting the Musée des Antiquités et Monuments Français in Paris, where the tomb of the young duchess was exhibited, bearing the inscription "*Rien ne m'est plus, Plus ne m'est rien*" ("Nothing is left me, I am myself nothing"), which also appears in the painting, written on the parchment scroll open on the table. Empress Josephine was much drawn to the work, buying it in 1805 for the Malmaison gallery.

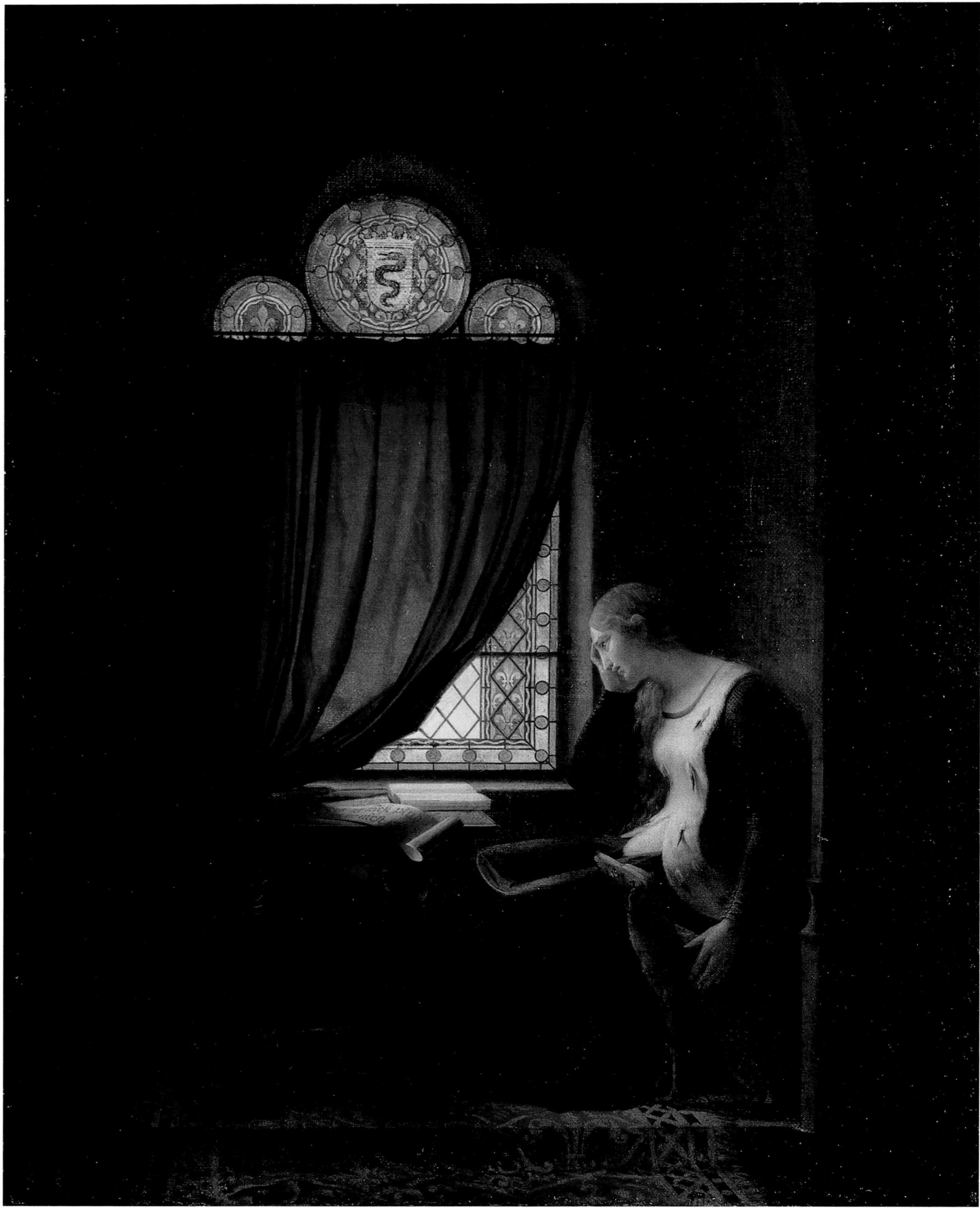

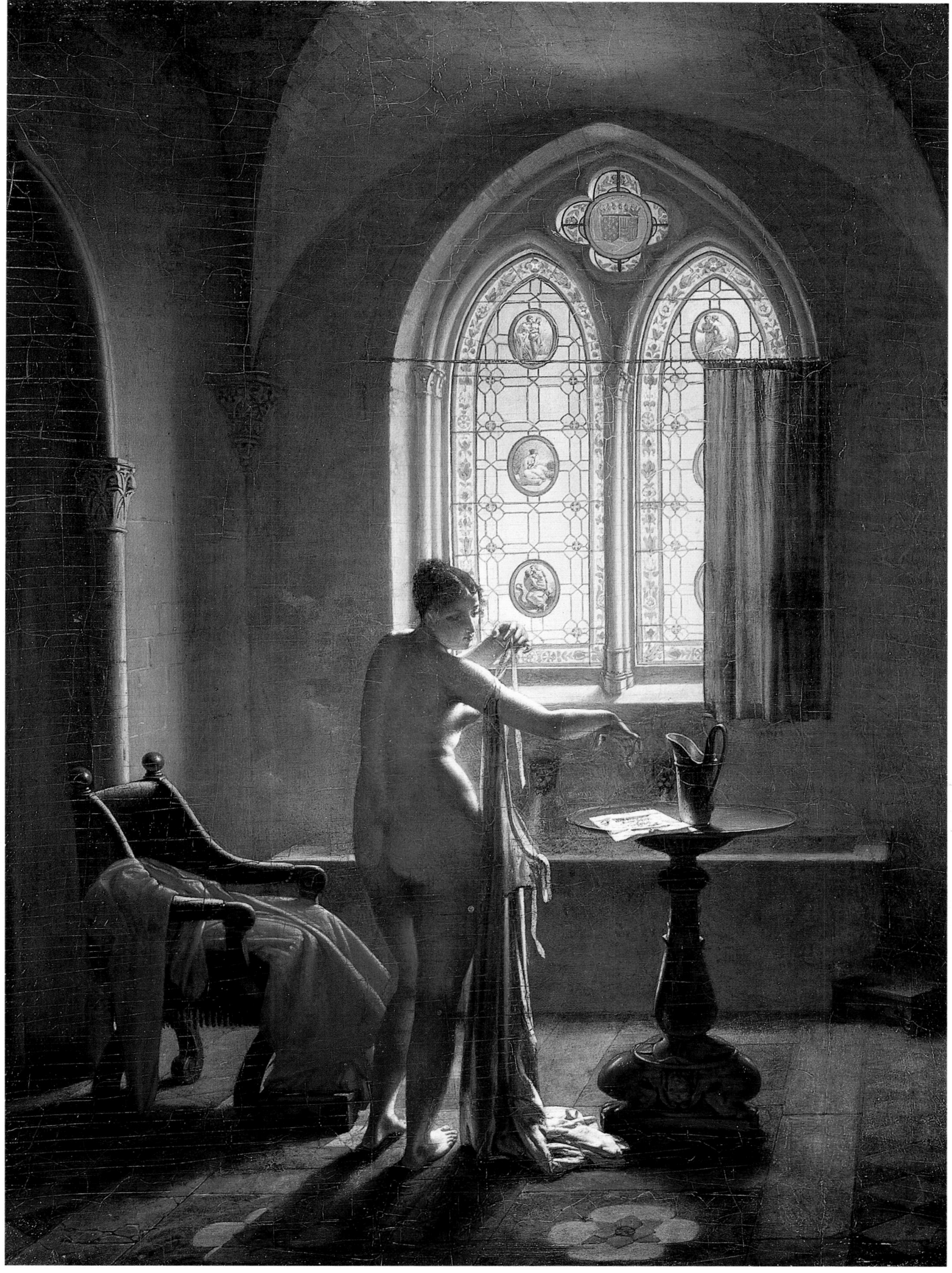

Jean-Baptiste Mallet
Gothic Bathroom
1810, oil on canvas
40.5 x 32.5 cm
Château Musée de Dieppe, Dieppe

Many components of Romantic taste and culture converge in this painting, blending to create a particularly effective atmosphere. The young woman undressing to take a bath stands in a room whose neo-Gothic style evokes that of a church, which is exactly what the stained-glass windows would suggest—such windows were exclusive to churches in the Middle Ages—except that they present scenes of love. Mallet thus uses extreme subtlety to successfully intertwine themes allusive to chivalrous love with religious faith and the medieval revival, sealing it all with the touch of sensuality provided by the female nude.

Karl Friedrich Schinkel
Medieval City on a River
1815, oil on canvas
95 x 140.6 cm
Nationalgalerie, Berlin

The trip he made to Italy between 1803 and 1805 left the young Schinkel enthusiastic, fascinated by medieval buildings, most of all the cathedral of Milan, with its strongly Gothic outline. In his career as an architect Schinkel made no practical application of his passion for the great Gothic cathedrals, but he loved to create their images in paintings like this one, inventing panoramas of ancient cities dominated by the towering spires of churches. The Gothic is perceived as a symbolic skyward thrust, thus mirroring the Romantic aspiration toward ideals of beauty and perfection, which are further suggested here in the sense of harmony between the sky and the earth, connected by a rainbow, while the presence of the people proceeding toward the cathedral fills the view with a sense of the joyous participation in religious life.

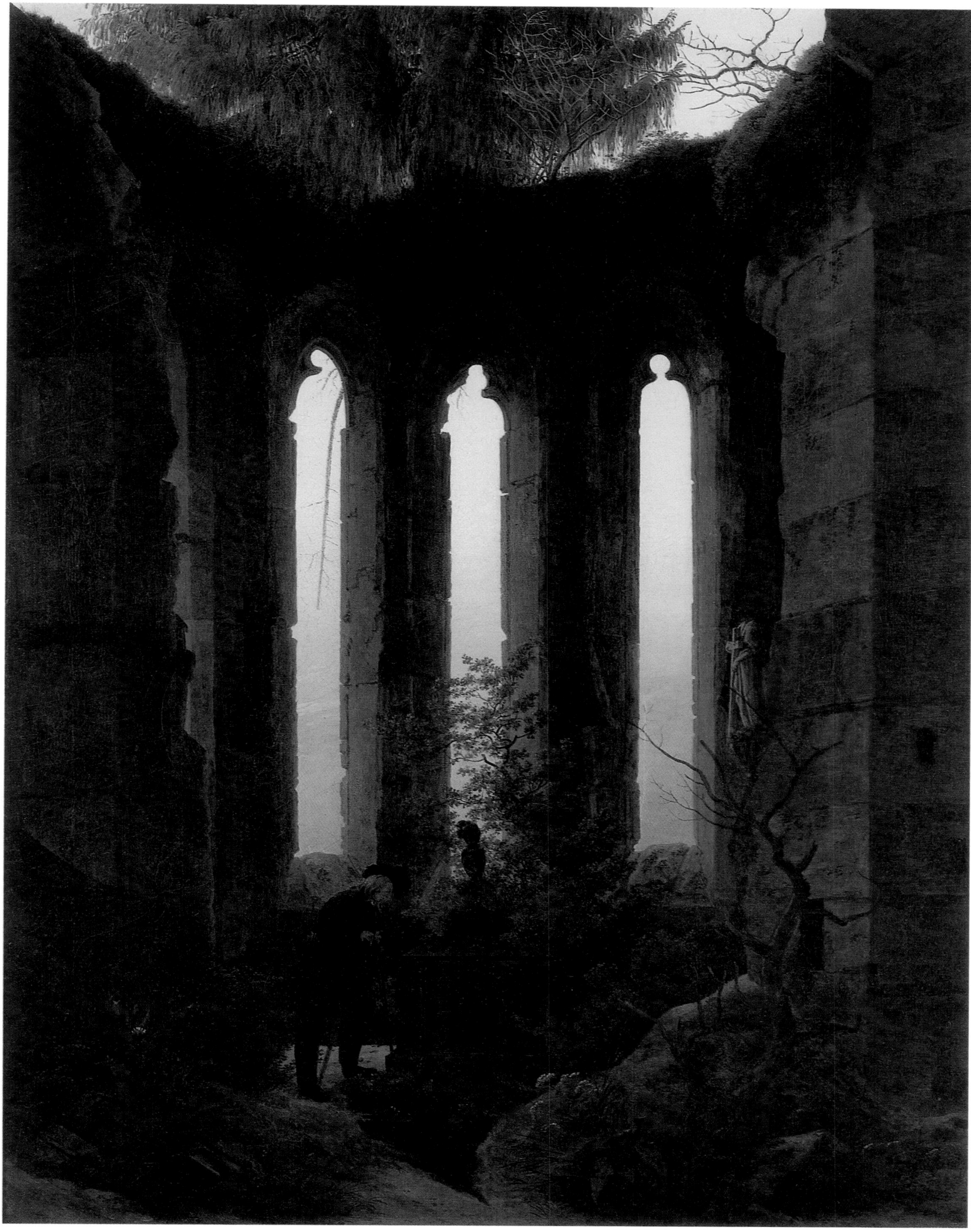

Caspar David Friedrich
The Tomb of Ulrich von Hutten
1824, oil on canvas
93.5 x 73.4 cm
Staatliche Kunstammlungen, Weimar

This work involves two layers of reading, one historical and one allegorical-political. In a sort of stage scene formed by high Gothic windows that are the remains of a building in ruins, a man pauses beside the tomb of Ulrich von Hutten, a humanist and poet, follower of Luther, and outstanding figure in German political history, who died in exile in 1523. In 1823 Germany celebrated the third centenary of his death, but the date also coincided with the tenth anniversary of the beginning of the wars of Prussian independence, to which Friedrich made explicit reference by inscribing on the monument the names of those spiritual heirs to von Hutten who had opposed the restoration or had been its victims.

Charles Lock Eastlake
The Champion
1824, oil on canvas
123.2 x 174.8 cm
Museum and Art Gallery, Birmingham

An English artist active in Rome from 1816 to 1830 and drawn to historical themes, Eastlake provided a personal description of the subject of this painting without, however, indicating any literary derivation. The central figure is a knight, perhaps distantly based on the Italian condottiere Giovanni delle Bande Nere. He is about to leave his castle to go to war on the invitation of the turbaned figure to the left, while the woman marks this moment of separation by giving him a sash as token of her love. The painting follows several basic elements of Romantic art, such as the theme of chivalric love, the taste for things exotic, the celebration of battle in the name of an ideal, and the value of Christian faith, as suggested by the figure of the friar to the right. The gleaming armor reveals Eastlake's passion for sixteenth-century Venetian art.

Pierre Révoil
Francis I Dubbing His Grandson Francis II a Knight
1824, oil on canvas
140 x 180 cm
Musée Granet, Aix-en-Provence

Like Fleury Richard, Révoil was a member of the Troubadours movement. He was commissioned to make this canvas by the count of Artois, the future Charles X, who wanted to celebrate an important episode in the history of the French monarchy. The scene presents a stately ceremony that unites three generations of the Valois dynasty: King Francis I; his son Henry II, who took the throne in 1547; and Francis II, born in 1544 to the marriage of the dauphin to Catherine de' Medici, shown here in the arms of his aunt Marguerite of Valois, the king's sister. The painting is purposefully descriptive, with that excess of erudition that was the occasional failing of the Troubadours; in fact, Révoil created the various figures on the basis of old portraits, listing them one by one in the Salon guidebook. To seal the setting with historical accuracy he put on the walls the *Holy Family* and the *St. Michael* by Raphael, works that Pope Leo X had sent the king as a gift in 1518.

Giuseppe Bezzuoli
Charles VIII Entering Florence
1829, oil on canvas
290 x 365 cm
Galleria d'Arte Moderna di Palazzo Pitti, Florence

During the Risorgimento period in Italy, the firm resolution with which the Florentines had prevented King Charles VIII of France in November 1494 from taking control of their city was seen as an important model of political behavior. Bezzuoli used it as a source for moral reflection on the leading players, emphasizing the haughtiness of the sovereign and his followers, the dismay of the simple citizens, and, to the right, the firm resolve and decisive expressions of Machiavelli, Pier Capponi, and Savonarola, who opposed Charles VIII.

Massimo D'Azeglio
The Carroccio (The Battle of Legnano)
1831, oil on canvas
90 x 130 cm
Galleria Civica d'Arte Moderna and Contemporanea, Turin

The historic struggle of Italy's free communes against the invasion of Frederick Barbarossa was of enormous contemporary interest on the eve of the Risorgimento movement, which aimed to drive out foreign dominators. The image of the *carroccio*, the communal battle wagon, was given a precise political significance, directed at reawakening a sense of national spirit in Italians.

GIUSEPPE SABATELLI
Farinata degli Uberti at the Battle of the Serchio
1842, oil on canvas
305 x 395 cm
Galleria d'Arte Moderna di Palazzo Pitti, Florence

The story of the battle fought between Guelfs and Ghibellines in 1262 along the Serchio River near Lucca is narrated in the *Istorie fiorentine* ("Florentine Histories") by Scipione Ammirato (1647): Farinata degli Uberti, the Ghibelline victor of the encounter, had given safety to a young wounded enemy, the Guelf Cece dei Buondelmonti, pulling him onto the rump of his horse; Farinata's cruel brother, Asino degli Uberti, rushed over and made the magnanimous gesture meaningless by killing Buondelmonti with the blow of a mace. The canvas presents the fury of the warrior striking at his enemy and Farinata's last attempt to save the youth from death. Sabatelli emphasized the dramatic tension of the moment through the torsion of the bodies, the tension in the faces, and the excited postures of the horses. Purists accused him of excessive drama, while those who looked to painting for moving paragons of virtue were enthralled.

Francesco Podesti
Henry II, King of France, Fatally Wounded, Blesses the Marriage of His Sister Margaret of Valois with Emmanuel Philibert, Duke of Savoy
1844, oil on canvas
178 x 280 cm
Ducal Castle, Agliè

This canvas was part of a series of works celebrating the house of Savoy made at the request of Maria Christina, queen of Sardinia, for the castle of Agliè early in the 1840s. This painting illustrates the union of the Savoy dynasty with the royal house of Valois, sanctified in 1559 by the marriage of Duke Emmanuel of Savoy to Margaret of Valois, a union that was blessed, as indicated by the title, by the dying ruler (fatally wounded in a tournament). The subject had immediate political significance, since Emmanuel Philibert had been the ruler who had joined all of the Savoy duchy under the capital at Turin; the painting was thus meant to reflect—but in a

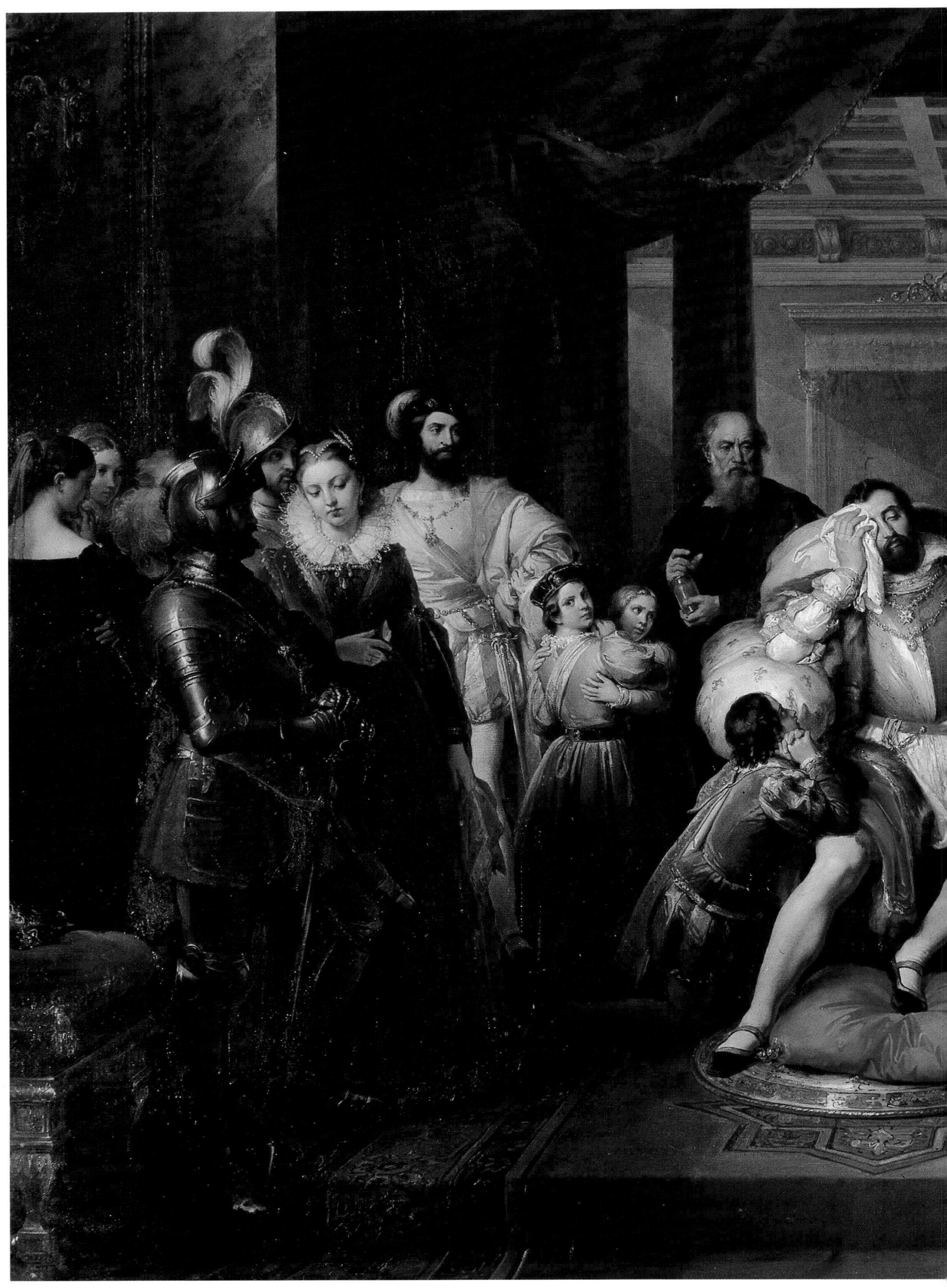

totally disguised form—the spirit of Risorgimento aspirations for a united Italy under the house of Savoy. The crowded scene is presented with minute detail rendered with virtuosic skill by Podesti, a painter from Ancona who specialized in historical subjects. Clothes, jewels, hairstyles, and weapons are reconstructed with historical accuracy in an effort to present an image as faithful as possible to historical reality. The composition has a sense of animation and reveals a theatrical layout that the artist reinforced by employing gestures that critics found excessive. The work also reflects the lively spirit of revival that just two years earlier, in 1842, had enlivened the great masked ball in historical Savoy costumes given at the court of Turin on the occasion of the marriage of Victor Emmanuel to Maria Adelaide.

Paul Delaroche
The Sons of Edward
1830, oil on canvas
181 x 215 cm
Musée du Louvre, Paris

In 1483, on the death of his father Edward IV, king of England, the thirteen-year-old Edward V was named successor to the throne but was immediately imprisoned in the Tower of London, together with his younger brother, Richard, duke of York, by their paternal uncle, Richard, duke of Gloucester, who shortly after their mysterious deaths had himself made king as Richard III. The disturbing tale of the two unfortunate heirs to the English throne struck Delaroche, fascinated like all the Romantics by the search for historical truth. The setting is reconstructed with accuracy in the smallest detail, with Renaissance furnishings and clothes and even a small dog to give the scene greater verisimilitude. The sense of drama is most clearly expressed in the dazed expression of the young king, who leans against his little brother, who seems sad and weary but not frightened. The painting enjoyed enormous success and inspired the French dramatist Casimir Delavigne to write the tragedy *Les Enfants d'Édouard* (1833).

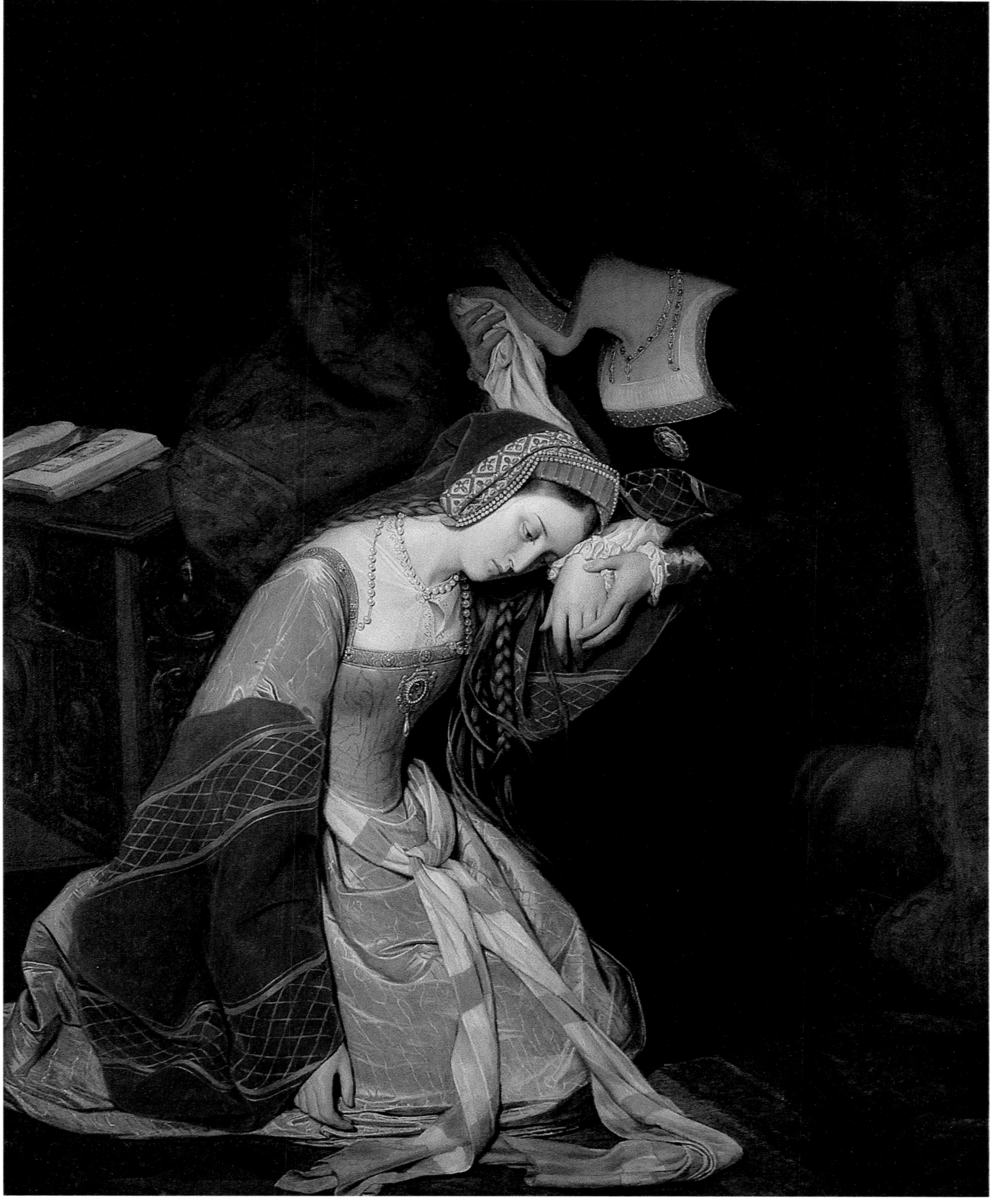

ÉDOUARD CIBOT
Anne Boleyn in the Tower of London in the First Moments of Her Arrest
1835, oil on canvas
162 x 129 cm
Musée Rolin, Autun

The histories of the queens of England, most particularly the moving story of the imprisoned queen, enjoyed great vogue in the Romantic culture of the 1830s. The fascination of the subject was at least partially a result of the novels of Sir Walter Scott, and Anne Boleyn became one of the favorite figures of painters of the period, making her way even into the musical repertory of the period when Gaetano Donizetti wrote the music for a dramatic opera about her in 1831. This painting, an expression of that special climate, shows the unfortunate queen, the second wife of Henry VIII, who was decapitated in 1536 by order of the king, accused unjustly of adultery and incest. She appears here almost bloodless in her controlled desperation; the pallor of her face contrasts with the elaborate beauty of her dress, while the missal behind her is open to a page with an illustration of Calvary.

THOMAS COLE
The Departure
1837, oil on canvas
100.3 x 160 cm
Corcoran Gallery of Art, Washington, D.C.

Painted in pendant with *The Return*, this canvas reveals the contacts between Cole, an American of English origin, and Europe. The landscape, the usual subject of his paintings, here gives way to a "Gothic fantasy" that reflects his participation in the taste of the Gothic revival, which he witnessed during a trip to England in 1831.

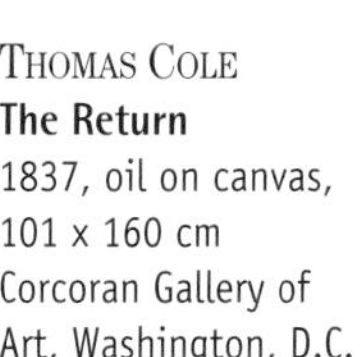

THOMAS COLE
The Return
1837, oil on canvas,
101 x 160 cm
Corcoran Gallery of Art, Washington, D.C.

In *The Departure* the landscape is dominated by a castle that overlooks a beautiful gulf encircled by green fields that give the sense of the serene passing of life. In this work a group of knights returns from war, but the atmosphere is melancholy, pervaded by the moving scene of the fallen warrior being transported.

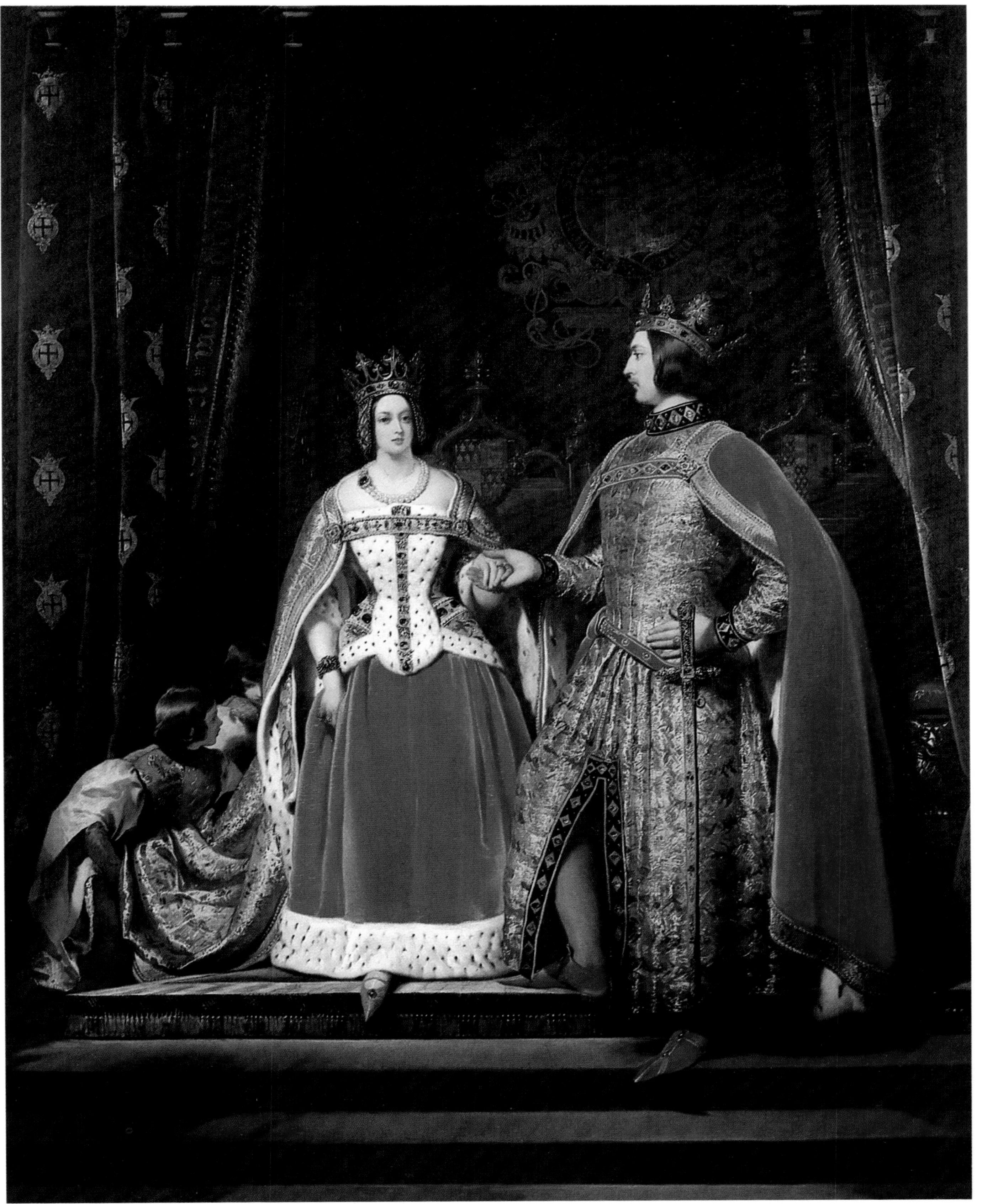

EDWIN HENRY LANDSEER
Queen Victoria and Prince Albert at the Costume Ball, May 12, 1842
1842–46,
oil on canvas
142.6 x 111.8 cm
Royal Collection, Windsor

On May 12, 1842, a magnificent masked ball was held at Buckingham Palace, with more than two thousand guests, all of it in keeping with the medieval revival that was then very much in style. In fact, another two such balls were held, in 1846 and 1851, each dedicated to a different historical period. On this occasion the rulers intended to celebrate their illustrious fourteenth-century ancestors, reliving for one day the chivalric pomp of the English royal court. Victoria dressed in the clothes of Queen Philippa of Hainault and Albert impersonated Edward III (1312–1377), founder of the Order of the Garter. The costumes were designed with great historical accuracy by James Robinson Planché, authoritative court historian, who saw to the smallest detail not only in the recreation of clothes, jewels, and shoes but also of the throne (which appears behind Victoria and Albert), in the heraldic devices scattered about, and even in the dances.

The years of the birth and spread of Romanticism were a period of major events throughout the world. In Europe, the first half of the nineteenth century saw the formation and collapse of governments and states at a relatively rapid rate, from the Napoleonic Empire to the Congress of Vienna of 1815, from the Restoration to the waves of revolutionary uprisings that shook Europe in 1848. Since the Renaissance, history painting had been considered the noblest artistic genre, for it presented examples of morality and exalted behavior; with the coming of Romanticism, this primacy grew only greater, with an ever larger repertory of subjects to deal with, even when considering only the presentation of contemporary history. In keeping with longstanding tradition history paintings were usually large in size, to celebrate in the most striking way events worthy of commemoration and narration, and usually employed epic tones since the subjects were crucial moments like battles, peace treaties, and dramatic episodes. Such had been the case for several centuries, but the affirmation of the individual fed by Romantic thought brought about a radical change in the way of looking at history. Théodore mind of a man face to face with death. That same year in Spain, a country that had experienced the violence of the French repression of the patriotic movements in Madrid, Goya did not hesitate to make clear the heroism of the Spanish rebels with a totally different version of the traditional myth of the hero, completely humanized and immersed in a sense of terror. It was thus on well-tilled soil that in 1818 Géricault planted the colossal undertaking of the *Raft of the "Medusa,"* a canvas of almost thirty square meters, which sharply divided public opinion at the Salon of 1819 since for the first time a contemporary news event, disturbing

Pierre Narcisse Guérin, *Henri de la Rochejaquelin*, 1817, oil on canvas, 216 x 142 cm; Musée Municipal, Cholet

Contemporary

Géricault is usually credited with having smashed this convention in 1819 with his *Raft of the "Medusa."* In reality, he only exploited the opening made in 1808 by Antoine-Jean Gros, who in *Napoleon on the Battlefield at Eylau* (see page 51) had dared to present the wounded and dead on the Russian battlefield with direct realism. The presentation of suffering in a celebratory painting drew some criticism—although the work won the artist the nomination to baron of the empire—but a few years later, when the collapse of Napoleon dragged with it the fates of thousands of soldiers, their sacrifice was viewed in a different light, and the antiheroic vision of history was no longer the cause of scandal. In this way Géricault in 1814 arrived at painting his *Wounded Cuirassier*, creating an emotionally compelling image of the state of

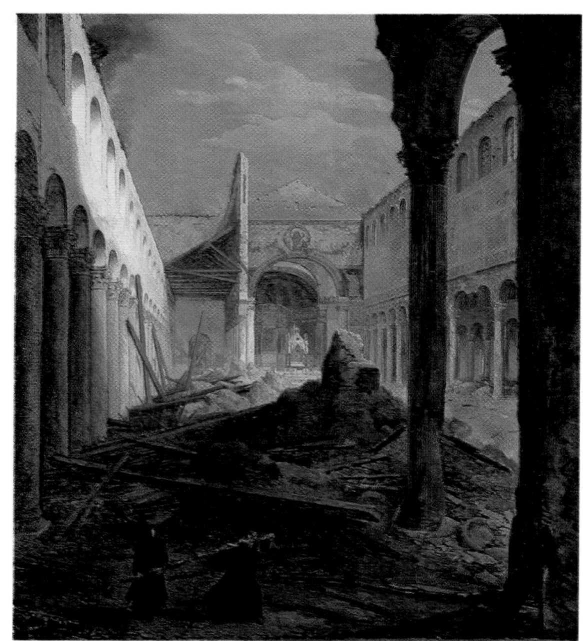

Léopold Robert, *Interior of the Basilica of San Paolo fuori le Mura after the Fire of 1823*, 19th century, oil on canvas, 85 x 74.5 cm Musée d'Art et d'Histoire, Neuchâtel

and presented in all its grim unpleasantness, had been raised to the level of an historical event and presented on a canvas of a format until then reserved for the celebration of heroic deeds. The indignation of the orthodox critics was silenced five years later by the success the painting enjoyed in England, followed by its acquisition by the Louvre, proof of how much times had changed and of how well Romanticism had opened the road to emotion. Eight years later, another shipwreck was memorialized in a canvas more than four meters long painted by Théodore Gudin. Military history and politics had not been swept from the scene. Aside from commissioning an entire series of paintings celebrating his dynasty, Louis XVIII commissioned a cycle of portraits of the French generals who had fought in the Vendéan

history

insurrection of 1793–96, a cycle that included *Henri de la Rochejaquelin* by Pierre Narcisse Guérin and the portrait of Jacques Cathelineau by Girodet (see page 65). In England Turner echoed these French works in scenes denouncing the horrors of war, including *The Field of Waterloo*, which while dealing with an English victory was accompanied by verses written by Lord Byron lamenting those who fall in battle. A poet who wrote of solitary heroes and rebels, Byron became himself a participant in the politics of the time, sacrificing himself in the great cause to which he dedicated the last years of his brief existence, the rebellion of Greece, which began in 1821 with the Greek war of independence against the Turks and went on through nearly a decade of bloody clashes. In Italy Ugo Foscolo, Giovanni Berchet, Francesco Hayez, and other Romantics took up the cause of Greek independence, and in France Eugène Delacroix expressed his solidarity with the Greeks in his *Scenes from the Massacre at Chios*, which drew strong criticism in terms of style when it was exhibited at the Salon of 1824 but was also seized on as an example by the critic Auguste Jal since in it Delacroix took on a theme from modern Greece instead of once again celebrating ancient Greece. Two years later, when Delacroix wanted to pay homage to the four thousand citizens of Missolonghi who had put up a heroic and desperate resistance against the Turkish fleet, he abandoned the chronicle-style layout and made a symbolic image of a Greece overcome but ready to rise again. He employed a similar layout in his later masterpiece, this time dedicated to events in his own homeland, the July Revolution of 1830 during which the people of Paris revolted against the government, causing Charles X to flee and abdicate. They were forced to wait for the 1848 uprising to see their dream fulfilled. In *Liberty Leading the People* Delacroix presented in a form both symbolic and realistic the events of July 28, 1830, the day on which the Parisians had taken to the streets and planted the tricolor atop barricades; the woman who bears the flag to battle, a personification of Liberty,

Carlo Bossoli, *The Austrians Abandon Milan from Porta Tosa*, circa 1848, tempera on paper; Museo del Risorgimento, Milan

may in fact make a reference to the statue of the Venus of Milo, discovered in 1820 and first displayed in the Louvre one year later. The enormously compelling power of the painting is confirmed by the fact that the government bought it—despite the crude realism of the figures in the foreground and the fact that it shows French soldiers being trampled by French people—but the political reasoning behind the acquisition was clear: the work, with its dangerous incitement to action, was never displayed in public and appeared in the halls of the Palais du Luxembourg in 1863 following the artist's death. The image of the Revolution returned in scenes recording the events of 1848. In some cases artists sought to capture the dramatic spirit of the uprising, as in *The Austrians Abandon Milan* by Carlo Bossoli; in others, they tried to give a face to the new government. In France, Dominique Papety won the competition to create the symbolic figure of the Republic with a surprising canvas, laid out in a style that, while keeping within the Néo-Grec context, managed to anticipate a strikingly *fin de siècle* taste.

Dominique Papety, *The French Republic*, 1848, oil on canvas, 273 x 185 cm; Musée du Petit Palais, Paris

Louis-Léopold Boilly
The Departure of the Volunteers in 1807
1808, oil on canvas
84.5 x 138 cm
Musée Carnavalet, Paris

Exhibited at the Salon of 1808 this canvas offered an interpretation of the war that was far different from that which, in those same halls, resounded from such canvases as *Napoleon on the Battlefield at Eylau* (see page 51). Boilly, a painter of narrative and domestic genre scenes, did not want to join in political celebrations and in this case presented a scene of volunteers heading off to war as seen from the emotional point of view an ordinary citizen. The ragtag crowd of recruits making its disorderly way out Paris's Saint-Denis gate has no relationship to a triumphal march; nothing about it awakens admiration, at least not like the orderly ranks and splendid uniforms of the imperial army. The blind man tapping his cane and moving ahead against the current at the far right of the painting confers an implicit sense of disillusion with the Napoleonic campaigns.

Anne-Louis Girodet-Trioson
The Revolt at Cairo
1810, oil on canvas
356.2 x 499.7 cm
Musée National des Châteaux de Versailles et de Trianon, Versailles

The revolt that broke out at Cairo in 1798 against the French troops of Napoleon who had conquered the Nile Valley is presented by Girodet in a way that makes clear that his sympathies are on the side of the invaded populace. Ignoring the theories according to which Napoleon had come to bring civilization and justice to a land reduced to a state of wildness, the artist presents the desperate battle between French and Egyptians giving full dignity to the figures of the Orientals. Thus the Mameluke holding up a fallen pasha while fighting off the attack of a French officer is ennobled by his classical-style nude figure, just as the beauty of the man on the ground at left presents the fascination of an entire people. Even the elegant Napoleonic uniforms do not seem to equal the beauty of the clothes worn by the collapsing pasha on the right.

Francisco Goya
The Second of May 1808
1814, oil on canvas
266 x 345 cm
Museo Nacional del Prado, Madrid

With the fall of Napoleon in 1814, Goya decided to paint the most heroic moments of the Spanish resistance. The clash between Mamelukes of the French cavalry and the people of Madrid at the Puerta del Sol in the center of the city is rendered with extraordinary clarity: the compact crowd thickens toward the foreground, where the battle is at its most desperate, as indicated by the gesture of the man on the right stabbing his enemy's white horse.

Francisco Goya
The Third of May 1808
1814, oil on canvas
266 x 345 cm
Museo Nacional del Prado, Madrid

On the night of May 3, 1808, the popular insurrection against the Napoleonic troops that had invaded Madrid was put down in blood, with soldiers commanded by Murat slaughtering the Spanish patriots, in this case by firing squad on the Principe Pío hill. Goya fills the canvas with the sense of the tragedy, using an effect of light that makes the viewer's eyes converge on the desperate faces and gestures of the doomed.

THÉODORE GÉRICAULT
The Wounded Cuirassier
1814, oil on canvas
358 x 294 cm
Musée du Louvre, Paris

Purposefully antiheroic and at the same time epic in its affirmation of an ideal, this painting presents one of the most novel lines of thinking connected to Romanticism, the awareness of the individual destiny of humans, their vulnerability in the face of history, their lonely suffering. The painting was made during the months that saw the beginning of the political and military decline of Napoleon, the hero *par excellence*, and it was displayed in Paris in 1814, the year of Napoleon's abdication: the work thus echoes the fall of the superman. The wounded cuirassier makes his way with difficulty down a steep slope, struggling to control his horse, which rears back in fear; the animal is presented in a monumental pose that contrasts with the uncertain and unsteady pose of the officer, portrayed without celebratory lights, forced to confront his fate alone.

JOSEPH MALLORD WILLIAM TURNER
The Battle of Trafalgar, as Seen from the Mizen Starboard Shrouds of the "Victory"
1808, oil on canvas
171 x 239 cm
Tate Gallery, London

The naval battle between the British fleet led by Horatio Nelson and a combined French and Spanish fleet, which took place on October 21, 1805, at Trafalgar, a little to the north of the Strait of Gibraltar, was the first great defeat of Napoleon. The admiral was mortally wounded during the engagement, and his body was brought back to England aboard the *Victory*, which reached the mouth of the Thames about two months later. Turner was on hand to witness the arrival and immediately made the sketches and notes needed to turn out in a short time this painting commemorating Nelson, who had become a British national hero. The work was ready in 1806, but it had to be worked on and refinished before it was shown to the public two years later. Absolutely innovative as a painting of a naval battle, the canvas communicates the sense of the action as seen from nearby, creating a strong sense of emotional involvement in the death of the great admiral.

Joseph Mallord William Turner
The Field of Waterloo
1818, oil on canvas
147.5 x 239 cm
Tate Gallery, London

It was the custom at the exhibitions of the Royal Academy for paintings to be accompanied by short literary citations concerning the subject presented. Turner accompanied this work with verses from Byron's poem *Childe Harold* in lament of the dead from a battle, which in the painting appear piled up in the foreground. This is what he wanted to emphasize in the canvas, in an image relating the consequences of war. After receiving the commission for the painting, Turner set off to personally visit Waterloo, in Belgium, so as to view the site where Napoleon had been defeated two years earlier. It took him sixteen days to get there, August 1–16, 1817. He did not use the notes he made for a documentary reconstruction of the encounter, but rather to evoke a scene of total desolation, with the field illuminated by the glare of the signal light that helped family members seek through the fallen for their loved ones.

Horace Vernet
Peace and War
1820, oil on canvas
55 x 46 cm
Wallace Collection, London

Like that of Géricault and Gros, Horace Vernet's vision of war was hardly triumphal, and he was more interested in the observation of the reality of the effects of military campaigns on individuals. Accused of having an anti-Bourbon spirit, this canvas was rejected by the Salon of 1822. The subject is unusual, unexpected, and certainly critical of the "post-Waterloo" period. A veteran of the Grande Armée, having returned to work in the fields, has unearthed a helmet with his plow. In his hands he holds a Legion of Honor, which speaks of the war, as does the cross atop the uncovered grave to the left, onto which Vernet casts a sharp, unreal light, arriving from a source outside the scene and thus emphasizing the sense of dark resentment that wraps the whole.

Théodore Gudin
Fire aboard the "Kent"
1827, oil on canvas
256 x 421 cm
Musée de la Marine, Paris

The *Kent*, a large vessel of the India Company, left England in 1825 for the Bay of Bengal, with more than six hundred persons on board; after a few days fire broke out during a raging storm in the Bay of Biscay. The English brigantine *Cambria* was nearby and rushed to save the dozens of women and children traveling aboard the *Kent*, transferring them to lifeboats with a system of cables. This is the moment Gudin immortalizes, presenting the fury of the stormy sea with striking immediacy, such that it takes on apocalyptic tones, with the ship rolling to the side and the precarious state of the boats at the mercy of the waves, rendered in spectacular perspective.

THÉODORE GÉRICAULT
The Raft of the "Medusa"
1819, oil on canvas
491 x 716 cm
Musée du Louvre, Paris

The tragic event occurred off the Senegal coast in July 1816: the French frigate *Medusa*, with 149 men on board, sank. Struck by this tragedy, Géricault decided to evoke it in a canvas of colossal size, a format that had never before been used for episodes outside the major events of history. The painting presents the fifteen survivors who, after twelve days on a raft, spot the *Argus*, the ship that will save them, but which in that moment seems to move away, throwing them into despair. In images of great impact the artist relays the desperation of the shipwrecked men, presenting their agonies with crude realism, the living in close contact with the bodies of their

dead and dying companions. To create the dying he made direct observations of sick people at the end of life, and for the dead he made sketches of the heads of executed people. In this way Géricault accomplished his ambitious project for a monumental composition constructed with classical balance, most evident in the pyramidal arrangement of the figures on the raft. It is a scene in which heroism is not presented in terms of military exploits but in the struggle of the individual to survive. The painting was the source of disputes at the Salon of 1819 but enjoyed great popularity in London and Dublin, where the public paid to see it, becoming one of the first expressions of Romanticism, most of all because of its disturbingly expressive power and the epic tone given an item from contemporary news.

EUGÈNE DELACROIX
Scenes from the Massacre at Chios
1824, oil on canvas
419 x 354 cm
Musée du Louvre, Paris

The Greek War of Independence was marked by many tragic events, including the Turks' ruthless massacre of the inhabitants of the Greek island of Chios in March 1822. The episode had a strong effect on public opinion in France, and the young Delacroix made it the subject of a large canvas, beginning work on it in 1823 and presenting it at the Salon the next year. The painting awakened contrasting reactions from critics. The work dealt with a political subject of enormous actuality, that of the oppression of peoples, and did so by taking formal and expressive liberties, including the use of bright colors that met with disapproval from the academic critics but were applauded by the supporters of the new Romantic sensibility. Delacroix emphasized the drama of the scene with the twisting mass of wounded bodies, but he also inserted strongly exotic elements, as in the rendering of the clothes and the Oriental character of some of the figures, elements that belong to the modern aesthetic.

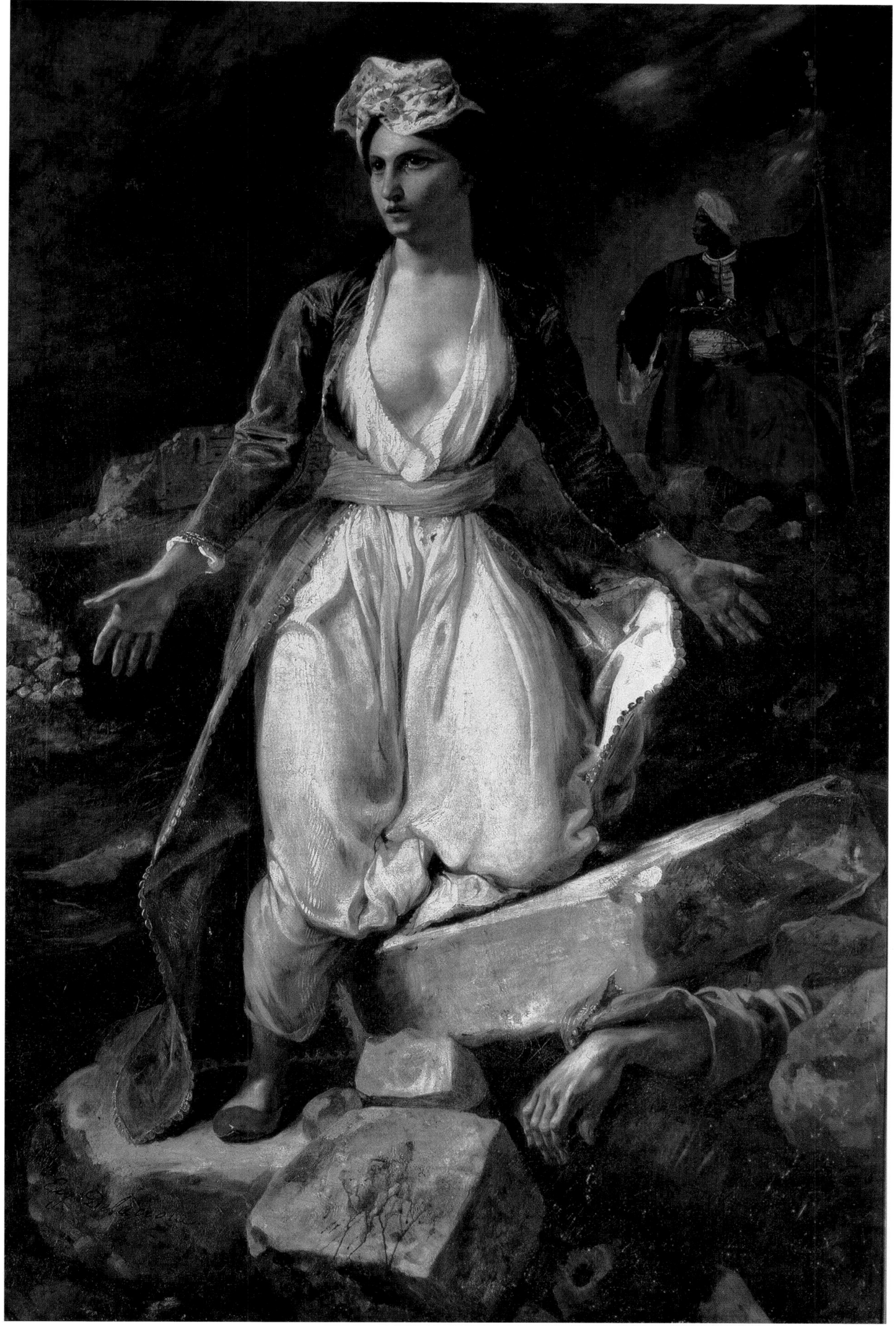

Eugène Delacroix
Greece on the Ruins of Missolonghi
1826, oil on canvas
209 x 147 cm
Musée des Beaux-Arts, Bordeaux

The subject of the liberation of Greece from Turkish oppression was of great importance to the Romantics. The Greek city of Missolonghi was besieged twice during the Greek War of Independence, attracting the assistance of foreign volunteers, including Lord Bryon, who died there in 1824 after going to Greece to join in the struggle against the Ottomans. Delacroix presents an allegorical personification of Greece on the day after the surrender of Missolonghi, April 22, 1826, following a dramatic siege: the woman wears traditional Hellenic dress and, defeated but ready to rise again, she rests on the masonry of the destroyed city. The sense of the slaughter is given by the blood spattered on the stone in the foreground and by the hand of a victim buried beneath the ruins, while in the background obscured by a dark sky stands the triumphant figure of a Turk with his gaudy uniform planting his Ottoman flag.

EUGÈNE DELACROIX
Liberty Leading the People (July 28, 1830)
1830, oil on canvas
260 x 325 cm
Musée du Louvre, Paris

It took Delacroix a little more than three months to make this large canvas. He had not participated in the desperate insurrection that shook Paris from July 27 to 29, 1830, but he wanted to immortalize the insurrection with which the people had tried to reestablish the republic and after which the abdication of Charles X had been followed by the unexpected parliamentary monarchy of Louis Philippe. With a singular ability to blend the realistic with the epic, Delacroix presents the people advancing weapons in hand to assault the barricades, led by the allegorical figure of Liberty, a young half-nude woman holding aloft the French flag against a background darkened by the swirling smoke of battle. The bright red and blue of the tricolor stand out here and there on the clothes of the wounded and dead, which the artist places in the foreground, employing a stark but touching realism similar to the dramatic Romanticism of Géricault.

Antoine-Jean-Baptiste Thomas
The Procession of San Gennaro at Naples during an Eruption of Vesuvius in 1822
1822, oil on canvas
95 x 128 cm
Musée National des Châteaux de Versailles et de Trianon, Versailles

Having been an eyewitness to this spectacular and, to a foreign artist, highly picturesque event, Thomas made, almost from life, a snapshot of Neapolitan life. At first glance the scene seems to take place outside chronological time: the simple clothes worn by the figures seem to have no relationship to the styles of the period, while the hooded monks and the representatives of the clergy further emphasize the scene's historical universality. The erupting Vesuvius stands out in the background. The volcano's frequent activity during the decades around the turn of the century constituted one of the main attractions for travelers and for those drawn to the picturesque.

Giovanni Migliara
The Town Guard of Milan Attempts to Disperse the Crowd from Palazzo Reale
1814, oil on canvas
55.5 x 74 cm
Museo di Milano, Milan

Almost a live news report of April 20, 1814, this canvas presents the uprising of the people of Milan against Napoleonic domination, which had just come to an end. With the collapse of the Napoleonic kingdom of Italy, of which the city of Milan had been capital, the Austrians returned the city to Hapsburg rule. Migliara, skilled narrator, resists any emotional involvement in the scene; the monuments that mark off the piazza and the members of the crowd—officers, aristocrats, the poor—are presented in the smallest detail, and the throng of the citizens in its unstoppable surge is illuminated by a strong light that favors the analytical observation of every element of the scene.

FRANCESCO HAYEZ
The Inhabitants of Parga Leaving Their Homeland
1826–31,
oil on canvas
201 x 290 cm
Civica Pinacoteca Tosio Martinengo, Brescia

In 1818 Britain ceded the Greek city of Parga to the Turkey of the Ali Pasha of Ioannina, awakening strong indignation among the supporters of Greek independence all across Europe. In 1826 Hayez was asked to make a painting on a subject of his choosing, "provided it was animated by lively passion," and he decided to take on this subject from contemporary history and particular actuality, on which both Ugo Foscolo in 1819 and Giovanni Berchet in 1823 (in the poem *Fugitives of Parga*) had spoken out. Hayez reconstructed the landscape and costumes with the greatest possible fidelity, creating a scene of enormous choral impact, with its pathetic tones that had the scope of moving the viewer to reflect on the suffering of a people. In that sense the work anticipates the role of painting proposed a few years later by the Italian patriot Giuseppe Mazzini, since it awakens patriotic sentiments in the heart of the viewer and inspires reflection on the lessons offered by history.

Horace Vernet
Italian Brigands Surprised by Papal Troops
1830, oil on canvas
86.3 x 131.5 cm
Walters Art Gallery, Baltimore

The brigand was one of the most appealing subjects in paintings in the 1830s. A figure living on the margins of society and battling against it, the brigand often assumed a halo of mystery that endeared him to the Romantic heart. Horace Vernet was in Rome around 1830, and aside from studying works by the great masters of the past, he sometimes painted subjects he knew would have more immediate appeal on the art market, such as this lively scene of a contemporary event. The painting presents the crucial moment in the capture of a brigand by papal officers. The composition is arranged in such a way that it includes an evocative landscape view, which contrasts with the dramatic excitement of the arrest in the foreground, with the clash between the outlaws and the guards, to which the artist adds a touch of the folkloristic in the costumes of the people, based on those of the Ciociaria district south of Rome.

Eugenio Agneni
The Shades of Great Florentines Protest the Domination of Foreigners
1857, oil on canvas
73.2 x 103.2 cm
Galleria Civica d'Arte Moderna e Contemporanea, Turin

An artist who led an adventurous life, on many occasions subject to political persecution because of his militant activities in the wars for Italian independence, Agneni was in Paris when he made this canvas. In it he uses touches of strong visual impact to treat the subject of exile, which he had so dramatically experienced and which he presents here in an allegorical form within a dreamy vision. Set against the background of a scenic nocturnal view of the piazza of the Uffizi in Florence, the painting is crowded with the souls of great figures of Italian history, either struck by the same condemnation or voluntarily distancing themselves from their homeland, among whom can be recognized in the foreground Dante and Machiavelli, Petrarch, Michelangelo, and even Boccaccio and Leonardo da Vinci, who rush against the foreign invasion, indicated symbolically, at the lower left, by a rifle and kepi on the ground.

Nineteenth-century society was regulated according to precise hierarchical rules, with the rhythms of daily life firmly established in accordance with the prevailing values of family, religion, and morality. Many details from certain aspects of daily life in Europe have been lost and would be difficult to retrace were it not for their appearance in paintings presenting the less noble aspects of history, the paintings of daily life that were made for a middle-class public. With the rise of the merchant and industrial class the style of decorating homes with paintings of the contemporary world became more widespread, creating a market for landscapes, portraits, and scenes set in the modern world. There was an increase—and most of all in the Anglo-Saxon world, as indicated by Charles Leslie or William Mulready—in paintings made to enliven domestic walls with pleasing images, sometimes with striking moral tones, sometimes directed at merely presenting on canvas a scene of simple daily life, but not for that reason without the fascination of a peaceful world. Not surprisingly, this point of view was extended to the sphere of court portraiture, as indicated by the painting in which Edwin Landseer

Friedrich Wilhelm Doppelmayr, *Family Group*, 1831, watercolor; Germanisches Nationalmuseum, Nuremberg

Daily life

portrayed *Windsor Castle in Modern Times*, in which the antics of the dogs, among them the adored Eos (see page 74), as well as heaps of dead game, reflect the prince consort's passion for hunting, while the atmosphere seems to be that of a simple well-to-do family in which the wife appears before her husband bearing a bouquet of flowers. The cult of the family, basic nucleus of society, was an important component of Victorian England, but the same spirit can be found in the painting of the countries of central and northern Europe in the first half of the nineteenth century. A watercolor made by Friedrich Wilhelm Doppelmayr in 1831 presents a delicate family group in an interior that is extremely interesting from the stylistic point of view. The meticulous reproduction of the pictures, curios, and furnishings set in perfect order around the room along with the display of family harmony, made clear by the gestures and facial expressions, all create a fine example of Biedermeier taste. Today the term designates an aspect of style that from the 1820s to the middle of the century characterized in part the painting and decorative arts of Germany, Austria, the Scandinavian countries, and even Russia; the word is from a concept of the "ordinary simple man," *Biedermeier* in German, which summarized in itself the most expressly bourgeois virtues, such as loyalty, simplicity, sincerity, morality, submission to authority, and the desire to not stand apart in any way. The Biedermeier is thus without any of the traits of the Romantic; it knows nothing of the passionate intellectual, the extravagant genius, the aristocratic disdain for mediocrity, or the sense of rebellion against tyranny. The term *Biedermeier* found a concrete visualization in Gottlob Biedermeier, a humorous and satirical character of a modest and tranquil Swabian master, created in 1855 and used as a pseudonym by

Edwin Henry Landseer, *Windsor Castle in Modern Times*, 1841–45, oil on canvas, 113.3 x 144.5 cm; Royal Collection, London

and Biedermeier

two poets, Adolf Kussmaul and Ludwig Eichrodt, to publish various works that exalted and satirized the family values and domestic concerns of the lower middle class; in the twentieth century *Biedermeier* came to indicate the style of furniture in Germany during the Restoration period, which imitated in undertones the Empire style; it later came to be applied to a style of middle-class life found in art, music, and literature. Among the leading exponents of Biedermeier painting were the German Georg Friedrich Kersting, the Danes C. W. Eckersberg and his student Chirsten Købke, and the Viennese Friedrich von Amerling. Aside from the inevitable differences related to the personalities of the artists, they had in common a style that was linear, without sharp color contrasts or strong perspective backgrounds. Domestic interiors were their favorite settings, usually characterized by comfortable furnishings in peaceful arrangements, by the orderly arrangement of curios, which are sometimes quite abundant, as in the style of homes that have been inhabited by several generations of the same family. The Biedermeier spirit is calm and serene, sometimes with an undertone of suffused melancholy, but always centered in the reassuring space of the home, preferably between the walls of the living room or the bedroom, in keeping with the anecdotal domestic vein, a mirror of good feelings. The Biedermeier style made sporadic appearances in Italy, sometimes in support of the taste of a ruler like the Austrian Marie Louise, Napoleon's second wife and regent of the duchy of Parma after the Restoration of 1815, sometimes as the cultural baggage of northern European artists in Rome. Although in a diluted form, traces of it can be made out in the various canvases signed by such Danish painters as Constantin Hansen or Ditlev Conrad Blunck, the latter the author of a lively group portrait in one of the many Roman osterias selected as the favored haunts by northerners in Rome. The life of the artists themselves offered particularly appealing views of daily life. Quite often, and most of all during their stays in a foreign city, their atelier was inside their home, if it did not in fact constitute the single rented room, perhaps a cramped mansard, the genial disorder of which matched the bohemian artist's Romantic spirit. Thanks to a wonderful canvas by Jean Alaux it is possible to look around between the domestic walls where Ingres lived for ten years in Rome, certainly far more comfortable than the cluttered garret in which Tommaso Minardi lived early in the century (see page 36) or the chaotic and tumbledown mansard painted with a humorous spirit by Carl Spitzweg. Daily life was also composed of open-air amusements, and Europe's cities offered a wide variety; there was no need to wait for carnival, which was particularly lively in Rome. In London, for example, before the Crystal Palace, taken down after the Great Exhibition in 1851 and moved to Sydenham in 1854, became a great amusement park, the puppet theaters set up in the streets were the source of daytime amusement for citizens of all ages, both young and old pausing in their afternoon stroll to watch the drama, as in the lively painted snapshot in which Benjamin Robert Haydon presents a sort of catalog of laborers, pickpockets, and the many other types of London society.

William Mulready, *Interior with Portrait of John Sheepshanks in His Residence in Old Bond Street*, 1832, oil on panel, 50.8 x 40 cm; Victoria and Albert Museum, London

Charles Robert Leslie, *Garden Scene*, 1840, oil on canvas, 30.5 x 40.6 cm; Victoria and Albert Museum, London

MARTIN DRÖLLING
Kitchen Interior
1815, oil on canvas
65 x 81 cm
Musée du Louvre,
Paris

Exhibited at the Salon of 1817, this painting was immediately acquired by the French government. The revival of antique Dutch painting was then spreading both in France and in England, and the works of Drölling, who had always drawn his inspiration from that repertory, enjoyed much success. In this simple domestic interior the sixty-year-old painter carefully reconstructed every detail of the kitchen, with its sense of the peaceful passage of time; the women sewing and the child playing with the kitten seem almost taken by surprise as they perform their usual daily activities. The slight disorder, such as the egg shell on the floor and the towel draped over the table, heighten the scene's sense of immediacy, infusing it with the feeling of calm, familiar peacefulness.

C. W. Eckersberg
Portrait of Bella and Hanna, Eldest Daughters of M. L. Nathanson
1820, oil on canvas
125 x 85.5 cm
Statens Museum for Kunst, Copenhagen

After earning himself a certain notoriety as a landscapist during his stay in Rome, Eckersberg returned to his homeland to become one of the leading exponents of the Biedermeier style. The young women in this painting were the daughters of the well-to-do Danish merchant Mendel Levin Nathanson; in this portrait the artist gives much importance to chromatics, creating a composition that has been compared with the schemes of classical art, which he had only recently studied during three years spent as a student of David as well as during his later stay in Rome. What emerges most powerfully from the painting is the direct impact of Biedermeier culture, with the detailed but cold rendering of the rigidly proper clothes, the use of furniture, the parrot in its cage, more a decorative animal than a companion and often present in domestic settings of the upper middle class.

JEAN ALAUX
The Atelier of Ingres in Rome
1818, oil on canvas
55 x 46 cm
Musée Ingres, Montauban

Ingres arrived in Rome in 1806, and from 1810 to 1820 he lived in an apartment on the via Gregoriana, inside which he had his studio. Jean Alaux was a student in Rome during those same years and became close friends with Ingres. In this lively painting he manages to capture both aspects of those rooms, the home and the studio. The foreground presents the domestic sense, with Ingres' wife—Madeleine Chapelle, whom he had married in 1813—presented in the act of turning toward her husband, perhaps having just returned from outside, as the hat and shawl resting on the dresser might indicate; on the other side of the door is the atelier, with various sketches of Ingres' works, including the preparatory study for *Christ Giving the Keys to St. Peter* (Musée Ingres, Montauban), recognizable in the pale frame on the shelf in the background. The painter is not shown busy at his easel but rather sitting with his violin in his hands.

Kapiton Zelentsov
In the Rooms
circa 1830,
oil on canvas
37 x 45.5 cm
Tretyakov Gallery,
Moscow

By the 1830s the style trends that had taken the form of the Biedermeier had traveled from central Europe to the lands of Russia, inducing various painters there to create peaceful scenes of domestic life, such as this painting by Kapiton Zelentsov, a student of Aleksey Venetsianov, one of the leading artists active in Moscow during the first half of the century. The canvas presents a series of rooms organized along clear lines of perspective; the statue of Venus near the window to the left—similar to the Medici Venus that Napoleon took from Florence and then returned—and the many paintings on the walls immediately indicate the inhabitant's relationship to art. All is in perfect order, the airy rooms are full of light, and the small dog on the right adds a touch of daily reality.

CHRISTEN KØBKE
The Landscape Painter Frederik Sødring
1832, oil on canvas
42.2 x 37.9 cm
Den Hirschsprungske Samling, Copenhagen

They were friends and shared the studio, Købke and Sødring, both of them Danes, both of them with a strong inclination toward landscape painting. Much of this is made clear from the engravings hanging on the walls in this portrait, which is one of the few portraits from Købke's career, since he made them only of people dear to him—this work was a gift to Sødring on his twenty-third birthday. The format is small, but is expanded through the insertion of so many components, from the chair with the striped seat on which Sødring sits to the consol table crowded with objects. Leaning against the wall to the lower right is a wood-and-leather stool for sketching outdoors; the inevitable easel is partially visible in the mirror on the wall. The painter's amused expression seems to confirm the close friendship between the two artists, while his dress offers an interesting example of the style of the period.

WILHELM BENDZ
Interior on Amaliegade
1830, oil on canvas
32.3 x 49 cm
Den Hirschsprungske Samling, Copenhagen

It is a room like many others, that of the artist's two brothers, with objects of various types and a slight sense of disorder, revealing the different character traits of the two young men. Bendz does not portray them posed but as though taken unaware, captured while immersed in their separate thoughts.

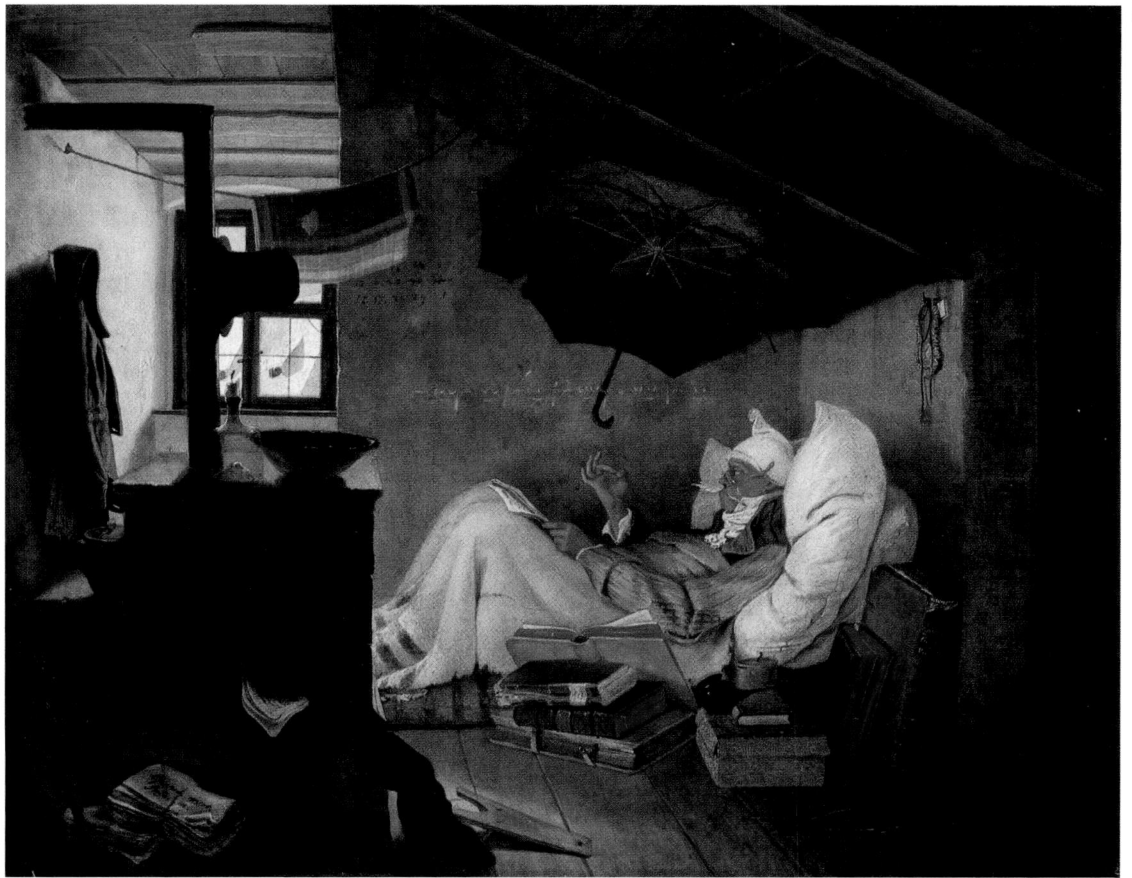

CARL SPITZWEG
The Poor Poet
1839, oil on canvas
36.2 x 44.6 cm
Neue Pinakothek, Munich

An amusing view of the bohemian life of a penniless poet: shut up in his chaotic, tumbledown garret, the poet takes shelter in bed, shielded by an umbrella from the rain that drips from the ceiling and drawn up under the covers as he works away, with the manuscript of the third volume of his works resting on the floor with the title *Operum meorum fas*[iculum] *III*.

Caspar David Friedrich
Woman at the Window
1822, oil on canvas
44 x 37 cm
Nationalgalerie, Berlin

A woman seen from behind looks out a window at what one intuits to be a landscape, in this case the River Elbe, its banks lined with poplars. In fact we know that the room is the artist's studio in Dresden, and thus the woman, whose face we cannot see, is most probably his wife, Caroline. The image of tranquil peace is in keeping with the meditative sentiment of many female figures in Romantic paintings, but in Friedrich it goes beyond the anecdotal domestic style, taking on mystical meaning by way of religious symbolism and alluding to the contrast between life and death, between earthly existence and eternal life. Just as a closed room receives light through the window, life is illuminated through reflection on Christ, indicated by the cross formed by the wooden window frame. Exhibited at Dresden in 1822, this painting inspired the German poet Friedrich de La Motte Fouqué to write the verses of his *Reise-Erinnerungen*.

Georg Friedrich Kersting
In Front of the Mirror
1827, oil on panel
46 x 35 cm
Kunsthalle, Kiel

A serene sense of calm and domestic simplicity animates this small canvas, which has the power to evoke the rhythmic life of women in the nineteenth century. The work was made by one of the closest friends of Caspar David Friedrich in Dresden, but unlike Friedrich, Kersting does not attempt a symbolic representation, concentrating instead on achieving an effect of delicate intimacy. He portrays a bourgeois interior with a few pieces of furniture and a warm light, only in part from the window open on the landscape. The young girl seen from behind wears a house dress and is busy braiding her long hair to go out for a stroll, as indicated by the coat and showy yellow hat. The protagonist of the painting is not the girl, whose face is seen only in its reflection in the mirror, but the thoroughly feminine gesture, which is presented in its daily dimension.

Giuseppe Molteni
Grandfather Showing His Granddaughter the Herm of Marie Louise
1830, oil on canvas
99.1 x 130 cm
Galleria Nazionale, Parma

Molteni's decision to give this painting to the duchess of Parma, in November 1831, turned out to be truly wise, since it marked the beginning of his professional rise. Marie Louise of Austria, widow of Napoleon and regent of the duchy of Parma from 1816 to 1847, was greatly pleased by the canvas, so much so that the next year she commissioned Molteni to make her portrait. The scene, implicitly celebrative of the ruler, was in her favorite style, much in keeping with the Biedermeier sensibility. An elderly middle-class man, learned and well to do, at least wealthy enough to have a house jacket trimmed with fur, gives his granddaughter an affectionate lesson in honor of the duchess. The girl turns toward the herm of Marie Louise carved by Canova and decorated with a garland of flowers while her grandfather consults the *Principal Monuments Erected to Her Majesty Marie Louise, Duchess of Parma, Piacenza, and Guastalla*, printed in Parma in 1822.

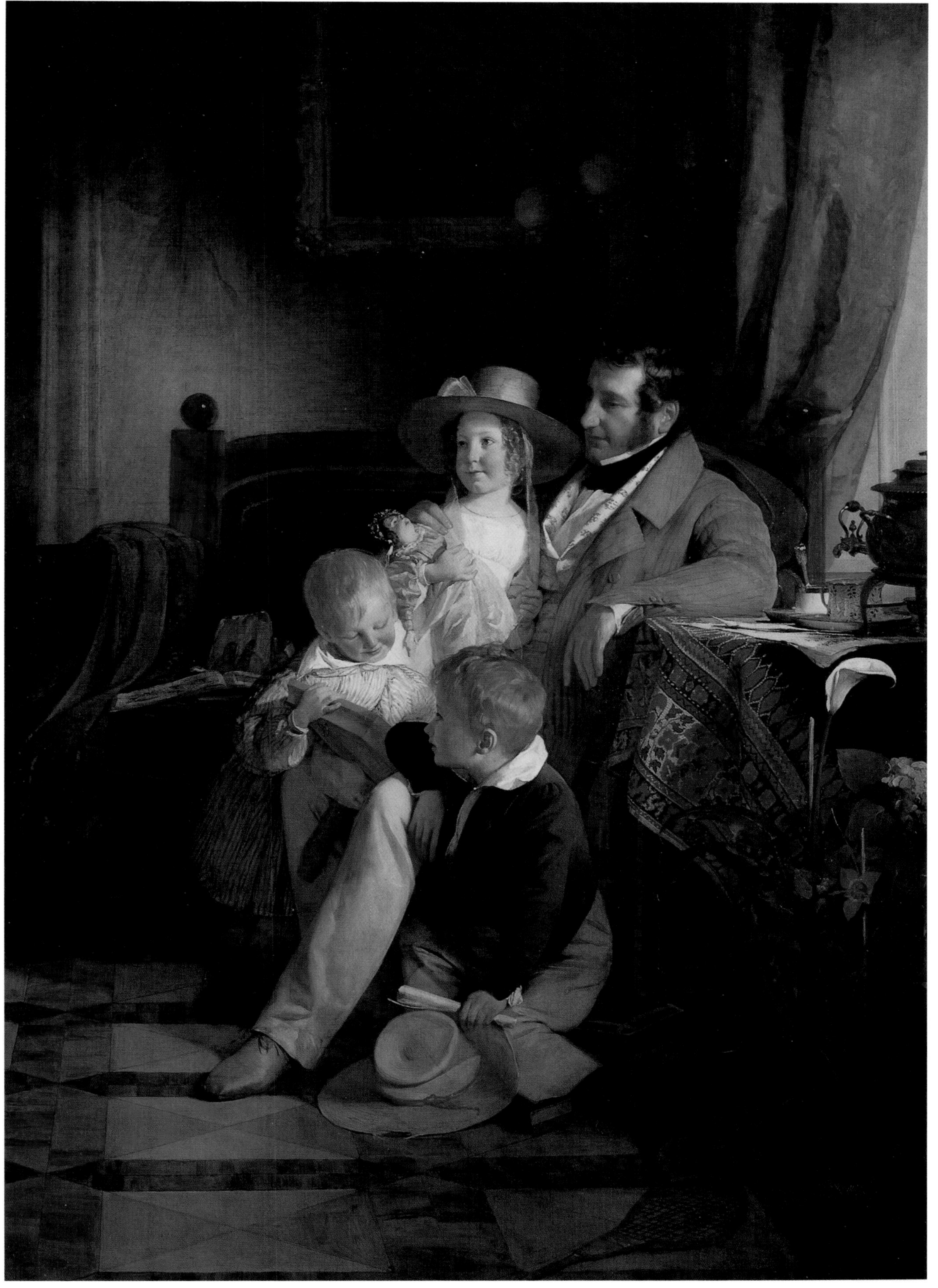

Friedrich von Amerling
Rudolf von Arthaber with His Children
1837, oil on canvas
221 x 156 cm
Österreichische Galerie, Vienna

Large-scale portraits like this were usually displayed in the most important room of a house, the living room or reception area, most of all if the work portrayed family members. Rudolf von Arthaber, well-to-do Viennese cloth merchant, was one of the artist's leading clients; a widower, he wanted to have himself portrayed together with his children but without excluding from the group the memory of their mother, symbolically present in the small portrait that the youngest daughter holds in her hand, offering it to the melancholy gaze of her father. Despite this touching insertion, the atmosphere is warm and lively, animated by the spontaneity of the children with their house clothes and their games, and also by the elegant notes of the furnishings, such as the samovar, porcelain cups, and the rug, against which the indoor plants stand out.

BENJAMIN ROBERT HAYDON
Punch or May Day
1835, oil on canvas
150.5 x 185 cm
Tate Gallery, London

Punch and Judy shows were the popular puppet shows in nineteenth-century England. Punch, the English version of the Italian character Pulcinella, had arrived on the far side of the Channel a little after the middle of the seventeenth century in the form of a marionette worked by strings, but otherwise preserving all his character traits and comical aspect. With the passage of time he made his way into the repertory of puppets, often sharing the stage with his nagging wife, Judy. Together they were the leading characters in amusing plots that most often ended in a thrashing. This is what Robert Benjamin Haydon wanted to present in

this canvas, assembling a cross-section of city life typical of the neighborhoods of London, whose streets were often animated by these shows. The puppet theater is on the left, with a good thrashing already in progress; gathered in front of this spectacle is an audience of adults and children. Meanwhile a fruit vendor displays her merchandise, and a pickpocket attempts to profit from the general distraction. Having presented his amusing genre scene the artist goes further, putting alongside it images allusive to the traditional May Day holiday and, in the background, two elements providing quite different views of life's realities: a pair of newlyweds in a carriage and, behind them, a funeral carriage.

Ditlev Conrad Blunck
Danish Painters at the Osteria La Gensola in Rome
circa 1836,
oil on canvas
71 x 94 cm
Der Nationalhistoriske Museum pä Frederiksborg, Hillerød

This painting recreates the brio of one of the many Roman osterias that were the favored haunts of foreign artists living in the city during the early decades of the nineteenth century. The Danish painter Blunck and various colleagues were in the habit of getting together in this locale in Trastevere, and thanks to writing on the back of the canvas they are all identifiable. To the right, presented three-quarters with white hair, sits Bertel Thorvaldsen; the man turning to speak to the standing host is the mayor of Copenhagen and patron of the painting; farther back the painter Albert Küchler plays with a dog. The setting is presented in all its homely simplicity, with the rustic serving ware, the well in the left rear, the maids, the fat cook by the fire, and the domestic animals, all presented with a lively sense of immediacy.

Constantin Hansen
A Group of Danish Artists in Rome
1837, oil on canvas
62.3 x 74 cm
Staten Museum for Kunst, Copenhagen

Hansen lived in Italy for nine years, from 1835 to 1844, and his studio in the center of Rome became a meeting place for friends and Danes passing through the city. This canvas presents an occasion on which the friends got together to celebrate the return of Gottlieb Bindesbøll from a trip to Greece and its region. Seated on the floor and wearing a red fez he tells the story of his travels while the others drink coffee and smoke the pipes he has brought back for them from Turkey. The atmosphere is without animation, the listeners seem almost bored, with only the spaniel expressing visible interest. The room is furnished with the bare essentials, including only a few pieces of furniture. Atop these stand out porcelain cups and an oil lamp, and studies by Hansen hang from the walls, including a few architectural sketches, such as the layout of a building leaning against the wall to the right and above it his *View of the Temple of Vesta*, today preserved in Copenhagen.

Karl Frederich Heinrich Werner
Carnival on the Corso
1848, watercolor on paper
73 x 131 cm
Collezione Antonacci, Rome

A German artist who came to Rome to study ancient monuments, Werner dedicated himself to portraying typical moments from the daily life of the city, such as this lively view of the masked parade during carnival along the Corso, a street near the Villa Medici, which can in fact be seen above, at the end of a narrow street. Since the Renaissance in Rome, carnival carriages and shows ran along this route, and until the 1830s it was also the race course (*corso*) for the Barbary horse race, which had been abolished by the time of the painting. The chaotic and colorful atmosphere is recreated in such

minute detail that this watercolor is an invaluable document in the history of street festivities. The citizens crowded on balconies do not merely watch the parade go by but actively participate by tossing down materials of all sorts. The paraders, on foot or in carriages, stop in front of improvised scenes performed by various masked characters, Pulcinella, Zanni, and Harlequins, figures inspired by the protagonists of the ancient *commedia dell'arte*, as well as men and women in Chinese or folkloristic costume. Standing out among all these many historical carnival heroes is the "wild man," seated on a carriage at the center. This personage tied to ancient traditions, a feature of the ritual spring celebrations for many centuries, made his final appearances in the nineteenth century.

Throughout the history of art, rebellion against the rules imposed on students in art academies has often led to the formation of new, innovative movements. So it was that the young artists who broke with the Vienna Academy of Fine Arts in 1809 laid the basis for one of the first manifestations of Romanticism. Between 1804 and 1806 various German intellectuals, including Friedrich Schlegel and Bettina and Clemens Brentano, and artists like Ludwig Schnorr von Carolsfeld, Franz Pforr, Friedrich Overbeck, and Ludwig Vogel had arrived in the Austrian capital. The pre-Romantic theories that these German philosophers and writers brought with them were not well received in the local academic spheres. Unwilling to put up with the scholastic exercises imposed on students, which included actual painting only as the final step, Overbeck and Pforr decided to break away. In 1808, gathering like-minded students around themselves, they formed a group that agreed to meet every two weeks

Julius Schnorr von Carolsfeld, *Clara Bianca von Quandt*, 1822, oil on panel, 37 x 26 cm; Staatliche Museen Preussischer Kultursbesitz, Gemäldegalerie, Berlin

of Rome with long beards and hair, for which reason they earned the name of Nazarenes. Aiming at a revival of the "primitive" religious paintings of the German Middle Ages and the early Renaissance, up to the works of the young Raphael and Dürer, they invented a style that emulated antique religious art and applied this style even to portraits, preferring to work in fresco since it had been the technique used "from the great Giotto to the divine Raphael." The group came to include Wilhelm Schadow, Philip Veit, Julius Schnorr von Carolsfeld, brother of Ludwig, Joseph Anton Koch, and Peter Cornelius, who arrived in Rome in 1812. All of them worked on the wall decoration of Roman palaces, including the Casino Massimo. The presence of the Nazarenes in Rome influenced the formation of Purismo, a trend that took form around 1830 on the initiative of Tommaso Minardi and his student Antonio Bianchini, author in 1842 of the movement's programmatic text, *Del Purismo nelle Arti;* the movement drew support from the sculptor Pietro Tenerani and,

Nazarenes, Purists,

to discuss their work; one year later, on July 10, following the model of the medieval guilds, they founded the *Lukasbund*, the Brotherhood of St. Luke (Luke being the patron saint of painters). In 1810 they moved to Rome—where Ingres had been living for four years—not only to make life studies of works by the great masters of the past but also because that city was the center of primitive Christianity. Animated by religious fervor and conceiving art as a tool for moral education, they sought to bring back the medieval society founded on the values of the Catholic church (a sentiment that included nationalistic nostalgia) and lived following the precepts of poverty and humility. In keeping with these principles, the young artists adopted a humble life-style, living as a community in the ruined monastery of San Isidoro and wandering the streets

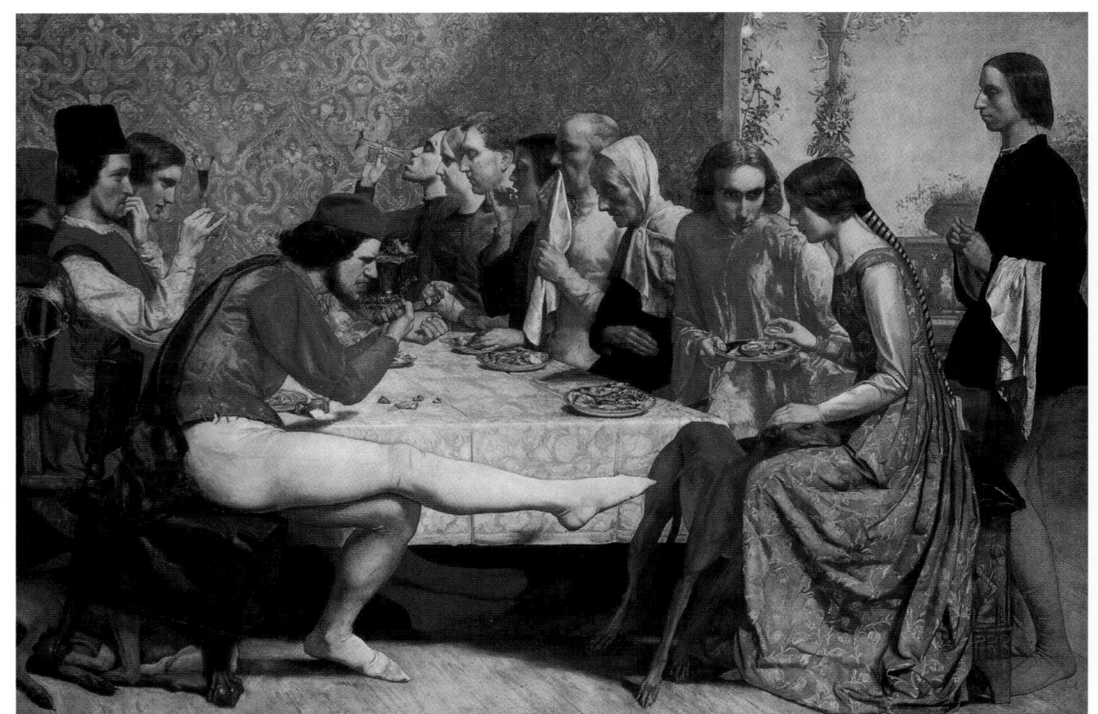

John Everett Millais, *Isabella*, 1848–49, oil on canvas, 102.9 x 142.9 cm; Walker Art Gallery, Liverpool

and Pre-Raphaelites

not surprisingly, from Overbeck. The term *purismo* ("purism") was derived from a literary movement of the period that sought the preservation of purity in the Italian language through study of the fourteenth-century dialect of Tuscany; applied to art, the intention was that of creating antiacademic art loaded with religious messages and modeled on the painting of the fourteenth century and early Renaissance, taking as the primary model Raphael up to the period (1510–11) in which he painted the *Dispute of the Holy Sacrament* in the Vatican. As Bianchini wrote, the aim of Purist art was to "speak to the soul" and to the "exterior beauty of settings." The 1842 manifesto repeated the theme of ideal beauty proposed by Minardi a decade earlier, a theory of particular importance not only within the Roman sphere but also in Tuscany, where Lorenzo Bartolini, with the theory of natural beauty, and the last Italian works by Ingres (in Florence from 1820 to 1824) had led to sharp disputes. Luigi Mussini was a Tuscan exponent of Purismo; following the example of Ingres, he supported the primacy of the art of Raphael, directing himself toward a true cult of the form and eventually surpassing the Nazarenes and Roman Purismo. He discarded the idea of imitating the ancients and proposed instead that it was important to rework the great masters from Giotto to Raphael—the only artists who in his judgment had "been able to reconcile and unite the severe purity of the fourteenth century with the greatness of the sixteenth"—in an autonomous way. Raphael was of central importance to yet a third Romantic movement, but in the case of the Pre-Raphaelites the great artist marked a true dividing line, for these artists proposed a return to the simple and primitive art prior to Raphael. The Pre-Raphaelite Brotherhood came into being in September 1848 in London. Once again young art students—John Everett Millais, William Holman Hunt, Dante Gabriel Rossetti, and his brother William Michael, with other artist friends—were presenting proposals that challenged academic teaching. They were united in their enthusiasm for painting with dreamy, angelic tones far removed from the modern images of cities besieged by the growth of industrial factories; embracing the widespread myth of the Middle Ages, they suggested a return to nature and to a firm social and religious order. The group followed strict rules, often made portraits of one another to give their figures more strength (four appear in Millais's *Isabella*), and established a peculiar classification of the great artists of history, their "List of Immortals," which placed Jesus Christ at the top, followed immediately by Shakespeare, beneath whom came the author of Job and Homer, Dante, Robert Browning, Edgar Allan Poe, and so on. Their first exhibit at the Royal Academy, in the spring of 1849, had a promising reception, but the next year the sensual, melancholy symbolism of their paintings was attacked, and their simplified and realistic renderings of religious themes were judged nearly scandalous. They were saved by the art critic John Ruskin, who rushed to their support and used his authority to return the young Pre-Raphaelites to public acclaim. In a letter to the *Times* of May 13, 1851, he responded to an article that had appeared in that paper ten days earlier that had expressed contempt for the group; extolling their painting, Ruskin expressed his full approval of painters who sought to present "the actual facts of the scenes they desire to represent, irrespective of the conventional rules of picture-making." Having become the movement's soul, Ruskin infused in the Pre-Raphaelites faith in the social function of art, in the importance of sentiment, and in the profound aspirations of the individual. Social realism was an important element in the group, as expressed for example in *The Last of England* by Ford Madox Brown, which presents the dignified anguish of a couple forced to emigrate.

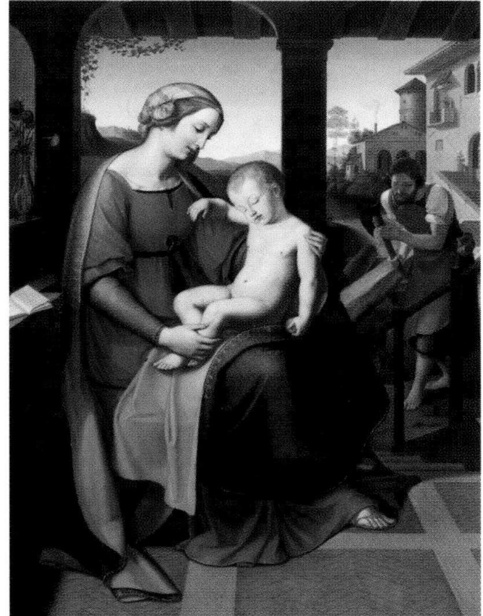

Wilhelm Schadow, *Holy Family beneath a Portico*, 1818, oil on canvas, 142 x 102 cm; Bayerische Staatsgemäldesammlungen, Munich

Ford Madox Brown, *The Last of England*, 1852–54, oil on panel, 82.5 x 75 cm; Museum and Art Gallery, Birmingham

Friedrich Overbeck
Franz Pforr
1810, oil on canvas
62 x 47 cm
Nationalgalerie,
Berlin

Overbeck and Pforr, who met as students at the Vienna Academy of Art, were the founders of the Brotherhood of St. Luke in 1809 and later the Nazarene movement. In this painting, made the year of their arrival in Italy, Overbeck portrays his friend in accordance with the criteria of their stylistic and compositional revival, the goal of which was a return to the simple aesthetic values of the mid-fifteenth century. The artist gives great importance to the setting: the youth, whose clothes evoke the Renaissance style, looks out from a sort of window decorated with an improbable terracotta frame, while behind him is a view of a Gothic city. Domestic details, such as the cat and the young woman knitting while reading, blend with religious symbols, such as the grapevine, the skull in the relief, and the vase of lilies, transforming the image of a young woman reading into a religious metaphor allusive to the Annunciation.

Franz Pforr
Entry of Rudolf von Hapsburg into Basel in 1273
1810, oil on canvas
90.5 x 118.9 cm
Städelsches Kunstinstut, Frankfurt

Pforr was one of the most active members of the Nazarene group, and this canvas is one of the first works with a medieval subject painted in a deliberately archaic style meant to evoke that of medieval miniatures. The flat perspective, bright colors, and simplicity of the forms attempt to create a sense of the artistic past that was associated with a political situation gazed upon with longing by Pforr: the German unity that existed under the Holy Roman Empire and in the golden age begun under the Hapsburg dynasty, of which Rudolf had been the first emperor.

FRIEDRICH OVERBECK
Italia and Germania
1811–29,
oil on canvas
94 x 104 cm
Neue Pinakothek,
Munich

The two allegorical figures represent the hoped-for union between the Italian and German civilizations. To the left is Italy, behind whom appears a Romanesque church; to the right is Germany, identified by the group of Gothic buildings as well as by her blonde hair.

PETER CORNELIUS
Joseph Recognized by His Brothers
1816, fresco
236 x 290 cm
Nationalgalerie,
Berlin

This fresco was part of the wall decorations of the Roman residence of the Prussian consul Salomon Bartholdy. It is an eloquent example of the style of Cornelius, who attempted the philological reconstruction of the style of Raphael and of the Umbrian and Tuscan painters of the late fifteenth century.

Joseph Anton Koch
Dante Attacked by Three Wild Beasts
1825, watercolor and pen with gray and brown ink
36.9 x 43.5 cm
Museum Boymans-van Beuningen, Rotterdam

On the basis of this preparatory drawing, finished in watercolor, Koch made a fresco on a wall of the so-called Dante Room in the Casino Massimo, located near the Lateran in Rome. The patron, Marchese Carlo Massimo, wanted to decorate his villa with cycles dedicated to the principal masterpieces of Italian literature, and Koch here illustrated the celebrated opening of Dante's *Inferno,* with the poet facing three beasts: the leopard, the lion, and the she-wolf. He made cunning use of the presence of the doorway in the wall to create a singular narrative effect, crowning it with the words written over the door to the afterworld: "Abandon all hope, you who enter." Koch's Nazarene style is marked by the use of bright colors, evocative of Italian Renaissance frescoes and suitable for the narrative function of the decorations.

Peter Cornelius
The Five Wise Virgins and the Five Foolish Virgins
1813–16, oil on canvas
114 x 153 cm
Kunstmuseum Düsseldorf im Ehrenhof, Düsseldorf

Religious painting was the area of greatest interest to the Nazarenes, who hoped to bring about a revival in religious representations. Cornelius was very much a part of this, and he used the theme of a parable from the Gospel of St. Matthew (25:1–3) as the means for experiments in search of the most appropriate visual language for the communication of the text's meaning, which could be presented on a symbolic plane. In this instance there is the substitution of the figure of the bridegroom with Christ surrounded by saints and the fathers of the church, an allusion to the broadest reading of the biblical text. Cornelius based the architectural space and the poses and profiles of many of the figures on Renaissance examples, such as the foolish virgins grouped in the background of the composition, comparable to certain figures in the *Fire in the Borgo* by Raphael in the pope's private rooms in the Vatican.

William Dyce
Madonna and Child
1838, oil on plaster
78.7 x 60.3 cm
Castle Museum, Nottingham

The Aberdeen-born artist William Dyce was deeply involved in Renaissance religious art and became active in the revival of fifteenth-century art not only in terms of painting but also church music and architecture, which he was involved in for the Anglican Church. He became associated with the Nazarene group during his second trip to Italy, in 1827, and began painting devotional images that enjoyed immediate success with reformers in the Church of England. He too found in the youthful painting of Raphael the clearest signs of the blending of art and faith and often drew his inspiration from that repertory; in this case the Raphael model of reference was probably the Tempi Madonna (Alte Pinakothek, Munich), which he had seen in 1837, the simplicity of which he exalted in the rigid profiles of the figures and the landscape.

Filippo Agricola
Constance Monti Perticari
1821, oil on panel
91 x 79 cm
Galleria Nazionale d'Arte Moderna, Rome

The young woman was the daughter of the poet Vincenzo Monti; she had married the Pesaro-born writer Giulio Perticari. Monti dedicated a sonnet to the portrait that begins with the lines "The more I contemplate it, the more I wander through that wonderful canvas." The artist, of neoclassical training, indicates here that he adhered to the Purismo current, distinguishing himself in the explicit derivation of the compositional scheme from Raphael. More precisely, Agricola sought to make a work capable of evoking, by citing the pose, gaze, and rendering of the face, several of the great master's female portraits from the early sixteenth century. Even the hairstyle and jewelry of the young Constance, like the style of the dress—although it reflects the Empire style still in vogue in the early 1820s—recall Renaissance-type iconographic precedents.

LUIGI MUSSINI
Holy Music
1841, oil on canvas
150 x 104 cm
Galleria dell'Accademia, Florence

Among the outstanding works of Tuscan Purismo, this canvas presents an allegory of religious music in much the same way that a Florentine or Umbrian painter of the fifteenth century would have done. The classical-style architectural layout, background landscape, and most of all the winged figure with the music scroll are elements derived directly from various Renaissance works, and in fact Mussini had begun his artistic training with the study of those works. Only the excessive reverence in the expression on the skyward-directed face reveals the nineteenth-century approach. Mussini made the canvas while studying in Rome, where he assimilated the ideals of the Nazarene revival, reworking them in light of the rigorous design principles spread by Ingres during his long stay in Rome.

Pietro Tenerani
Abandoned Psyche
1818, marble
height 118 cm
Galleria d'Arte Moderna di Palazzo Pitti, Florence

Tenerani was among the artists who signed the Purismo manifesto, published in 1842, but he had embarked on his career nearly twenty-five years earlier with this sculpture, displayed in the Campidoglio in 1819. The work enjoyed immediate success and was bought by the Florentine Marchioness Carlotta Medici Lenzoni, who just managed to get in her offer before Prince Metternich, who therefore had to settle for a replica, which he immediately ordered from Tenerani. The noblewoman proudly displayed the sculpture in her Florentine home, where it was admired by her many visitors, including Giacomo Leopardi and other Romantic writers. In its composed simplicity this delicate figure marks a moment of reflection on the evolution of sculpture, which in the second decade of the century was slowly moving away from the rigid norms of the neoclassical and opening itself to the observation of nature in all its manifestations.

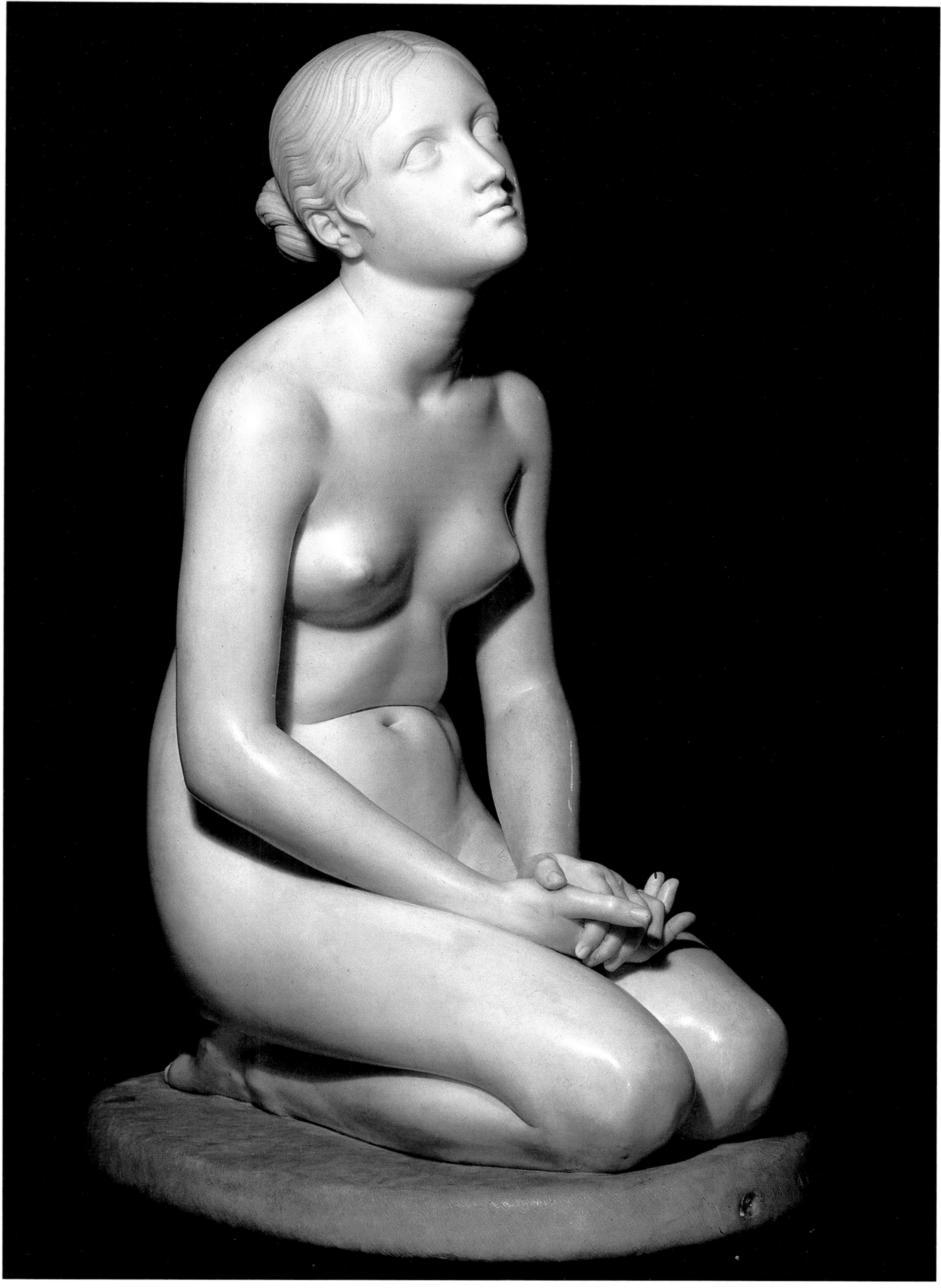

Lorenzo Bartolini
Trust in God
1835, marble
height 93 cm
Museo Poldi Pezzoli, Milan

Bartolini lived in Paris from 1799 to 1808, often visiting David's studio, where he worked alongside Ingres, nearly his contemporary in age, sharing his admiration for the art of the Italian Renaissance. On his return to Italy he played an important role in freeing sculpture from the canons of neoclassicism and moving it toward the direct observation of nature, thus putting it in tune with Romantic sensibilities. With this delicate image of *Trust in God* he translates a spiritual concept by way of a tender adolescent nude. The restrained emotion on the face and the pose of the figure met with success at the Brera exhibition, but at the same time indicate the artist's secondary position in terms of the innovations then taking place in northern Europe.

Dante Gabriel Rossetti
The Girlhood of Mary Virgin
1848–49, oil on canvas
83.2 x 65.4 cm
Tate Gallery, London

This painting was exhibited at the first show held by the Pre-Raphaelites, at Hyde Park in 1849, a few months after the foundation of the confraternity, the Pre-Raphaelite Brotherhood, the initials of which, P.R.B., Rossetti added beneath his name at the bottom left of the canvas. Son of an Italian patriot exiled in London, the artist was twenty years old when he made this painting, and in it he united the themes dearest to him, both evangelical and familiar, portraying in the sacred scene his mother, his sister Christina, and the elderly house servant Williams. In this canvas Rossetti adopted the criteria of naturalness, formal severity, but also the luminous return to nature advocated in those years by John Ruskin, who was to be among the most vocal supporters of the Pre-Raphaelite movement.

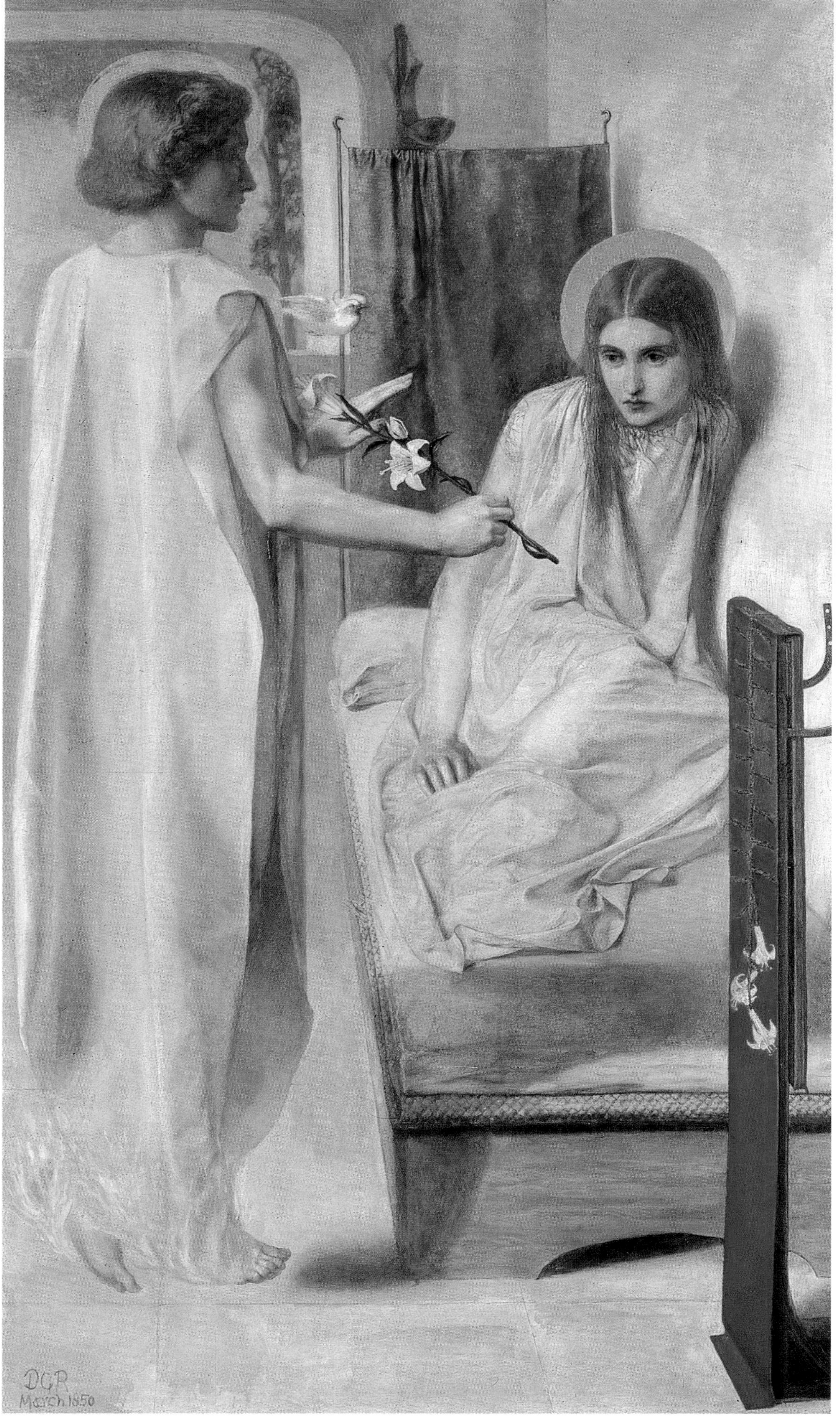

Dante Gabriel Rossetti
Ecce Ancilla Domini! (The Annunciation)
1849–50,
oil on canvas
mounted on board
72.6 x 41.9 cm
Tate Gallery, London

When he set to work on this painting Rossetti had behind him the success of the Pre-Raphaelites' first pubic exhibition. Determined to explore the language he was developing, he came up with this modern Annunciation, which is only partly faithful to the traditional iconography of the scene. He eliminated the Virgin's reading stand and Bible and the other furnishings usually present in the setting, opting for a prevalence of pale tones, most of all white, as symbols of purity, and reducing the chromatic range to the bare minimum. In this way Rossetti hoped to exalt the spiritual and emotional meaning of the event, with the calm statuary angel, feet hardly touching the floor, and the troubled response of Mary, drawing herself back on her bed in a decidedly modern gesture. The artist was greatly disappointed by the unexpected criticism directed at this work, so much so that from then on he only rarely displayed his paintings in public.

JOHN EVERETT MILLAIS
Christ in the House of His Parents (The Carpenter's Shop)
1849–50,
oil on canvas
86.4 x 139.7 cm
Tate Gallery, London

Millais was twenty when he made this work, his first important painting, which was exhibited at the Royal Academy in 1850. The subject almost seems to continue the discussion begun by Rossetti in his *The Girlhood of Mary Virgin* (see page 168), and it was probably inspired by a sermon heard at Oxford in the summer of 1849 on a verse from the book of the prophet Zechariah. The canvas uses simple and universal language to present a quiet domestic scene that is interwoven with symbolic allusions. At the center is Jesus, being consoled by his mother for having injured the palm of his hand; blood falls onto his feet in a clear prefiguration of his Crucifixion, much like the pliers and nails visible on the work table behind him. The small bowl of water carried with such care by the young John to the

right preludes the Baptism that he, as an adult, will administer to Jesus. As the setting for the scene the young Millais used a carpenter's workshop in Oxford Street, and it seems that to create the flock of sheep he bought two sheep heads from a butcher and portrayed them in variations. The result is a highly analytical presentation with realistic details, such as Joseph's dirty hands, which not did, however, please the public. In fact the attacks from critics were ferocious: the painting, judged by some to be blasphemous, caused a scandal at the exhibition precisely because of the excessively "vulgarized" interpretation of a sacred subject such as that of the Holy Family. Charles Dickens thundered against Millais in *Blackwood's Magazine*. Queen Victoria, curious at the uproar, had the painting temporarily removed from the exhibition and brought to her palace so she could examine it in person.

JOHN EVERETT MILLAIS
The Bridesmaid
1851, oil on panel
27.9 x 20.3 cm
Fitzwilliam Museum, Cambridge

According to old English superstition, if the bridesmaid passed a piece of wedding cake through the ring nine times she would have a vision of her future love. This is the gesture being performed by this young girl, with her absorbed, almost dreamy expression. Millais created the mood by experimenting with dramatic effects of chromatic contrasts. The painting is dominated by the girl's long hair, the orange tones of which almost invade the image, fading toward yellow on the silk dress but recalled in full by the fruit on the plate in the foreground.

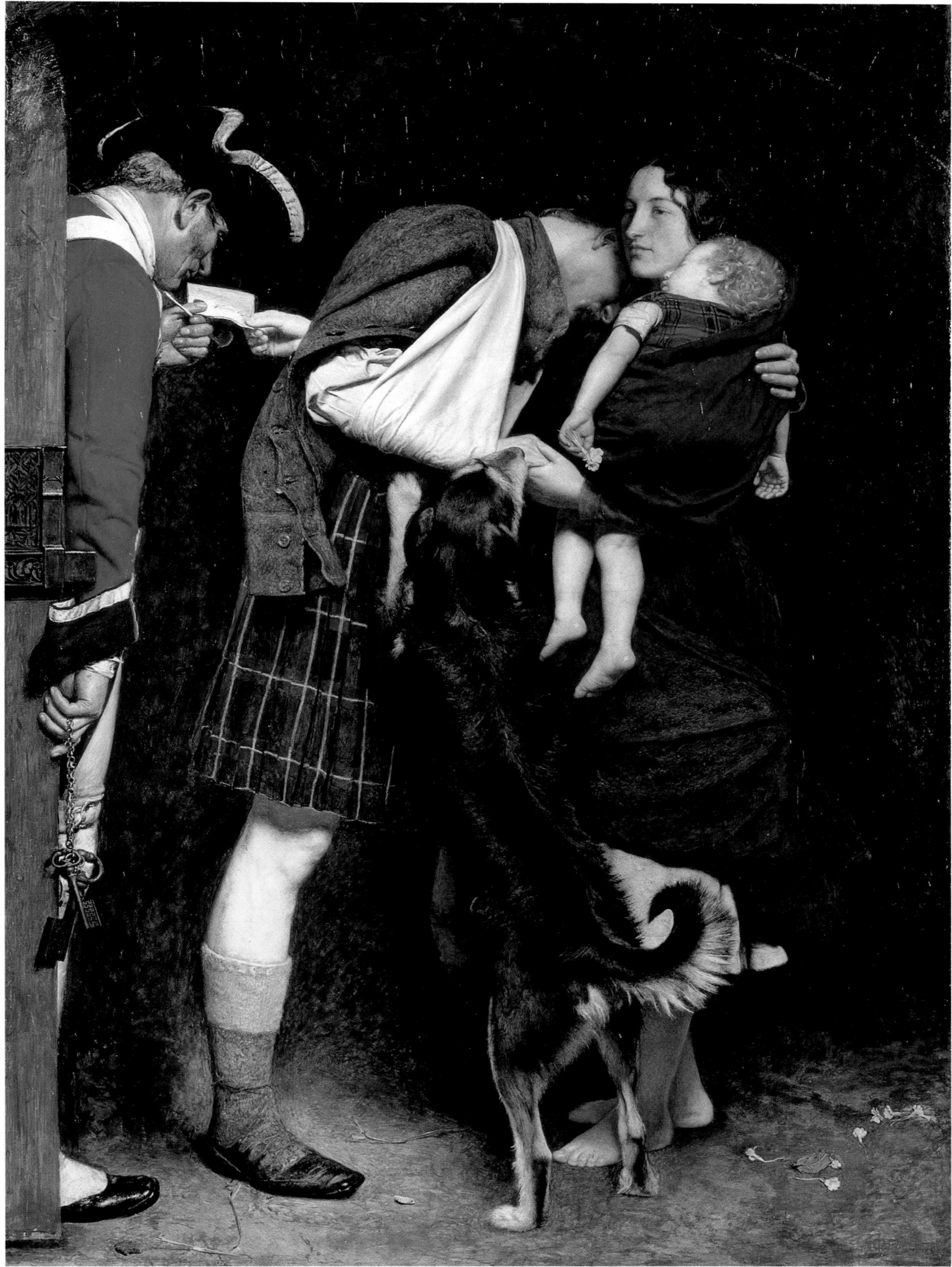

John Everett Millais
The Order of Release, 1746
1852–53,
oil on canvas
102.9 x 73.7 cm
Tate Gallery, London

In the fall of 1852 Millais decided to make a painting on a Scottish subject and came up with this episode, perhaps drawing inspiration from a story by Sir Walter Scott: a highlander imprisoned following the Jacobite rebellion of 1745 is freed from prison after almost a year thanks to the efforts of his wife. In fact, the scene is focused on the woman's intense and eloquent expression; John Ruskin's wife, Effie, posed for the face. Millais filled the moment of the reunion of the man and his family with strong emotions, extending even to the dog. He also made the scene as historically accurate as he could, making sure of the details of the setting and most of all employing the right kinds of fabrics, for which he consulted books in the library.

William Holman Hunt
The Light of the World
1853, oil on canvas transferred to wood
125.5 x 59.8 cm
Keble College, Oxford

In keeping with the standards the Pre-Raphaelites imposed on themselves, Hunt painted this at night, working in the open by the light of the moon. When exhibited at the Royal Academy in London in 1854, the painting was accompanied by a passage from the Book of Revelation (3:8). In this verse, Christ stands at a door and knocks, waiting to see who will open the door to him. This type of Protestant icon was neither well received nor fully understood by critics, but Ruskin wrote a letter to the *Times* explaining its symbolism and defending it as the most noble work of religious art ever made. The allusions to biblical texts include those to the gospels, most of all the passage in John (9:5–12), in which Jesus says, "I am the light of the world." Ruskin also noted that the closed door is covered by climbing plants in allusion to the human soul, while the light of the lantern indicated the light of conscience.

Arthur Hughes
Home from the Sea
1856–62,
oil on panel
50.8 x 65.1 cm
Ashmolean Museum,
Oxford

Hughes began work on this painting at Chingford in Essex in the summer of 1856 and exhibited it the following year at the Pre-Raphaelite show under the title *A Mother's Grave* (changing it in 1862). This is in fact the subject of the painting, although at first glance it does not awaken a sense of tragedy but seems instead to present a simple moment of youthful sorrow in a flowering field. In reality, as one learns from the words of the painter himself, the scene presents a young sailor who, learning of the death of his mother on his return from sea, weeps on the grass under which she is buried; beside him sits his sister, a figure added by Hughes in 1862 in anticipation of another exhibition. The delicacy of the setting, full of color and domestic simplicity, diminishes the sense of anguish of the protagonist; at first glance, the church and simple country graveyard offer a pleasant image, with the little lambs that leap among the headstones, which stand out against the green of the grass, along with the flowers and rosebushes.

Images of

Sacred images are perhaps the oldest in the history of painting. From the beginning of the Christian era, all of Western art was based for centuries on the presentation of religious subjects, whether made for public devotion in churches or for private worship. By the first half of the nineteenth century the number of pictorial genres had grown enormously, and the production of religious images had undergone a slight decline, a result of the suppression of monasteries during the Napoleonic epoch. The production of these works did not cease, however, and it resumed during the Restoration. In the first decades of the century, and most of all in France and Italy, the production of biblical and evangelical subjects occupied an important part of academic training, creating a stylistic imprint that long adhered to traditional aesthetics and compositional criteria. No programmatic efforts were ever made to close the field to innovation, but until the 1820s paintings with religious subjects did not make any important contributions to the artistic evolution of the time, with the exception of such cases as Caspar David Friedrich, who broke onto the Romantic scene with subjects imbued with profound faith, such as the Tetschen Altar. This work is full of symbolic allusions explained by the artist himself, such as the fir trees on the hillside, whose nature as evergreens is symbolic of the Christian hope necessary to sustain humanity, while the Christ, seen from slightly behind and illuminated by the rays of the setting sun, is an allusion to God's abandonment of earth. While strongly representative of Romantic sentiments, Friedrich was a singular case, his personality uniting spirituality, devotion, and the worship of the divine perceived through the natural world.

François Gérard, *Saint Theresa*, 1827, oil on canvas, 172 x 96 cm; Infirmerie Marie-Thérèse, Paris

He was not a painter of religious scenes but performed the role of great innovator in terms of the relationship between art and religion, most of all in Germany. *The Penitent Magdalene*, sculpted by Antonio Canova in 1796, was displayed at the Paris Salon of 1808 and is thus from roughly the same period as the Tetschen Altar. While it is absolutely different from the altar in terms of artistic genre and geographic area, it is quite similar in terms of its precocious use of Romantic notions to express the narration of a sacred theme. Indeed, Stendhal judged it to be one of the great masterpieces of modern times. Completely extraneous to traditional iconography, Mary Magdalene is rendered in an image of physical perfection that adds greater fascination to the work's expressive intensity. The statue was acquired by the Milanese Baron Angelo Sommariva, and he designed an emblematic location for it, a setting with violet walls illuminated by an alabaster lamp, so as to create a vaguely disturbing atmosphere, a mixture of the sacred and the profane. The sphere of Romantic painters did not include specialists in religious art, but many of the leading masters made works for worship or for the wall decoration of churches, and there were also canvases commissioned by private persons. One example is *Hagar Cast into the Wilderness by Abraham* painted by Horace Vernet for Alphonse Clarke, who paid four thousand francs; there is also the *St. Theresa* painted by François Gérard on a commission from Madame Récamier for the Infirmerie Marie-Thérèse, the charity asylum created by the wife of François-René de Chateaubriand in 1819. In France, after the Restoration, Charles X and his municipal authorities took on the task of commissioning new altarpieces for churches, as a political means to diminish the memory of the destruction of monuments and paintings in church buildings carried out during the Revolutionary period; in a similar vein the ancient tradition of private patronage for places of public worship was revived. Such patrons expected a certain kind of religious painting, characterized by the sort of official decorum found in great history paintings, both eloquent and majestic. Within that sphere, great

Antonio Canova, *The Penitent Magdalene*, 1796, marble, height 96 cm; Palazzo Bianco, Genoa

John Martin, *Belshazzar's Feast,* 1820, oil on canvas, 95.3 x 120.6 cm; Yale Center for British Art, Paul Mellon Collection, New Haven

masterpieces were made with completely different intentions that reveal Romantic values. Outstanding examples are the heartfelt *Crucifixion* by Pierre-Paul Prud'hon, which was taken directly into the Louvre

the sacred

collection instead of being placed in the church in Metz for which it had been painted, and the *Vow of Louis XIII*, which announced Ingres' triumphant debut at the Salon of 1824, where it was exhibited before being placed on the altar of the cathedral of Montauban: the canvas contained a clear self-celebratory message of the reign of Charles X. The work's clear derivation from the work of Raphael reflects Ingres' feelings for the Italian Renaissance master, but such sentiments cannot be compared to the neoprimitive taste of the Nazarenes, Purists, or Pre-Raphaelites, all of whom dedicated themselves to religious painting in a far more purposeful way. As seen in the preceding chapter, the goal of German artists like Friedrich Overbeck, Franz Pforr, and Wilhelm Schadow, as well as that of the Scottish William Dyce in his youthful period, was the renewal of religious sentiment, which they hoped to achieve by creating simple, easily understood images capable of communicating evangelical virtues. To accomplish this goal they based their stylistic and figurative language on the simple but convincing style of fifteenth-century Italian art. Having adopted this style they soon brought it with them from Rome back to Germany, such that in 1819 Friedrich Schlegel wrote: "Now even the protestants look favorably on embellishing their churches with devotional images." The "return to the sources" was also a feature of the Italian Purismo movement, which was animated by the same conviction that harmony and simplicity could reinforce the sentiment of purity that is inherent in devotional images. The history of the emulation of "primitive" (medieval or Renaissance) art, the styles of which were applied to religious themes during the Romantic age, reached its conclusion in Britain with various works by the Pre-Raphaelites following their debut on the artistic scene. With the approach of the middle of the century, religious painting began to expand, following certain highly evocative Romantic notions. John Martin, who became famous for his "Illustrations to the Bible" and for the sensation he caused at the British Exhibition of 1821 with his highly original *Belshazzar's Feast*, made an apocalyptic version of the sublime with his *The Great Day of His Wrath.* Paul Delaroche ended his career with four masterpieces of highly religious and spiritual content, dictated by profound personal suffering, including the extraordinary *Young Christian Martyr.*

François-Joseph Navez, *Hagar and Ishmael,* 1822, oil on canvas, 221 x 171 cm; Koninklijke Museen voor Schone Kunsten, Brussels

Caspar David Friedrich
The Cross in the Mountains
1808, oil on canvas
115 x 110.5 cm
Staatliche Kunstsammlungen, Dresden

This work is also known as the Tetschen Altar because it was commissioned by Count Franz Anton Thun-Hohenstein for the chapel in his castle at Tetschen, Bohemia. The theme of the Crucifixion emerges without giving the canvas a devotional tone, but the religious nature of the scene reaches the highest levels of mystical sensibilities because of the extraordinary luminous effects with which the artist expressed the sacredness of nature, a concept that was to characterize all of his later production. Accused by some critics of having used a landscape as an altarpiece, Friedrich put himself at the center of a lively debate with this canvas, which in fact earned him notoriety as a leading light of Romantic ideals. The frame was carved by the sculptor Karl Gottlob Kuhn on a design made by the painter employing symbolic plant motifs.

Giuseppe Boccaccio
The Baptism of Christ
circa 1830,
oil on canvas
70 x 95 cm
Museo Glauco Lombardi, Parma

Although it doesn't reach the emotionally charged drama of Friedrich's *Cross in the Mountains* (opposite), this canvas is also an example of a religious subject presented within a landscape. Made early in the third decade of the nineteenth century, it reflects the artistic taste of the Parma court under Marie Louise, which Boccaccio adapted by fitting it to the traditional layout scheme of contemporary landscape painting. And in effect this is a landscape painting, since the holy scene with Christ and John the Baptist would not stand out from the composition were it not for the powerful ray of light that comes in from the upper left to isolate the two figures, leading the viewer's eyes to the event of the Holy Baptism.

Pierre-Paul Prud'hon
Crucifixion
1822, oil on canvas
278 x 165.5 cm
Musée du Louvre,
Paris

Commissioned for Metz cathedral, this work, although partially unfinished, awakened such enthusiasm that the Louvre decided to purchase it. Prud'hon, emotionally distressed for more than a year following the suicide of Constance Mayer, his student, lover, and collaborator since 1803, had taken a completely traditional scene and imbued it with a sense of profound emotional involvement. The canvas reveals Prud'hon's great passion for seventeenth-century Italian painting, in particular for the style of Caravaggio and his followers. It is from that art that he drew the violent illumination of the Crucifixion, which contrasts with the background immersed in darkness, as well as the realistic treatment of the suffering Christ on the cross and the intense drama with which the religious theme is interpreted.

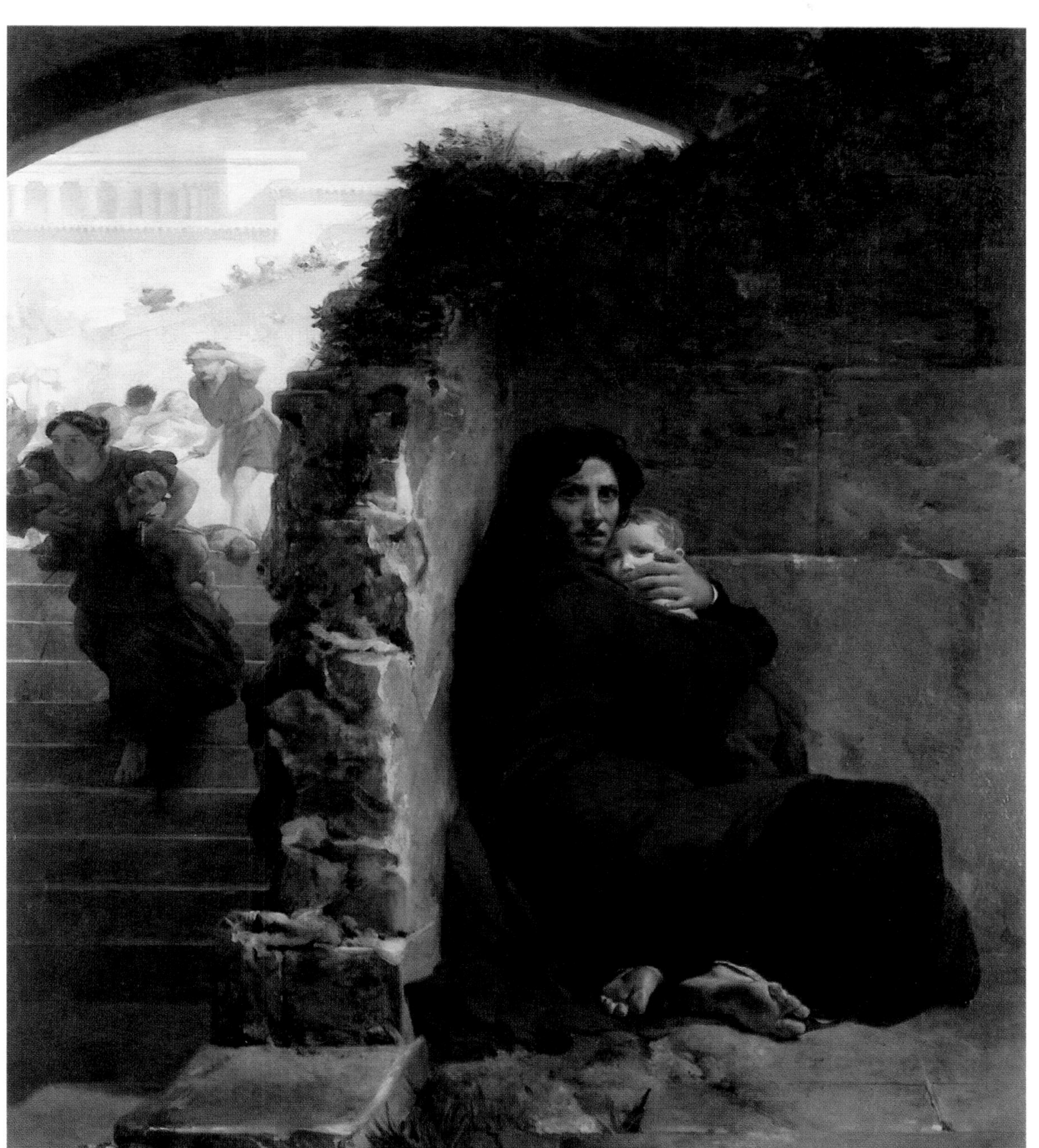

Léon Cogniet
The Slaughter of the Innocents
1824, oil on canvas
265 x 235 cm
Musée des Beaux-Arts, Rennes

This canvas was displayed at the famous Salon of 1824, the exhibition with which Paris confirmed the triumph of the Romantic movement. In this work Cogniet presents a very original version of the ancient story of the slaughter of the innocents, dividing the composition in half and using only half for the traditional scene of collective panic. He did so in order to concentrate on a single figure packed with the true meaning of the terrible event, thus creating an image of sensational expressive power that fit perfectly with the host of other Romantic masterpieces at that year's Salon. The viewer's attention is drawn to the terrified face of the young mother, crouching in the shadows, pulling back against the wall in an effort to save her child. Despite its religious subject, the work was not necessarily meant to serve as an altarpiece; it was in fact bought for 7,000 francs by a well-to-do banker.

Jean-Auguste-Dominique Ingres
The Vow of Louis XIII
1824, oil on canvas
421 x 262 cm
Cathedral of Notre-Dame, Montauban

The canvas was commissioned from Ingres by the city of his birth, Montauban, and he painted it in Florence during his stay there in the summer of 1820. Exhibited at the Salon of 1824, it was his first great success and won him the Legion of Honor, presented to him by the king in person. Although conceived as an altarpiece, the work had a strong political message: it evoked the solemn gesture with which in 1638 Louis XIII had consecrated to the Virgin the kingdom of France (on the throne of which Charles X now sat). The king is shown from behind in the act of offering the Virgin the crown and scepter; thanks to the artist's exceptional skills, the mantle he wears seems almost tangible. Echoes of the style of Raphael, whom Ingres saw as the model of perfection and to whom he turned for inspiration, are quite clear, both in the Virgin and Child group and in the two angels holding up the cartouche with the subject of the painting and the date of the historical event.

Jean-Auguste-Dominique Ingres
The Martyrdom of St. Symphorian
1834, oil on canvas
407 x 339 cm
Cathedral of Saint-Lazare, Autun

After his success at the Salon of 1824, Ingres was commissioned to make an altarpiece for the cathedral of Saint-Lazare in Autun. The bishop chose the subject and the details of the painting, which was to present the moment in which the young Christian Symphorian, being led to the temple of Cybele to be sacrificed to the goddess, took leave of his family under the walls and city gate of the ancient city of Autun. Ingres created a scene with an unusual dynamism, based on the crowd of people and Roman soldiers around the martyr. This novelty did not please critics, who accused the artist of design excesses and of bodies rendered too vigorously, more similar to models by Michelangelo than to the perfection of Raphael. This awakened the admiration of the Romantics, but their praise was not enough to console Ingres who, embittered, decided that he would never again exhibit his works at the Salon.

Horace Vernet
Hagar Cast into the Wilderness by Abraham
1837, oil on canvas
81 x 65 cm
Musée des Beaux-Arts, Nantes

Hagar, the handmaid who had given Abraham a son, is driven out into the wilderness with the young Ishmael, where the intervention of an angel will save them from death. The biblical subject offered an example of moral cruelty since Hagar was cast off only when Sarah, Abraham's wife, was no longer sterile and could give her husband legitimate heirs. Vernet presents the moment of the separation, with the implicit condemnation of the young woman and the child to die of thirst in the desert, but he does so without dramatic accents. Only the resolute gesture of the patriarch alludes to the decision he has made; the scene has no signs of emotional turmoil or desperation. Instead, the artist dedicates much care to the rendering of the physical setting, making use of his recent trip to Algeria. During that trip he had decided that the dress and customs of the local populations had remained unchanged over the centuries and thus reflected those of the ancient biblical world.

Francesco Hayez
The Penitent Magdalene
1833, oil on panel
118 x 151 cm
Civica Galleria d'Arte Moderna, Milan

When, sometime around 1830, Hayez found himself asked to paint a penitent Magdalene, the sculptural version by Canova from 1796 (see page 176) was among the most praised works of Romantic culture. Hayez was also aware of another version of the subject by Canova, the *Fainting Magdalene,* made between 1819 and 1822, which may have inspired the more relaxed pose he used here, which also reveals the nudity of the figure, unleashing attacks from the more avowedly moralistic of the critics. The painter was accused of having "profaned" the very values of penitence and modesty that were held to be implicit and obligatory in the presentation of this figure from biblical history.

Tommaso Minardi
The Madonna of the Rosary
1840, oil on canvas
108 x 82 cm
Galleria Nazionale d'Arte Moderna, Rome

Minardi completed this canvas—which he had been commissioned to make about five years earlier by an English lord, who had died in the meantime—a short time before the manifesto of Purismo, which he signed in 1842. Indeed this canvas expresses the basic concepts of Purismo, of which he was a front-line representative in Italy. A supporter of the idea that through harmony and simplicity painting could inspire a new purity in art, most of all in devotional images, Minardi believed contemporary artists should draw inspiration from the works of the young Raphael and Leonardo, since these offered ideal examples of aesthetic and religious purity. For many years Minardi dedicated himself to making compositions similar to this one, beginning with his stay in Perugia in 1810, during which he began making copies of Raphael.

Francesco Hayez
Jacob, Meeting Esau and Bowing to Him Seven Times, Shows Him the Flock and Camels That He Sent Him as a Gift, and at the Same Time Presents to Him His Wife and Children
1844, oil on canvas
208 x 300 cm
Civica Pinacoteca Tosio Martinengo, Brescia

This painting aroused a negative response from the official critics in Milan, who claimed that the attitudes and poses of the figures lacked verisimilitude, meaning the work contravened its principal purpose, that of presenting instructional examples of religious values. The painting's weighty title, not unusual for similar works of the period, reveals in of itself the didactic role conferred on art. The canvas does reveal important changes in Hayez's style, in keeping with the novelties proposed by the Purismo movement, presenting chromatic choices aimed at creating an appealing atmosphere, to which the painter added a patina of Oriental style.

Simon Saint-Jean
Holy Water Stoup; Notre-Dame-des-Roses
1850, oil on canvas
127 x 90 cm
Musée National du Château, Compiègne

From his youth the Lyons-born Saint-Jean was passionate about the painting of flowers and still lifes, and he earned himself fame in France and Europe in general for his radiant compositions. The genre had fallen somewhat out of style with the arrival of Romanticism in the nineteenth century, for which reason it was only the more appreciated as being rare. The beautiful drooping roses in the foreground are the true protagonists of this painting, in which the religious setting is almost an excuse for creating an image that blends the sense of ancient time, expressed by the building wrapped in ivy, with religious devotion, expressed by the sacred group in the niche, and the hope of life that reflowers, for which there are the roses. A vision of enchanting delicacy, it has a strong element of sentimentalism capable of drawing the spectator into a sort of spiritual embrace.

PAUL DELAROCHE
Young Christian Martyr
1855, oil on canvas
170 x 148 cm
Musée du Louvre, Paris

A young Christian, having refused to venerate the pagan divinities, has been thrown into the Tiber with her hands tied, and now two passing pilgrims spot her body as it is carried along on the current. So runs the description provided by the artist in 1857 for the exhibition of the painting, which he called "the saddest and most sacred of my works." The canvas belongs to the later period of Delaroche's career, when his work often revealed the anguish he suffered following the death of his wife, Louise Vernet, in 1845. Reminiscent perhaps of the *Ophelia* by Millais (see page 345), but far different, this image of a martyr presents extraordinary pictorial subtleties, such as the light that spreads from the halo across the water, revealing its exceptional transparency and reinforcing the scene's nocturnal effect. The result is a sense of magic transcendence with which Delaroche attempted to bring about a renewal of religious painting, achieving here a result that seems to anticipate symbolism.

Giovanni Dupré
Dying Abel
1842, marble
length 235 cm
Hermitage,
St. Petersburg

Giovanni Dupré
Dying Abel
1851, bronze
length 220 cm
Galleria d'Arte
Moderna di Palazzo
Pitti, Florence

The bronze version was made on the request of Grand Duke Leopold II of Lorraine, after the marble original had been sold to Maria, duchess of Leuchtenberg, daughter of Czar Nicholas II, when she was visiting Florence in 1842. The work was at the center of numerous debates among critics at the time, who for several years had been divided in opposing camps based on their opinions of the principle of naturalism, which Lorenzo Bartolini proposed, in favor of an art inspired directly by nature. The statue was the cause of scandal since some critics suspected Dupré of having made it by molding it directly on the body of his model; at the same time, however, the artist was praised by others for having opened the way toward a lyric sensuality, in which sense the statue was hailed as a universal symbol of the struggle of good against evil.

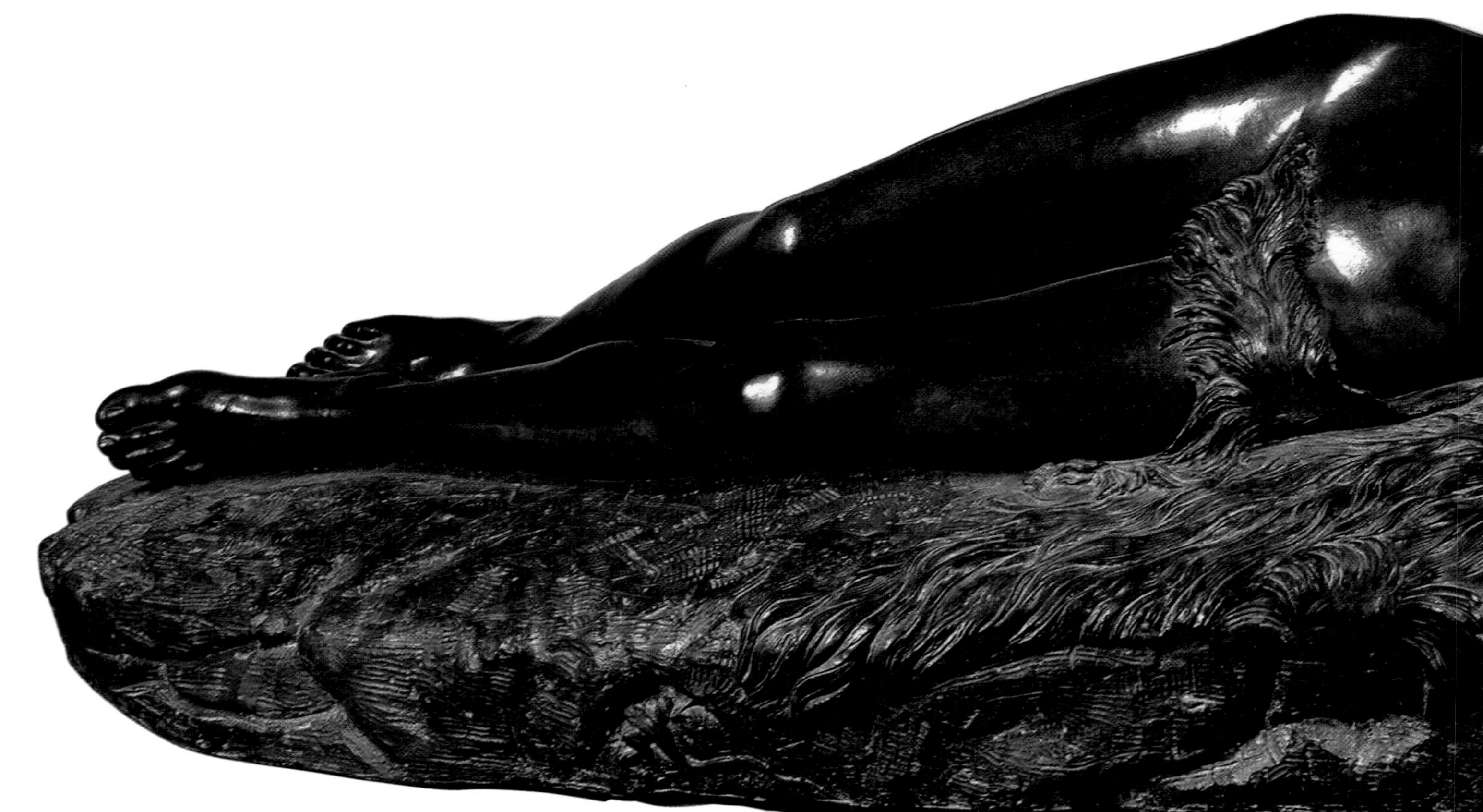

JOHN MARTIN
The Great Day of His Wrath
1851, oil on canvas
196 x 303 cm
Tate Gallery, London

A late masterpiece by Martin, who for many years had been among the most famous and beloved of Romantic painters in Europe, this canvas has the fascination of grandiosity. The Last Judgment is presented with all the astonishing expressive powers of which Martin was master, being a dedicated specialist in the representation of catastrophic themes used as a theater of exciting spectacular effects. In Martin's hands, the traditional Dies Irae takes on swirling tones in a composition that blends visionary painting and the painting of the sublime, with a landscape overcome by the forces of nature, the sky rent by lightning, mountains exploding into terrible masses that plunge down upon a landscape devastated by fires and explosions, while the ground itself cracks apart to swallow the last survivors before the end of the world.

JEAN-LÉON GÉRÔME
The Age of Augustus: The Birth of Christ
1855, oil on canvas
620 x 1,015 cm
Musée d'Orsay, Paris

In 1852 the French government commissioned Gérôme to paint a large-scale work on a subject of his choosing. It was the crucial year in which the political ascent of Napoleon III culminated in the restoration of the empire, and the artist thought of rendering homage to him by identifying him symbolically as the "new Augustus." He drew inspiration for this picture from a passage in the *Discourse on Universal History* (1681) by the French bishop Jacques-Bénigne Bossuet (1681), a text based on a vision of history supported by Providence; he

selected the moment in which the entire world knelt to Caesar Augustus, the sole ruler of the empire. In a canvas of exceptional size, perhaps one of the largest today in existence, the artist posed the victorious figure of Augustus enthroned before the temple of Janus, surrounded by artists and politicians, while all the people of the world, portrayed with rigorous scientific accuracy in their different ethnic types and costumes, gather to acclaim him. In the center foreground, a singular nativity sanctifies the achievement of peace under his rule with an exuberant effect of light. Religion and politics are blended in a spectacular and symbolic composition that was among the leading attractions of the Universal Exposition in Paris in 1855.

The appeal of the

The allure of the Orient and other far-off lands has always been a latent aspect of European civilization. As early as the Renaissance the exotic culture of ancient Egypt had become the subject of studies, and the Near East had drawn the attention of European artists, including Gentile Bellini, who traveled to Constantinople around 1480 and made a portrait of Sultan Mehmed II (National Gallery, London) that he brought back to Venice. As diplomatic contact between Europe and the Middle East intensified, the fascination of the exotic made its way into various aspects of European culture. There were the so-called Turkish dances along with the Oriental-style costumes that so often appeared in the theatrical presentations and court festivities in the principalities of Europe. At the end of the eighteenth century European painting was swept by a powerful wave of interest in things Oriental. The primary cause was Napoleon's campaign in Egypt in 1798, which was disappointing in military results but surprisingly successful in cultural results, setting off great interest in the Egyptian world. Entire expeditions of archaeologists and scholars were sent to record every aspect of local life in Egypt, and with them went artists who put together a wealth of documentary images, all of which were added to the decorative repertory of the Empire style, which was soon awash in "Egyptomania." Founded by Napoleon himself, the Institut d'Egypte produced a monumental twenty-four volume *Description of Egypt*—a major contributor was Dominique Vivant Denon, author of the *Voyage dans la Bassse et l'Haute Egypte* (1802)—and it met with immediate success. Artists and decorators made ample use of its illustrations, drawing on them to cover the neoclassical lines of furniture, ornaments, and jewels with sphinxes, obelisks, and pyramids. It was only a short step from the passion for Egyptian iconography to the exaltation of the Orient in general, and Romantic scholars and artists were overwhelmed by the fascination for exotic settings and began describing that unknown world on the basis of their personal sensibilities. Their works were not necessarily the fruit of direct experience; some artists, such as Ingres and Hayez, never went to the Orient and drew their atmospheric descriptions from the pages of Chateaubriand (*Itinéraire de Paris à Jerusalem*, 1811), Victor Hugo (*Les Orientales*, 1829), and most of all Lord Bryon. Indeed the English poet, who began writing verse narratives to meet the public's passion for things Oriental on the advice of Madame de Staël, ended up dedicating a large part of his production to the subject, becoming so sympathetic to the spirit of the Hellenic people that he dramatically set off to join them in their struggle for liberation from the Turks. Many painters, driven by the Romantic appeal of the unknown, of the mysteries of the desert, and perhaps most of all eager to find exotic settings, managed to make the journey to those distant lands. David Roberts, John Frederick Lewis, Ippolito Caffi, Alberto Pasini, Prosper Marilhat, and Théodore Chassériau are only a few of the many who made the trip. Among the first to depart was Alexandre-Gabriel Decamps, who, along with fellow painter Louis Garneray, went in 1828 to Navarino, site of the battle in which the British, French, and Russian fleets had defeated a Turkish-Egyptian fleet a year earlier. Following a

David Roberts, *View of Cairo*, 1843, oil on canvas, 76.2 x 62.2 cm; Victoria and Albert Museum, London

Ludovico Lipparini, *The Death of Marco Botzarsi*, 1841, oil on canvas; Museo Sartorio, Trieste

year at Smyrna in Turkey he returned to France with a load of drawings and studies on which he drew for his paintings immersed in Oriental light. Eugène Delacroix presents a singular case, since he was infatuated with Orientalism well before he made his first trip to North Africa, in 1832. Inspired by the thrilling images of Byron's poems, he did not hesitate to paint scenes of unrestrained if not morbid sensuality, works that were greeted by critics with predictable indignation. The extremism in his vision of the East underwent a radical change, moving toward a more documentary realism, following his visit to Morocco and Algeria as a member of a diplomatic mission sent by King Louis Philippe to convince the sultan of Morocco to support him in his efforts to annex Algeria to France. For Horace Vernet the encounter with the inhabitants of North Africa, in 1833, was nothing short of enlightening: in those people the painter recognized the direct heirs to the peoples of the Bible. Their customs and laws, according to Vernet, had not evolved, preserving intact a millennial civilization. For this reason Vernet—and various other artists, such as Decamps and Chassériau—believed that he could achieve unequaled levels of perfection in his paintings of biblical subjects by accurately portraying those people, their clothes, woman of the house, but it soon came to designate a slave or concubine in a harem, thus taking on a load of sensual connotations. Symbol of beauty and sensuality, by the early years of Romanticism the figure of the odalisque had come to embody several basic elements of painting, such as the representation of the female nude and exoticism. The

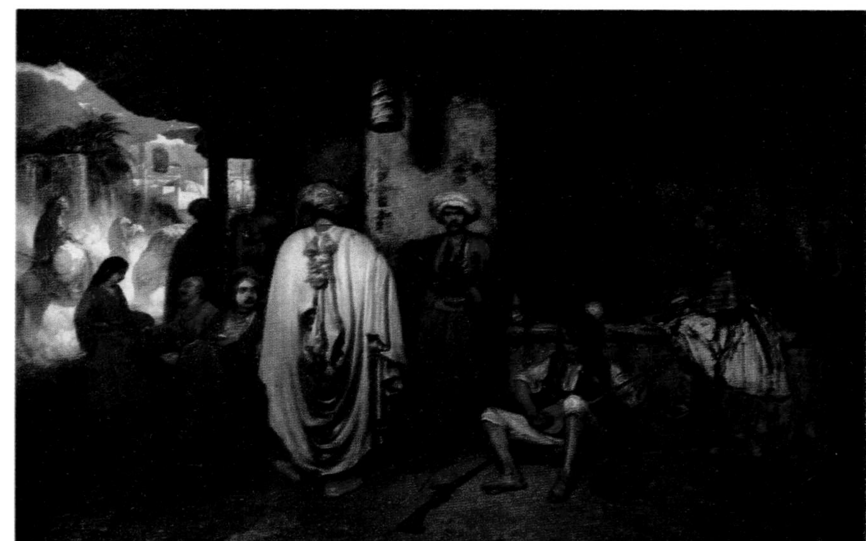

Alexandre-Gabriel Decamps, *A Turkish Patrol on the Route to Smyrna*, 1833, oil on canvas, 91 x 155 cm; Musée Condé, Chantilly

Orient and of the exotic

and their landscapes. In 1848 he published a book on the subject, setting off an important process of mingling religious themes with scenes of the exotic. Indeed, the sacred iconography of the Romantic age, most of all in France and Italy beginning in the 1830s, is drenched in highly effective Oriental tones. These also made their way into the painting of both ancient and contemporary history, such as the *Death of Marco Botzaris*, painted by Ludovico Lipparini to commemorate the death of the Albanian hero who died in 1823 fighting the Turks at Karpenisi and whose troops later came under the command of Lord Bryon at Missolonghi. The figurative appeal of the Middle East was by no means limited to ethnographic studies; works with greater impact resulted from the increasing interest given the dreamy, sensual world of harems. The major figure in this realm was the odalisque. In Ottoman Turkey this word was applied to a servant of the

John Frederick Lewis, *A Guest in the Harem*, 1858, watercolor on paper, 60.6 x 47.7 cm; Victoria and Albert Museum, London

description of a harem had been the subject of a book still in vogue early in the nineteenth century, the *Letters of Lady Mary Wortley Montagu* (1763), and Ingres may have drawn inspiration from that book for his series of odalisques, beginning with the lost canvas made for Queen Caroline Murat of Naples, probably made in 1811 and intended as the pendant for the famous *Grande Odalisque* in the Louvre. By the time he painted the *Odalisque with a Slave* for his friend Charles Marcotte in Rome, hidden beauty and sensuality were no longer the sole protagonists of the harem, which was now the scene of figures with great exotic appeal. Finally, at the age of eighty-two, the almost obsessive repetition of the model led to the famous *Turkish Bath* (1862; Musée du Louvre, Paris), the initial version of which so scandalized Empress Eugènie for the excessive number of nudes that Napoleon III had it returned to the painter.

Marie-Guillemine Benoist
Portrait of a Negress
1800, oil on canvas
81 x 65 cm
Musée du Louvre, Paris

Born Leroulx-Delaville and also known as Madame Benoist, from the name of her husband, this painter was a student of Elisabeth-Louise Vigée-Lebrun and of David. The extraordinary rendering of chromatic contrasts, which makes the white of the drapery stand out sharply against the uniform background and the model's bronze skin, demonstrates a sense of pictorial values that reveals her artistic training. Exhibited at the Paris Salon of 1800, this portrait earned the painter great success. Six years after the abolition of slavery in France, the painting conferred further social dignity on the black population, exalting the beauty of the woman through the beautiful contrasts of her nude body with the white gown and her headdress with the solid tone of the background.

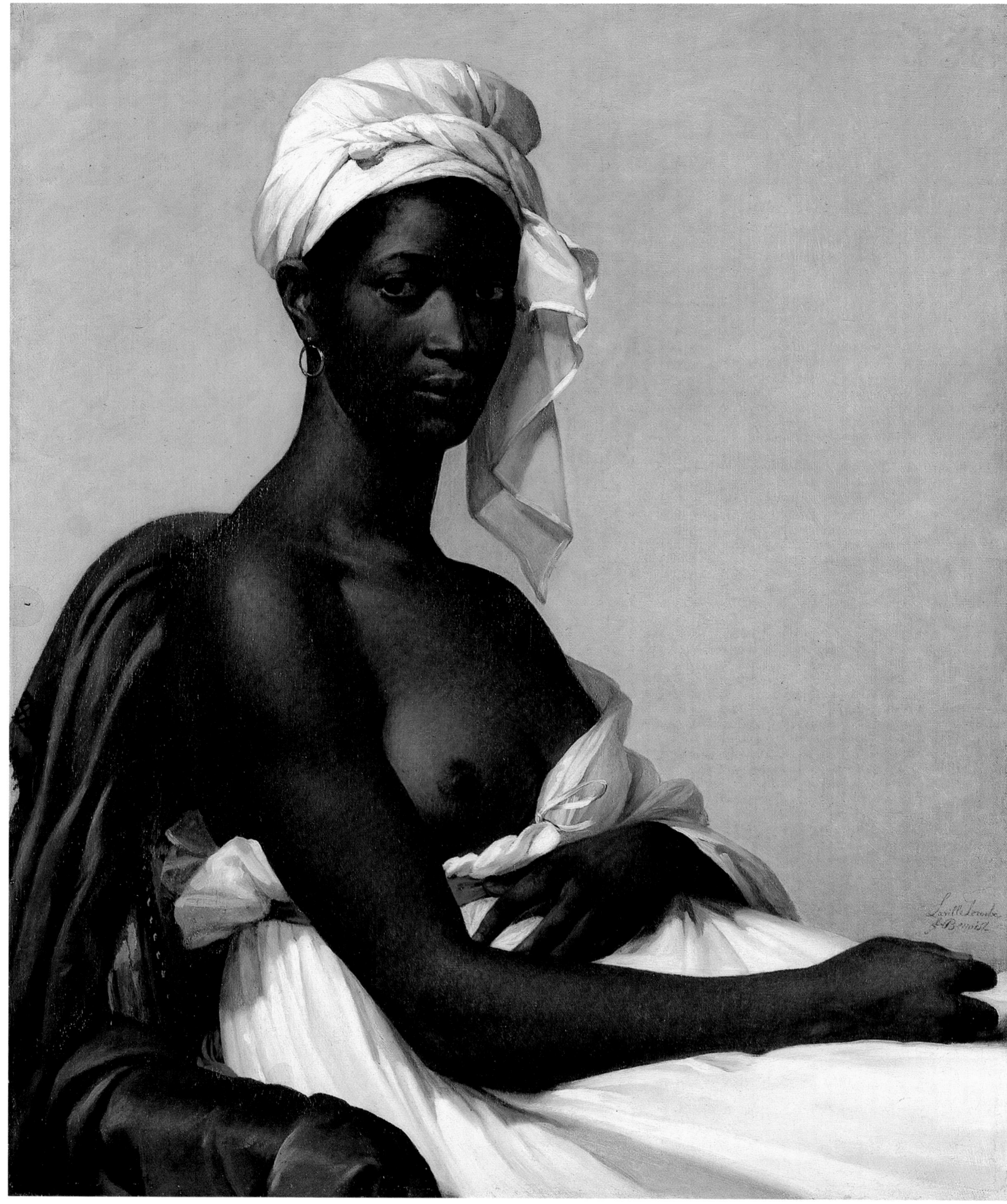

Jean-Auguste-Dominique Ingres
Grande Odalisque
1814, oil on canvas
91 x 162 cm
Musée du Louvre, Paris

It was probably on the request of Caroline and Joachim Murat, the rulers of Naples, that Ingres made this famous canvas, dealing with a subject whose exotic nature was just beginning to fascinate the public both in France and Italy. He interpreted the theme with sophisticated elegance, giving surprising importance to the luxurious fabrics, the peacock-feather fan, the jewelry. The sensuality of the image remains on an abstract plane, with emphasis given the virtuosic, elongated line of the woman's body. The perfect face of the odalisque revives the ideals of female beauty found in the works of Raphael, a connection reinforced by the striking repetition of the turban and hairstyle of Raphael's famous *Fornarina*. Critics found fault with the work, accusing the artist of having created a sort of "false anatomy," claiming that to accentuate the sinuous length of the woman's back Ingres had used a greater than natural number of vertebrae.

Eugène Delacroix
The Death of Sardanapalus
1827, oil on canvas
342 x 496 cm
Musée du Louvre, Paris

According to ancient legend—brought back into vogue in 1821 by the tragedy on the subject by Lord Byron—Sardanapalus, last king of the Assyrians and notorious for his luxury, ordered his eunuchs to kill his concubines, horses, and dogs, and then committed suicide so as not to surrender to the forces besieging his city. The episode offered the pretext for a scene of sensuality and drama pervaded by horror but also packed with wanton Oriental sexuality. Delacroix used extreme freedom in assembling the composition, which is crossed by a diagonal line inspired by the pictorial space of Rubens. The work was rejected by the official critics because of its absence of perspective and the immorality of its subject. In reality, with its swirling mass of figures and free use of color, the painting overturned the traditional criteria of painting and made full use of the expressive power of Romantic sensibilities, for which reason it earned praise from such intellectuals as Victor Hugo.

Eugène Delacroix
Women of Algiers in Their Apartment
1834, oil on canvas
180 x 229 cm
Musée du Louvre, Paris

Delacroix's trip to Morocco and Algeria in 1832 revealed to him a world he found enormously congenial. He was fascinated by its colors, its bright luminosity, by the dress of the people and their customs. This canvas is the fruit of that emotional and spiritual immersion in a new world. Here he creates a simple atmosphere dense with intimacy, in which the clothes and jewelry of the women, together with their serene expressions, suggest a quiet sensuality. The work marked a new phase in Delacroix's painting, centered on the description of an almost magical Orient, distanced from the more voluptuous and disturbing vision of previous years. This canvas was bought at the Salon of 1834 by King Louis Philippe.

Jean-Auguste-Dominique Ingres
Odalisque with a Slave
1839–40,
oil on canvas,
72 x 100.3 cm
Fogg Art Museum,
Cambridge

At a distance of more than twenty years from his *Grande Odalisque*, Ingres returned to the theme of the harem and its sensual atmosphere, and did so with his usual refinement, increased in this case by close attention to the construction of the setting. The protagonist, in an alluring pose, is surrounded by objects of daily life, including a feather fan, cushions, silks, and a narghile. Beside her a slave plays an instrument, farther back is a black eunuch, both dressed in a way that attracts attention, and not only because of the Oriental style but because of the striking fabrics and accessories, reproduced in detail. Ingres made the canvas between 1839 and 1840 for his friend Charles

Marcotte in Rome. Disappointed and indignant over the clamorous failure in 1834 of his *Martyrdom of St. Symphorian*, Ingres had sworn to never again exhibit a work at the Salon (and until 1855 he didn't). He had then left Paris, accepting the offer to direct the French Academy in Rome. When Ingres returned to France in 1841, King William I of Württemberg contacted him and asked him to make a copy of the work, and by 1842 Ingres had already completed it (Walters Art Gallery, Baltimore). The space of the original version, shown here, is marked off with geometric motifs, from those of the balustrade to the patterns on the rear wall and the carpet, against which the sinuous lines of the odalisque stand out. The replica differs from the original by opening the room to a sophisticated garden, including an artificial lake with swans, some of which Ingres had his student Paul Flandrin paint.

Gaspare Landi
Harun el-Rashid in His Tent with the Wise Men of the East Who Accompany the Army
1813, oil on canvas
268 x 335 cm
Museo Nazionale di Capodimonte, Naples

As part of the decorations made for the Quirinal Palace under the direction of Napoleon, Landi was commissioned to paint a large work showing some great figure from history whose glory would reflect that of the emperor. Harun el-Rashid, a caliph who lived at the time of Charlemagne, dying in 809, had been one of the most powerful rulers of the Abbasid dynasty, cruel in reality but transformed by legend into a symbol of justice and magnificence. Landi, a painter of neoclassical training, seeking to celebrate not only the caliph's gifts as a military strategist but also his cultural values, presented him surrounded by instruments of knowledge while interrupting a meeting in his tent to listen to one of the learned men of his court. For the accurate rendering of the costumes Landi was assisted by Dominique Vivant Denon, who had become an expert on Oriental customs after Napoleon's Egyptian campaign.

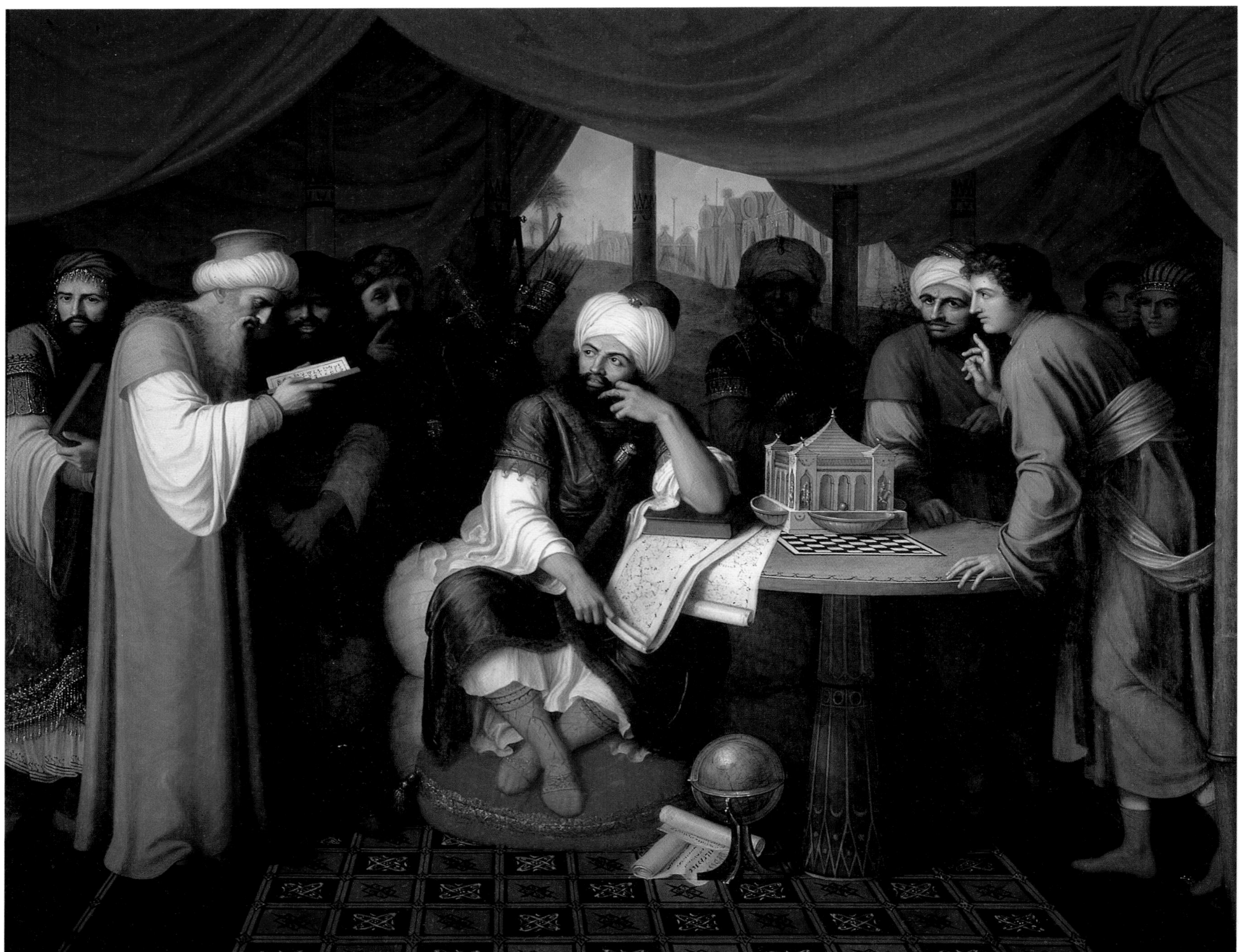

Horace Vernet
Arab Chiefs Tell a Story
1834, oil on canvas
98 x 137 cm
Musée Condé, Chantilly

Contact with the Arab populations of North Africa thrilled Vernet, beginning with his first trip to the region, in 1833. The artist saw the simple lives and ancestral habits of the local populations as the unchanged repetition of rhythms, uses, and images dating back thousands of years. He saw those people as the depositary of a type of existence that had been frozen in time and was therefore of great fascination. Vernet made two versions of this composition, the first in 1833 (Wallace Collection, London) and this second version one year later in Rome on the request of Count Gourieff. The two works differ in only a few details; for example, instead of the two dogs on the left, the original has a couple. With an exceptional atmospheric rendering that prefigures the language of realism, Vernet portrayed the Bedouins seated under a tree while in the distance a group of French soldiers refers to the political realities of the moment.

HORACE VERNET
The Lion Hunt
1836, oil on canvas
57.1 x 81.7 cm
Wallace Collection, London

In the spring of 1833 Vernet obtained permission from King Louis Philippe to take a leave of absence from his position as director of the French Academy in Rome in order to go to Algeria, at the time facing French conquest. He was astonished by the fascination of the places he visited and used the experience as the source for many works, among them this lion hunt, which he had personally witnessed in the Sahara on May 28, 1833, and which he painted on his return to Paris. He chose the dramatic moment when the lioness charged wildly at the hunter who had just killed the lion, while another hunter, riding a camel, grabbed the pair of cubs. Details of costume and almost blazing light reflected off the sand render the immediacy of a memory recorded from life.

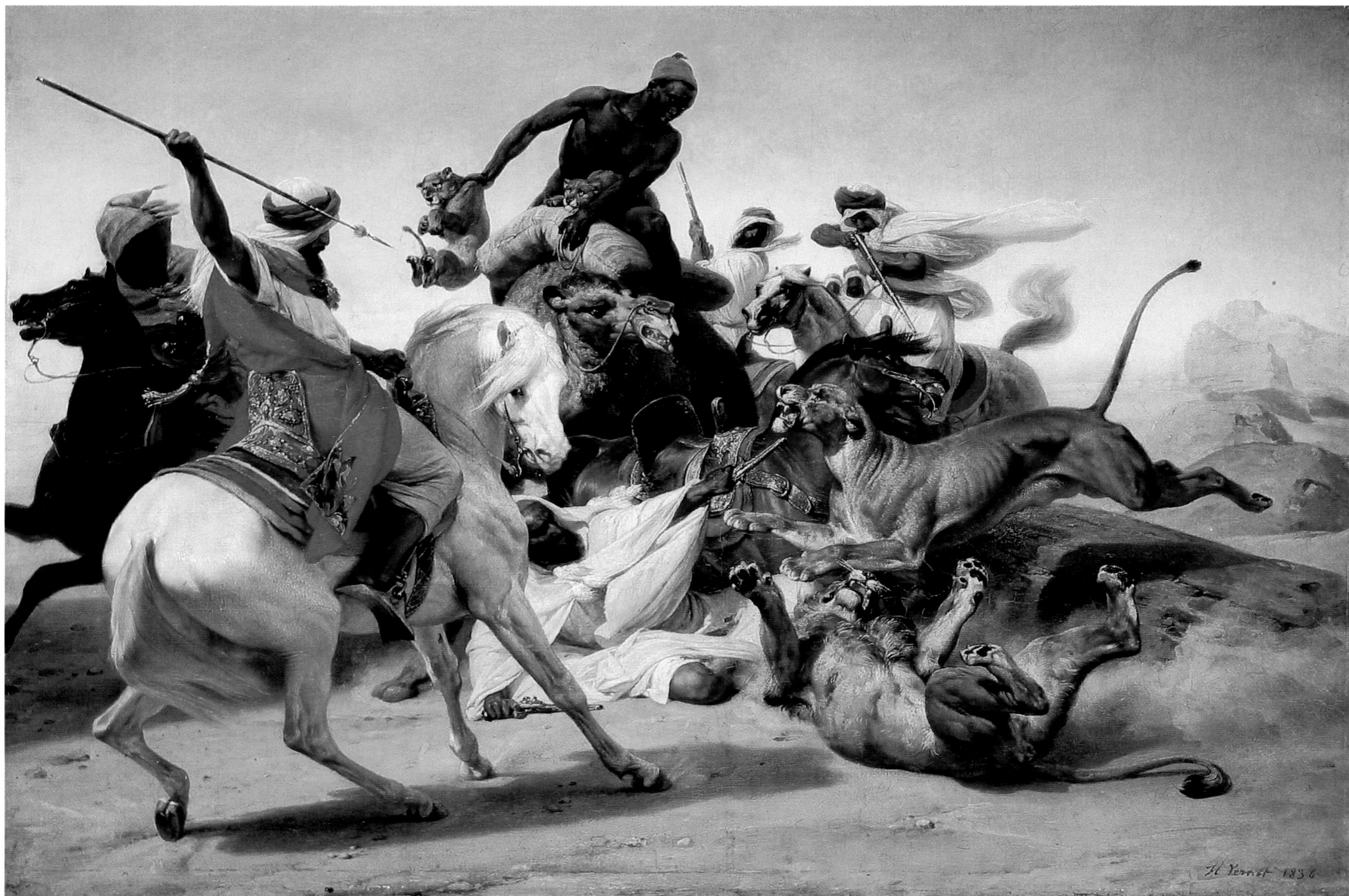

Eugène Delacroix
The Sultan of Morocco and His Entourage
1845, oil on canvas
377 x 340 cm
Musée des Augustins, Toulouse

The original title of this work was *Moulay Abd er-Rahman, Sultan of Morocco, Leaves His Palace of Meknès, Surrounded by His Guard and Principal Officials*. The artist had personally witnessed this scene during a trip to Morocco in the spring of 1832 in the company of his friend Charles de Mornay, members of a diplomatic mission sent by King Louis Philippe. Thirteen years passed before Delacroix did this painting, for which he used his old notebook of sketches and designs made in North Africa; the primary source for the painting is a study (still in existence) in which he portrayed the meeting between the sultan and the French delegation, although he left the delegation out of the composition. The work shows the artist's stylistic evolution, now moving toward the use of a steady, crystalline luminosity and the almost geometric distribution of color, with a modern contrasting of complementary tones.

Théodore Chassériau
The Toilet of Esther
1841, oil on canvas
455 x 355 cm
Musée du Louvre, Paris

Student of Ingres and then of Delacroix, Chassériau developed a highly singular style that was very different from those of his masters, but at the same time expressive of the values of Romanticism. In this famous canvas he presents a biblical subject that is relatively common in European painting, the beautiful Jewish woman Esther, here busy caring for her body. Chassériau, born in Santo Domingo of a probably mestizo mother—and thus perhaps even more intimately drawn than his peers to a taste for exoticism—transformed the biblical figure into an image of great fascination, characterized by a strong Orientalizing component, suggested by the pose, almost like that of a dancer, and the appearance of the two servants. The exotic imprint, so in keeping with the point of view and style of the period, led the more moralistic and traditional members of the public to accept unusual images, and even blatantly sexual female nudes, without scandal.

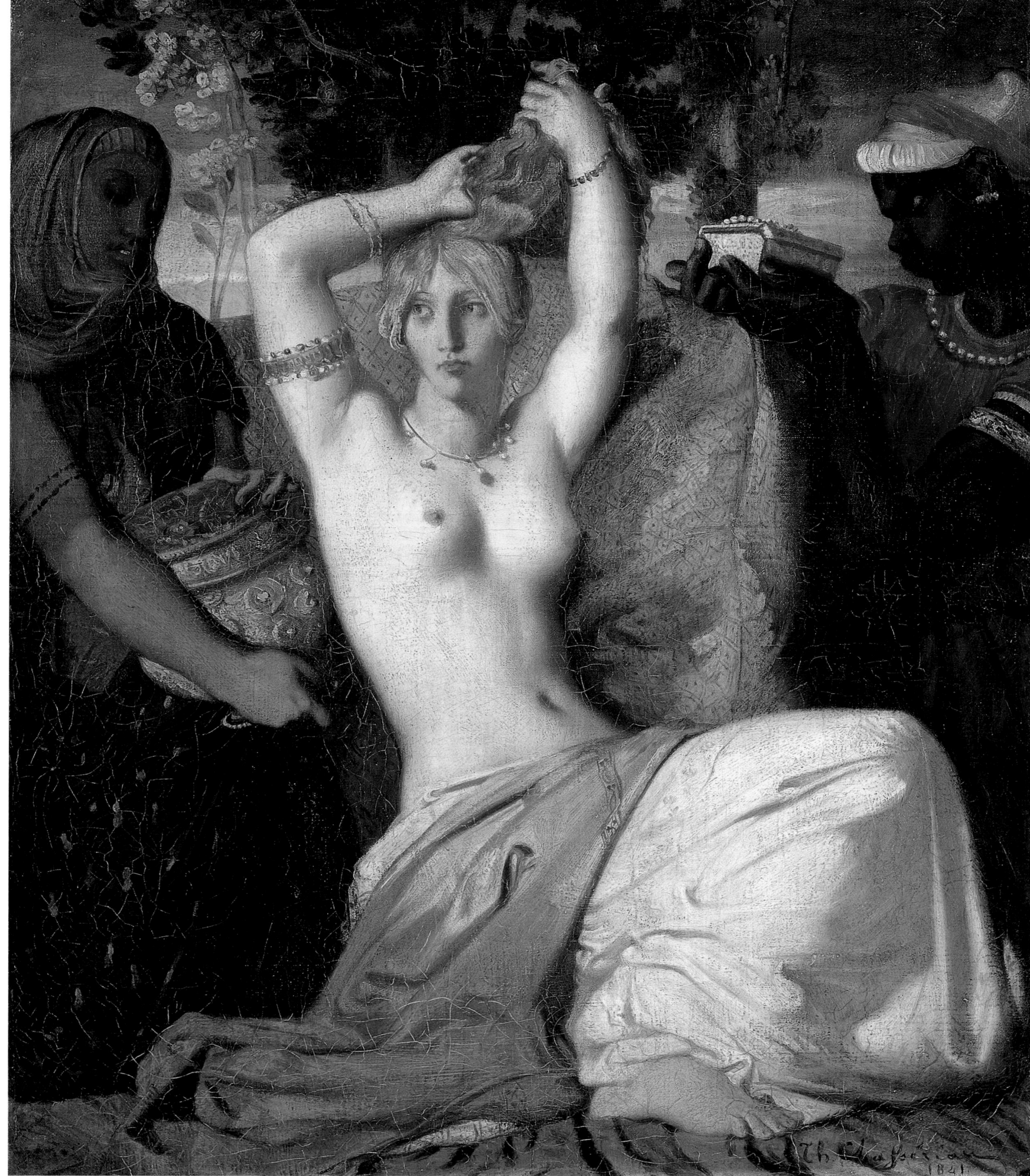

THÉODORE CHASSÉRIAU
Ali-Ben Hamet, Caliph of Constantine and Chief of the Haractas, Followed by His Escort
1845, oil on canvas
325 x 259 cm
Musée National des Châteaux de Versailles et de Trianon, Versailles

The Salon of 1845 did not go well for Chassériau. He was so enraged by the rejection of his *Cleopatra with the Asp* that he destroyed almost all of the painting; the other painting he presented, this portrait of Caliph Ali-Ben Hamet on horseback, was reasonably well received but had to withstand comparison to the *Sultan of Morocco and His Entourage* by Delacroix (see page 205), the artist Chassériau most admired in that period. Perhaps it was this direct comparison with a work by the most talented and appealing illustrator of the Oriental world that put Chassériau's work in shadow, judged by some a *coloriage* because of its original use of strongly contrasting colors. Baudelaire liked it, however, seeing in it the pride of the great masters.

Giacomo Trécourt
Self-Portrait in Oriental Costume
1842, oil on canvas, 80.5 x 65 cm
Musei Civici, Pavia

Made by the Italian artist Giacomo Trécourt, born in Bergamo, this work is quite an unusual self-portrait. He presents himself wearing a showy turban but strangely does not direct his eyes at the spectator, which is natural for someone observing himself in a mirror. It is precisely that frowning and troubled gaze directed into the distance that is the fascination of this painting, since it gives the figure a sense of adventurous mystery well in keeping with his Oriental dress. The artist does not present an accurate reflection of his features, but elaborates them to make them more exotic, thus making his portrait agree with the modern artistic trends, which had arrived on the Italian artistic scene a little late. Furthermore, it seems that the origin of this canvas was the *Portrait of Carlo Prayer in the Costume of Alp*, a hero in Lord Byron's "The Siege of Corinth," painted by Hayez in 1832 (private collection).

CHERUBINO CORNIENTI
The Last Farewell of Paolo Erizzo to His Daughter
1842, oil on canvas
166 x 223 cm
Private collection

History painting too was effected by the Orientalist style, which began spreading through Italy during the 1830s. Cornienti, a Romantic artist known for biblical and historical scenes, here transforms a grim event from the Renaissance into an image tinged with Middle Eastern suggestions. In 1470 the Venetian Paolo Erizzo, betrayed by Mehmed II, was condemned by the Turks to an atrocious death (he was sawn in half). The painter presents Erizzo's heartrending farewell to his daughter with a strong theatrical impact but gives more emphasis to the Ottoman setting than to the careful description of details. The work was therefore accused of lacking completeness, of being more of a sketch than a painting, while in reality Cornienti had given proof of his modern style.

Ippolito Caffi
View of the Egyptian Desert with Obelisk
1844, oil on canvas
31.5 x 44.5 cm
Museo Civico, Belluno

The painters of scenes set in the Orient had not always actually visited such locales. Seeking inspiration for their paintings, many turned to the enticing pages of narrators or novelists who described the evocative atmospheres, customs, colors, and dress of those distant peoples. Such was not the case with Ippolito Caffi, who beginning in the 1830s and most of all between 1843 and 1844 spent months traveling in the Middle East, where he was taken most of all by Egypt. The result was many paintings like this, in which he fixed in an almost extemporaneous way impressions of light and landscape, fiery skies, camels, and caravans in the desert, following an already modern viewpoint: one that put less emphasis on the more sensual or adventurous aspects of the vision than on the almost scientific reconstruction of a totally different climate and civilization.

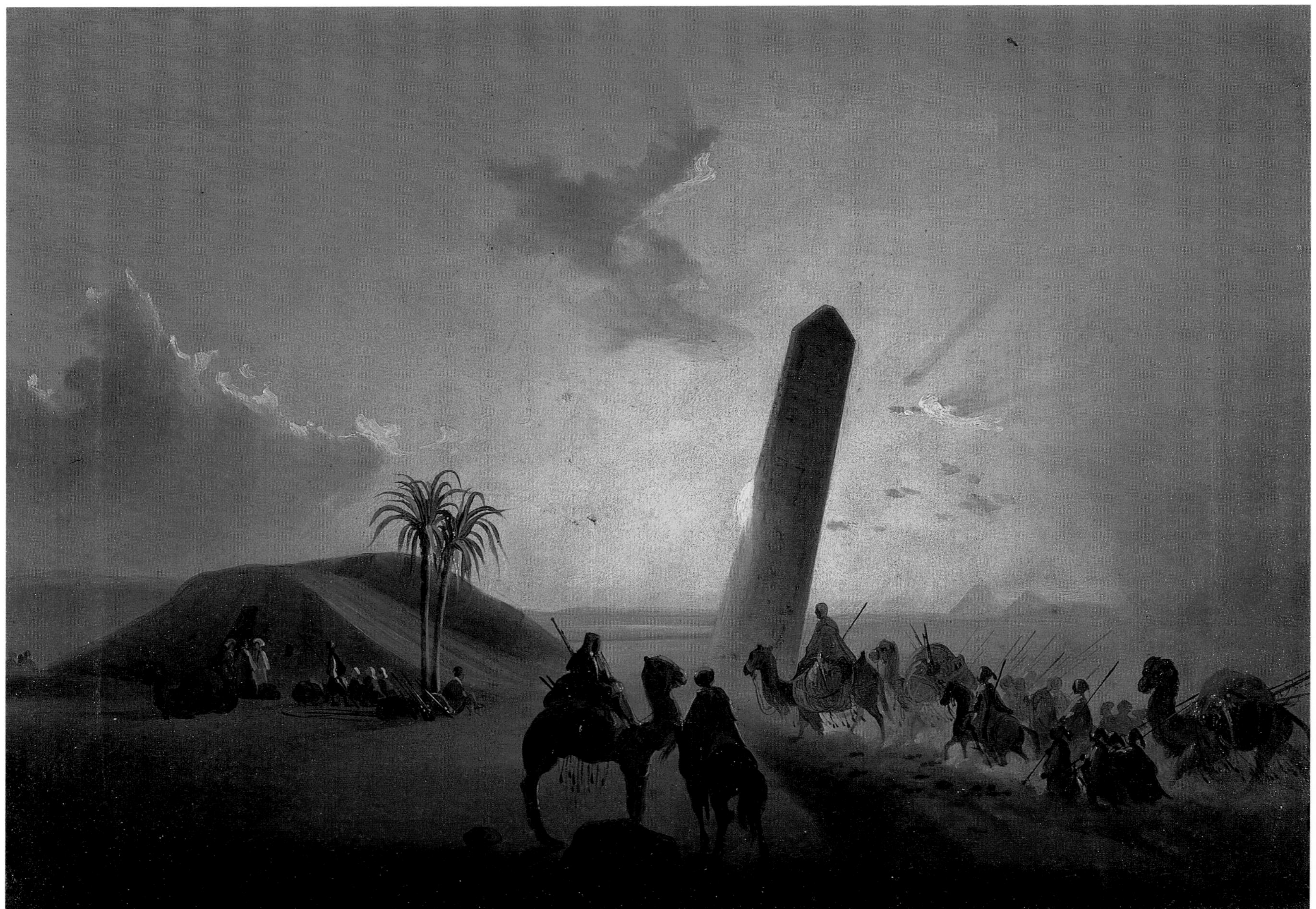

Karl Blechen
Interior of the Palm House
1832, oil on paper applied to canvas
65.6 x 49 cm
Museum Georg Schäfer, Schweinfurt

In 1830 the explorer and botanist Alexander von Humboldt convinced King Frederick William III of Prussia to buy a precious set of palms from the Foulchiron Collection put on sale in Paris. To provide an adequate setting for the valuable specimens, the king commissioned Karl Friedrich Schinkel to build the Palm House near the palace of Sans Souci on the Pfaueninsel ("Peacock Island") in Potsdam, to the southwest of Berlin. This is one of the two views of the elaborate greenhouse that the ruler commissioned of Blechen to give to his daughter Charlotte, czarina of Russia. In terms of the architectural elements, colors, and types of decorations, the atmosphere is absolutely Oriental, so much so that the painter was inspired to accentuate the work's sultry, exotic tone by adding a group of odalisques to the scene, arranged near the central palm.

Jacques-Laurent Agasse
The Nubian Giraffe
1827, oil on canvas
127 x 101.5 cm
Royal Collection, Windsor

Born in Switzerland but a student of David in Paris, Agasse moved to England in 1800, becoming famous as a painter of animals. For that reason King George IV commissioned him to portray this giraffe, which together with other exotic animals was part of the royal menagerie. Since the Renaissance, owning rare animals from distant locales had been a favorite way for princes to show off, and during the early nineteenth century the habit only intensified, thanks to the increase in commercial exchanges between the West and the East. Most of the painting's appeal is its accurate presentation of the Oriental clothes of the two guardians of the giraffe, which contrast with the black suit and top hat of the man on the right, identified as Edward Cross, a well-known importer of exotic animals and provider to the British royal court.

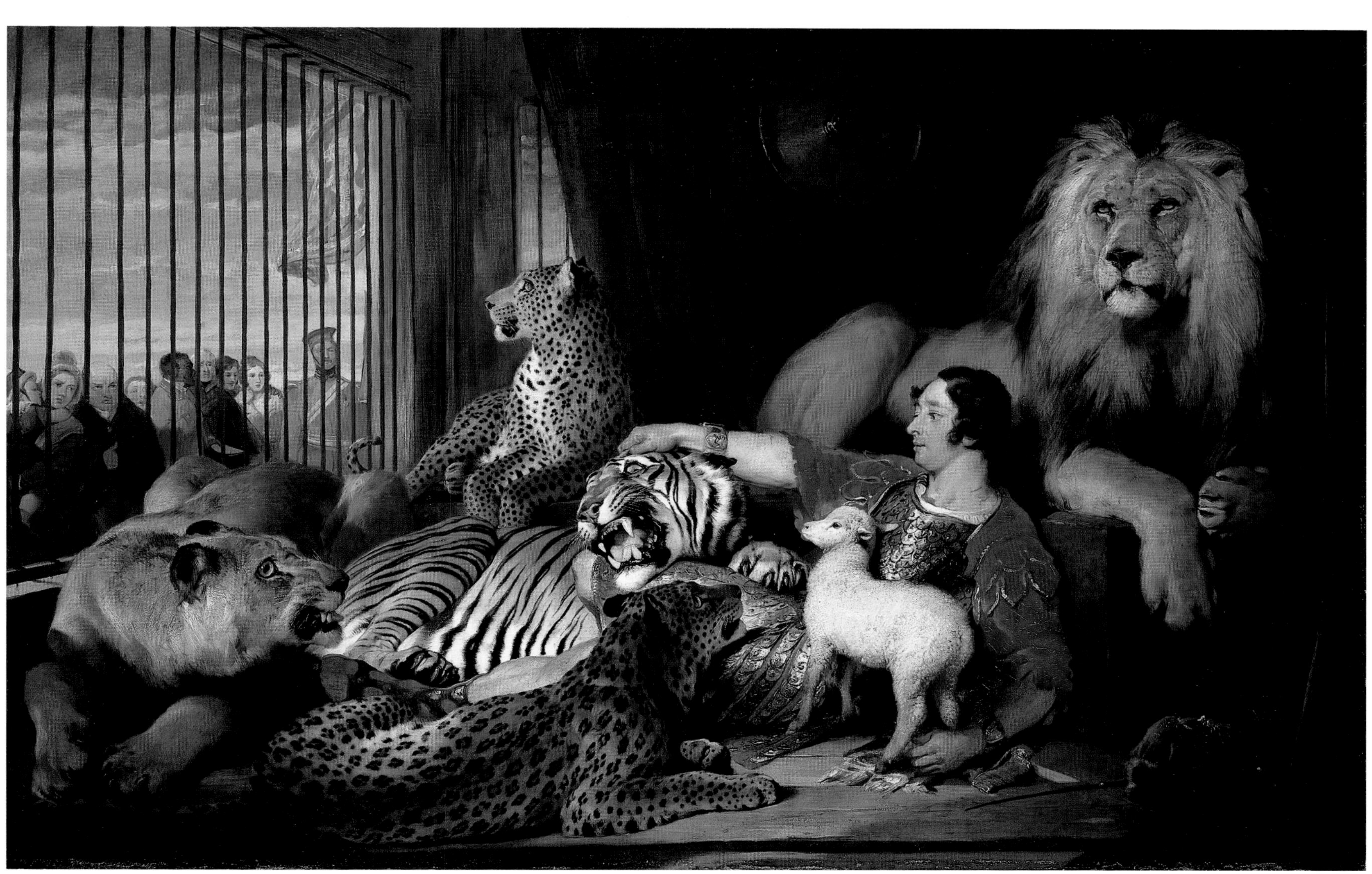

EDWIN HENRY LANDSEER
Isaac van Hamburgh and His Animals
1839, oil on canvas
113 x 174.6 cm
Royal Collection, Windsor

Isaac van Hamburgh was an American lion tamer of Dutch origin who in 1839 excited Londoners with performances held in two theaters in the capital. Queen Victoria attended these shows at least five times in two months, noting in her diary her astonishment at the tamer's daring, including a quarter of an hour spent closed in a cage together with ferocious wild beasts. She commissioned Landseer to capture this memory of the event. The artist portrayed Van Hamburgh in the cage with the exotic animals—two leopards, a lion, a lioness, and a tiger—dressed in a sort of ancient-style breastplate, which increased the scenic effect of the spectacle. The trepidation that seized the public is indicated not so much by the expression and calm tone with which the trainer keeps the five animals at bay as by the scratches that the painter put on his neck and right arm.

By the nineteenth century little of this planet had not been visited by European explorers, but an appealing air of mystery still tinged certain corners of the world. Of these lands the Americas had the closest contact with Europe, although many Europeans still saw them as exotic. In their eyes, following the American Revolution the New World broke in two; there was the United States, still perceived as a political extension of Europe since England and France had once divided its territory, and there was Central and South America, which the Spanish government kept inaccessible, preventing entry to adventurers and explorers. Rare bits of news made their way out of that region, enticing tales of cannibalism or descriptions of the astonishing Amazonian forests. In 1799 Alexander von Humboldt and Aimé Bonpland obtained permission to visit South America and made an extraordinary documentation of the fauna, tropical vegetation, and the monuments and customs of the indigenous peoples. They assembled this information in twenty-three illustrated volumes published in Paris (1805–34). In the eyes of Europe, North America too still possessed curiosities and unexplored corners. Books that described the daily life of the Native Americans—from *Bouquet's Expedition against the Ohio Indians in 1764* by William Smith (1766) to *The History of the American Indians* by William Hauley (1775) to the famous *Domestic Manners of the Americans* by Frances Trollope (1832)—were guaranteed to sell. Of all the subjects related to North America, the presentation of Native Americans most interested artists, but with the advent of the Romantic culture the image of Native Americans underwent a radical change. The traditional identification of them as "noble savages," associated with Enlightenment theories of the primordial world and a mythical golden age, was abandoned as they came to assume the features of Romantic heroes. Thus the protagonists of the paintings by Joseph Wright of Derby and Benjamin West are still immersed in an idealized aura, and the clear intention is to exalt Native American virtues (as in Wright's *The Indian Widow*, 1785). They are also presented in noble attitudes, such as the almost Michelangeloesque pose of the Native American in West's *The Death of General Wolfe*. West also painted *Penn's Treaty with the Indians*, celebrating the 1682 treaty between the Lenape Indians and the English Quaker William Penn, founder of Pennsylvania. Quite different is the image made popular by Romantic artists and men of letters, such as Girodet, Delacroix, and Chateaubriand (who spent five months in Florida in 1791). In their works, the Native Americans become figures animated by great passions. They are aware that their way of life is doomed to end soon, and that awareness gives them an aura of true tragedy. That sense of solitude, melancholy, and powerless resignation in the face of inevitable death came to incarnate the European view, part of an appreciation of the destructive consequences of progress understood as civilization imposed on a still uncontaminated world. American artists were front-line participants in this drama of a people in danger of extinction. Outstanding in this sense was George Catlin, who made expeditions to the Great Plains during the 1830s, assembling an exceptional pictorial documentation of what he saw. Using an encyclopedia style similar to that of the contemporary naturalist John James Audubon, he recorded the life of the Native Americans, paying close attention to every aspect, from clothes to ceremonies to daily habits, enormously aware that he was saving from imminent loss at least a visual memory of those peoples. The enormous exhibition of his works that Catlin gave in 1837 in various cities in the eastern United States, involving more than five hundred paintings (of which 310 were portraits of chiefs), was later exported to London and Paris, accompanied by a further attraction,

Benjamin West, *Penn's Treaty with the Indians,* 1772, oil on canvas, 192 x 273 cm; Pennsylvania Academy of Fine Arts, Philadelphia

John Vanderlyn, *The Landing of Columbus in 1492,* 1837–47, oil on canvas, 365 x 548 cm; Capitol Rotunda, Washington, D.C.

tribal dances performed by actual Native Americans that the painter had brought with him. The exhibition arrived in Paris in 1845. Delacroix visited the show together with George Sand, and both were enthralled by the dances, which show up in the writer's *Le Diable de Paris* (1846), which includes a detailed description of the moment in which the warriors, dressed in their ritual war paint and playing strange instruments, burst into the hall, making her relive the most frightening scene in *The Last of the Mohicans.* First published in 1826, this American best-seller by James Fenimore Cooper had also conquered the European public, contributing to the consolidation of the growing culture of the United States, still without a clear identity despite having won political independence in 1783. In that regard, Thomas Cole, who was born in England but had emigrated to America with his family at age seventeen, becoming American by adoption, came to play an important role on the artistic front. Founder of the Hudson River

Carl Wimar, *The Lost Trail,* circa 1856, oil on canvas, 49.5 x 77.4 cm; Museo Thyssen-Bornemisza, Madrid

century. The events of the nation's past, including scenes of the first European explorations of the continent, became part of the national repertory, as in *The Landing of Columbus in 1492* painted between

The New World

School, so-named for the excursions that he often organized along the Hudson River Valley together with other painters, Cole was a talented landscapist who looked on the great wilderness scenes of North America from a Romantic stance, sometimes presenting the quietly sublime aspects of their majesty, sometimes presenting the enthralling beauty of a still primordial nature. Cole moved to the Catskill Mountains north of New York City and elaborated the pictorial layout that gave birth to the first school of American landscape painting, which after Cole's premature death in 1848 was carried on by his followers, among them Asher B. Durand and Frederic Edwin Church. The artistic production of the young United States grew progressively greater toward the middle years of the

Frederic Edwin Church, *Niagara Falls,* 1857, oil on canvas, 107.3 x 230 cm; Corcoran Gallery of Art, Washington, D.C.

1837 and 1847 by John Vanderlyn for the Capitol Rotunda in Washington, D.C., and the paintings in which Robert Weir recreated important events from the explorations of Henry Hudson, the first European to explore, in 1609, the river that today bears his name. Painters also turned to the subject of the life of the pioneers and prospectors who crossed the country in search of homes or wealth. Europe also observed the social evolution of the new continent, praising Abraham Lincoln's abolition of slavery. Slavery had been abolished in French territories in 1794 only to be reestablished in 1802; the traffic of slaves from Africa and the West Indies was "abolished" in 1815 by Louis XVIII with a decree that went into effect only in 1831. Only by a proclamation of 1848 was slavery finally abolished.

Joseph Wright of Derby
The Indian Widow
1785, oil on canvas
101.6 x 127 cm
Museum and Art Gallery, Derby

Planned as one in a series presenting exemplary women, the painting was well received at the London exhibition of 1785 in part because of the novelty of its subject. Wright of Derby never visited America and never saw the populations of Native Americans, and he based his art on the *History of the American Indians* written in 1775 by William Hauley, who had spent forty years in the North American territories. The canvas illustrates the author's description of the period of mourning prescribed for the wife of an Indian chief, obliged to spend an entire month outdoors, without shelter from the sun or inclement weather, seated in front of a tree on which were draped the dead warrior's weapons and belongings. Wright translated the isolation, pain, and sorrow of the woman in a stormy landscape with a swirling sky; he took care in the documentary reproduction of the objects, including the headdress, using actual examples from America as models.

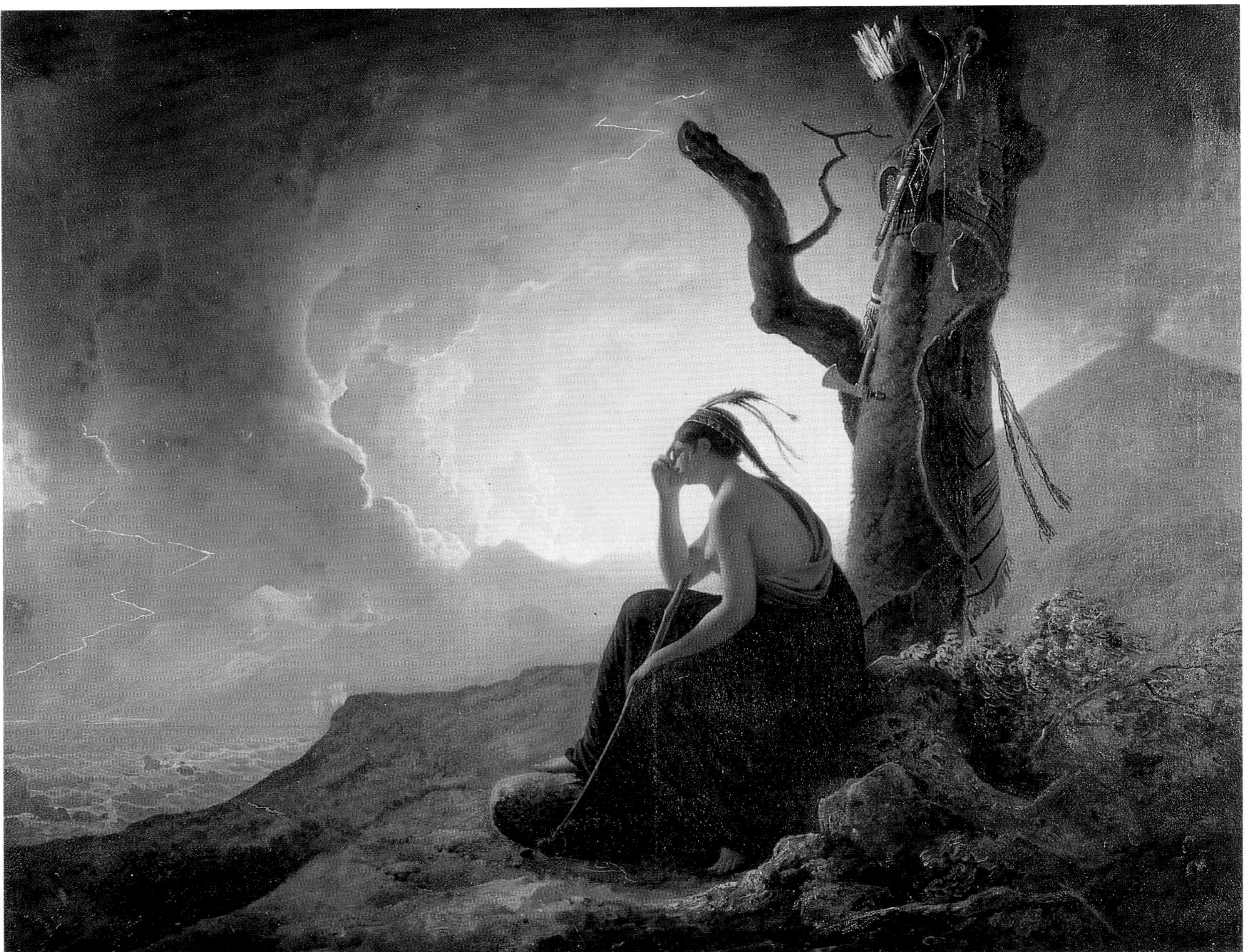

Anne-Louis Girodet-Trioson
The Burial of Atala
1808, oil on canvas
207 x 267 cm
Musée du Louvre, Paris

This painting presents the dramatic conclusion of a story by Chateaubriand, *Atala* (1801): Chactas, an Indian of the Natchez tribe, mourns the death of Atala, a young Christian girl who, falling in love, has committed suicide in order to avoid breaking her vow of chastity. Assisted by the friar Aubry, he is about to bury her. The work presents a view of the New World different from that of the Enlightenment and is pervaded by a thoroughly Romantic emotional involvement: the American Indian is no longer conceived as a noble savage but rather as an individual capable of strong emotions equal to those of any other man. Girodet concentrates the dramatic tension of the moment in the gesture of the young man hugging the feet of his beloved and in the expression on the face of the friar, and he illuminates the body of Atala with a warm, almost supernatural light.

BENJAMIN WEST
The Death of General Wolfe
1770, oil on canvas
152.6 x 214.5 cm
National Gallery of Canada, Ottawa

An American painter active at the royal court in London, West made many paintings based on historical themes or contemporary events, such as this scene of the death of General James Wolfe during the battle of Quebec in 1759, an episode from the French and Indian War. In presenting the event, West followed the style of the period in the use of a still classical layout, but he added an interesting use of the formal language of religious art, which contributes to emphasizing the drama of the scene. The wounded general is stretched out on the ground and surrounded by his officers in a pose based on the layout of a Lamentation on the Dead Christ; another classical touch is the "meditative" pose of the Native American placed in the left foreground, one of the first appearances of a Native American in a European-style history painting.

Robert W. Weir
The Landing of Henry Hudson
1838, oil on canvas
170 x 270 cm
David David Gallery, Philadelphia

Over the course of the nineteenth century America developed its own national repertory of history paintings, to which Weir dedicated various works. In this canvas he presents the English explorer Henry Hudson, who made several important expeditions between 1608 and 1611 in his effort to find the Northwest Passage. In 1609 he sailed his ship, the *Half Moon*, into the mouth of the Hudson River, an event here witnessed by the local Native Americans.

Eugène Delacroix
The Natchez
1835, oil on canvas
90.2 x 116.8 cm
Metropolitan Museum of Art, New York

Once again (see page 217), the source of this painting is Chateaubriand's story *Atala* (1801). The canvas is not meant to be a simple pictorial transcription of the story since Delacroix's intention was to evoke the tragedy of a people being destroyed and left without a future. He drew his inspiration from the closing pages of the story, in which the narrator comes upon a young Native American couple that has paused beside Niagara Falls with their dying child. Survivors of the slaughter of their tribe, the Natchez, at the hands of the French, the two first fled to safety with a nearby tribe of the Chickasaws, staying there until the "whites" took over that land too. Forced to flee, the woman gave birth to a son, but because of the hardships endured was unable to keep the child alive. Delacroix reduced the ethnographic elements to a minimum so as to concentrate on the human participation in the suffering.

George Catlin
White Cloud, Head Chief of the Iowas
1844, oil on canvas
70.2 x 58 cm
National Gallery of Art, Washington, D.C.

Intrigued by a delegation of Indian chiefs visiting Philadelphia, where he was working as a portraitist, Catlin moved to Saint Louis, a city on the frontier near the Mississippi River, and in the next thirty years made five trips to study the life and habits of the Native American populations. The result was a large collection that included 200 scenes of daily life and hunting, artistic artifacts, notes, and 310 portraits of Indian chiefs. In 1837, he presented this material to the public in his Indian Gallery. As emerges from this face of White Cloud, Catlin did not present Native Americans as barbaric wild men but as individuals full of pride and dignity. He paid scientific attention to the accurate recording of clothes, headdresses, and customs with the intention of preserving at least a visual memory of the "noble race," condemned to a sad fate.

Francis Danby
The Upas, or Poison-tree, in the Island of Java
1819, oil on canvas
168 x 235.4 cm
Victoria and Albert Museum, London

Among the news that reached Europe from the distant, still unexplored wild lands was a notice published in the *London Magazine* of December 1783 describing a tree on the island of Java that was so poisonous that it killed any living thing within the range of fifteen meters. The name of the plant was *upas*, the term for the substance the Javanese used to make arrow poison. There was no truth to the report, but in 1789 Erasmus Darwin, grandfather of the famous Charles, contributed to the spread of this false "scoop" by inserting it in his book about the emotions of the vegetable world (*The Loves of Plants,* part of his *Botanic Garden*). The description of the tree in that book served as the inspiration for this painting by Francis Danby. The tree, with its thin trunk, is presented at the center of a disturbingly desolate rocky valley, illuminated by just enough spectral moonlight to reveal the tree's most recent victims.

John Glover
Sunset at Ben Lomond
1840, oil on canvas
77 x 114 cm
Musée du Louvre, Paris

Like George Catlin, John Glover dedicated part of his life to recording the customs, rituals, and images of the life of a people facing tragedy as the result of western colonization. In 1831 he and his sons arrived in Tasmania, the large island to the south of Australia, which had become a British colony. The artist took to heart the gradual destruction of the indigenous civilization and saw the extinction for which it was destined. In dozens of paintings he recorded the faces and habits of the aborigines, such as this moment in which at sunset some of the aborigines bathe in the river while others light a fire near the banks. Glover paid close attention to the plants of the island, presenting them with the same documentary clarity he used for the inhabitants and their ceremonies.

THOMAS COLE
Landscape Scene from "The Last of the Mohicans"
1827, oil on canvas
64.5 x 89 cm
Wadsworth Atheneum, Hartford

In 1826 James Fenimore Cooper published *The Last of the Mohicans,* a highly successful novel set in 1757, during the French and Indian War. At the time, Thomas Cole was a young landscape artist who, in search of untouched landscapes, had just begun to paint grandiose views of the Hudson River Valley and areas in New England. He was immediately drawn to the book and painted several scenes from it, including this image in which Cora kneels at the feet of Tamenund. The episode takes place in the final chapter of the novel when Cora, captive of the Hurons, allies of the French, implores the chief Tamenund to free her while Uncas, last of the Mohicans, a tribe allied with the English, attempts to save her. The scene is almost marginal within the vast, majestic landscape, although the ritual circle of the Native Americans confers a sense of further sacredness on the whole.

THOMAS COLE
View from Mount Holyoke, Northampton, Massachusetts, after a Thunderstorm (The Oxbow)
1836, oil on canvas
131 x 193 cm
Metropolitan Museum of Art, New York

A masterpiece and among of the best known works by Cole, this view was made from the peak of Mount Holyoke in western Massachusetts, so as to portray the spectacular twist in the Connecticut River (the "oxbow" of the title). The landscape to one side presents its wilderness state, emphasized by the recent passage of a storm and the geological details of the site, which constituted one of what Cole and his followers called the natural antiquities of America (as opposed to the manmade antiquities—the ancient ruins—of Europe); to the right the view runs across a broad, orderly valley that presupposes human intervention. Cole was fascinated by the still largely uncontaminated places of North America and wanted to celebrate them, in this case with the contrast of the storm and the area of serenity, thus exalting the sublime, religious sense of nature.

François-Auguste Biard
The Slave Trade on the West Coast of Africa
circa 1840,
oil on canvas
162 x 228.6 cm
City Museums and Art Galleries, Wilberforce House, Hull

It is possible that Biard, a tireless traveler, actually witnessed a scene like this, involving one of the many slave markets along the African coast. The human drama is not the main subject of the painting, which is more a view of daily life, showing cruel aspects but for the most part without finding fault. The suffering and humiliation of the individuals are not given dramatic tones, since Biard limits himself to presenting the episode in a documentary style. The work was exhibited in London, where the abolition of slavery was a topic of great importance, and it was then given to Sir Thomas Fowell Buxton, a leading social reformer in the World Anti-Slavery Convention, which met in the English capital in 1842.

George Caleb Bingham
Fur Traders Descending the Missouri
1845, oil on canvas
73.7 x 92.7 cm
Metropolitan Museum of Art, New York

Were it not for the people aboard this canoe, the image might be mistaken for one of the many Romantic landscapes showing lakes or rivers in Europe. The location here is instead the American West, and these are two fur traders moving down the nearly motionless waters of the Missouri River together with their cat. The painting is open to a kind of double reading, on the one hand realistic, on the other unnatural. Bingham shows great sympathy in the reproduction of the more adventurous aspects of the figures, including their somewhat shabby work clothes, but he also puts them in unexpected positions, posed as though for a studio portrait, with the almost dreamy look of the boy at the center of the boat, his attitude perfectly matching the sense of peace that pervades the setting.

Fables and

Fables and love stories made up some of the most popular reading material for the nineteenth-century public. Amorous emotions and intrigues, "elective affinities," and a fascination with the supernatural fueled both Romantic literature and Romantic painting in a rising crescendo that ran from the outset of the century to reach its true culmination in Victorian England. The German writers who were the founders of the Romantic movement laid the basis for this current of thought. They looked on the genre of fables with great enthusiasm, drawing inspiration from the ancient popular legends of the Germanic world. The authors of dramatic love stories included Friedrich Leopold von Hardenberg, who wrote under the pseudonym Novalis (1772–1801), Clemens Maria Brentano (1778–1842), and even Johann Wolfgang von Goethe (1749–1832), who wrote poetic compositions set in the world of the fairies, such as *Der Erlkönig* ("Ballad of the Elf King") of 1782, which probably served as the inspiration to Julius Schnorr von Carolsfeld in 1825. The Romantic movement's ideological program theorized by the Schlegel brothers and their circle also included the return to popular German traditions. The goal was that of rediscovering the German people's ancient religion and reinvigorating it so it could serve the reawakening of the national consciousness and the expulsion of the Napoleonic invaders. The brothers Jakob and Wilhelm Grimm and Brentano were dedicated to the recovery of those tales and legends. The Grimm brothers transcribed the fairy tales directly from the oral tradition of the people and assembled them in collections, which they began publishing in 1812. Both brothers contributed to the *Zeitung für Einsiedler* ("Newspaper for Hermits"), founded by Clemens Brentano and Achim von Arnim in Heidelberg around 1808. The paper's goal was to retrieve the medieval patrimony of popular German culture and revive the ancient national spirit through folk tales and songs from all levels of society. These were published in part by Brentano in the three volumes (1806–08) dedicated to Goethe under the title *Des Knaben Wunderhorn* ("The Boy's Magic Horn"), followed by *Rhine Fables*, written in 1814 but published posthumously in 1847. Another member of the Heidelberg group was the painter Philipp Otto Runge, a man with an eclectic personality who exhibited enormous creative talent during the early period of the German Romantic movement. Like Caspar David Friedrich, and only three years younger, Runge was born in Pomerania in northern Germany; he studied at the Copenhagen Academy, after which he spent several years in Dresden. He and Friedrich became friends and developed a deeply mystical sense of landscape, firmly believing that painting nature was a way to approach the divine; even so, their paintings were very different. In Friedrich sentiments are filtered through the landscape, and his figures, even if timidly immersed in a magical, loving embrace, as in *On Board a Sailing Ship* or *A Man and Woman Contemplating the Moon*, are seen from behind, letting the nature that surrounds them be the protagonist of the work. The same relationship with the landscape can be found in painters like Carl Gustav Carus or the American Asher B. Durand, who in *Kindred Spirits* dealt with one of the most common Romantic themes, that of interpersonal relationships, a subject made popular by the famous novel by Goethe *Die Wahlverwandtschaften* ("Elective Affinities"). Nothing of this appears in the paintings that Otto Runge made during his short life.

Francis Danby, *Scene from "A Midsummer Night's Dream,"* 1832, watercolor, 19.7 x 27.9 cm; Oldham Art Gallery, Oldham

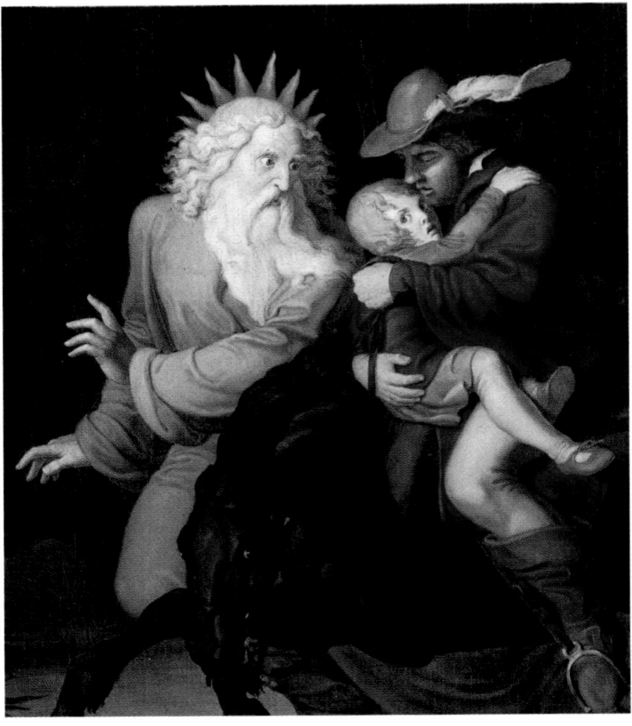

Julius Schnorr von Carolsfeld, *The Ballad of the Elf King* (detail), 1820–25, oil on canvas, 53.2 x 65.8 cm; Schack-Galerie, Munich

He investigated the study of symbols, theories of the meaning of colors, and a type of painting directed stylistically toward the decorative style of medieval miniatures, attempting to obtain an ideal blend of poetry, sentiment, music, and allegory. He moved into an almost esoteric mysticism in the cycle of works made to illustrate the *Four Times of Day* in symbolic form, and, convinced of the immense importance of childhood as a repository of the purest sentiments, he made works based on the world of fables, as shown by *The Nightingale's Music Lesson*. Both of these aspects of Runge's work were translated in a concrete form by the founders of German Romantic opera. Such composers as Carl Maria von Weber sensed the strong appeal of the supernatural, telling tales of ghosts, enchantments, and poisoned rings in their musical creations. Weber's *Euryanthe* (1823) and *Oberon* (1826) are both examples of this. The subject of the latter is from Shakespeare's *A Midsummer Night's Dream*, which enjoyed singular fortune in English Romantic painting, from Fuseli (see pages 15 and 328) to Francis Danby to Joseph Noel Paton. Other texts then in vogue, including *The Faerie Queene* (1595) by Edmund Spenser, furnished excellent models for paintings of fairies, sprites, goblins, and elves. In

sentimental tales

some cases, such characters are the sole protagonists of the painting, as in Richard Dadd's surreal masterpiece, *The Fairy Feller's Master-Stroke*. This artist, given to fits of insanity and violent behavior—he stabbed his father to death and spent his last years in asylums—brings to mind the interrelationships between the interior world and the invisible occult world presented in the works of E.T.A. Hoffmann, the German Romantic novelist and composer who proposed overcoming the mediocrity of daily existence by opening the self to the supernatural invisible world inhabited by spirits, fairies, ghosts, demons, and witches with their occult magic. This fondness for the unknown and the mysterious, for the enchanting and the sentimental, also shows up in French Romantic paintings, although without the total immersion in the sense of the fabulous seen in Germany. The French painters who demonstrated the greatest interest in peeking behind the secret curtain of the past were the group known as the Troubadours. The fairy tale of "Little Red Riding Hood" came to be selected as the outstanding symbol of French national mythology. For Fleury Richard it became the means for expressing a nostalgic vision of a distant world. Pierre-Auguste Vafflard opted instead for an ancient legend that came back into vogue in nineteenth-century France, that of Emma and Eginhard, set at the Carolingian court. It was love, or better the agonizing suffering experienced by the lover, that was the central theme of the favorite literature of the nineteenth century, and the subject found immediate success in Romantic painting. Here again it was the British who were the most receptive to the display of emotions and sentiments in the usual domestic settings. Among the artists who dedicated themselves to such works were Johann Peter Hasenclever, Charles West Cope, Francis Danby, and the Pre-Raphaelite Arthur Hughes, who fixed in enthralling views of daily life images of young girls absorbed by their thoughts, trembling in anticipation of an arrival or collapsing in bitter tears over the heartbreak of a departure.

Charles West Cope, *Palpitation*, 1844, oil on wood, 76.2 x 57.8 cm; Victoria and Albert Museum, London

Johann Peter Hasenclever, *Sentimental Girl*, 1846, oil on canvas; Kunstmuseum, Düsseldorf

Philipp Otto Runge
Morning
1808, oil on canvas
108.9 x 85.4 cm
Kunsthalle, Hamburg

This painting was part of a cycle made to illustrate the *Four Times of Day* seen as the "four dimensions of the creative spirit." Conceived as a medieval illuminated page, the painting presents morning understood as the "boundless illumination of the universe." Light, symbolized by the lily, accompanied by the advancing figure of Aurora, announces the coming of the Holy Spirit. Runge and Friedrich were among the founders of German Romantic painting; Runge did not himself make a great many paintings, but he played an important role in developing theories supporting the existence of a profound relationship among poetry, music, and painting, and he saw the painter as capable of giving life to the mysterious forces of nature, revealed through allegory and the symbolic meaning of colors.

Georg Friedrich Kersting
Woman Winding Wreaths
1815, oil on canvas
40 x 32 cm
Nationalgalerie, Berlin

A young girl winds oak leaves into wreathes that she will then hang from the branches of trees; carved into the trunks of the trees are the names of soldiers fallen in a distant battle for national liberation. The image is simple, the flavor domestic, as appears from the girl's calm attitude and her work basket. The painting dates to 1815, the crucial year of the post-Napoleonic restoration, and with this work the artist (who had served as a volunteer in 1813) hoped to offer strength to the German spirit and to inspire remembrance of the nation's heroes, celebrating the importance of memory as a sign of love and recognition.

Caspar David Friedrich
A Man and Woman Contemplating the Moon
1830, oil on canvas
34 x 44 cm
Nationalgalerie, Berlin

The exclusive subject of Friedrich's paintings, as well as of his philosophical writings, was the deep tie that he saw between human emotions and the spirituality of nature. In paintings he often made use of elements to which tradition had given symbolic values, such as the moon, ancient emblem of hope. The couple that pauses to contemplate it seems wrapped in the magical silence of the place, framed by a tree that bears signs of the passing of time that confirm it is a living being and thus a participant in human sentiments. Friedrich had already painted a very similar canvas in 1819 (Gemäldegalerie, Dresden) in which the two figures, once again seen from behind, are his student August Heirich and his brother-in-law Wilhelm.

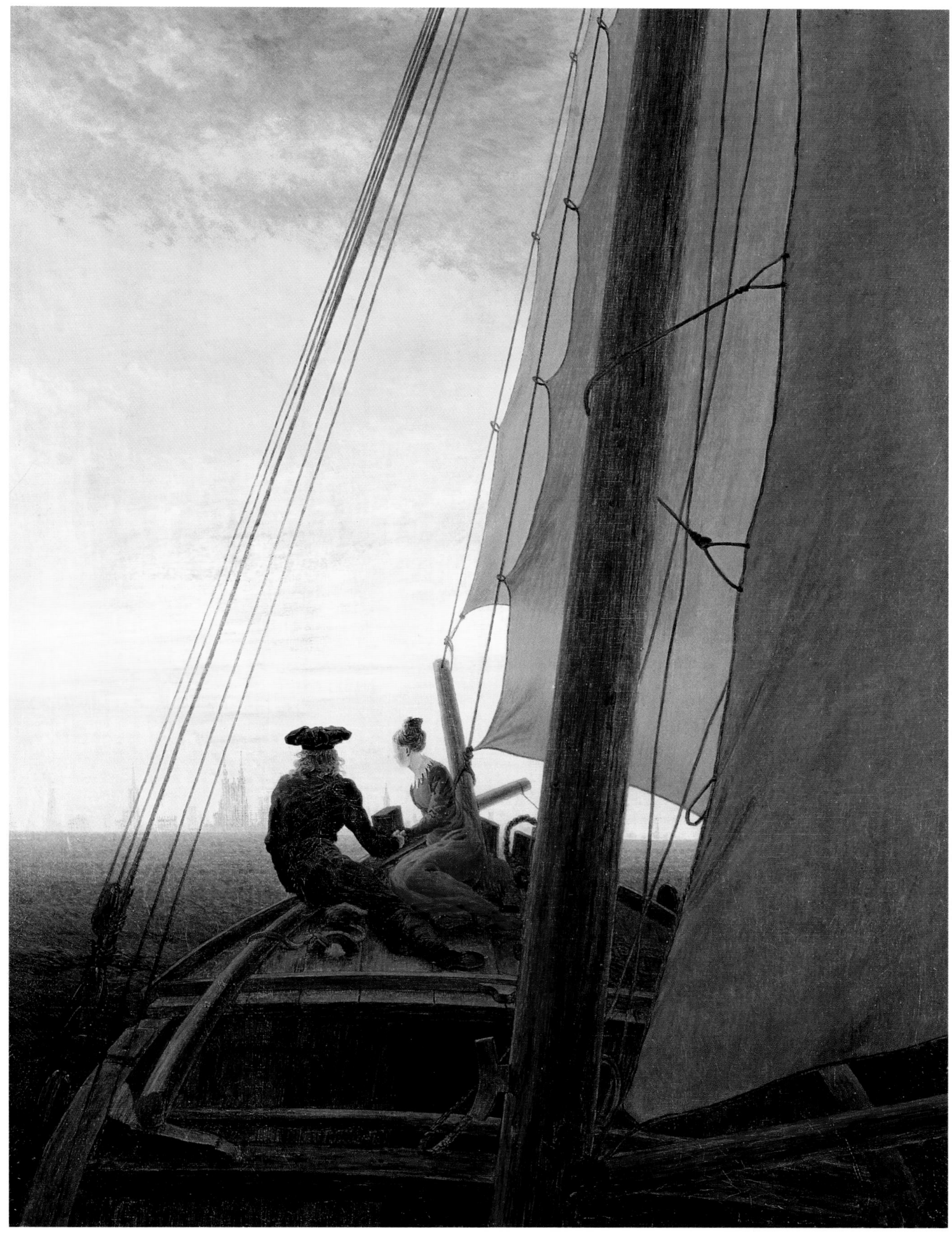

Caspar David Friedrich
On Board a Sailing Ship
1818–20,
oil on canvas
71 x 56 cm
Hermitage,
St. Petersburg

This canvas was made between 1818 and 1820, and the hypothesis has been made that the young couple are in fact the artist himself and his wife, Caroline, shortly after their honeymoon. In any case their tranquil pose and their gazes directed at the soft tones of twilight converge in creating an atmosphere of profound intimacy and calm, full of emotion, which the spectator is drawn to and also involved in by way of the location of the point of view, which seems to be somewhere on the deck of the ship.

Caspar David Friedrich
Sunset
1830, oil on canvas
25 x 31 cm
Hermitage,
St. Petersburg

As in many paintings by Friedrich, the figures in this work are seen from behind, in this case as they contemplate the sea, a stretch of mountains, and the setting sun. The two figures represent humanity in general presented in an attitude of silent observation of the world before them. But Friedrich did not consider the observation of nature to take place on an exclusively visual plane, writing, "Close your bodily eye so that you may see your picture first with your spiritual eye."

KARL GUSTAV CARUS
Pilgrim in a Rocky Valley
circa 1820, oil on canvas
28 x 22 cm
Nationalgalerie, Berlin

Friend of Goethe, Friedrich, and the philosopher Schelling, Carus painted in his free time from his profession as doctor and botanist. Even so he became one of the leading theorists of the Romantic aesthetics of nature. He succeeds here in imbuing a small canvas with the spiritual sense of nature. A pilgrim, seen from behind, makes his way along a path, perhaps with difficulty; the image does not communicate the idea of weariness but rather of what Carus identified as the correspondence between the motions of the soul and the atmosphere of the surrounding landscape. The beautiful light that marks with the first star the passage between day and night seals the painting as symbolic of spirituality, of the revelation of the divine that the painter perceived in nature.

ASHER B. DURAND
Kindred Spirits
1849, oil on canvas
112 x 91.6 cm
New York Public Library, New York

One of the leading members of the Hudson River School of landscape painters, Durand painted this canvas in memory of his friend Thomas Cole, who had died prematurely the preceding year. Durand presents the painter Cole in the company of the poet William Cullen Bryant, standing atop a rock to admire a beautiful view of the Catskill Mountains. The two friends are presented as symbols of the spiritual affinity that unites Romantic artists and poets in the sense of the interpenetration of the individual and nature. The two figures are presented in conversation, but their human presence is discreet, blending into the scene of trees, the stream, and the surrounding rocks, putting them in complete harmony with the spirit of the place.

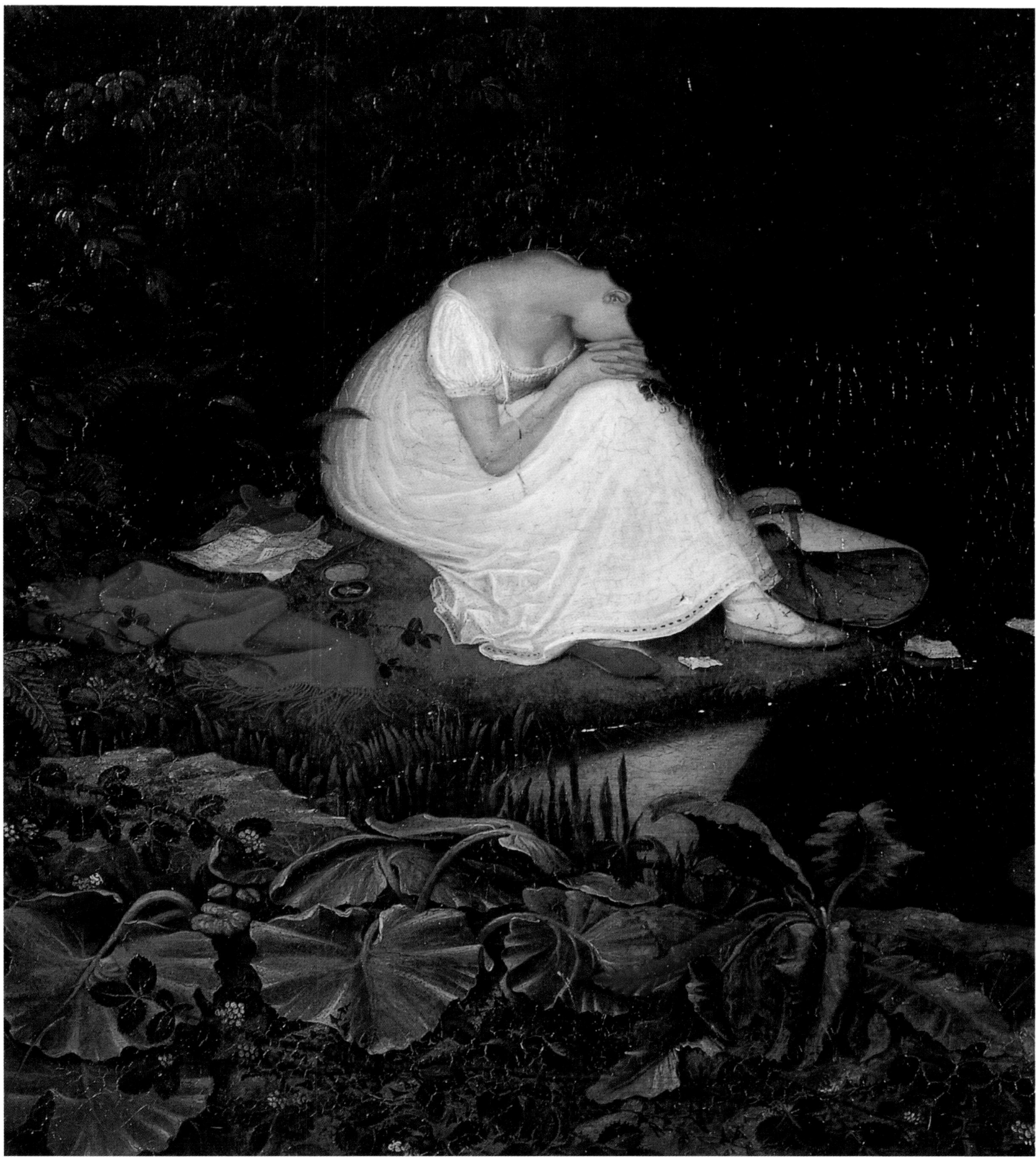

FRANCIS DANBY
Disappointed Love
1821, oil on canvas
81.2 x 62.8 cm
Victoria and Albert Museum, London

Painted during the years in which Danby lived in Bristol, the painting may present a secluded area along the banks of the River Frome near Stapleton. The stretch of bank and the pond offer shelter to an unhappy young woman, withdrawn alone to cry over a disappointment in love, as suggested not only by her posture but by the miniature portrait beside her and the shreds of a torn-up letter. The leaves in the foreground seem to wilt in response to the young woman's sorrow; it is not impossible that Danby had been influenced in that sense by the works of Erasmus Darwin, who in 1789 had written in *The Loves of the Plants* the theory, today confirmed, that plants have the ability to experience emotional reactions.

Arthur Hughes
April Love
1856, oil on canvas
88.9 x 49.5 cm
Tate Gallery, London

In November 1855, when this canvas was not yet finished, John Ruskin saw it in the painter's studio and was so enthusiastic about it that he immediately returned with his father to convince him to buy it. Unfortunately for Hughes, short of money like all young artists, the purchase did not end well, but the work met with great success the next year when it was exhibited at the Royal Academy, accompanied by six verses from *The Miller's Daughter* (1833), a poem by Alfred Tennyson concerning the languid pains of love. The painting was not meant to illustrate the verse; the verses were used to complement the painting in its delicate evocation of the emotions and quarrels of lovers. Hughes created an image of extreme freshness in which the beautiful details of the petals and leaves of ivy, symbols of love and eternity, and the tonal effect of the fabrics are rendered with photographic clarity.

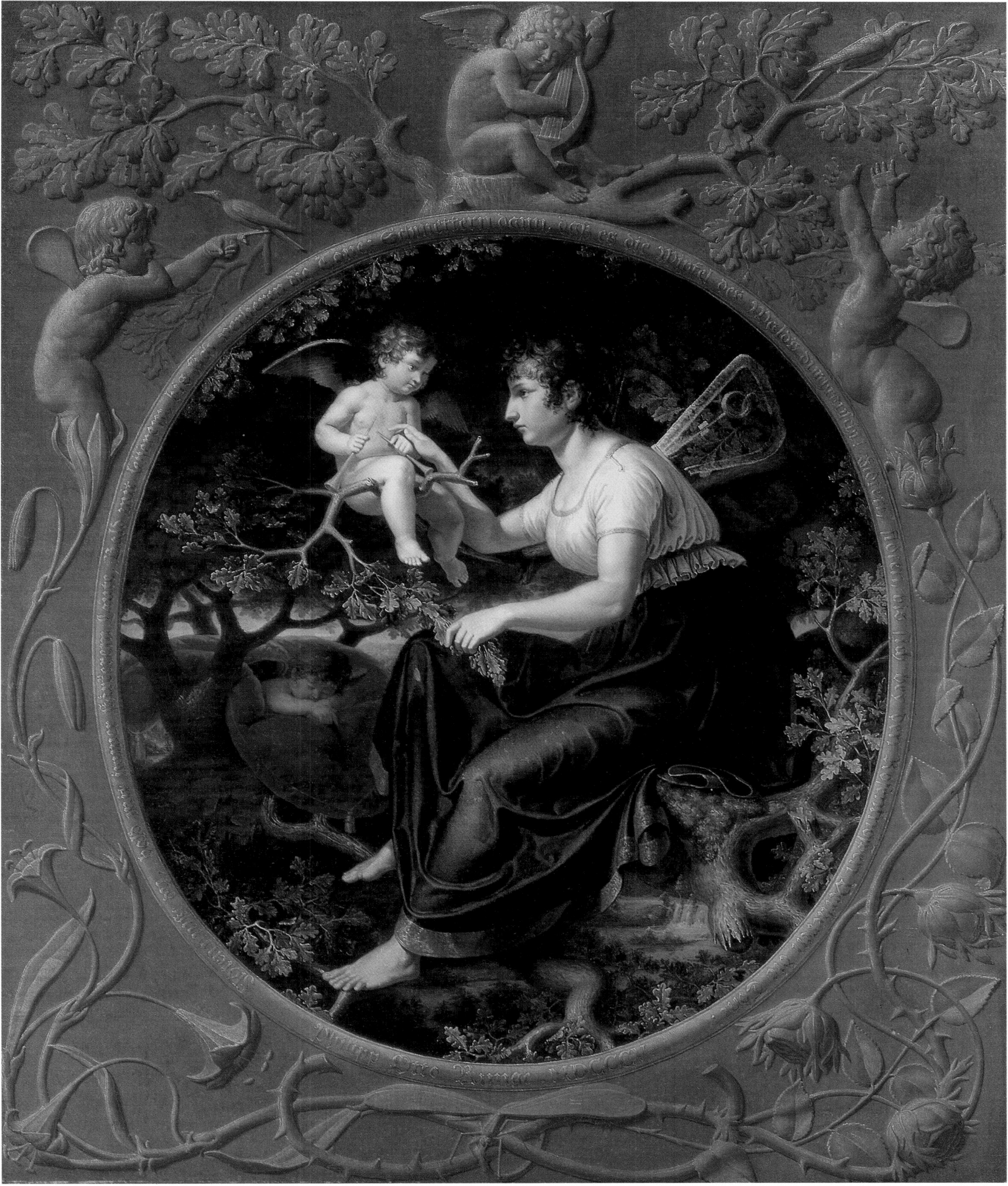

Philipp Otto Runge
The Nightingale's Music Lesson
1805, oil on canvas
104.7 x 88.5 cm
Kunsthalle, Hamburg

Runge made this painting as a declaration of love for his young wife, Pauline, and the canvas is full of references to poetry, myth, and music. The subject is taken from an ode by the poet Friedrich Klopstock: at nightfall, when the nightingale begins its song, Psyche teaches the song to Cupid, telling him how beauty awakens the power of love. Even the frame is interwoven with symbolic references, such as the climbing plants, cherubs, and oak leaves that join to wrap around the forest scene in the oval. Like many Romantics, Runge was particularly fond of the world of fables because of the density of Christian, mythological, and esoteric symbols in them, a subject to which he dedicated much of his studies.

Pierre Antoine Augustin Vafflard
Emma and Eginhard; or, The Stratagems of Love
1809, oil on canvas
100 x 81 cm
Musée Ancien Evêché, Évreux

Emma, daughter of Charlemagne, is betrothed to a Greek prince but secretly loves Eginhard, court chaplain; the two lovers are discovered by the emperor when the girl, to keep her lover's footprints in the snow from revealing their nocturnal meeting, carries him across the courtyard toward her room.

Pelagio Palagi
Orombello and Beatrice de Tenda in the Castle of Binasco
circa 1845,
oil on canvas
64.5 x 53 cm
Galleria d'Arte Moderna, Bologna

The clandestine meeting of the two lovers, Michele Orombello and Beatrice, wife of Filippo Maria Visconti, duke of Milan, is full of poetry and grace: the red stockings and the pose of the young man, the angle at which the tender embrace is made, and the castle in the background give this tragic medieval tale the tones of a fable.

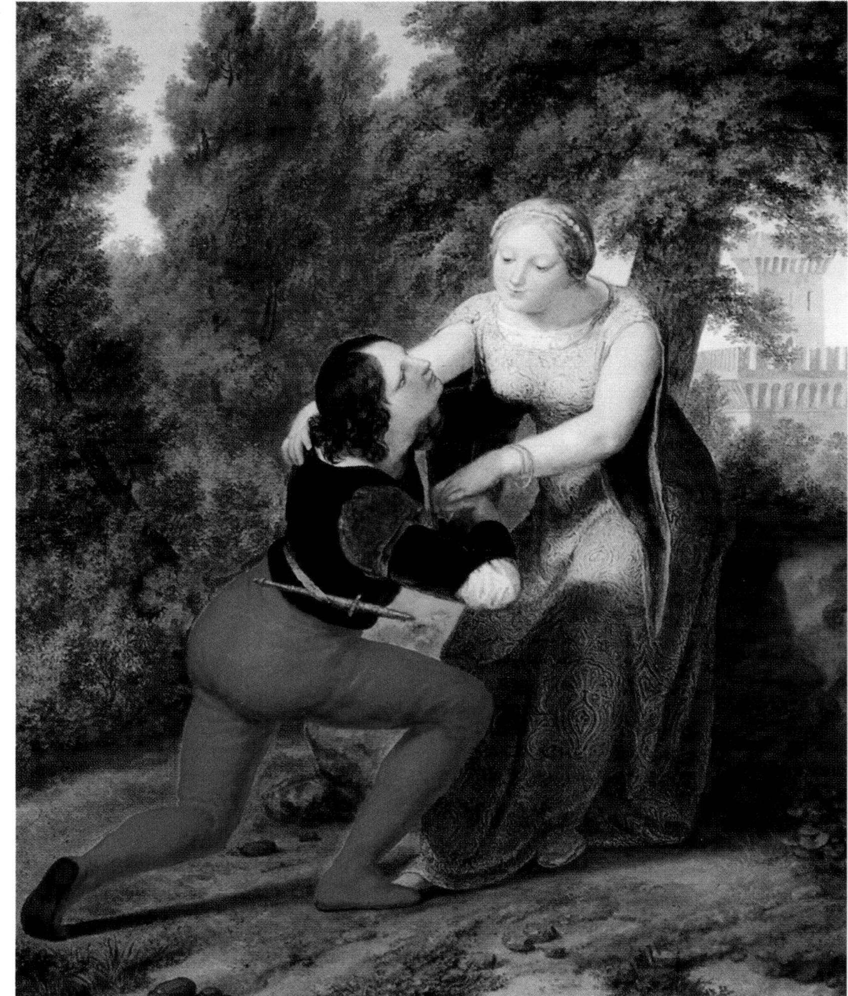

Francis Danby
Children by a Brook
circa 1822,
oil on canvas
34.5 x 46 cm
Tate Gallery, London

The light sweetly filtering through the branches of the trees, the children playing with the water, and their simple timeless gestures give this scene the feeling of a fable. The house visible through the open gate confers a sense of serene tranquility on the woods, crossed by the stream, while the girl with the pitcher acts as the chromatic fulcrum of the composition. All these aspects reinforce the delicate poetic effects with which Danby imbued some of his youthful works, painted when he lived in Bristol and, as with this work perhaps, inspired by the landscape near Stapleton.

Alexandre-Gabriel Decamps
The Witches of "Macbeth"
1819, oil on canvas
29.4 x 40.4 cm
Wallace Collection, London

As a witch drops a toad into the caldron, she is carefully watched by a cat on the right and an owl on the left. The painting follows the text of Shakespeare's *Macbeth* (Act IV, Scene 1), in which three witches, moving around a cauldron, prepare a poison that calls for many ingredients, including a toad held for thirty-one days and nights "under a cold stone." The subject was taken up by many Romantic artists, such as Ary Scheffer and Delacroix, from whom Decamps may have drawn his inspiration, although the atmosphere he creates here is even richer in magical suspense and has more illustrative appeal, while the evanescence of the figures emphasizes the sense of mystery. Not even Chassériau and Corot, when they painted the same scene in the second half of the 1850s, succeeded in immersing their paintings in equally dark and fabulous tones.

FLEURY RICHARD
Little Red Riding Hood
1820, oil on canvas
35 x 47 cm
Musée du Louvre, Paris

As can be deduced from the clothes on the floor, the wolf has already eaten the grandmother. Now he plans to devour Little Red Riding Hood. Richard, leading artist of the Troubadours group, loved to locate his scenes inside old monuments that would be recognizable to the public. In this case he placed the fairy tale by Charles Perrault (1628–1703) in an abandoned church, perhaps a building that still existed in the area around Lyons at the time of the painting. The canvas thus combines two subjects dear to the artist, the world of fairy tales and the Middle Ages, both of them symbols of a distant past.

JOHN EVERETT MILLAIS
Ferdinand Lured by Ariel
1849, oil on panel
64.8 x 50.8 cm
Bridgeman Art Library, London

This painting is a delightful transposition in fabulous tones of an important moment in *The Tempest* by Shakespeare (Act I, Scene 2): the spirit Ariel, helped by elves, lures Ferdinand, son of the king of Naples, to his master, Prospero. Millais made the painting in the summer of 1849 during a vacation spent with his friend George Drury at Shotover Park, near Oxford. For the image of the prince he used as model an illustration from the *Historical Costumes* by Camille Bonnard, in which he found the image of a young fifteenth-century Italian male. In this work Millais blended the Pre-Raphaelite style with the colors and magic of Victorian painters of fairies.

Richard Dadd
The Fairy Feller's Master-Stroke
1855–64,
oil on canvas
54 x 39 cm
Tate Gallery, London

This extraordinary assembly of fairies, sprites, gnomes, and other mysterious creatures takes place around the woodcutter who, seen from behind, is about to split a hazelnut and use it to make a new carriage for Queen Mab. With the exception of Oberon and Titania, visible above and recognizable by their crowns, all the figures were creations of Dadd's imagination, an unfortunate artist who spent most of the last years of his life in asylums and who transferred to this canvas the vision of a magical world, free of the logic of proportions and packed with fascination and mystery. It is a sort of fantastic transposition of the figures that populate the games and tales of childhood; Dadd worked on it over the period of nine years, using highly detailed preparatory studies to create a masterpiece that became the reference model for the illustration of fairy-tale books in later decades.

From visionary-
to the exploration

Henry Fuseli, *Silence,* 1799, oil on canvas, 63.6 x 51.5 cm; Kunsthaus, Zurich

One of the most fascinating aspects of the Romantic sensibility is its exploration of the human psyche and soul. In this realm Romanticism revealed its most direct relationship to the rationalism of the Enlightenment. Interest in the more recondite mechanisms of the human mind dates to the last decades of the eighteenth century—the period of the Enlightenment. It was then that study of psychic phenomena was given full dignity as a science, freed from the prejudices of superstitions. During the same period, and also within the sphere of the Enlightenment, various inroads were made that gave access to the more obscure dimensions of the inner world of the mind, but in the face of what lay there such explorations came to a halt, with the admission of the existence of a mystery related to death, to the visions of dreams, and to the night. The night attracted the attention of the artists of the early Romantic period, whose works reveal a preference for nocturnal scenes, for the subjects of dreams, for magic and the forces of the occult. These sentiments came together in a book by Johann Kaspar Lavater, *Physionomische Fragmente* (1775–78), which investigates physiognomics, the art of determining character on the basis of facial features. The book was printed in France in 1781 under the title *Essai sur la physiognomie*, with most of the illustrations made by Henry Fuseli. Both natives of Zurich, Fuseli and Lavater had met when young and in 1762 had collaborated on a small pamphlet against political corruption that had earned them so much enmity from the local authorities that they had been forced to leave the city. When they returned to Zurich, the ties of friendship between them had not weakened, but Fuseli's infatuation for Lavater's niece, Anna Landolt von Rech, and her father's adamant opposition to the relationship, forced the painter to move to London in 1779. There he made illustrations for Lavater's book and in 1792 contributed to the English translation of the work. These studies on physiognomy were enthusiastically embraced by more than a few of the early Romantics, including Goethe, and they inspired the reflection on the relationships between animal form and human expression that appears so frequently in Fuseli's pictorial production. Acute explorer of the psyche, but most of all of the dreamlike aspects of the unconscious, Fuseli dedicated extraordinary masterpieces to subjects of a visionary character, to the emotions brought on by terror or by nightmares. Not surprisingly, a Romantic myth took shape around him, for he devoted his entire life to giving visible form to the outstanding imaginative creations of the poets and intellectuals of the early nineteenth century. Scenes of the fantastic were also a constant and fascinating element in the art of William Blake. Indeed Blake combined the fantastic with a singular talent for rendering the dynamics of metamorphosis, creating mystical suggestions often intended to be symbolic, visionary creations, and he achieved these thanks in large part to the extraordinarily virtuosic line that distinguished all of his works. The Dane Nicolai Abraham Abildgaard, the artist who brought the neoclassical style to his homeland, was also attracted by visionary themes, and his meeting with Fuseli in Rome (where they both went in the 1770s) was important in that regard. In Spain the creative inspiration of Francisco Goya ended the nineteenth century with an engraving with an emblematic title, *The Sleep of Reason Produces Monsters*, which

William Blake, *The Ancient of Days,* 1827, watercolor and ink, 23.5 x 16.8 cm; Whitworth Art Gallery, Manchester

fantasy painting of the psyche

belongs to the series of *Los Caprichos*, published between 1797 and 1799. Sinister creatures of the night invade the mind of the artist, abandoned without the protection of reason in a sleep that opens the way to dreams and nightmares. Goya was a tormented artist and he died in solitude; much of his work includes images connected to themes of the occult, fears related to the unconscious, to insanity. In Fuseli, the supernatural was blended with the sensual; in Goya, scenes of magic and irrational forces often assume a deformed outline on the edge of caricature, with preference given demonic and hallucinating expressions that sometimes reinforce the fantasy element, sometimes emphasize the horror produced by human suffering, as in the case of the paintings showing scenes of the insane closed in asylums. Romantic thought supported the notion that creative art was itself of an irrational nature, the product of an altered state of mind, an expression of the unconscious or the subconscious, as indicated by Théophile Gautier's tale *The Opium Pipe* (1838) or Hector Berlioz's *Symphonie Fantastique* (1830). This notion was further supported by the theory expressed by Edgar Allan Poe and repeated by Baudelaire in 1855 in a text praising Delacroix: "The effect of opium on the senses is to endow the whole of nature with a supernatural interest that gives every object a deeper, a more deliberate, a more despotic meaning." Such were the sensations that Charles Gleyre experimented with toward mid-century and that Adolf von Menzel further investigated in a more internalized form, in a direct movement toward symbolism. Romantic art reflects other attempts to understand the human soul. Ingres and his student Flandrin approached the subject in an elegant, highly sophisticated form, presenting the relationship between the individual and the unknown by way of the sphinx, the symbol *par excellence* of that enigma. A large portion of the works of Caspar David Friedrich deal with the intimate colloquy between man and nature, along with the profound yearning for the infinite. The Romantic age also saw the flowering of paintings dedicated to melancholy, which was the characteristic sentiment of the epoch. Fuseli captured the subject in the ingenious image *Silence*, which appeared on the cover of his book *Aphorisms, Chiefly Relative to the Fine Arts*, published in 1818. Melancholy was also presented by Constance Marie Charpentier in an image of moving sorrow and by Francesco Hayez in an image of languid apprehension. Malaise was examined from other angles. The disconcerting portraits of the mentally ill that Géricault painted between 1820 and 1824 were meant not only to be tools for clinical observation for his friend Dr. Georget, founder of social psychiatry, but to be real images of the alienation of the psyche. The Romantic imagination gave much attention to insanity, particularly since it was understood as a mental and spiritual condition very similar, in terms of intensity of suffering and social isolation, to genius. And so it was that the yearning to represent the extreme forms of emotion led some artists to high levels of inner turmoil and to works that were not always well received or even fully understood. Such was the case with Auguste Préault's bronze *Slaughter* (1834), the work that marked the beginning of his career.

Auguste Préault, *Slaughter*, 1834, bronze, 109 x 140 cm; Musée des Beaux-Arts, Chartres

Francisco Goya, *The Sleep of Reason Produces Monsters*, 1796–98, engraving, 18.2 x 12 cm; Civica Raccolta Bertarelli, Milan

Henry Fuseli
The Nightmare
1791, oil on canvas
76 x 63 cm
Goethe Museum,
Frankfurt

"Dreams are one of the least explored regions in art." Related to Fuseli's statement is a series of paintings he began work on in 1781 dedicated to the presentation of nightmares. Understood as visualizations of the most unexplored realms of the human soul, a revelation of the recondite facets of the psyche, the nightmare was a subject well suited to the presentation of the unknown by way of visionary and fantastic forms. Fascinated by the mystery of the supernatural, Fuseli created a composition that blends sensuality and monstrosity in an ambiguous dimension; a woman sleeps, her body in a pose of total abandon. Atop her chest sits a beast half-dwarf and half-animal, while the terrifying head of a horse thrusts its way through the curtains, itself a visual pun on the idea of the nightmare—the mare of the night.

Nicolai Abraham Abildgaard
Culmin's Ghost Appears to His Mother
1794, oil on canvas
62 x 78 cm
Nationalmuseum, Stockholm

Abildgaard was born in Denmark in 1743 and died in 1809, so his works make him an important precursor of the investigation of the human psyche and its more disquieting dream manifestations. In this work he uses a visionary or at least strongly dramatic style of painting to take on the subject of the night, nightmares, and spectral apparitions. Making use of only a limited number of compositional elements—the two figures, dogs, a night sky, a sliver of moon—he nevertheless manages to confer extraordinary expressive power on them through the play of lines and light effects. The ghost of the young warrior Culmin, with an opalescent consistency, appears stretched out, as at the moment of his death, beside him his shield, and the diagonal line of his nude body contrasts with the curving, almost spiraling body of his mother, on whom is concentrated the light that arrives from the opposite side of the shadows.

Francisco Goya
The Witches' Sabbath
1798, oil on canvas
44 x 30.5 cm
Museo Lazaro Galdiano, Madrid

This canvas belongs to a series of eight paintings the duchess of Osuna commissioned from Goya for her personal study in her country residence located near Madrid, called Alameda. The small cycle was composed of scenes of witchcraft, a particularly popular subject in Spain at the end of the century, both as an aspect of popular culture and as a recurrent motif in the theatrical repertory of the period. Although the setting is not especially frightening, Goya presents the horrid ritual of the witches, who, according to popular superstition, offered a child in sacrifice to the goat, a stand-in for the devil since ancient times. This is not the only case in which Goya took on the theme of witchcraft, for he was especially fascinated with it as an allegorical expression of the perversion of the human soul.

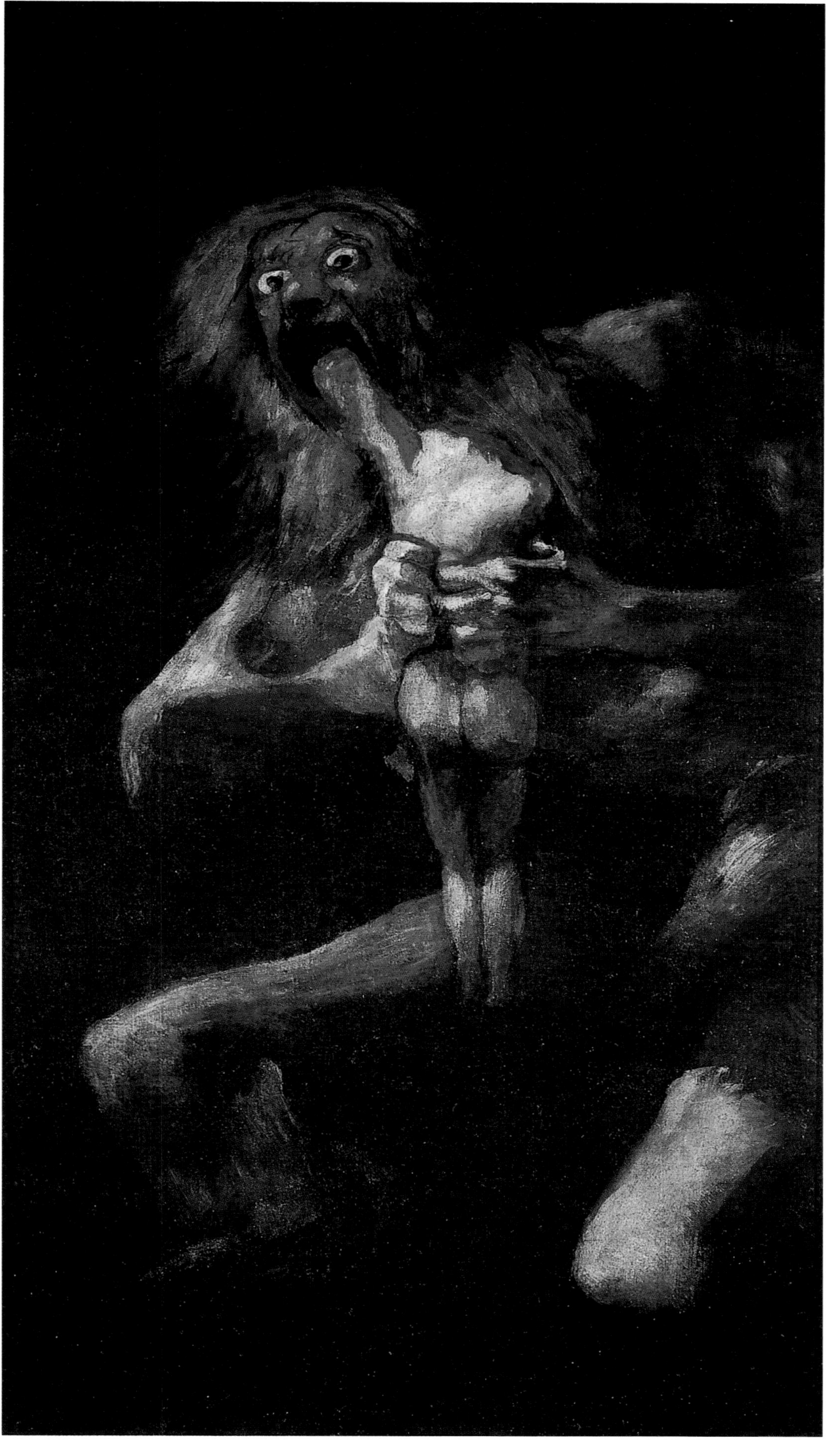

Francisco Goya
Saturn Devours His Children
1823, oil on plaster transferred to canvas
146 x 83 cm
Museo Nacional del Prado, Madrid

Oppressed by solitude and by the deafness that had isolated him from the world for years, and deeply troubled by the persecutions carried out by King Ferdinand VII's regime, Goya expressed his desperation in paintings with hallucinatory, visionary tones, taking on obsessive themes like this image of Saturn, the Lord of Olympus, who devoured his own children to prevent one of them from one day taking his throne. Goya painted the scene with such powerful deformation that it creates a terrifying effect, allusive to the fears of the unconscious, to the monstrousness of violence. This work belongs to the series of "Black Paintings" (1820–23)—so-called for the predominant dark colors and the strong chromatic contrasts—originally made for the walls of his country house, where he lived out the last years of his life in a state of exasperation.

WILLIAM BLAKE
Illustration from Dante's "Divine Comedy": Hell, Canto 5
post 1817, pen and watercolor on paper
36.8 x 52.2 cm
Museum and Art Gallery, Birmingham

This watercolor is Blake's powerful representation of the "hellish hurricane, never resting" that appears in the fifth canto of Dante's *Inferno*. The incessant wind that swirls the souls of sinners in endless torment is translated in a powerfully dynamic image. The famous lovers Paolo and Francesca are not presented as the sole protagonists of the scene but as part of the swirling circle of the those whose sin was lust. Their souls appear before Dante slightly separate from the vortex of the other damned, forever united by their love. The artist concentrates on the bright light and the sense of strong emotion in this supernatural vision.

THÉODORE GÉRICAULT
Delusion of Military Command
1822, oil on canvas
81 x 65 cm
Sammlung Oskar Reinhart, Winterthur

Géricault made portraits of various mentally ill patients for his friend Dr. Étienne-Jean Georget, psychiatrist at Paris's Salpêtrière hospital. These works, which present the physiognomic effects of mental illness, are located on the border between Romantic investigation of the soul and realistic clinical observation of the individual.

EUGÈNE DELACROIX
Insane Woman
1822, oil on canvas
41 x 33 cm
Musée des Beaux-Arts, Orléans

Painted at the same time that Géricault made his portraits of the mentally ill, this work by Delacroix is another expression of the Romantic interest in insanity. The artist used this portrait as the model for the face of the woman with the desperate expression who appears on the right of the *Scenes from the Massacre at Chios* (see page 130).

Constance Marie Charpentier
Melancholy
1801, oil on canvas
130 x 165 cm
Musée de Picardie, Amiens

After studying first with Gérard and then with David, Constance Marie Charpentier met with success in the decades around the turn of the century. In this canvas she takes on the theme of melancholy, a popular subject in the art of the Renaissance and repeated in the neoclassical period. Originally treated as an allegorical figure, melancholy later became an ornamental motif in funereal reliefs. The nineteenth century saw yet another version of melancholy as indicated by this canvas, in which Charpentier, as early as 1801, presented the new Romantic sensibility, directed at grasping the flavor of an indefinable emotion that blends languid meditation, forlornness, and subtle restlessness, well expressed both by the pose of the woman and by the large weeping willow that fills the background.

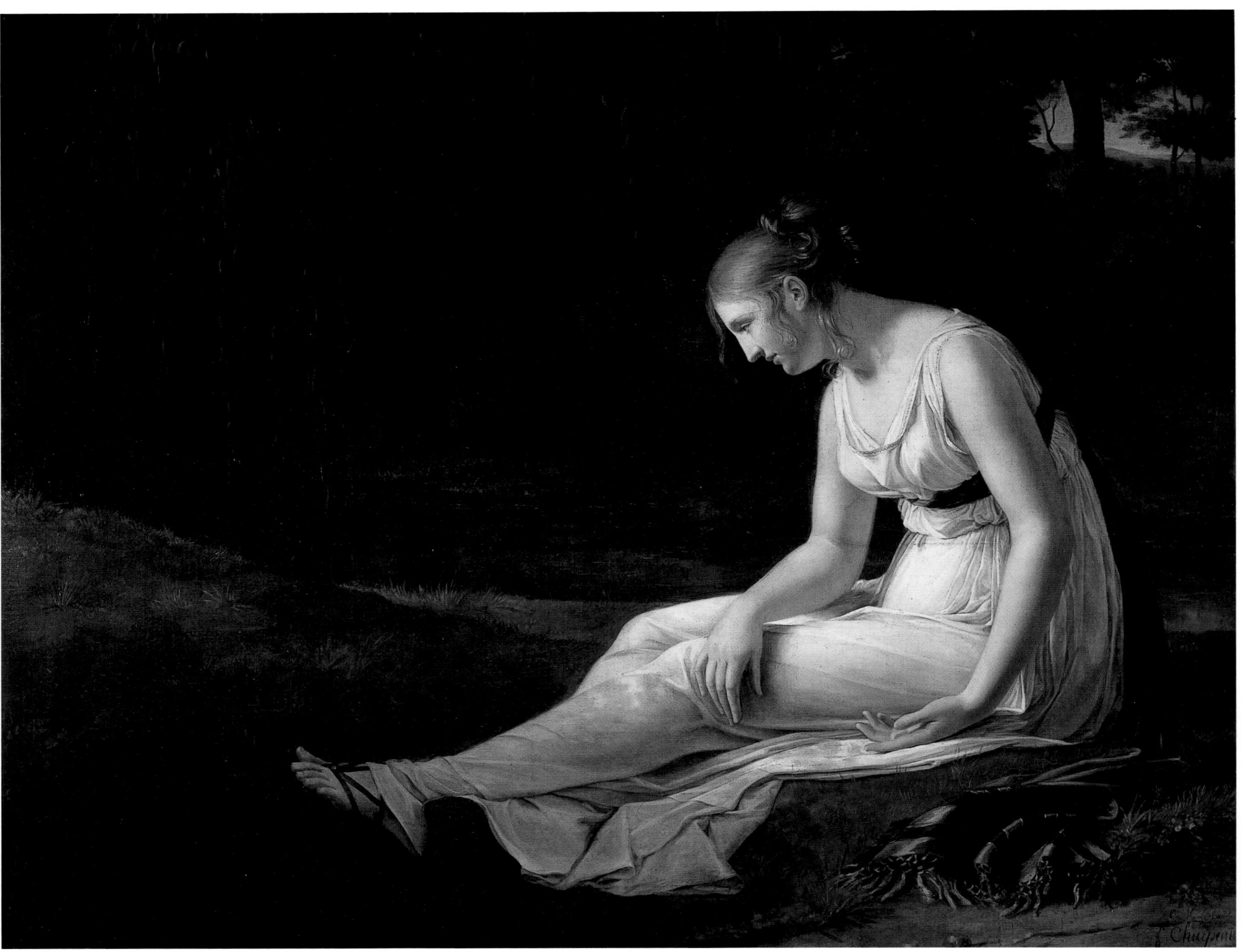

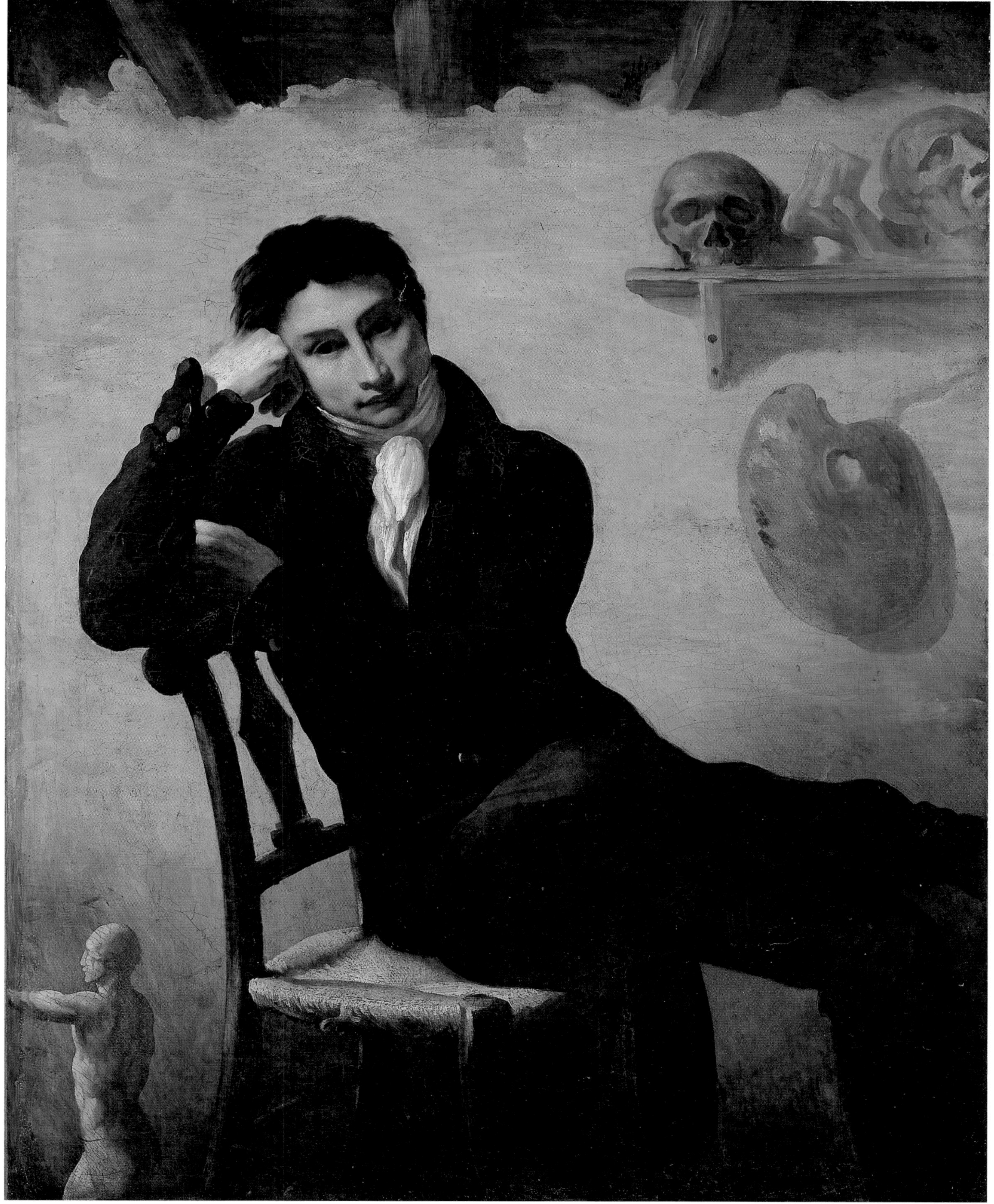

Théodore Géricault
The Artist in His Studio
1818, oil on canvas
146.5 x 101.5 cm
Musée du Louvre, Paris

The profession of artist is indicated by the palette hanging on the wall to the right and by the small sculpture standing at lower left; nothing else in the work, except its title, indicates the occupation of the seated young man. His languid pose and melancholy gaze delineate the profile of the "elect spirit" in which Friedrich Schlegel recognized the Romantic artist at the beginning of the nineteenth century. The sense of solitude and the simplicity of the setting also recall the bohemian atmosphere of the rooms in which young artists lived during their years of study, while Géricault uses the skulls on the shelf above, possibly plaster models, to send a symbolic message about the fleeting nature of life.

Jean-Auguste-Dominique Ingres
Oedipus and the Sphinx
1808, 1827,
oil on canvas
190 x 147 cm
Musée du Louvre, Paris

An example of the tragic destiny of man, Oedipus unknowingly killed his own father and then, becoming king of Thebes in his father's place by solving the riddle of the sphinx that terrorized the country, unknowingly married his mother. Midway between the heroic classicism of the nude and the sense of a universe ruled by the monstrous forces of pagan divinities, this painting reached its definitive version in 1827, when Ingres added the disturbing detail of the foot and bones at the lower left and the terrorized face on the figure to the right. Thus this canvas unites the image of the state of the soul from two different epochs: the impassive calm of Oedipus as he meditates on the riddle of the sphinx, the mysterious ambiguity of the monster, and the sense of transcending natural laws that already hangs over the protagonist.

Hippolyte Flandrin
Young Male Nude
1836, oil on canvas
98 x 124 cm
Musée du Louvre, Paris

The influence of Ingres, under whom Flandrin studied, can be seen in the formal perfection of this nude, but the skill with which the artist reveals the interior sense of the youth is entirely his own. The youth is curled up on himself as though to indicate closure from the external world, his profile forming an elegantly geometric line that stands out against the sea without, however, detaching him spiritually. There is no contemplation of nature in this scene, rather a concentration on the individual, who nevertheless feels a part of nature. The youth's nudity accentuates the sense of total immersion, a profound contact with the world surrounding him that permits him to concentrate on listening to his interior voice.

CASPAR DAVID FRIEDRICH
Monk by the Sea
1809, oil on canvas
110 x 171.5 cm
Nationalgalerie, Berlin

"A magnificent thing it is, in infinite solitude by the sea, under a sullen sky, to gaze off into a boundless watery waste. . . . Joined to this sentiment is the fact that one has wandered out there, that one must return, that one wants to cross over, that one cannot, that one lacks here all life and yet perceives the voices of life in the rushing tide, in the blowing wind, in the passage of clouds, in the solitary birds. . . . Nothing could be sadder or more discomfited than just this position in the world: the single spark of life in the vast realms of death, the lonely center in the lonely circle." So wrote the dramatist Heinrich von Kleist, who was among the first restless spirits of Romanticism, commenting on this painting in October 1810. Made as a pendant to the

Abbey in the Oaks (see page 268), the canvas enjoyed great success; both works were bought by King Frederick William III of Prussia at the suggestion of the young crown prince, later known as "the Romantic on the royal throne." It was during these same years that Friedrich was affirming his idea of art as the visual expression of emotions and states of mind, which here is made clear in all its evocative force. In the tiny and almost invisible figure of the monk (seen from behind, as are almost all the human figures in Friedrich's paintings) contemplating the vastness of infinite space, the artist succeeds in expressing the profound yearning of the individual to achieve harmony with the cosmos, the perception of the divine that drives man to immerse himself in the spirituality of nature, his sensing himself infinitely small in the universe.

FRANCESCO HAYEZ
A Melancholy Thought
1842, oil on canvas
138.6 x 104 cm
Private collection

The subject of melancholia fascinated Romantic philosophers, writers, and painters alike. Hayez presented meditations on the subject in several famous masterpieces. In this work he presents the more intense and sensual side, transforming the female personification of melancholy into a portrait that seems to concentrate on the subject's psychological condition. The young girl's fixed and empty stare contrasts with the joyful burst of color of the flowers, and her sense of anguish is reflected in the almost distorted carelessness of the position of her arms, on which the folds of her chemise and dress rest in disorder. The somewhat disheveled tone that results from her posture, joined to the rest of the image, with its unquestionable sensuality, concur in emphasizing a sense of disillusion and fragility, aspects of the Romantic concept of women in the society of the time.

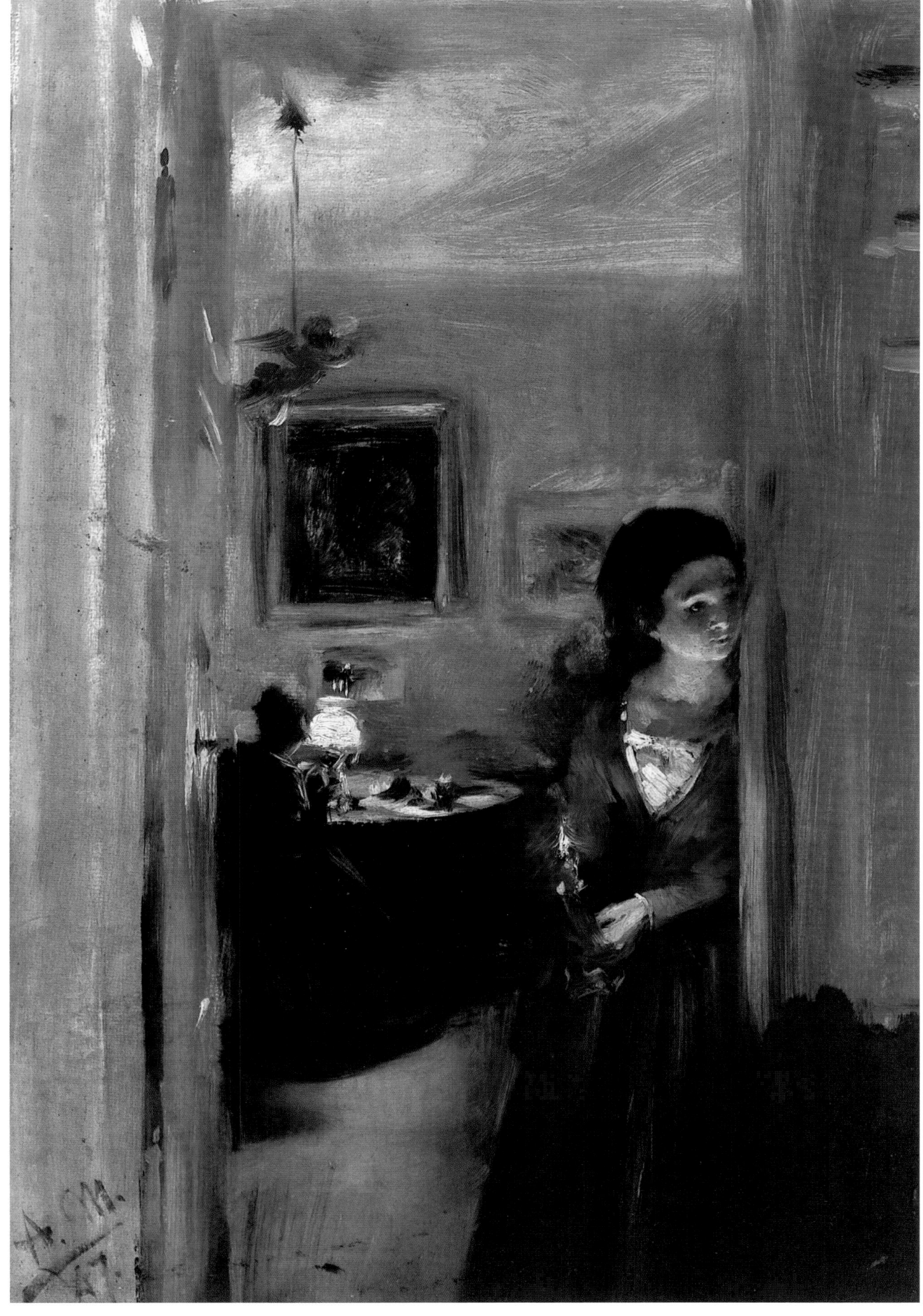

Adolf von Menzel
The Artist's Sister with a Candle
1847, oil on paper
46.1 x 31.6 cm
Neue Pinakothek, Munich

During the 1840s, the presentation of light in domestic interiors became one of the motifs that most interested this German artist, whose works were quite unrelated to the Biedermeier style popular with many of his colleagues. He was drawn to the study of atmospheres generated by artificial light in homes and by the psychological image of the figures immersed in them. In this case von Menzel portrays a family view with a room illuminated by various light sources, including an oil lamp on the table—at which a figure sits, seen from behind, sewing—as well as the candle held by his sister. The girl is not portrayed with sharp definition, but her position, with the flame illuminating her face from below, reveals an enigmatic state of mind composed of restless melancholy and an almost furtive dealing with unhappy thoughts.

Antoine Joseph Wiertz
La Belle Rosine (The Two Beauties)
1847, oil on canvas
140 x 100 cm
Musée d'Art Moderne, Brussels

A skeleton hangs from the ceiling, identified as "La belle Rosine" by writing on a slip of paper glued to the skull. Looking up into the skull's eyes is a beautiful young girl, half naked, flowers and peals wound in her hair, a ring shining from her finger. By means of this modern allegory Wiertz presents the ancient theme of death's triumph over life and beauty. The sensibility and style of the work locate it halfway between Romanticism and realism, and several decades after it was made it was very popular with the symbolist painters. Located in an artist's atelier, as indicated by the palette, easel, and plaster models located along the bottom of the painting, this image combines the unsettling language of the macabre *memento mori* with the presentation of a female body, the two aspects separated by a total absence of emotional involvement, by the state of absorbed meditation on the face of the girl.

Charles Gleyre
Evening: Lost Illusions
1843, oil on canvas
156 x 238 cm
Musée du Louvre, Paris

Seated on the quay, a man watches a ship move off into the golden light of sunset bearing with it his youth, his dreams, the joys of companionship. Gleyre here presents with a poetic richness the theme of solitude and the fleeting nature of life, which so often inspired the Romantic imagination. In conceiving this work Gleyre may have drawn on a personal experience: eight years earlier he had fallen into a kind of dreamy hallucination while seated on the banks of the Nile. The painting has a singular evocative power that thrilled the French public, along with such intellectuals as Baudelaire.

In 1756, Edmund Burke, the Anglo-Irish political writer and statesman, published his *Philosophical Enquiry into the Origin of Our Ideas of the Sublime and Beautiful*, destined to lay the basis for one of the most spectacular aspects of Romantic painting. In this work Burke examined the theories and concepts related to the sublime and the beautiful in relationship to the emotions provoked in the spectator: "Whatever is fitted in any sort to excite the ideas of pain, and danger, that is to say, whatever is in any sort terrible, or is conversant about terrible objects, or operates in a manner analogous to terror, is a source of the Sublime; that is, it is capable of producing the strongest emotions which the mind is capable of feeling." Nature above all possessed the power to produce this sense of the sublime. Sometimes incommensurable in its vastness, fearsome in its awesome power, almost annihilating man himself, nature can awaken the sensation of the sublime by manifesting its overwhelming greatness. The direct opposite of this was beauty, founded on just proportions and pleasant harmonies that awaken completely different passions. The sense of the sublime could be unleashed by witnessing a terrifying scene caused by nature even from a distance, thus even from a position of tranquility. The sublime as an aesthetic notion was at the center of heated debates during the second half of the eighteenth century. From the original sense of a very deep emotion, the step was taken to applying the term to the powerful response caused by a work of art. In 1793 Jacques-Louis David wrote that "it is not only with the enchantment of the eyes that great works of art reach their end; they reach it by penetrating the soul, by impressing on the spirit a profound impression similar to reality." Thus was the concept of the sublime added to Romantic thinking and Romantic passions; it came to be part of the collection of ideas concerning the relationship between the soul and nature, between painting and inner experience, that the Romantics had inherited from the preceding century, but it was augmented by the concept that art too could be a vehicle of sublime sensations. With Caspar David Friedrich, one of the century's masters of landscape painting, the antithesis between the beautiful and the sublime came to an end, reduced to a single concept: "You must move toward the sublime and the magnificent if you want to reach the beautiful." For Friedrich the sublime was not unleashed by the perception of a hostile and awesome nature, by the agitation caused by a powerful cataclysm, but resulted instead from the intimate interpenetration of man with nature itself, from the capacity to identify oneself with the infinite greatness, thus involving a diminished sense of oneself. To sense the vastness of space, the sense of the infinite produced by a limitless horizon: this, to Friedrich, was to experience the sublime, or better, following the words of Immanuel Kant, to experience "That which is absolutely great, that which is great beyond all comparison" and which man in his finiteness cannot ever equal. Kant continued with examples of such natural phenomena as "hurricanes leaving desolation in their track, the boundless ocean rising with rebellious force," and other events that "reduce our power to resist such force to an insignificant smallness." Only rarely in Friedrich is the sublime achieved by way of a disastrous spectacle; rather, it is combined with the sense of the divine that the artist achieves by evoking the infinite and listening to its spirit: "Preserve a pure, childlike sensibility and follow without question your own inner voice, for it is the divine in us, and does not lead us astray." *The Sea of Ice* confronts the viewer with the sublime power of an inviolate and untouched nature—almost vindictive when challenged by humans—but in many other canvases Friedrich sought to penetrate the

Caspar David Friedrich, *Moon Rising Over the Sea*, 1820, oil on canvas, 55 x 71 cm; Nationalgalerie, Berlin

Francis Danby, *Sunset at Sea after a Storm*, 1824, oil on canvas, 89.6 x 142.9 cm; Museum and Art Gallery, Bristol

The sublime

James Ward, *Gordale Scar*, 1813, oil on canvas, 76.8 x 101.9 cm; Art Gallery and Museum, Bradford

infinite vastness of landscapes to reveal a sacred silence. This happens in his *Wanderer on the Sea of Fog*, with its figure of a solitary wanderer, a figure dear to Romantic culture that found echo in the poetry of William Wordsworth (*The Prelude*, 1805) and the paintings of Carl Gustav Carus (see page 235). Other painters created images expressing similar experiences. There were the English artists Francis Danby and James Ward; the latter in 1813 portrayed *Gordale Scar*, a large and spectacular crevice in the rocks in Yorkshire. The northern European artists who came in contact with Friedrich in Dresden, such as the Norwegian Johan Christian Dahl, were affected by his passions but failed to match his lyricism, associating the concept of the sublime more often with such traditional scenes as storms and heavy seas. In France and England, the image of the cataclysm was the predominant expression of the sublime. The sublime made its appearance in American painting thanks to the fertile imagination of Thomas Cole, who succeeded in transforming the limitless vastness of American landscapes into visions of overwhelming beauty, probably refashioning them in the light of the masterpieces of the English artist John Martin. It was Martin, along with William Turner, to represent the most fascinating heights of painting of the sublime in the United Kingdom: frightening storms that wipe away all they encounter are a recurrent theme in Turner, from *Fall of an Avalanche in the Grisons* (1810) to *Snow Storm: Hannibal and His Army Crossing the Alps* (1812), up to the later *Snow Storm—Steam-Boat off a Harbour's Mouth Making Signals in Shallow Water* (1842; Tate Gallery, London), the result of a personal experience of Turner's, who had witnessed a snow storm while lashed to the mast of a ship for four hours in order to observe it. Even more spectacular and scenographic were the paintings of terrible natural catastrophes made by John Martin and often rendered as apocalyptic visions, most especially *The Great Day of His Wrath* (see page 191), the work that ended his extraordinary career. In France, Girodet presented an early and extraordinary example of the sublime in his *Scene of the Deluge* of circa 1806; other expressions of the sublime in France show up in narrations of shipwrecks, paintings that were based on contemporary events, such as Eugène Isabey's *Fire Aboard the "Austria."* More dramatic expressions of the sublime appear in the endless expanses of ice in the Arctic regions, seen around 1840 by the adventurous François-Auguste Biard as part of an expedition to the North Pole. The astonishment of those never-before-seen landscapes was presented as something both ineffable and disturbing.

John Mallord William Turner, *The Fall of an Avalanche in the Grisons*, 1810, oil on canvas, 90 x 120 cm; Tate Gallery, London

Caspar David Friedrich
Wanderer on the Sea of Fog
1818, oil on canvas
94.8 x 74.8 cm
Kunsthalle, Hamburg

A man, seen from behind, stands atop a rocky crag and contemplates the peaks of mountains immersed in fog. Solitary, he looks off toward a horizon lost in the distance among clouds, thus experiencing the mystery of the infinite. It is the kind of panorama that allows every wanderer to capture the sublime grandeur of nature and to feel it invade his soul. This painting, ranked among Friedrich's most important works, reflects the Romantic concept of nature understood as a place for the individual to achieve a spiritual experience. The painting, which may well have originally commemorated a death, can also be taken as a symbolic representation of the overcoming of earthly life and the elevation of the spirit to God.

Caspar David Friedrich
Chalk Cliffs at Rügen
1818, oil on canvas
90 x 70 cm
Museum Oskar Reinhart, Winterthur

In January 1818 Friedrich married Caroline Bommer, and Rügen, an island in the Baltic Sea off the German coast, was a stop on their honeymoon. The sea is here framed by the wild profile of the cliffs, which descend straight downward, almost creating a sense of dizziness. Friedrich undoubtedly attributed allegorical roles to the three figures, perhaps allusions to the three theological virtues (Faith, Hope, and Charity) on the basis of the colors of their clothes (blue, green, and red) or as aspects of human life symbolized by their gestures or the directions of their gazes. The protagonist of the painting is the relationship between humans and the spectacular grandeur of nature, the artist's astonishment in front of the enchantment of the sea, the horizon lost in the distance, the sense of the sublime that it inspires.

Caspar David Friedrich
Abbey in the Oaks
1810, oil on canvas
110.4 x 171 cm
Nationalgalerie, Berlin

This work was created as a pendant to *Monk by the Sea* (see pages 258–59), but Friedrich had conceived it several years earlier, as indicated by a drawing he made showing his own funeral. In fact, that funeral is the allegorical center around which this composition wheels, with monks busy at a burial in the center. The pessimistic tone connected to that scene finds its response in the morning light that pervades the canvas, symbolic of the eternal life to which the artist turns, animated by a faith in God that sometimes put him in opposition to the Church as an institution. Indeed, the monumental ruin of the abbey (perhaps the remains of the church of Eldena) may refer to that lack of confidence in things ecclesiastical. Thanks to the success of the two canvases, Friedrich was made a member of the Berlin Academy in November 1810.

Giovanni Battista De Gubernatis
Stormy Landscape with Castle with Four Towers and Large Mullioned Window above the Door
1803, watercolor on paper
46 x 59 cm
Galleria Civica d'Arte Moderna e Contemporanea, Turin

The sublime and the picturesque, the two central concepts of the Romantic vision, blend in this appealing view. The lightning flashes that illuminate the stormy landscape achieve an effect of almost unreal light, perfectly in keeping with the atmosphere of suspense. The work is thus related to the literary genre of the Gothic romance, the popularity of which had begun spreading across Europe at the beginning of the century and in which storms and medieval castles were inevitable elements. In 1803, the year of this painting, De Gubernatis gave a series of lectures at the Turin Art Academy on the concept of the beautiful in the picturesque, an indication that he was particularly up to date in the debates related to the medieval revival. This watercolor may be related to a sketch for a theatrical setting, which would explain the descriptive tone of its title.

Caspar David Friedrich
The Sea of Ice
1824, oil on canvas
96.7 x 126.9 cm
Kunsthalle, Hamburg

In search of the Northwest Passage, the English explorer William Edward Parry led an expedition to the North Pole (1819–20). Two ships were involved, the *Hecla* and the *Griper*. The undertaking ended in a dramatic shipwreck in the Arctic seas, an event that became well known all across Europe. Friedrich drew on the tragedy to create an extraordinary painting, in which he visualized not only the insurmountable power of nature but also the sacredness of such untouched regions as the Arctic, the borders of which humans were not supposed to cross. This painting is also known by another

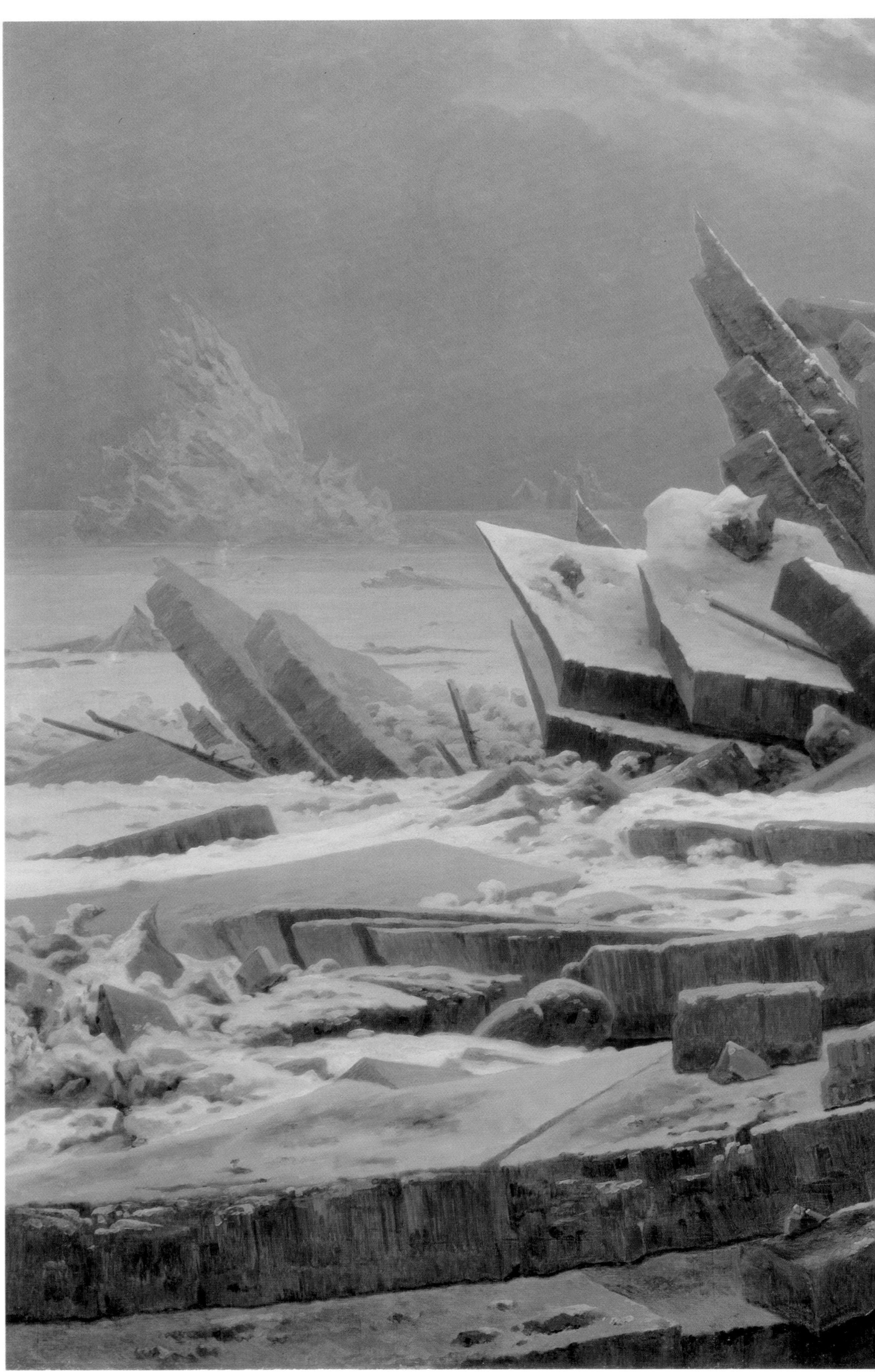

title, *The Wreck of Hope*, which also expresses the symbolic value the painter gave the image. The stern of the sunken ship, visible to the far right, is only a marginal insert, the true protagonist of the painting being the unexplored, primordial, and thus sacred landscape, violated by the curiosity of man. Behind the foreground blocks of broken and jagged ice extends an endless icy sea engulfed in silence, beyond all measurements of space or time, a metaphor for the eternity of God. And it was precisely in that sense of immensity that Friedrich perceived the sublime, in the limitless enormity of nature and its power to make all human attempts to dominate or resist it insignificant.

Caspar David Friedrich
Large Enclosure
1832, oil on canvas
73.5 x 102.5 cm
Gemäldegalerie, Dresden

In this canvas Friedrich presents the large reserve of Ostra, located to the northwest of Dresden near the confluence of the Weisseritz and Elbe rivers. The broad layout conveys a sense of large distances, an effect the artist believed necessary in landscape paintings. In 1830, only two years before making this canvas, he had written observations on the criteria of certain modern landscapists, noting that "what in nature is separated by

great distances is suffocated in paintings in a narrow space, saturating the gaze of the spectator and giving him a negative and disturbing impression. It is the water that gets the worst of this, with the sea reduced to a puddle." He added that the painter should "present nature as it is, simple, noble, and large." This painting does exactly that. The sensation of vastness is amplified: the beautiful gradations in the clouds stand out against the sunset sky, reflecting the areas of the land that have been invaded by water with a kind of visual symmetry.

Caspar David Friedrich
Seashore in Moonlight
1836, oil on canvas
134 x 169 cm
Kunsthalle, Hamburg

The sun setting on the sea is a very common motif in Friedrich's repertory, an image he created in a variety of versions. This canvas of 1836, also known by the title *The Moon Behind Clouds on the Shore of the Sea,* is one of the last he made, as confirmed by his friend Carl Gustav Carus, who in November of the next year proposed that the Dresden gallery buy it since it was the artist's last work. Although still alive, Friedrich had suffered a stroke and was in such precarious health that he quit making drawings and watercolors. This large work represents a dramatically broad view of a beautiful cloud formation in

movement over the sea, with the light of the moon filtering through the clouds. The result is a work of spectacular and imposing impact between the sky and the sea, with the involvement of the coastline, its outline made jagged by the irregular surface of the rocks. The vision fixed to the canvas by Friedrich succeeds in relating the overwhelming power of nature even in its more benign manifestations; the vastness of the sky and the sea seem to join in drawing the viewer's gaze outward to the infinite. Inside this view the ships constitute fixed points that further indicate the dramatic movement of the clouds, in turn highlighted by the moonlight, as though to emphasize that the normal events of human activity take place within the eternal vastness of space.

Giuseppe Pietro Bagetti
The Sacra of San Michele
circa 1821–28, watercolor on paperboard
65 x 99 cm
Palazzo Reale, Turin

The majestic architectural complex of the ancient abbey of San Michele della Chiusa, better known as the Sacra of San Michele, stands atop a mountain near Turin; between the end of the eighteenth century and the early nineteenth, it attracted the attention of scholars and medievalists, but it soon became a favorite stop on Romantic itineraries. Bagetti was an expert topographer as well as a landscape painter, but in making this view he interpreted the scene not with the analytical eye of the expert observer, but also in light of the new sensibility that was inspiring efforts to reproduce atmospheric disturbances in order to create views of nature capable of unleashing the sensation of the sublime. In an unreal light that gives it the sense of being a reflection, the Sacra stands out sharply against a mysterious background that cannot be identified as natural sky, while the mountain itself assumes impressive tones that intimidate the observer, provoking a new emotion.

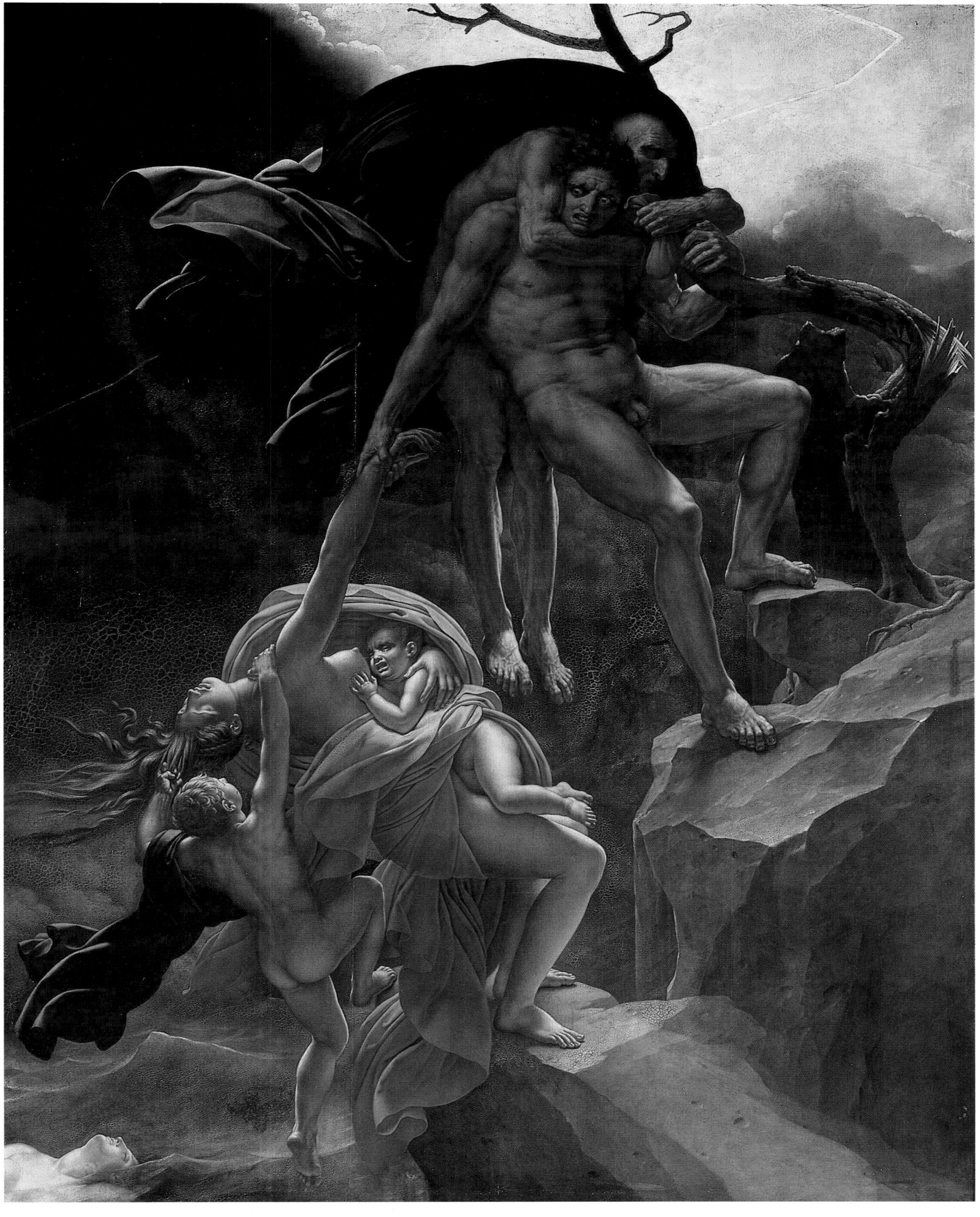

ANNE-LOUIS GIRODET-TRIOSON
Scene of the Deluge
circa 1806,
oil on canvas
61 x 47 cm
Musée Magnin, Dijon

This painting is a small-format copy of the large canvas, today in the Louvre, that appeared at the Salon of 1806. The work's complete title was *Scene of the Deluge: A Family about to Be Swallowed by the Storm*. Girodet hastened to add that the subject of the painting was not the biblical flood but a scene with universal application, a calamity that strikes the earth, canceling the destinies of humans and confronting the individual with a life-or-death choice. The man struggling to cling to the land must decide whether to save his elderly father on his back or his children, who are clinging to his wife, herself about to succumb to the force of the storm. Girodet presents the intimate drama of the man divided between past and future in the most spectacular and symbolic of forms, that which the Romantics recognized as the expression of the sublime: the unleashed fury of nature, to which the individual cannot resist but that awakens strong emotions in the soul, including terror and fright.

JOSEPH MALLORD WILLIAM TURNER
Snow Storm: Hannibal and His Army Crossing the Alps
1812, oil on canvas
146 x 237.5 cm
Tate Gallery, London

The official subject of this canvas is the crossing of the Alps by Hannibal in 218 B.C. with a large army, including thirty-seven elephants. The exploit had been emulated in 1800 by Napoleon, who boasted of having followed in the footsteps of the great commander. The imminent campaign in Russia, which in 1812 presaged further expansion of the French Empire in Europe, drove Turner to question the Napoleonic rhetoric of heroism. In this painting the Carthaginian commander—but the thought runs immediately to Napoleon—having challenged nature, is punished by a violent snow storm that strikes his army. The power of man is annihilated and made useless, soldiers and elephants hardly distinguishable in the swirling vortex of the storm, crushed beneath a sky that seems to collapse on top of them, hurling them into obscurity.

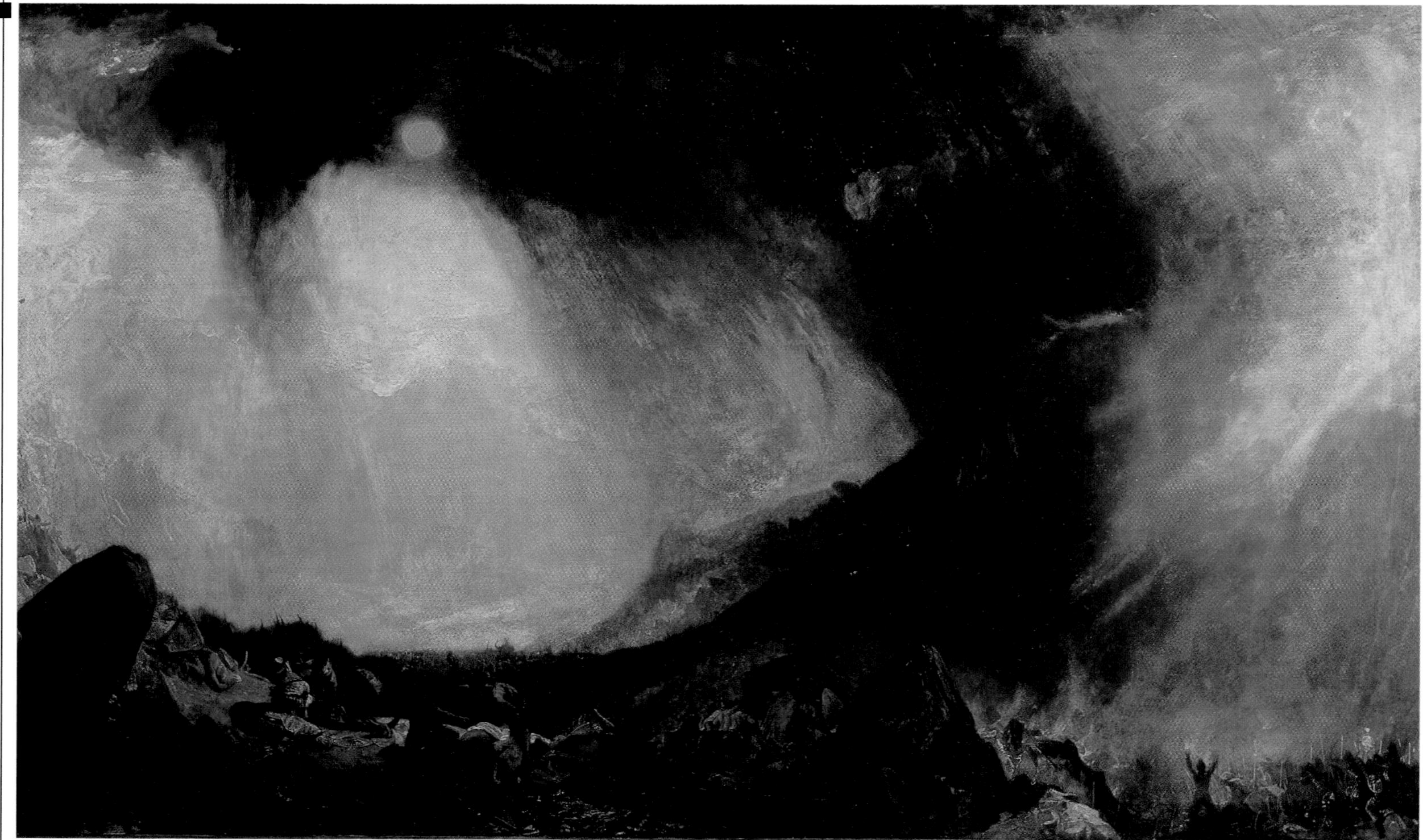

JEAN-BRUNO GASSIES
Scottish Landscape
1826, oil on canvas
60 x 78 cm
Musée Rolin, Autun

A man advances in a blast of wind, around him gray rocks and clouds and more and more mountains to the limits of sight. His figure is small, almost insignificant, in comparison to the vastness of the landscape, one of those austere and imposing places dominated by an uncontested nature.

JOHN KNOX
Loch Lomond
1835, oil on canvas
62.2 x 157.5 cm
Art Gallery, Glasgow

Scotland's misty landscapes were rendered even more alluring by the novels of Sir Walter Scott; Loch Lomond inspired different reactions in different artists, some portraying its picturesque aspects, some fascinated by its mysterious vastness, which seemed to swallow up visitors.

John Martin
The Bard
1817, oil on canvas
127 x 101.5 cm
Yale Center for British Art, New Haven

Emblematic figure in the Romantic movement in Britain, the bard was the ancient poet of the Celtic Welsh, the medieval people oppressed by King Edward III. Martin draws on that long-ago time to create a dramatic vision centered on the solemnity of the landscape and the myth of the last man, the sole survivor of a calamity. The bard, fleeing the army that winds its way along the banks of the river, has reached the edge of a cliff; his flapping cloak reinforces his heroic gesture of victory, spiritually reflected in the immense height of the mountains, the peaks of which seem to rise beyond the sky. Every element of the landscape communicates a sense of majesty. In this case the sublime is presented not by a terrible catastrophe but by the grandeur of a nature that can offer shelter and salvation to a human in flight from evil.

Johan Christian Dahl
Morning after a Stormy Night
1819, oil on canvas
74.5 x 105.6 cm
Neue Pinakothek, Munich

Son of a Norwegian fisherman, Dahl was a dedicated painter of marine scenes. He moved to Dresden in 1818 and met Friedrich, the two of them becoming close friends. It was certainly because of him that Dahl was drawn to scenes like this, in which he displayed extraordinary skill in bringing out the sublime power of the waves and the wind, which dominate this view. The tragedy of the shipwreck is revealed by the ship swallowed by the waves but most of all by the man seated on the rocks with his dog: tiny in proportion to the gigantic masses above him, the sailor emphasizes the desperate impotence of man in the face of the power of the sea, the protagonist of this painting, with the waves of the sea still swirling.

THOMAS COLE
Expulsion:
Moon and Firelight
1828, oil on canvas
91.3 x 121.9 cm
Museo Thyssen-Bornemisza, Madrid

The title refers to the expulsion of Adam and Eve from Eden, a subject later presented by Cole in another canvas (Museum of Fine Arts, Boston) of which this was a first compositional stage, although it achieves a high level of completion and offers a symbolic version of the sublime. Holding true to his preferred genre, Cole presents the sacred subject but gives the landscape a preponderant role. In fact, it has an exclusive role in this work, since every trace of the biblical narration has been eliminated to give space to the sense of abandonment and terror unleashed as divine punishment. The view of daylight at the upper right may be a faint hint of the distant, forever-lost Paradise, from which, by passing through the blazing fire of sin and rage, one reaches the mouth of the cave and the rock bridge over the abyss. Going farther the sense of desolation increases, with the shadows that fall on the sea offering a view of the moon and the spectral branches of a dead tree that burst from a terrain marked by blood to the left.

François-Auguste Biard
Madgalene Bay: View from the Peninsula of the Tombs to the North of Spitzbergen; Effect of Aurora Borealis
1841, oil on canvas
130 x 163 cm
Musée du Louvre, Paris

In 1839 Biard took part, together with his fiancée, Léonie d'Aunet, in an expedition to the North Pole. They were enormously moved by the dramatic vistas, such as the spectacle, at once magical and sinister, presented by the bay, scattered with the bones of seals and walruses left by fishermen; an unreal landscape, it troubled their minds, awakening sensations beyond words.

Eugène Isabey
Fire Aboard the "Austria"
1858, oil on canvas
242 x 430 cm
Musée des Beaux-Arts, Bordeaux

The wreck of the *Austria* took place in the middle of the Atlantic on September 23, 1858; almost five hundred people died, the survivors numbering only a few dozen. Isabey presents the last moments in an apocalyptic image in which the cold, unnatural light reinforces the violence of the storm and leads the viewer to a sense of the sublime.

On October 23, 1821, John Constable wrote to a friend: "I have not been idle, and have made more particular and general study than I have ever done in the summer. But I am most anxious to get into my London painting room, for I do not consider myself at work without I am before a six foot canvas. I have done a good deal of skying. I am determined to conquer all difficulties, and that most arduous one amongst the rest." The artist, one of the leading English exponents of Romantic landscape painting, rejected the traditional models of "finished" painting, with the application of paint and forms designed to create a finished look, preferring an immediate vision of nature. Constable was particularly passionate about the rendering of atmospheric effects, most of all clouds and sky. During the preceding century the English had given much space to landscapes, most of all in keeping with the new theories of the sublime and the picturesque, but

The presentation

with the nineteenth century a new approach began to take shape, based on the criteria of scientific investigation. This shows up in Constable himself, who, to give one example, painted the trunk of a tree with such precision that today it seems, at first glance, to be a photograph (*Study of the Trunk of an Elm*, 1820–23; Victoria and Albert Museum, London).

Caspar David Friedrich, *Oak Tree in the Snow,* 1829, oil on canvas, 71 x 48 cm; Nationalgalerie, Berlin

The realistic detail with which he portrayed the English countryside fascinated the French, critics and public alike, when his works were shown in France for the first time, at the famous Salon of 1824. Stendhal was enchanted by the sense of "verity" in the paintings, which however did not prevent the magic of the light from standing out forcefully, revealing the artist's Romantic sensibility. No longer conceived in conventional or idealized terms, landscape painting absorbed one by one the various intonations of Romanticism, and it took to heart the opinions on nature of Friedrich von Schiller, who stated in 1794, "We want the art of landscape to have the same effect on us as music," and it was no coincidence that the painters of the "sublime" turned to the landscape for their masterpieces. In his choice of views and panoramas Caspar David Friedrich did not look for originality, but he used such scenes to transmit the profound sense of the divine that he saw in the sea, the sky, the large open and uninhabited spaces. For him, "the role of the artist does not consist in the faithful representation of the sky, water, rocks, and trees; his soul and his sensibility must be reflected in nature." He also observed that "If the painter knows only how to imitate dead nature, or more precisely, can produce only a dead imitation of nature, then he is little more than a trained ape." The Romantic landscape was also allegorical and fantastic, as in Turner's canvases and watercolors, which draw the viewer into fascinating vortexes and swirling atmospheres with such heightened luminosity that the real landscape is overcome. His interpretations of nature were unmistakably his own, his vision completely individual, yet it resounded in the works of Friedrich and his German followers, whose works were in part a response to that part of Europe that approved of progressive urbanization. The enthusiasm for the majestic landscape, for the vastness of boundless horizons, and for the powerful energy of a nature that was still wild and uncontaminated also resounds in the stupendous views of the American landscapes made by the members of the Hudson River School, founded in the 1820s by Thomas Cole. The opposite of

Frederic Edwin Church, *Twilight in the Wilderness,* 1860, oil on canvas, 101.6 x 162.6 cm; Art Museum, Cleveland

of the landscape

such visions still survived in certain environments that clung to landscapes with an eighteenth-century layout, but at the dawn of the new century even such views began taking on a new warmth. As early as the opening decades of the nineteenth century the views of the Roman countryside or ruins of the city created by foreign painters in Rome were showing a greater touch of vitality, an attention to the realities of daily life or inserts of sentimental taste that reflected the change that was underway. In Italy too the turn was made toward a new sensibility, and the opening to the mystery and enchantment of solitary nature slowly began to take effect. This can be seen in the works of Giuseppe Pietro Bagetti, a famous topographer who presented visions that were completely extraneous to his technical skills, and it also shows up in such artists as the Neapolitan Gabriele Smargiassi, who slowly developed a sentimental naturalism, and the Venetian Ippolito Caffi, who began with a matrix still based on the Canaletto style to reach a taste for fascinating nocturnes, arriving at an almost concise style with which he transformed numerous views of Venice into visual sensations, opening Italian landscape painting to the popular Oriental horizons, such as those he made during trips to Egypt and the countries of North Africa. Massimo D'Azeglio and Carlo and Giuseppe Canella also participated in the creation of the Italian Romantic landscape. D'Azeglio created the genre of the "historiated landscape," an intellectual blend of historical romance and landscape setting; Canella moved from the panoramic-style landscape of eighteenth-century tradition toward the assimilation of the most sentimental aspects of contemporary art as expressed in literary culture. Certain works by other Italian artists reveal a more "touristy" vein, such as the mosaic table made by Michelangelo Barberi for Grand Duke Alexander of Russia, son of Czar Nicholas I, in 1839. An important step in the evolution of the genre was taken in France in the 1830s. During the time when the practice and study of landscape painting still drew artists from every part of Europe to Italy, a group of Parisian painters went instead to the nearby forest of Fontainebleau, beginning the so-called Barbizon School, named for a meeting place and site for *en plein air* painting used by Théodore Rousseau and some of his friends, including Charles-François Daubigny, Constant Troyon, and Alexandre Decamps. The style of painting developed in these outdoor excursions was to be the departure point for realism, breaking away from the academic landscape painting still imposed by the French schools and directed toward a vision more in keeping with the point of view of the English and German Romantics. The *barbizonniers*, as the members of the group came to be called, immersed themselves in the great silences of nature, finding there a sort of condition of ideal life and rediscovering the poetry of the individual in close contact with it. For decades they profited from this pictorial research, gradually moving the objective from the grandiosity of trees and forests to an increasingly evocative study of life, of *en plein air* atmospheric renderings, which laid the basis for the "realistic" landscape painting that was the prelude to Impressionism.

Michelangelo Barberi, *Chronological Rome Table,* 1839, table in mosaic of colored enamel, diameter 109 cm; Hermitage, St. Petersburg

Gabriele Smargiassi, *Landscape of Sorrento with Shepherds and Flocks,* 1839, oil on canvas; Palazzo Reale, Naples

Hendrik Voogd
Italian Landscape with Pines
1807, oil on canvas
101.5 x 138.5 cm
Rijksmuseum, Amsterdam

Among the many artists who went to Italy from all over Europe at the end of the eighteenth century was the Dutchman Hendrik Voogd, who arrived in Rome in 1788 and spent the rest of his life there. By the time of this painting he had assimilated the style of such seventeenth-century landscape artists as Claude Lorrain, which he had studied for years, working out a style that already revealed a Romantic sensibility, in particular in the sentimental character that bursts from the luministic rendering. The strong effect of backlighting highlights the majesty of the pines and sweetly shades the field without diminishing the importance of the human figures, although their presence in the scene is of secondary importance.

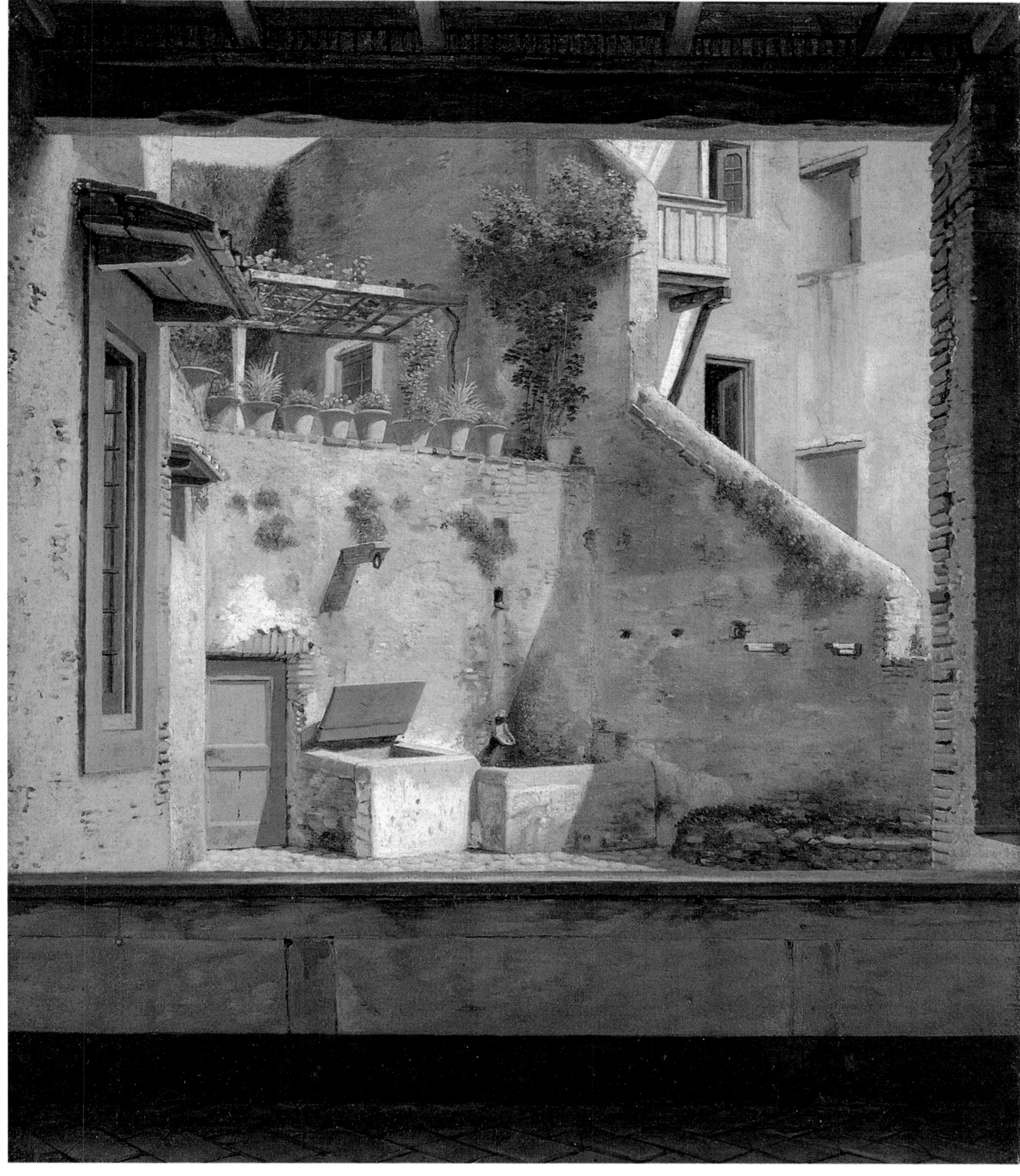

C. W. Eckersberg
Roman Courtyard
circa 1814,
oil on canvas
33.5 x 27.5 cm
Kunstmuseum, Ribe

A Danish artist born in 1783, Eckersberg was in Rome from 1813 to 1816, where he learned highly important lessons about landscape painting that he then exported to Copenhagen, where there was not yet a specific teaching post in the discipline of landscape painting. This canvas reflects the typical city view taken in its natural simplicity, free of any historical or artistic motivations, but essentially meaningful in being a view of daily life. The simplicity of the objects that compose the whole almost anticipates the type of extemporaneous view that was to characterize the great step toward realism.

Antoine-Félix Boisselier
View of Lake Nemi
1811, oil on paper applied to canvas
32.5 x 48 cm
Phillips Collection, Washington, D.C.

Boisselier was not yet twenty when he came to Rome to visit his brother Félix, who was studying at the Villa Medici. The young painter made this fascinating view of one of the regular stops on the excursions outside the city taken by landscape artists, both local and foreign: Lake Nemi, located in the Latium hills to the south of Rome. The work is painted on paper like an *en plein air* study from life, but its execution is extremely refined; Boisselier pauses on each detail of the landscape, which is animated by the presence of the boat and by the smoke from a fire in the distance. The trees and bushes in the foreground are rendered with subtle precision, such that the water and hills can be made out between the leafy branches. The protagonist of the painting, however, is the wonderful warm light, the golden sky, and the pink hues on the hillsides, which give the scene a profound sense of emotional and sentimental involvement.

CASPAR DAVID FRIEDRICH
The Temple of Juno at Agrigento
1830, oil on canvas
52 x 72 cm
Museum für Kunst und Kulturgeschichte, Dortmund

Isolated from the emptiness that surrounds its base, almost as though it rose above an enormous stage, this temple dominates a solitary valley immersed in total silence. Looking down on this ancient sacred place is a distant moon, a presence that for Friedrich was symbolic of Christianity.

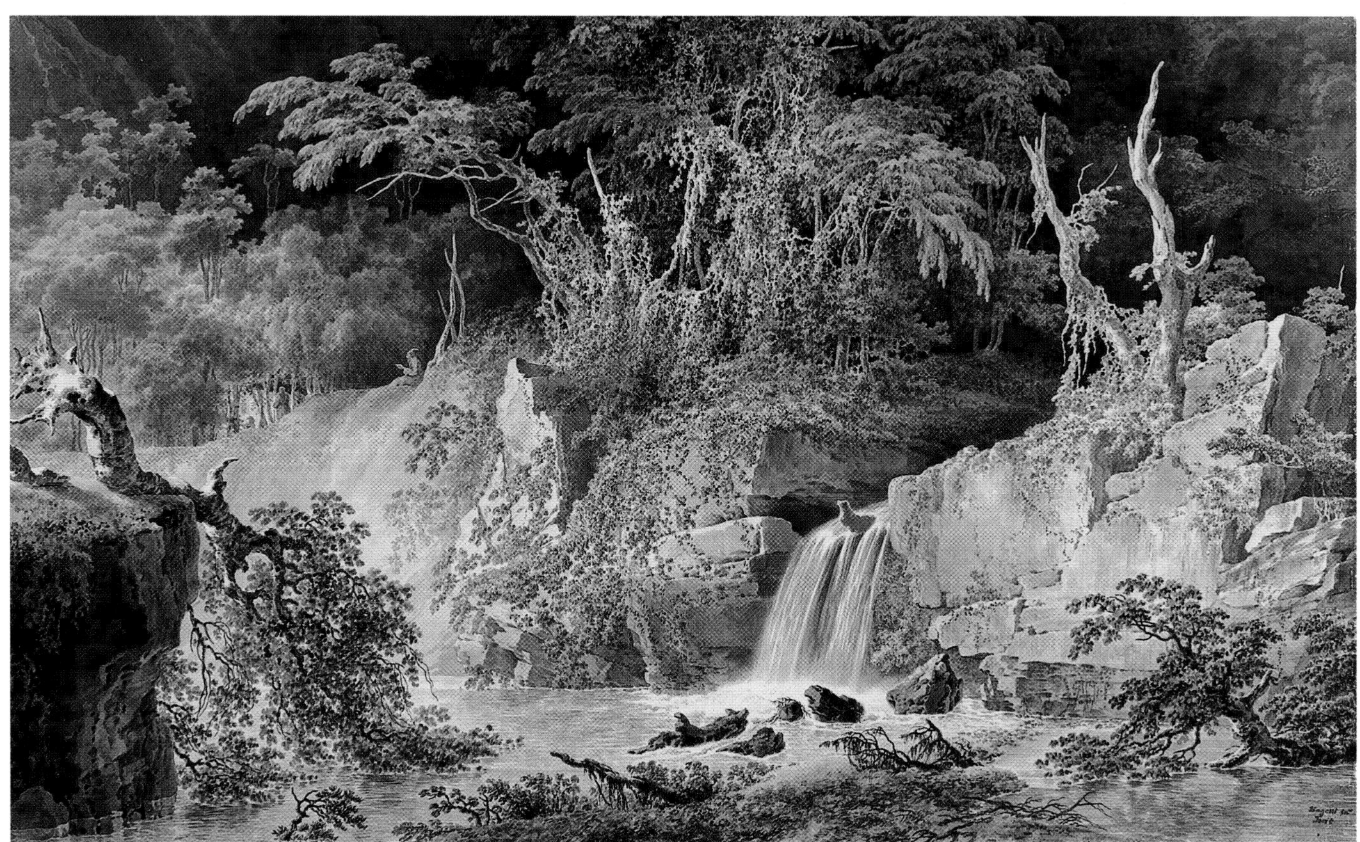

GIUSEPPE PIETRO BAGETTI
Landscape with Waterfall (Woodland with Monk)
circa 1815,
India ink and watercolor on paper applied to paperboard
58.2 x 90.2 cm
Galleria Civica d'Arte Moderna e Contemporanea, Turin

A celebrated topographer, Bagetti portrayed this still-unspoiled area of woodland with the analytical attention he was known for. The uprooted tree to the left and the effect of frost that makes the plants and bushes opalescent give the site a tone of mystery and wildness.

NIKANOR CHERNESTOV
In the Colosseum
1840, oil on canvas
29.5 x 22.5 cm
Russian State Museum, St. Petersburg

This view of the Colosseum by the Russian painter Chernetsov is in some ways similar to many others, but it differs by the sense of quiet emotion that pervades it. It is the figure of the man standing to the side, the artist's inseparable brother, Grigory, that provides the catalyzing function, expressing and communicating, in his absorbed gaze toward the arches, the power of the magical silence of the place. Also here ruins and weeds are caressed by a warm Romantic light, but the intimate spiritual fusion between artist and ruins that so often appears in such works is replaced by a contemplative tone that evokes, although without achieving it, the perception of the sublime in the face of the eternity of history.

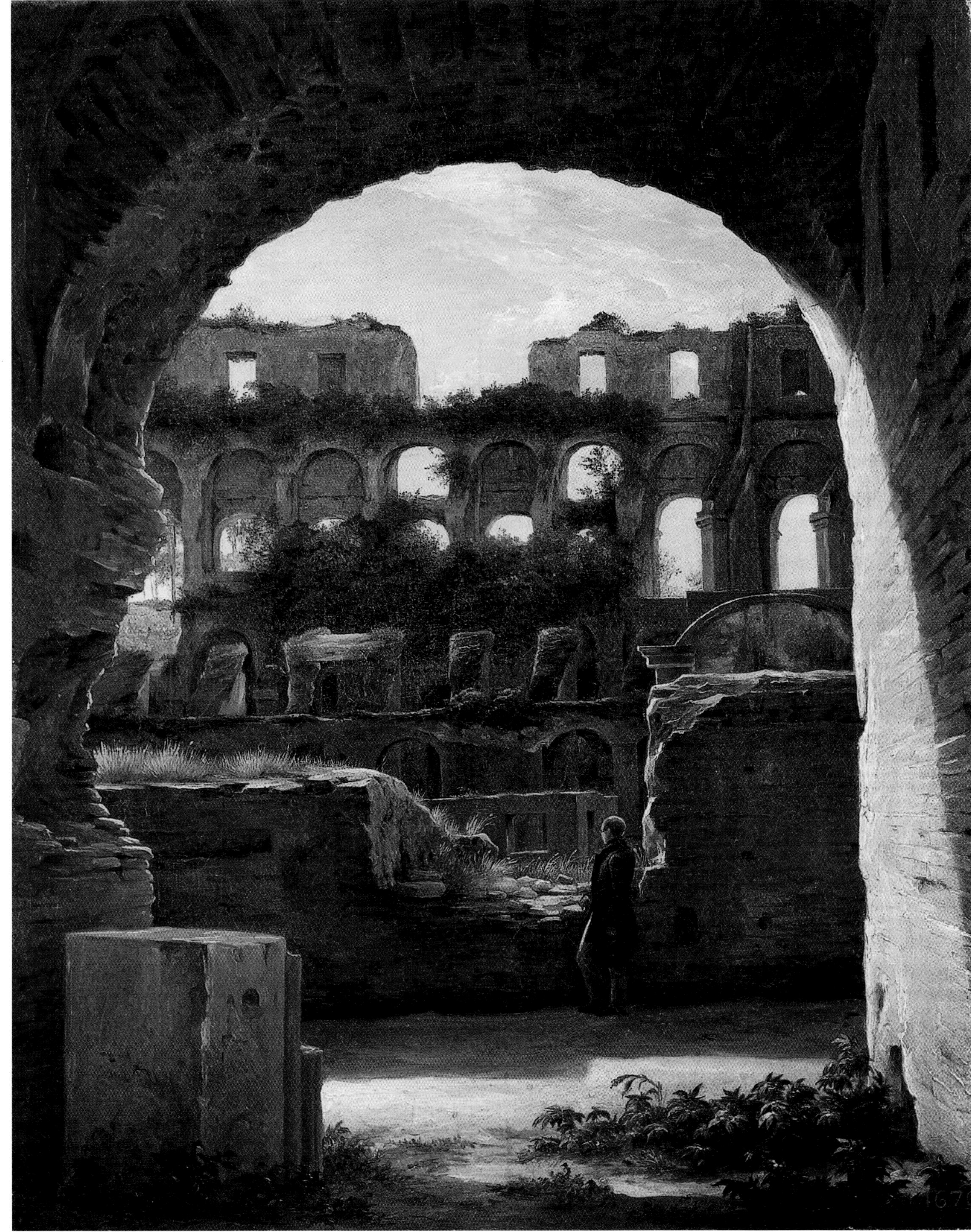

Auguste-Xavier Leprince
The Susten Pass, Switzerland
1824, oil on canvas
81.5 x 105 cm
Musée des Arts Décoratifs, Paris

A delightful snapshot of a hike in the mountains; an Alpine guide with three tourists making a stop so that one of them can make a picture of the goats and shepherd they have met along the path. In the background is a panorama with snowy peaks, a favorite goal of the Romantic excursionist.

Massimo D'Azeglio
View of Lake Como, Branch of the Lecco
1831, oil on canvas
103 x 137 cm
Private collection, Milan

In 1831 D'Azeglio met and married Giulia, daughter of Alessandro Manzoni. Thus the title's reference to Manzoni's *The Betrothed,* which is set in this area of Italy, becomes even more interesting. The book was published in 1827 and became one of the period's great best-sellers. The sentimental spirit of this painting, with the pink light and the simple gestures of the peasants on the road, evokes the pages of the novel.

Anton Sminck Pitloo
Castel dell'Ovo, Naples
1820, oil on canvas
76 x 103 cm
Galleria Nazionale d'Arte Moderna, Rome

Recently arrived in Naples on the invitation of Count Orloff, a Russian diplomat, Pitloo was Dutch by origin but immediately integrated in the life of the city, so much that he opened an important painting school there in the year in which he made this canvas. The work was made for the competition for the chair in landscape art at the Fine Arts Institute, which he was awarded in 1824, and it reflects a style that blends diverse elements: on a still classical base that evokes the warm atmospheres of the seventeenth-century landscape tradition, Pitloo establishes a scene in the manner of northern European landscapes, characterized by the sharply detailed presentation of the panorama.

GIUSEPPE CANELLA
Full Moon
1840, oil on canvas
49 x 74 cm
Galleria d'Arte Moderna e Contemporanea, Brescia

Canella was a landscapist who for many years employed a documentary style still influenced by the eighteenth-century panoramic style, but in his late production he moved toward a typically Romantic sensibility, creating works like this. The quiet nocturnal atmosphere includes a few figures in contemplation of the magnificent spectacle of the moon, which is reflected on the water, awakening in the viewer a profound sense of involvement. In 1854 Federico Odorici compared this painting to the calm magic of certain poems by Giacomo Leopardi.

THOMAS COLE
The Falls of Kaaterskill
1826, oil on canvas
109 x 92 cm
Warner Collection of Gulf States Paper Corporation, Tuscaloosa

With Thomas Cole, founder of the Hudson River School, the basis was laid for the artistic identity of the United States, not yet defined nearly a half century after the declaration of political independence in 1776. Barely twenty, Cole distinguished himself in Philadelphia as a landscape artist; around 1825 he moved to New York, and from there, in the company of other young painters, he made trips along the Hudson River Valley and into the Catskill Mountains, making images of the wilderness, with its expressions of power, majestic beauty, and vastness. The result was the first manifestation of American Romantic painting. What stands out in this canvas is the energy of the water pouring down the rocks, framed by the brightly colored trees, the height of which becomes perceptible only in relation to the almost indistinguishable figure standing to the right of the falls.

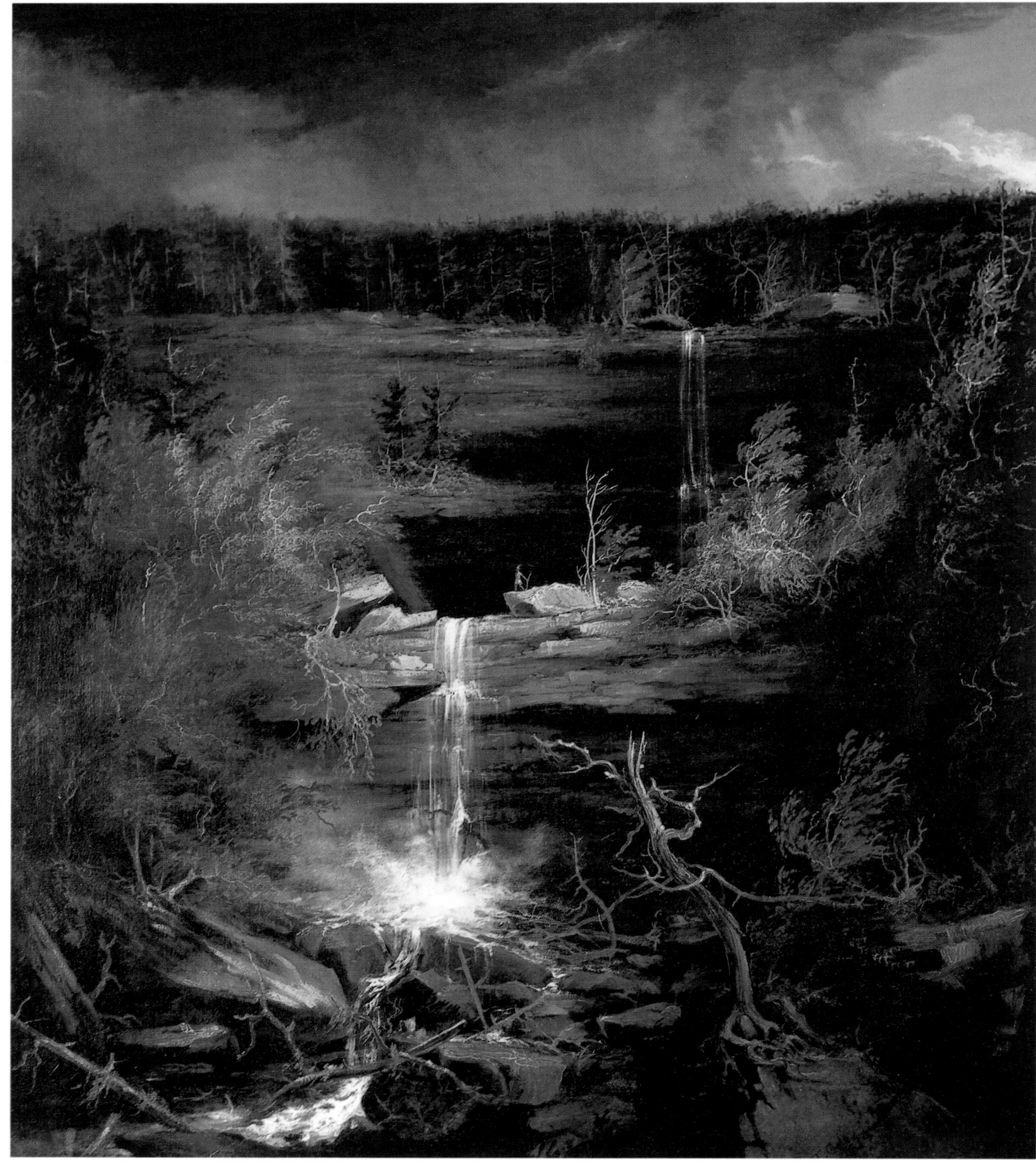

John Constable
The Hay Wain
1821, oil on canvas
130.2 x 185.4 cm
National Gallery,
London

Throughout his life Constable was closely tied to his native Suffolk and often drew his inspiration from the area, which is also the location of this famous canvas. Constable made the painting in his London studio, basing it on many sketches he had done on the spot. The entire work rings with the familiar, from the small farm house to the barking dog to the banks of the river and the horses pulling the wooden wagon through the water; in the distance to the right grain harvesters are at work in the fields. Constable's passion for country life was always filtered through a strongly lyric and sentimental point of view, making him one of the leaders of English Romanticism. He did not neglect realistic details in his views, and in fact presented them with a close analysis that contributed to the lively sense of his works. This canvas did not excite the public at the Royal Academy of 1821; three years later, at the famous Parisian Salon of 1824, it met with unanimous admiration.

JOHN CONSTABLE
Salisbury Cathedral from the Meadows
1831, oil on canvas
151.8 x 189.9 cm
National Gallery, London

Especially fond of the Gothic cathedral of Salisbury, Constable painted it several times over the arc of his career. Here it is viewed from the northwest, an area set amid thick woods crossed by the River Avon. The whole offers an image full of the intense lyricism for which this English artist's landscapes are known. Constable was attracted to naturalistic details, reproducing them with almost photographic clarity, but he was primarily drawn to a contemplative vision of the world of the countryside, surmounted by skies animated by moving clouds and crossed, as in this case, by a rainbow, which may have been added later. To the sense of immediacy and freedom of his landscapes, Constable added a refined technique employing vibrant brushstrokes that seem the fruit of rapid execution but that he perfected by way of a scrupulous reworking of sketches made from life.

Ippolito Caffi
Snow and Fog on the Grand Canal
circa 1840,
oil on canvas
26 x 42 cm
Galleria d'Arte Moderna di Ca' Pesaro, Venice

A painter who led an exciting life, Caffi spent several periods in Venice, where he made dozens of views of the city's most beautiful corners and captured moments of poetic enchantment, such as this view of the Grand Canal. The snow that covers the roofs of the palazzi and houses and the docked gondolas offers an unusual image, sweetly melancholy and antiquated, as in a Flemish landscape. Made before the long series of trips to the Orient that Caffi undertook early in the 1840s, the canvas is representative of the style of Romantic landscape that he contributed to popularizing in northern Italy. In doing so Caffi applied a modern vision with atmospheric phenomena to a mixture of eighteenth-century panorama views and academic-style landscape painting; the result was a freer style, better suited to capturing the tones of personal emotion.

ALEXANDRE DESGOFFE
"Palet" Players
1849, oil on canvas
155 x 198 cm
Musée du Louvre, Paris

Student of Ingres and brother-in-law of Paul Flandrin, Desgoffe was popular among his contemporaries but later fell into obscurity. He represented the continuation of the tradition of the classical landscape in the Romantic period: in this scene with its Arcadian flavor the figures are dressed in the antique style, and also antique is their game—a sort of bocce—which consisted in tossing stones or flat disks (*palets*) as near as possible a target located on the ground. In the distance can be seen figures resting on the ground near a stele, then shepherds, and then farther back the French city of Provins and the Durteint River. It is thus a real place, which the artist has filtered through a poetic and idyllic vision, locating it outside time but also in a transparent and clear light, not really so very distant from the new sensibility of Corot and the nascent realism.

Charles-François Daubigny
A Corner of Normandy
1859–60, oil on canvas
26 x 45 cm
Musée du Louvre, Paris

Member of the group known as the Barbizon School, Daubigny was among the promoters of the Romantic infatuation for landscapes painted from life, or *d'après nature*. Like his Barbizon School friends, he was hostile to the industrialization of the cities, to the progressive distancing from nature caused by the urgent pressure of progress. He often traveled in the French countryside, making paintings with lyric and nostalgic tones, as appears in this view, immersed in a dreamy, transparent light that closely anticipates the luminous creations of realism. The rejection of modern civilization induced him in 1856 to build a covered boat, the *Bottin*, which for a while became his permanent home and aboard which he explored the canals and rivers of the Seine basin, stopping to make pictures whenever the view attracted him, as with this beautiful Norman landscape.

Exhibitions, museums,

Toward the close of the eighteenth century the number of museums in Europe began to increase, thanks to a new conception of art collecting. Until then, only in isolated cases had a select group been given access to the artistic collections of princes or aristocrats. As early as the seventeenth century the Uffizi in Florence could be visited only by express permission of the grand duke of Tuscany. Many of Europe's principal museums grew from private collections like that of the Medici during the pre-Romantic age. In 1793, the Musée Royal des Arts was inaugurated at the Louvre; in 1777, the painter Hubert Robert had been named conservator of the French royal collection, with the task of setting up the Grande Galerie to make it a place to display works to the public. His position acquired greater importance under Napoleon, who entrusted to him the chore of enlarging the Louvre to accommodate the masterpieces stolen from conquered cities. We owe to him many interior views of the palace and also scenes that capture provisional arrangements, such as the monument erected to Jean-Jacques Rousseau (1712–1778) in the gardens of the Tuileries in 1794, when the ashes of the philosopher who supported the principles of equality that inspired the Revolution were displayed for one night under a small temple especially built on an artificial island in the park. Various museums were created during the period of the Napoleonic empire, such as the Prado in Madrid, established by a decree of Joseph Bonaparte. The British Museum, however, was assembled from the collections of private individuals. In 1753 the government procured the first nucleus, the collection of Sir Hans Sloane; this was followed, at the end of the century, by the acquisition of the collection of Sir William Hamilton, British ambassador to the Bourbon court of Naples and husband of Lady Hamilton, who became Horatio Nelson's lover. In 1816 came the collection of Lord Elgin, owner of the marbles from the Parthenon; and there were many others. After the Revolution another museum was set up in Paris, the Musée des Antiquités et Monuments Français, which displayed works of art from churches that had escaped the devastating fury of the Revolutionary uprisings. In 1792 these had been entrusted to the painter Alexandre Lenoir, and three years later he opened this museum to the public. On a solidly Romantic matrix, French history from the Middle Ages onward was brought to life by way of monuments and tombs. Before the establishment of the great museums, the public had few opportunities to see works of art. Those who did not have the good fortune to be friends with a collector could visit the ateliers of artists. The studios of painters and sculptors were always crowded with works of art, sketches and studies, canvases or statues about to be shipped off to a buyer or in need of one. Exhibitions offered another opportunity to see art. Art exhibitions began as special events held only in capital cities, but over the course of the nineteenth century their number increased, and they appeared in secondary cities. The supreme example was the Salon of Paris, created during the age of Louis XV, who inaugurated twenty-four of them between 1737 and 1773. Until the Revolution only artists from the Royal Academy were admitted to the Salon, but the Salon was later opened—in various phases, according to the orientation of the government—to outside artists. A major cultural event, with the king and high dignitaries presiding over its inauguration, the Salon usually opened in March and lasted three months. It did not always take place at the same time of year, and only beginning in 1833, in response to great request, was it made an annual event. As early as the eighteenth century it had been held in the Louvre, in the great

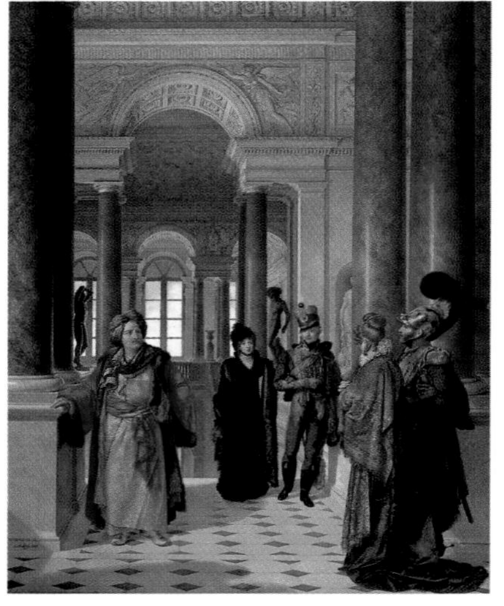

Jean-Baptiste Isabey, *The Main Stairs at the Museum of the Louvre,* 19th century, watercolor; Musée du Louvre, Paris

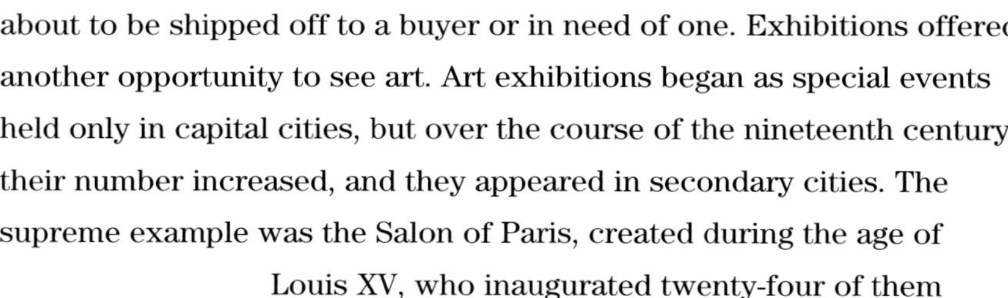

Hubert Robert, *Monument Erected to Rousseau in the Gardens of the Tuileries: Nocturnal View,* 1794, oil on canvas, 80.5 x 65 cm; Musée Carnavalet, Paris

square Salon that gave it its name; over time, the growing number of works presented (more than 1,800 in 1827) forced the exhibition to expand into the adjacent halls, where the displayed paintings eventually covered all of the available wall space. The cardinal event of the artistic scene, the Salon sometimes responded to government policy (sovereigns often commissioned subjects related to the ancient French monarchy), but it could also dictate artistic criteria, introduce a new talent, or present a convincing stage for the manifestation of a new trend. This happened at the Salon of 1824, which decreed the affirmation of the Romantic movement. It is also what happened at the world version of the Salon in 1855, the Universal Exposition, which, even with the exclusion of Gustave Courbet, gave its official sanction to the "pictorial trend that is disastrous for French art," better known as realism. Paris was also the scene of the first museum exhibiting works by living artists, the Luxembourg, which was set up in 1818 as a permanent exhibition of works acquired at the Salon. In Italy, the institutions that offered space to artists in which they could exhibit their works were the promotional

Wilhelm Bendz, *Model Class at the Art Academy*, 1826, oil on canvas; Statens Museum for Kunst, Copenhagen

to young artists, but also as meeting places for artists and intellectuals; to this was added the commercial aspect, which around the middle of

and the ateliers of artists

Joseph Paxton, *Crystal Palace*, 1851, print; Private collection

the century began assuming an increasingly prominent role. The growing importance of such events led to the great Great Exhibition held in London in 1851. Conceived as a kind of immense fair, the exhibition saw, for the first time in history, the peaceful gathering of all the nations of the world for commercial purposes. Between May 1 and October 11 it was visited by more than 6 million people, who saw exhibitions of artisan, industrial, and artistic products from every part of the planet arranged in a special building, the Crystal Palace, 563 meters long and 124 wide, it too a symbol of technical innovation. Designed by Joseph Paxton, an expert in greenhouse construction, the pavilion was made of glass and iron. It was built in Hyde Park and was dismantled at the end of the exhibition to be reassembled at Sydenham, where it became London's first amusement park and remained the principal entertainment spot for the city until it was destroyed by fire in 1936. After the English triumph of 1851, Europe's capital cities vied to be chosen as the site for later international expositions; in 1855 it was the turn of Paris, and so it went through the various major cities, including Florence in 1861 and Vienna in 1873.

societies of the fine arts, the first of which opened in Turin in 1842 and Florence in 1844, soon followed by versions in all the major centers. These were used not only as exhibition spaces and to provide assistance

Hubert Robert
Preparing the Grande Galerie of the Louvre
1796, oil on canvas
115 x 145 cm
Musée du Louvre, Paris

Made conservator of the Louvre in 1795, Robert followed the various phases of the museum's growth and designed the pilasters and skylights, such as those in the Grande Galerie. This was where Napoleon intended to display the collection of paintings enlarged with masterpieces carried off from Italy and other conquered countries.

Louis-Léopold Boilly
Meeting of Artists in the Atelier of Isabey
1798, oil on canvas
71.5 x 110 cm
Musée du Louvre, Paris

This large, animated group portrait numbers fully thirty-one figures—all identifiable—most of them painters, but also musicians, singers, and actors, assembled in the atelier of Jean-Baptiste Isabey, which like many ateliers was a meeting place for intellectuals and artists of all kinds.

Joseph Michael Gandy
View of the Dome Designed by John Soane
1811, pen and watercolor
119 x 88 cm
Sir John Soane's Museum, London

At the end of the eighteenth century the English architect John Soane (1753–1837) built a home in London, including within it an area set up as a museum, the Dome, twice the height of the other rooms, in which to display the many plaster casts, marbles, and fragments from antiquity in his collection. He wanted to illuminate these works with theatrical effects of hidden lighting, so as to create a strong sense of mystery, as presented magisterially in this work by Gandy. Soane appears in person on the balcony to the right, nearly hidden in the mass of works typical of past ages, works that are not arranged according to criteria of visibility but are placed close to one another and under and above one another to cover the wall, creating an effect of great fascination and also, as is made clear in this view, great unreality.

Archibald Archer
The Temporary Elgin Room
1819, oil on canvas
76.2 x 127 cm
British Museum, London

While serving as British ambassador at Constantinople, the British diplomat Thomas Bruce, seventh earl of Elgin—Lord Elgin—received permission from the Turkish government to remove certain sculptures from the Parthenon and save them from destruction by taking them to London. Elgin displayed the first group to arrive, in 1807, in the garden of his home. In 1816, finding himself in financial difficulties, the earl, with the support of a committee of experts, convinced Parliament to purchase the marbles for the British Museum, where they were put in a hall set up for that purpose, the Elgin Room, to let the public see them and artists study them to make copies. This is the subject of this reconstruction, in which the sculptures from the Greek temple, which are still preserved in the London museum, are displayed in a casual atmosphere.

NICOLAS GOSSE
Napoleon III Visiting the Site of the New Louvre
1854, oil on canvas
34 x 24 cm
Musée du Louvre, Paris

Son of Louis Bonaparte and Hortense de Beauharnais, Napoleon III was proclaimed emperor in December 1852. Under his reign the Louvre was enlarged following plans that dated back to Henry IV; in 1603 that king had approved a plan for the enlargement of the building, consisting of joining the palace of the Louvre to that of the Tuileries, but only the construction known as the Grande Galerie had been actually made. The plans were taken up again two and a half centuries later, in 1852, under the direction of the architect Louis Visconti. When Visconti died suddenly in 1853, he was replaced by Hector-Martin Lefuel. This painting by Gosse shows the worksite and its scaffolding to the right, with the emperor visiting the workers, who pause in their work. The Nouveau Louvre was inaugurated on August 14, 1857.

François-Joseph Heim
Charles X Distributing Awards at the Salon of 1824
1825, oil on canvas
173 x 256 cm
Musée du Louvre, Paris

This canvas (itself displayed at the Salon of 1827) presents an interesting view of Parisian artistic life, showing the final act of the Salon of 1824 with the prize ceremonies held in the Louvre on January 15, 1825. The king is shown handing a decoration to the sculptor Pierre Cartellier, named knight of St. Michael. That year's Salon was of particular importance and saw the unexpected triumph of Ingres with the *Vow of Louis XIII* (see page 182), recognizable at the center of the wall, which marked his return to France after a sixteen-year absence in Italy. To the right of the canvas by Ingres is the *Joan of Arc in Prison* by Paul Delaroche.

Paul Delaroche
James-Alexandre, Comte de Pourtalès-Gorgier
1846, oil on canvas
128 x 78 cm
Musée du Louvre, Paris

Close friend of Delaroche, the count of Pourtalès-Gorgier (1776–1855) had himself portrayed in the room of his Parisian residence in which he displayed a prestigious collection of antiquities and objets d'art. One of the leading collectors of his time, Pourtalès succeeded in buying masterpieces by leading Renaissance artists—today held in the major museums of the world—as well as works by contemporary artists, such as the *Grande Odalisque* by Ingres (see page 197). The sculptures behind him are identifiable: to the left is a *Hercules* in ivory at the time believed to be by Giambologna, at the center is a Renaissance bronze statue of Venus, to the right is a *Head of Apollo* in marble on a red porphyry base, today in the British Museum, that was admired by Madame de Staël and Prosper Mérimée for its expressive intensity. Delaroche made it stand out by doubling the image through the artifice of the mirror, thus also reinforcing the extraordinary photographic rendering of the portrait.

David Roberts
The Inauguration of the Great Exhibition, May 1, 1851
1852–54,
oil on canvas
86.4 x 152.4 cm
Royal Collection, Windsor

On May 1, 1851, the Great Exhibition opened in London. This was the first universal exhibition, a fair on a scale never before seen in which products of every type were presented: artistic, industrial, but most of all inventions, machines, and other expressions of technology. The exhibition was held in the Crystal Palace, a colossal glass-and-steel structure designed by Joseph Paxton and set up in Hyde Park, in which 14,000 exhibitions from throughout the world were arranged. The interior presented by this canvas offers a cross-section of the displays with a scene of the inaugural ceremonies, attended by Queen Victoria and Prince Albert with their children, Victoria and Albert, everyone entertained by an orchestra of two hundred instruments and six hundred singers.

SALVATORE FERGOLA
The Tarsia Grand Hall with the Products of Neapolitan Arts and Crafts on Display, May 30, 1853
1854, oil on canvas
102 x 140 cm
Museo Nazionale di San Martino, Naples

As the long title explains, a major exhibition of local arts and crafts was held in Naples at the end of May 1853. The undertaking was part of the Bourbon program of supporting local arts that had been initiated in 1825 by Francis I, who had begun the plan for biennial shows dedicated to the fine arts and artisan products. Fergola portrays here the hall that also hosted the exhibition of industrial arts in 1853, the so-called Tarsia Hall. Within its luminous and inviting interior the products are arranged on fabric-covered tables, but not in any particular order. Musical instruments, paintings, and porcelains are set in place casually, while standing out on the left is a series of products of the Biedermeier taste: compositions of dried flowers under glass that constituted one of the favorite furnishings for the middle class.

Hans Ditlev Christian Martens
Pope Leo XIII Visiting Thorvaldsen's Atelier in Rome in 1826
1830, oil on canvas
100 x 138 cm
Thorvaldsens Museum, Copenhagen

Bertel Thorvaldsen arrived in Rome in 1797 and stayed forty years. In 1825, Pope Pius VII died, and there were many who saw it as scandalous that Thorvaldsen, a Lutheran, was entrusted with the creation of the pope's funeral monument. When the new pope, Leo XIII, visited the sculptor's studio one year later he saw several statues for the tomb that were already ready.

François-Auguste Biard
Four o'Clock, "Closing Time" at the Salon
1847, oil on canvas
67.5 x 57.5 cm
Musée du Louvre, Paris

This lively view presents an almost caricatured image of the visitors to the Salon and in so doing seems to anticipate the throngs that fill museums today. Ordinary citizens, artists, officials, and families with children fight for space to get a look at pictures or, exhausted, elbow their way toward an exit.

Arie Johannes Lamme
The Great Atelier in Rue Chaptal in 1851
1851, oil on panel
58 x 74 cm
Musée de la Vie Romantique, Paris

Paris's Museum of Romantic Life is today located in a house that once belonged to the Dutch painter Ary Scheffer. When Scheffer first moved into the house, in 1830, he had two ateliers built at the entrance to the garden, one of which is presented here by his cousin Arie Johannes Lamme. The artist is presented on his stool working at a canvas while his wife, in the back of the room, is busy reading. Scheffer was always deeply involved in the artistic and intellectual life of Paris. For many years the house in rue Chaptal was the scene of regular Friday meetings of writers like Dickens and Lamartine, the lyric poet and writer of songs Pierre Jean de Béranger, and such composers as Liszt, Chopin, Rossini, and Gounod. Many of them were Scheffer's friends, and he made his atelier available to several of them so that they could display works that had been refused by the Salon.

GUSTAVE COURBET
The Painter's Studio: A Real Allegory Summing Up Seven Years of My Artistic and Moral Life
1855, oil on canvas
359 x 598 cm
Musée d'Orsay, Paris

"Mon cher ami," Courbet wrote to his friend Champfleury in 1854, "although assailed by hypochondria I have launched into an immense painting, 20 feet in length and 12 in height, that will show that I am still alive. . . . It is the moral and physical history of my atelier." Further on the letter gives a description of the figures that crowd the painting, divided in two parts. To the right are friends, fellow artists, and art lovers; to the left is the world of ordinary life, "the masses, wretchedness, poverty, wealth, the exploited and the exploiters, people who live on death." On the right are portrayed Baudelaire reading, the writer Champfleury, seated in profile, the merchant and collector Alfred Bruyas standing with the beard, behind

him Pierre-Joseph Proudhon, socialist philosopher, and others; on the other side are common types often met in works by Courbet and representative of ordinary life, including a Jew, a laborer, huntsman, Irishwoman, and others, including a skull on a newspaper because, as Proudhon said, newspapers are the cemeteries of ideas. At the center sits the painter himself observed by a child—the future—while he paints a landscape and smiles because of the useless presence behind him of a nude model, symbol of inspirational reality. This canvas played a leading role in the difficult debut of realism on the French scene. When it was rejected by the Universal Exposition in Paris in 1855, Courbet challenged the jury by having a hall built adjacent to the exhibition at his own expense. This was the famous Pavillon du Réalisme, in which this work along with another fifty paintings marked the beginning of the revolutionary break with official painting.

Steam, electricity, arrival of the

The eighteenth century was the century of Enlightenment, a period of great scientific discoveries. It was also the age of the industrial revolution, which had begun in Great Britain and had then made its way across Europe, becoming symbolic of progress itself. Within the industrial system the figure of the artist came to assume a new role, that of the creator or designer of models and objects distinguished by a certain stylistic character; however, the actual material execution of these was to be entrusted to other people, if not to machines. Emblematic of the period were institutions like the Birmingham Lunar Society, an association formed during the 1770s and so-named because its members assembled on nights when the moon was full so as not to have to return home in the dark. The society's members included intellectuals, politicians, scientists, industrialists, and artists, all of whom presented their creations or experiments to the other members. These included Josiah Wedgwood, who perfected a new procedure for the manufacture of porcelain, James Watt, inventor of the steam engine, and the painter Joseph Wright of Derby, whose paintings give a good sense of the kind of scientific demonstrations that were presented to the associates along with a sense of the fascination attached to the first industries, particularly when they were portrayed in their more spectacular aspects, as blazing forges in nocturnal landscapes. Wright was a member of a middle class that saw progress and industrialization as the means to achieve economic and political power. Thus his paintings avoid the negative side of science and industry, the very side that was presented by those who, like William Turner or Philippe Jacques de Loutherbourg (see page 25), blamed industry for contaminating the landscape and destroying the peace of life lived in accordance with nature. This sense of alarm was not expressed in Italy, where the landscape painting of the early nineteenth century still held to traditional concepts and where the first signs of industrialization were simply folded into idyllic atmospheres or included as aspects of the normal landscape, as is the case with Antonio Basoli, who portrayed factories on the outskirts of Bologna in the 1820s, giving them the face of pleasant daily reality. The nineteenth century saw a steady series of innovations and discoveries in many sectors, from physics to chemistry to engineering—to cite only three—that had immediate impacts on daily life, on production in the broadest sense, and on industry. The century opened with a scientific development of fundamental importance: in March 1800 Alessandro Volta wrote a letter to Sir Joseph Banks, president of the Royal Society, informing him of his invention of the electric pile (Volta's pile), an

Antonio Basoli, *Sulfuric Acid Factory,* 19th century, oil on canvas; Raccolte Cassa di Risparmio, Bologna

James Pollard, *Street Scene with Omnibus,* 1845, oil on panel, 24.7 x 32 cm; Museum of London, London

Nicola Cianfanelli, *Alessandro Volta Presents the Pile to the First Consul,* 1841, fresco; Museo della Specola, Florence

early type of battery. The next year Napoleon Bonaparte invited Volta to Paris to present his invention to the members of the French Institute and awarded him with a gold medal. Over the course of the next decades Volta's pile was applied to many technological fields. The electric telegraph, thanks to the contributions of Carl Friedrich Gauss and Wilhelm Weber in 1833 and of Samuel F. B. Morse in 1837, facilitated civil communication and also had an effect on military and diplomatic activities, as well as on the world's stock markets. During the same period the steam engine made its technological advance: invented early in the eighteenth century in England, by 1765 it had been perfected by James Watt and—based on the use of steam as motive force—had with real rain, behind which is real sunshine" and urged the public to come see the train "lest it should dash out of the picture." The realistic effects Turner achieved prefigured the coming affirmation of realism. At mid-century London led Europe in such important urbanistic innovations as its street system, sewer system, and plumbing, which brought water into the homes of citizens, including those of the least well off; the rail line guaranteed a daily round trip to the city for the residents of the suburbs and the countryside, while outlying areas were further connected to the center by means of an efficient bus and trolley system, visible, for example, in a painting by James Pollard of 1845. The United States was the source of new inventions destined to change the profiles of industry and society. These included such machines as Cyrus Hall McCormick's reaper of 1831 and Elias Howe's sewing machine of 1846, both of which were presented at the Great Exhibition in London in 1851. A new era opened in the sector of art with the birth of a technique that was soon in competition with painting, or at least was having a great effect on it: the camera, invented by Louis-Jacques-Mandé Daguerre in 1839. The daguerreotype, a silver-coated copper plate treated with iodine

and the camera

Alessandro Guardassoni, *Self-Portrait with Camera,* 1860, oil on canvas; Istituto Gualandi, Bologna

permitted notable advances in many industries, among them mining and textile manufacture, but most of all in transportation. By the beginning of the nineteenth century ships were steaming up and down rivers and lakes as well as across entire oceans. In 1814 George Stephenson constructed the first steam locomotive; nine years later, a steam-powered railroad came into being, the Stockton and Darlington Railway in England. This was followed in 1830 by the Liverpool-Manchester line, 160 kilometers long. Italy had to wait nearly fourteen years to see its first railroad, which was constructed between Naples and Portici and inaugurated on October 3, 1839, by King Ferdinand II, ruler of Naples and Sicily. The train slowly made its way into paintings, eventually becoming an everyday element of the landscape. Turner made one of the first examples in 1844: *Rain, Steam, and Speed—The Great Western Railway*, a work that excited critics with its extraordinary rendering of the speed of the locomotive. One wrote that Turner had "made a picture

vapor on which a positive image was impressed, offered a system to quickly capture any type of reality, and with the greatest precision. Many were drawn to this new means of portraying persons, objects, and landscapes. In 1857 an article in the *Revue des Deux Mondes* stated that photography could never replace the special relationship established between a painter and the person being portrayed, but in reality the new invention was taking over the world. In 1856, Félix Tournachon, the pioneer French photographer better known as Nadar, made use of two great inventions that were opening the way to the modern world: during a trip through the skies of Paris in a hot-air balloon he took photographs of the city from above, assembling a complete view. Honoré Daumier immortalized the scene in an emblematic cartoon entitled *Nadar raises photography to the dignity of an art.*

James Wright of Derby
An Experiment on a Bird in the Air Pump
1768, oil on canvas
182.9 x 243.9 cm
National Gallery, London

Son of a lawyer of Derby, Wright belonged to the London middle class and was particularly interested in the expansion of progress and industrialization. Many of his paintings present scientific experiments, and these are always located in highly evocative settings. This work presents an experiment with a vacuum pump, involving the withdrawing of air from a glass flask containing a white cockatoo. Wright used the experiment for the construction of a highly effective nocturnal scene, with the darkness of the room, the moon hidden by clouds, the lamp at the center of the table that illuminates only the faces. It is those faces that receive most of the attention, Wright taking care to present the various emotional reactions of the spectators to what is happening, the drama experienced by the children who fear for the life of the bird, the indifference of the young couple, interested only in themselves, the impatience of the man to the left, eager to witness the scientific result.

Benjamin West
Benjamin Franklin Drawing Electricity from the Sky
1816, oil on canvas
33.5 x 25.5 cm
Museum of Art, Philadelphia

Benjamin Franklin (1706–1790) and Benjamin West were friends; Franklin was the godfather of West's second son, born in 1772. In 1816 the artist made this posthumous portrait of his friend, presenting him as the scientist who discovered the lightning rod. His image assumes almost heroic tones, with his hair and his cloak flying in the wind of the thunderstorm, while he reaches to the key on the kite string, which is being held in place by several cherubs. In the background lightning crosses the sky. The layout of the work reveals the elderly painter's classical style, as does the presence of cherubs as technical assistants at the great scientific discovery; they are guardians of the very tradition that was being brought into question, according to the more conservative point of view, by innovations that threatened to introduce changes into daily life.

JOSEPH MALLORD WILLIAM TURNER
Lime Kiln at Coalbrookdale
1797, oil on panel
29 x 40.3 cm
Yale Center for British Art, New Haven

Turner was twenty-two when he painted this panel of a site that drew the attention of many artists in the pre-Romantic period. During the industrial revolution the town of Coalbrookdale in Shropshire became absorbed in the activities related to iron working. Foundries and lime kilns offered painters like de Loutherbourg and Turner opportunities to make impassioned nocturnal scenes, with the blaze emanating from the active kiln rendered even more intense by the surrounding shadows. An homage paid to picturesque taste is here transformed into a vaguely disturbing image, evoking a demoniacal cavern allusive to the loss of the identity of the countryside, condemned to change its face because of the growing invasion of industry. The work can thus be seen as an environmentalist statement from the end of the eighteenth century.

Joseph Mallord William Turner
Rain, Steam, and Speed—The Great Western Railway
1844, oil on canvas
91 x 122 cm
National Gallery, London

Turner never tired of making references to the relationship between the changes wrought by progress and the appearance of the landscape. The notion expressed in the title of associating speed and rain is in of itself eloquent, creating a contrast between the speedy pace of the machine and the cadenced rhythm of the English countryside, for centuries crossed only by rain. The steam locomotive advances along an iron road that runs over the railway bridge erected over the Thames near Taplow by the engineer Isambard Kingdom Brunel. The powerful sense of perspective lines is echoed, to the left, by the brief diagonal of another bridge, while the presence of water is merely suggested, revealed most of all by the ship and the sense of reflected light. The entire painting is immersed in singular luminous effects, which Turner achieves by treating the oil paint with techniques from the use of watercolors, imperceptibly blending rain, sky, water, and the locomotive itself as though they were being dematerialized in the rain.

Pelagio Palagi
Newton Discovers the Refraction of Light
1824, oil on canvas
167 x 216 cm
Pinacoteca Tosio Martinengo, Brescia

This painting was commissioned from Palagi by Count Paolo Tosio, a collector who in 1832 bequeathed the masterpieces in his collection to the city of Brescia. Tosio wanted a picture of Isaac Newton (1642–1727), the famous English mathematician and natural philosopher, but with reference not to his most memorable discovery (the laws of universal gravitation, which legend holds he intuited by observing an apple fall from a tree) but instead to another important discovery, related to the field of optics, his corpuscular theory of light. In a room furnished in late-seventeenth-century style, Newton sits at a table busy at his studies, but his attention has been

drawn to his sister's child, sitting behind him playing with soap bubbles. Newton is presented in the moment in which he takes note of the phenomenon of the colors that appear on the surface of the bubbles through the effect of refraction. In keeping with the requests of the count, Palagi presents the sense of wonder and the dawning awareness of discovery on the face of the scientist, but does so in a controlled way, without undue emphasis. In fact the work was highly praised by critics for not making use of the exaggerated expressions so common in painting of the time, and for having emphasized instead the meditative tone, the effect of the light that filters through the window, and for the presumed historical veracity in the reconstruction of the setting.

Louis Dupré, Sébastien-Louis Norbin
Chateaubriand Receives the Grand Duchess Hélène of Russia in the Gardens of the Villa Medici, April 29, 1829: Release of the Balloons
circa 1830,
oil on canvas
73 x 97 cm
French Academy, Rome

This painting presents the reception given at the French Academy in honor of the visit to Rome of Grand Duchess Hélène of Russia, which included entertainment given on the terrace of the Villa Medici and concluded with the release of several balloons. There was still a great deal of enthusiasm for the invention of the French brothers Joseph and Jacques Étienne Montgolfier, who in 1783 had made the first experiments with balloons, followed one year later by Jean-Pierre Blanchard's courageous balloon flight across the English Channel. The grand duchess, her father the prince of Württemberg, Chateaubriand, and Horace Vernet, recently nominated director of the academy, appear at the center of the painting; around them is a crowd of ordinary citizens, women of the court, an orchestra, and guests, while a balloon bearing the Russian coat of arms is about to be sent aloft to join two others already in the sky.

Salvatore Fergola
The Inauguration of the Naples-Portici Rail Line
1840, oil on canvas
124 x 219 cm
Appartamenti Storici, Palazzo Reale, Caserta

On October 3, 1839, King Ferdinand II opened the first stretch of railroad on the Italian peninsula, an eight-kilometer line connecting Naples and Portici. In immortalizing the great event, Salvatore Fergola filled his canvas with exquisite details, his purpose being to render every element of the celebration with "truth and exactness." As viewed from above the loggia of the Villa Frascati, the scene presents the carriages of the train, with all their decorative details, and the honorary guests, seated under the awnings to the right. The king and the court dignitaries took shelter in a pavilion set up atop the bridge that appears in the distance, which is also where the altar was placed for the solemn blessing of the iron road.

Salvatore Fergola
The "Real Ferdinando" at Sea
1828, oil on canvas
52 x 65 cm
Museo Nazionale di San Martino, Naples

This steamship, baptized with the name of the ruler of Naples, had been purchased in England during the reign of Ferdinand I (1815–25). It weighed 235 tons and could carry 200 passengers. Its maiden voyage, from Messina to Palermo, took place on June 20, 1824. Fergola portrays the ship in profile to show off its elegant lines and to emphasize its stability, even in heavy seas, as evinced by the choppy waves in the foreground. The ship is clearly in motion, as indicated by the long trail of smoke and the flags pulled taut by the wind.

FRANCESCO TRÉCOURT
The "Contessa Clementina" in the Port of Pavia
circa 1845,
oil on canvas
52 x 77.5 cm
Musei Civici, Pavia

The *Contessa Clementina* was one of the steamships that went into service along the river routes connecting Venice, Mantua, and Pavia in 1845. Property of the Milanese Perelli and Paradisi company, it was captained for a certain period by the Garibaldian Gaetano Sacchi. In 1859 the company that ran the line was forced to close, suspected of patriotic activities and complicity with secret societies. Francesco Trécourt, brother of the better known Giacomo, portrayed the ship at the center of a busy scene set in Pavia's river port.

Never have literature and art been so closely tied as they were during the Romantic period. Many writers, poets, and philosophers were close friends of painters or sculptors. Men of letters, among them Stendhal, Charles Baudelaire, and Théophile Gautier, were keenly aware of the world of art and left an enormous quantity of writing on it—including Baudelaire's frequent reviews of the Salons—not to mention the many others figures, including John Ruskin and Eugène Fromentin, who were active on both fronts. A story by Honoré Balzac that appeared in Paris in 1832 under the title *The Unknown Masterpiece* (and was included in his *Comédie Humaine* as *Étude philosophique*) can be taken as emblematic of this close relationship. The subject of the story is a great seventeenth-century painter named Édouard Frenhofer who is caught up in a dramatic effort to reconcile imagination and reality in art. In making the protagonist a typical Romantic painter, torn between aspiration for the absolute and the difficulties of achieving it, Balzac gave written form to the debates that were then dividing the art scene in two opposing camps. This debate dated back to the clashes between Ingres and Delacroix, between academism and the breaking of traditional rules, between classicists and Romanticists. Narrative literature was one of the supporting columns of Romantic culture, and the novel, a genre inherited from the preceding century, developed rapidly and spread not only across Europe but also in America, becoming such a popular form of entertainment that novels were serialized in newspapers and magazines. An example is the novel by Eugène Sue *Les Mystères de Paris*, published between 1842 and 1843 in the *Journal des Débats*. Novels also made their way into art, and sometimes quite rapidly. In 1827, a year after the publication of James Fenimore Cooper's *Last of the Mohicans*, Thomas Cole made paintings of some of that work's most dramatic scenes. In France, the historical novel *par excellence*, Victor Hugo's *Notre-Dame de Paris*, published in 1831, was immediately translated into painted scenes, including the singular work by Andrea Villa in which the cathedral of Notre-Dame includes a clock that actually runs, driven by a mechanism on the back of the painting. The first edition of *The Betrothed*, which in 1827 had already made Alessandro Manzoni (before the definitive version of 1840) famous, was soon the subject of illustrations and paintings, the prototypes of which were frescoes in lunettes in Florence in the personal bedroom of Leopold II of Lorraine inside the Meridiana Palace, the last enlargement of the grand ducal Pitti Palace. The novel was hardly the only literary genre to inspire artists during the first half of the nineteenth century: stories, poetry, and plays—ancient or contemporary—furnished an enormous panorama of texts that inspired many of the masterpieces of the period. On one side were the great names of European literature, such as Dante, Shakespeare, and even Ariosto, writers whose works had much in common with the Romantic

Claudius Jacquand, *Count Comminges Recognizes Adelaide,* 1836, oil on canvas, 163 x 208 cm; Musée des Beaux-Arts, Rennes

Novels and

Andrea Villa, *Notre-Dame de Paris,* 1831, oil on metal plate, 82.5 x 107.5 cm; Quartiere d'Inverno, Palazzo Pitti, Florence

literature

spirit. There were also the Homeric poems, the *Iliad* and the *Odyssey*, each packed with heroes to portray. To these was added the poetry of Ossian, the modern Homer born in 1760 in the imagination of the Scottish author James Macpherson who, by way of the figure of this Gaelic bard, sang of deeds that thrilled Goethe and Napoleon alike. So taken was the emperor with the legendary bard that he sought to surround himself with paintings of him. Thus came into being, one after another, the images of Ossian for Malmaison and for the Quirinal Palace commissioned from Gérard (1801), Girodet (1802), and Ingres (1813). At the same time, the Romantic repertory of literary subjects was dominated by contemporaries of the level of François-René du Chateaubriand—his texts were the sources for the *Burial of Atala* by Girodet (see page 217) and *The Natchez* by Delacroix (see page 220)—and Lord Byron, the idol of English artists and a source of inspiration for many French artists, chief among them Delacroix, who was deeply moved by the Orientalism of Bryon's poetry even before his 1832 visit to Algeria and who came to share Byron's fervor for the freedom of the Greek people. Within the sphere of paintings conceived as illustrations for a written text, the works of Dante and Shakespeare rank second only to the Bible. In 1786, Henry Fuseli, with Thomas Sandby, Benjamin West, George Romney, and other painters was involved in the ambitious project conceived by the engraver and print publisher John Boydell to create a collection of paintings illustrating scenes from Shakespeare to be displayed in a gallery, the Boydell Shakespeare Gallery, which opened in London in 1789. Fuseli undertook a similar plan on his own, a Milton Gallery, which numbered forty works in 1799. There is then the large collection of watercolors of Dante's *Divine Comedy* made by William Blake for John Linnell, an art patron who in this way alleviated some of the hardship of the last years of Blake's life. Other artists made images of the same text, and the many interpretations of the fifth canto, with the story of the lovers Paolo and Francesca, differ in layout from Blake's (see page 252) and are more directly explanatory of the importance Romanticism saw in the values celebrated by Dante. The 1835 version by Ary Scheffer presents the famous pair of tragic lovers in a scene tinged with sensuality. A painter fond of subjects of literary derivation, Scheffer drew inspiration more than once from the works of Goethe and also from the shadowy texts of the eighteenth-century pre-Romantics, such as the *Leonore* by the German poet Gottfried August Bürger, making his *Lenore—"The Dead Ride Fast"* of 1820–25 and in 1829 *Le Retour de l'Armée* (Dordrecht Museum, Dordrecht). Scheffer was not the only artist drawn to this macabre ballad. Horace Vernet made a canvas based on it (1839; Musée des Beaux-Arts, Nantes), Gérard de Nerval translated it in 1829, Victor Hugo drew inspiration from it more than once, and Franz Schubert composed a musical version. The three-act drama shown in Paris in 1764, *Les Amants Malheureux, ou Le Comte de Comminges* by François-Thomas de Baculard d'Arnaud, belongs to the "Gothic" current that laid the basis for the so-called Gothic romance, later more fully developed in England and France. Claudius Jacquand used its pathetic conclusion in a canvas of 1836, creating a scene with almost monochromatic tones in which Comminges, surrounded by his fellow brothers, discovers that the dead monk they are about to bury is in reality his beloved Adelaide, who had entered the Trappist monastery in disguise in order to be near him after he had taken the vows. There were also instances in which this trend was reversed, with a painting inspiring a literary work. So struck was Casmir Delavigne by Paul Delacroche's *Sons of Edward* (see page 114) that he wrote a tragedy of the same name.

François Gérard, *Ossian on the Banks of the Lora Calls on the Gods,* 1831, oil on panel, 26.5 x 26.5 cm; Kunsthalle, Hamburg

Ary Scheffer, *Paolo and Francesca,* 1835, oil on canvas, 166.5 x 234 cm; Wallace Collection, London

HENRY FUSELI
Titania,
Bottom, and Fairies
1793–94,
oil on canvas
169 x 135 cm
Kunsthaus, Zurich

Painted for the Boydell Shakespeare Gallery, the plan initiated in 1786 that was to include an illustrative cycle of the works of the great playwright, this canvas is based on the scene in *A Midsummer Night's Dream* (Act IV, Scene 1) in which Titania, queen the fairies, embraces Bottom with the donkey's head, while dancing fairies frame the group. In the background two fairies wear "modern" clothes as ladies in waiting, while a third with a stylish hat caresses Bottom's head. When Titania awakens she will tell her husband, Oberon, of having been in love with a donkey, and Puck will break the spell. Fuseli was fascinated by the supernatural and by fabulous figures, and in this subject was able to combine the two, adding yet another element dear to him, that of dreams, which he here rendered in a truly magical form, breaking traditional compositional schemes.

William Blake
"Like an angel dropped down from the clouds"
1809, pen and watercolor on paper
30.8 x 19.1 cm
British Museum, London

Based on *Henry IV, Part I* (Act IV, Scene 1), the painting is one of the illustrations Blake made for the Reverend Joseph Thomas, who wanted to include it in an antique edition of the works of Shakespeare. The passage is that in which Sir Richard Vernon describes how the "gallantly armed" Prince Henry "did rise from the ground like feathered Mercury, and vaulted with such ease into his seat, as if an angel dropped down from the clouds to turn and wind a fiery Pegasus and witch the world with noble horsemanship." Blake introduces a figure not in the text, that of the young nude woman with the book, perhaps a personification of the reader, stretched across a cloud above the falling angel and Pegasus. While the line of the figure is in keeping with the formally classical style, the almost abstract way in which the figure is included in the composition reveals Blake's orientation toward images with a symbolic tone.

Augustin-Alphonse Gaudar de La Verdine
Orlando Furioso
1804, oil on canvas
275 x 194 cm
Musée Municipal Bertrand, Chateauroux

Orlando, the hero of Ludovico Ariosto's epic poem, crazed by jealousy after discovering writing on the trunk of a tree that reveals the love between Angelica and Medoro, has torn off his armor and clothes in order to uproot the tree from the ground. The scene presents him in a larger-than-life size, his nude body expressing the height of muscular tension, illuminated by light that comes from the left. The work reveals inspiration drawn from models of classical statuary, such as the Belvedere Torso, which the artist was able to carefully study during the years he spent in Rome, where he made this painting and sent it to Paris as an examination entry. While maintaining ties to the formal canons of academic tradition, the young Gaudar presents a highly Romantic subject in this *Orlando Furioso:* the hero driven mad battling with nature.

Francesco Hayez
Rinaldo and Armida
1813, oil on canvas
198 x 295 cm
Gallerie dell'Accademia, Venice

When he painted this canvas Hayez was just over twenty and was in Rome on a scholarship to the Venetian Academy. He took the subject from *Jerusalem Delivered* (1575) by Torquato Tasso, an epic poem that was particularly popular with Romantic painters. The meeting of the two lovers is set in a garden that establishes the sentimental tone of the scene; the style of the painting is already recognizable as belonging to Hayez and reveals many of the components of the artist's training. In these years, aside from being interested in the sculpture of Canova, Hayez was making a thorough study of sixteenth-century Venetian art, most of all Titian. The lustrous surfaces of the helmet and shield, the body of Armida, and the rich folds of the fabric cast over the rock recall the style of Titian, which was composed of light and suffused with sensuality.

Jean-Auguste-Dominique Ingres
Angelica and Ruggero
1819, oil on canvas
147 x 190 cm
Musée du Louvre, Paris

The episode appears in Canto X of *Orlando Furioso* by Ludovico Ariosto (1532): Ruggero arrives to free Angelica, chained to the Isle of Tears and about to be devoured by a terrible sea monster, which the knight hastens to dispatch. Ingres created a composition of great effect, set in a night barely illuminated by a beacon, with strong light that frontally illuminates the scene; the shining armor of Ruggero, chiseled and elaborate, and the fearsomely terrible body of the hippogriff (half-horse and half-eagle) he rides contrast enormously with the nude, sensual body of Angelica, not unlike a statue of Venus. Despite the tension that pervades the scene, it has an almost unreal tone, thanks to Ingres' calligraphic meticulousness, which was judged archaic by the critics of the Salon. The work was painted for Louis XVIII and was made for the throne room in the château of Versailles.

ARY SCHEFFER
Lenore ("The Dead Ride Fast")
1820–25,
oil on canvas
56 x 98 cm
Musée de la Vie Romantique, Paris

The ballad of *Lenore* (1774) by the German poet Gottfried August Bürger (1747–1794) was made popular in France by Madame de Staël; she spoke enthusiastically of it in her *De l'Allemagne* (1818), and it was translated into English by Dante Gabriel Rossetti. The plot is exquisitely Romantic: as soldiers return from the Seven Years' War, Lenore waits in vain for her lover, Wilhelm, who appears instead at midnight wearing his armor and invites her to climb onto his black horse and marry him before the sun rises. Their frantic ride (during which he whispers, "The dead ride fast") ends at the cemetery in a scene populated with ghosts and the dead who leave their graves. Beneath his armor Wilhelm too is a skeleton, and he and the other dead vanish with the first light of dawn. Drenched in the dark fantasy style of a Gothic romance, the painting emphasizes the nocturnal tones of the scene, rendered almost monochromatic by the lunar glow, and the dynamism of the two lovers' precipitous ride.

Massimo D'Azeglio
The Death of Montmorency
1825, oil on canvas
149 x 202.4 cm
Galleria Civica d'Arte Moderna e Contemporanea, Turin

The subject is from *Malek Adel,* a novel by the French writer Marie-Sophie Cottin that had been translated into Italian in 1823, just two years before this work. D'Azeglio exhibited the painting in Turin in 1825 to great success, and it marked the beginning of a new genre, that of the "historiated landscape," a landscape adapted to the presentation of an historical event, not for a scene from daily life. The plot of the novel was based on a theme from the Crusades, soon to become an important source in the repertory of the so-called history painting. The death of Henri, duke of Montmorency and constable of France, is at the center of the composition, but the dominant element is the landscape, with its arcane and almost supernatural character, to which the palm trees add an element of exoticism.

Francesco Hayez
The Last Kiss of Romeo and Juliet
1823, oil on canvas
291 x 201.8 cm
Villa Carlotta, Tremezzo (Como)

The complete title of the painting describes it much like a stage direction: "The last kiss of Romeo and Juliet; obliged to flee, he is about to climb out the window; the background shows the coming dawn; the servant withdraws with the lamp; the architecture recalls the time in which these fortunate [*sic*] lovers lived." The long title makes clear how much the early nineteenth-century viewer, most of all in Italy, was led to appreciate the accurate structural and material reconstruction of a scene. Every element in this image was reproduced with historical accuracy, from the colored window panes to the lovers' stockings, from the devotional crucifix to the capitals of the columns, even to the so-called Savonarola-type chair. The protagonists of the famous tragedy by Shakespeare (Act III, Scene 5) were among the Romantic public's favorite figures, and Hayez continued to present them or cite them in paintings up to the famous *Kiss* of 1859 (see page 21).

Charles Lock Eastlake
Lord Byron's "Dream"
1827, oil on canvas
118 x 170.8 cm
Tate Gallery, London

An English artist of great descriptive gifts, Eastlake was one of the members of the current that long remained anchored to the neoclassical tradition. Even so, the choice of a subject like this reveals that he was also open to Romantic culture, emblematically represented by a poem like "The Dream," which Lord Byron composed in 1828. Eastlake based this canvas on the fourth stanza of the

poem, in which the symbolic voyage of the dream reaches a vision that blends the taste for ruins with Oriental motifs. In search of shade "from the noontide sultriness" the wanderer sits amid the fallen columns and ruins of ancient structures while camels and horses graze and other people slumber under a blue sky. Eastlake translates the almost paradisiacal mood with which the stanza ends in a scene of enormous calm outside time in which he succeeds in transferring all the dreamy sense of the poem to the imaginary landscape.

THOMAS COLE
The Cross in the Wilderness
1845, oil on canvas
61 x 61 cm
Musée du Louvre, Paris

Feelings of love and solitude but also the spirituality of nature and religion are the protagonists of this unique painting, which at first appears to be a tondo whereas the sharply outlined stone wall that frames the image is part of the painting and is of enormous importance. To the upper left on the wall Cole wrote out the title of the poem on which he based the painting, "The Cross in the Wilderness," composed in 1827 by Felicia Hemans, an English writer whose fame had spread to America. In the poem Hemans sings of the anguish of an Indian chief praying at the grave of a Christian; emotion and piety, the faiths of distant peoples, the delicate poetry of the landscape blend here in an atmosphere of profound spiritual harmony, perhaps an echo of Cole's conversion, since he had been baptized the year before at the age of forty-three.

Auguste Couder
Notre-Dame de Paris
1833, oil on canvas, oil on panel, with gilt-wood frame
163 x 128.5 cm
Maison de Victor Hugo, Paris

Designed as an old-style polyptych, this work is composed of ten canvases and a central tondo on panel, all of it inserted in a wooden frame made in a mixture of Renaissance and neo-Gothic style in keeping with the setting of the story, dated 1482. Couder, a student of Jacques-Louis David open to the various pictorial styles of the early nineteenth century, here presents a sumptuous celebration of *Notre-Dame de Paris,* the historical novel symbolic of Romanticism that brought Victor Hugo fame on its appearance in 1831. Couder presents several important moments in the various paintings and puts a portrait of the author at the center of the top, almost as though to indicate his divine position within modern literature. In the individual scenes, and most of all in the central one, the artist used an expressive style marked by high melodrama, thus fully in keeping with the tone of the novel.

NICOLA CIANFANELLI
Lucia and the Unnamed
1834, fresco
Palazzina della Meridiana, Palazzo Pitti, Florence

Commissioned by Leopold II, grand duke of Tuscany, this fresco decorated a room in the Meridiana Palace, the new wing connected to the Florentine royal residence, the Pitti Palace. It shows one of the outstanding episodes from *The Betrothed,* the first edition of which (1827) had already enjoyed great success and had greatly excited Leopold II. He requested the direct participation of the book's author, Alessandro Manzoni, in the creation of the nine scenes that he had selected from the novel to make the decoration for his room. Among these is the dialogue between Lucia and the Unnamed, which Cianfanelli set in an evocative nocturnal light, putting the profile of the domineering tyrant in shadow and illuminating the imploring gesture of Lucia, such as to make stand out the imminent repentance and the religious conversion.

Jehan Duseigneur
Orlando Furioso
1831, bronze
height 130 cm
Musée du Louvre, Paris

Exhibited at the Paris Salon of 1831, this statue drew immediate praise from Théophile Gautier, who proclaimed it a manifesto of Romantic art. Once again the subject is the hero of the famous poem by Ludovico Ariosto, the paladin of Charlemagne who falls prey to madness for the love of Angelica. Duseigneur, a sculptor who went against the formal rigid canons imposed by the academy, presents Orlando in the rage of madness while trying to free himself from the bonds that hold him prisoner, thus creating an image of great expressive force that made symbolic allusion to one of the most heartfelt themes of Romanticism: the efforts of every individual to give free reign to passion. The bronze casting was not made until 1867.

CARL CHRISTIAN VOGEL VON VOGELSTEIN
Dante and Ten Episodes from the "Divine Comedy"
1844, oil on canvas
232.5 x 176.5 cm
Galleria d'Arte Moderna di Palazzo Pitti, Florence

A German artist who spent a long time in Italy, becoming a supporter of the Nazarenes, Carl Vogel began this painting in Florence and finished it in Rome, drawing inspiration from both Dante's *Divine Comedy* and his *Vita Nuova*. Designed to resemble a Gothic polyptych—with a frame made of gilt carved wood topped by a cross and statues of the pope and emperor—the painting illustrates episodes from the *Inferno*, *Purgatorio*, and *Paradiso*, dividing them on three horizontal levels; at the center appears the enthroned Dante. The work thus uses the language of the medieval revival and blends the historical celebration of the figure of Dante—the national glory of Romantic Italy—with a moral message addressed to the viewer, who is induced to reflect on the spiritual path of the soul.

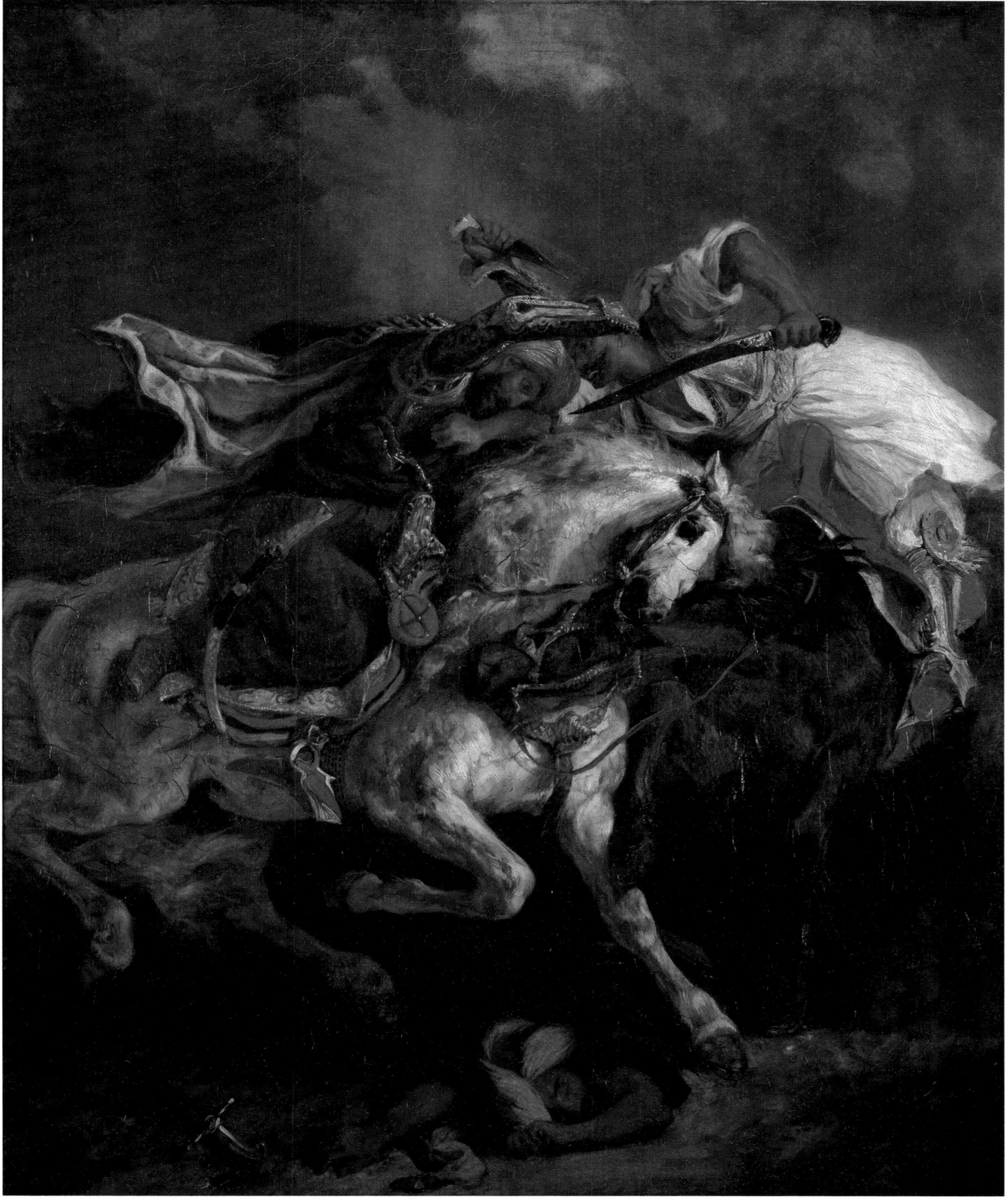

Eugène Delacroix
Combat of the Giaour and the Pasha
1835, oil on canvas
73 x 61 cm
Musée du Petit Palais, Paris

Attracted to the settings and costumes of the Near East and a great admirer of Lord Byron, Delacroix here illustrated an episode from one of Byron's poems, *The Giaour: A Fragment of a Turkish Tale* (1813). Set in late-seventeenth-century Greece, the poem narrates the strongly opposed love of a *giaour* (the Moslem term for an infidel) and Leila, a slave of the Pasha Hassan, barbarously killed for having betrayed him. The young Venetian giaour decides to vindicate the beloved woman, sets an ambush for the Turk, and fights a terrible battle with him that ends in Hassan's death. Delacroix began making preparatory studies for the painting in 1824, also making sketches from other sections of the poem, as can be read in his diary. The canvas, finished in 1826, is today in the Art Institute of Chicago, but in 1835 Delacroix made a replica with a few variations, which is this work, today in Paris. Delacroix's artistic evolution, including a renewed excessiveness, can be seen in this second version, animated by a frenetic dynamism that extends even to the swirling movement of the clouds.

Joseph-Désiré Court
Rigolette seeks to distract herself during the absence of Germain
1844, oil on canvas
112 x 80 cm
Musée des Beaux-Arts, Rouen

Between 1842 and 1843 the *Journal des Débats* published in installments a novel by Eugène Sue, *Les Mystères de Paris*; Court, a painter of history scenes and portraits, drew on it to make this painting, which found greater favor with the public than among critics and enjoyed immediate fortune when it was made into a print. The heroine, Rigolette, has just learned of the arrest of Germain, accused of theft, and she tries to while away the time until his release by busying herself with sewing. The setting is simple and didactic, with a modern middle-class house with a window open on the center of Paris, including a bridge over the Seine and, to the right, the cathedral. The artist presents few distractions in the room—the birdcage, the plant—and concentrates on the face of the woman, the model for which may have been Delphine Delamare, the woman who may have inspired the title character in Flaubert's *Madame Bovary*.

John Everett Millais
Ophelia
1852, oil on canvas
76.2 x 111.8 cm
Tate Gallery, London

A character in Shakespeare's *Hamlet*, Ophelia goes mad and throws herself in a stream (Act IV, Scene 7): Millais used this to create a composition of extreme fascination in which he portrayed with botanical precision dozens of plants and flowers, each with a precise symbolic meaning in terms of the young princess's emotions.

Alexandre Cabanel
Albaydé
1848, oil on canvas
98 x 80 cm
Musée Fabre, Montpellier

The figure of Albaydé appears in a collection of the poetry of Victor Hugo, *Les Orientales* (1829): Cabanel painted her in a singular way, full of a sensuality that contrasts with her melancholy expression and faraway gaze, but that perfectly anticipates the style of European painting at the end of the century.

Painting and drama have been linked since antiquity, as indicated by the scenes of theatrical stages that appear on Greek and Italic ceramics and as revealed by many Renaissance masterpieces, which often present scenes from the Gospels based on versions established by medieval miracle or mystery plays. Over the centuries images drawn from the theatrical stage made their way into paintings, in forms both direct and indirect. In the first half of the nineteenth century the range of typologies extended to include portraits of stage actors, presented in costume or not, illustrations of specific stage sets, the transposition of theatrical gestures or expressions to history paintings, and the use of subjects from contemporary plays as themes for paintings. In 1818 Ermes Visconti dedicated a chapter of his *Idee elementari sulla poesia romantica* to dances and pantomime, emphasizing how these forms of theatrical performance had come to blend poetry and painting, but this observation could easily have been applied to the other types of theatrical performance that were coming to constitute the preferred entertainment of the middle class. Romantic art was first defined in Germany, and the first gasps of Romanticism appear in Mozart, with the yearning for a spiritual world, the appearance of the demoniacal, and a fascination with the supernatural, aspects of which Karl Friedrich Schinkel employed in stage settings designed around 1815. These were joined to the ideas of the philosopher Friedrich Schelling, leading to plans for a complete art form that would summarize in itself music, poetry, and images to transport the spectator to a universe never before conceived. Such was the shared objective of the composer and pianist Carl Maria von Weber and the novelist and composer E. T. A. Hoffmann. In Italy the Romantic aesthetic began to take form with Gaetano Donizetti (*Anna Bolena*, 1830) and Vincenzo Bellini (*Norma*, 1831), with operas that, like contemporary painting, drew on history for their subjects, taking female figures from the heartless Middle Ages, such as Francesca da Rimini or Pia de' Tolomei, and having them act out tragic tales of love and death. The success of *Anna Bolena* is reflected in the many paintings showing famous sopranos in the costume of the unfortunate queen. The high point of the opera was the so-called mad scene, which involved a kind of pantomime of expressions of sorrow along with wild, hysterical gestures, as can be seen in both the canvas by Alessandro Guardassoni and in the portrait of *Giuditta Pasta in the Mad Scene of "Anna Bolena" by Donizetti* painted by Karl Pavlovich Briullov in 1834 (Museo Teatrale alla Scala, Milan), in which the singer appears in the costume she wore during the triumphant opening night in Bologna in 1830. Unlike the preceding century—in which excessive gesturing had been banned, for example, by Vittorio Alfieri in the performance of tragedies—the use of gestures came to be particularly cultivated in the Romantic theater. The codification made by Antonio Morrocchesi, the leading actor in the Alfieri repertory, in his *Lezioni di declamazine d'arte teatrale* of 1832, had been replaced by a style that adopted the most pathetic gestures easily recognizable in the figures of contemporary history painting, most of all those from the

Karl Friedrich Schinkel, *The Queen of the Night,* 1815, design on paper; Hochschulbibliothek, Berlin

Enrico Pollastrini, *Nello at the Grave of Pia,* 1851, oil on canvas, 147 x 185.5 cm; Galleria d'Arte Moderna di Palazzo Pitti, Florence

academic sphere. Francesco Hayez's paintings are particularly significant in that regard. His canvas of *Caterina Cornaro Deposed as Queen of Cyprus* (1842) makes an immediate echo of the musical work from the preceding year by Fromental Halévy, based on a text inspired by the tragedy written by Augustin Eugène Scribe. Such was the great appeal of the subject that both Donizetti, between 1842 and 1843, and Giovanni Pacini in 1846 translated it into music. In those same years Giuseppe Verdi was becoming the ideal Romantic composer. With his *Nabucco* of 1842 the passionate ideals of the Italian Risorgimento burst onto the Italian scene. On the opening night of *Macbeth*, performed at the Teatro della Pergola in 1847, Verdi, accused by some of having corrupted Italian *bel canto*, conquered the Florentine stage. A few years later Antonio Ciseri, one of the leading authorities in the academic field, introduced to Verdi by Giovanni Dupré, agreed to decorate a villa in Volterra with scenes from *Rigoletto*, which had been staged in Florence in March 1852. The Italian opera met with great success in Paris, where Rossini directed the Théâtre-Italien for three years, which saw the opening night of his *Siege of Corinth* in 1826 and in 1835 the debut of *I Puritani* by Vincenzo Bellini. The theater, built in 1783 and also known as the

French school, *The Théâtre-Italien of Paris at the Salle Favart in the Period of the Restoration*, 1815–30, oil on canvas, 53 x 74 cm; Museo Teatrale alla Scala, Milan

to dance on points—on the tips of her toes—so well that what had once been a technical tour de force became a basic feature of academic dance. This style was the perfect visual manifestation of the ethereal figure, an ideal expression of spiritual elevation that thrilled the Romantic public. On March 12, 1832, at the Opéra of Paris,

Melodrama

Salle Favart, served as the headquarters for Italian opera companies until its interior was destroyed by fire in 1838. During this period Paris saw the debut of another important aspect of Romantic theater, classical ballet. The apparently contradictory union of the two terms is instead quite meaningful, since with the perfection of the classical technique, rigidly academic and based on the Italian matrix, a great leap in quality was made that found its winning expression in the "Romantic" spirit. After the short period of the "coreodramma" of Salvatore Viganò, the early years of the century had seen the evolution of a complex formula of "dance tragedy." A fundamental change took place when the ballerina Marie Taglioni (1804–1884), daughter of an internationally famous choreographer, achieved such technical skill that she was able

Taglioni performed *La Sylphide*, a ballet created for her by her father (with a libretto by Adolphe Nourrit and music by Jean Schneitzhoeffer). *La Sylphide* presented two epochal innovations: the use of a plot no longer historical or mythological but drawn instead from a legend of the northern woods narrated by Charles Nodier, and the use of a white muslin skirt, the tutu, created for Taglioni by Eugène Lami and destined to become the symbol itself of the classical ballerina. Romantic ballet went on to become one of the most popular genres in the theaters of the world, thanks to dancers like Carlotta Grisi, heroine of *Giselle* in 1841, and Lucien Petipa, member of a family of choreographers that included Marius Petipa, composer at the end of the nineteenth century of such immortal ballets as the *Nutcracker*.

Francesco Hayez, *Caterina Cornaro Deposed as Queen of Cyprus*, 1842, oil on canvas, 121 x 151 cm; Accademia Carrara, Bergamo

Joshua Reynolds
Mrs. Siddons as the Tragic Muse
1789, oil on canvas
239.7 x 147.6 cm
Dulwich Picture Gallery, London

Dressed in her stage costume, the actress appears in the role of Melpomene, muse of tragedy, whose traditional attributes, a cup and a dagger, are held in the hands of Pity and Terror, standing behind her. Sarah Siddons (1755–1831), daughter of the actor Roger Kemble and wife of the actor William Siddons, performed as a tragic heroine for nearly thirty years, retiring from the stage in 1812. Reynolds portrays her seated almost regally in an unreal and evanescent atmosphere, with an extremely inspired sensibility that places her outside time. Critics at the beginning of the nineteenth century admired the expression of great modernity on the actress's face, and various Romantic intellectuals claimed the painting had the power of the sublime, in fact defining it "The most sublime portrait ever painted."

Francesco Hayez
Giovanni David in Theatrical Costume
1830, oil on canvas
224 x 164 cm
Accademia di Brera, Milan

Giovanni David (1790–1864), a Neapolitan tenor of great fame, is here presented dressed for his role in *Gli Arabi nelle Gallie,* a melodrama composed by Giovanni Pacini that was presented at Milan's La Scala opera house in 1827. Attached to the painting is a behind-the-scenes tale of amorous intrigue, for it was commissioned from Hayez by Countess Yulia Samoilova Pahlen, wealthy Russian art patron and collector living in Milan and also the lover of the composer Giovanni Pacini, who had abandoned Paolina Borghese (née Pauline Bonaparte) to be with her. The countess gave the painter precise instructions to put the soprano Stefania Favelli in the background, and in fact she appears seen from behind, kneeling at an altar. The year before this painting the singer had been portrayed in stage costume by Giuseppe Molteni, Hayez's great rival, and Hayez continued his competition with Molteni by presenting the sophisticated Arabian costume worn by David in extreme detail.

Giovanni Pagliarini
Imelda and Bonifacio
1835, oil on canvas
163 x 203 cm
Museo Revoltella, Trieste

The tragic love story of Imelda de' Lambertazzi and Bonifacio de' Geremei, set in medieval Bologna, was brought to light in 1830 in a book by the historian Defendente Sacchi that opera librettists turned to time and again for inspiration until the end of the nineteenth century. The canvas presents the moment that precedes the dramatic epilogue, with a scene more than reminiscent of the deaths of Romeo and Juliet: attempting to extract the poison from her lover's wound, Imelda falls victim to it herself. The melodramatic tones impressed by Pagliarini on the presentation of the two lovers seem tinged with theatrical staging, in which the gestures and gazes of the leading players concur in emphasizing what has occurred; even the setting seems to meet the requirements of the stage, while the painter unleashed his fancy on precious fabrics, the bright colors well in keeping with stage costumes.

Vincenzo Lucchini
Portrait of the Tenor Napoleone Moriani
1839, oil on canvas
88 x 72 cm
Museo Civico and Pinacoteca Crociani, Montepulciano

The tenor Moriani became famous in the 1830s for his interpretations of Donizetti's operas. In this canvas he is presented in the final scene of *Lucia di Lammermoor* in the role of Edgar of Ravenswood, about to be killed in a duel near the tombs of his ancestors.

Alessandro Guardassoni
Anne Boleyn Driven Mad at Feeling the Loss of Her Diadem
1843, oil on canvas
101 x 79 cm
Galleria d'Arte Moderna, Bologna

The so-called mad scene of *Anna Bolena* was one of the outstanding moments in the drama by Felice Romani, set to music in 1830 by Gaetano Donizetti. An event shrouded in gloom, the history of the queen unjustly condemned to death fascinated the Romantic age. The painting presents the desperation, disturbed expression, theatrical gestures, and beautiful stage costume.

Girolamo Domenichini
The Condemnation of Hugo and Parisina
1836, oil on canvas
118 x 159 cm
Galleria Civica d'Arte Moderna, Ferrara

Byron's tragic poem *Parisina* (1816) inspired numerous paintings and stage versions during the nineteenth century, beginning with Felice Romani's 1833 libretto for the opera by Donizetti. Domenichini must have based this painting more on the opera's second act than on Byron's text. The story weaves love and jealousy; the moment presented here precedes the macabre conclusion: Parisina, wife of the duke of Ferrara, loves young Hugo, who is in fact the duke's natural son. Two guards bring the couple before the furious husband, who condemns Hugo to death; the faithful Ernest, on his knees, pleads in vain for mercy. Parisina, forced to witness the beheading of Hugo, will not survive. The duke's emphatic gesture has been taken to indicate the moment in which, rejecting the entreaties of the older man, he pulls away, ordering, "Have this madman taken far away from me."

Francesco Hayez
The Secret Accusation
1848, oil on canvas
153 x 120 cm
Civica Pinacoteca Malaspina, Pavia

This canvas, along with several other paintings Hayez made in later years, is based on a novel written by Andrea Maffei, *La Vendetta*, knowledge of which facilitates understanding of the painting. Set in the Venice of the doges, the story involves secret love affairs, betrayals, and vendettas; the shadowy climate of the book is well expressed in the elegant image of this young woman. This is in fact Maria, distressed at having been betrayed by her lover; in her hand is the anonymous letter with which, on the advice of her friend Rachele, she will get her revenge, accusing her lover of political treason, thus causing him to be condemned to death. Every element of the painting is presented with theatrical accents: Maria's sensuality and her emotional tension are reflected in the ruffled black veil that covers her, just as the arches of the Doge's Palace seem to imprison her in her fatal intrigue.

ANDREA APPIANI JUNIOR
Ginevra Sees the Ship of Ettore Fieramosca
1857, oil on canvas
169 x 121 cm
Palazzo Reale, Turin

In 1833 Massimo D'Azeglio published the novel *Ettore Fieramosca; or, The Duel of Barletta,* and it became the source of many opera librettos. This painting does not present a scene of exciting action but rather one of the central moments of the story. The love between the hero and Ginevra, wife of Graziano d'Asti, ferocious murderer who in fact killed her father, blossoms without compromising the young woman's moral virtues and honesty; the two meet secretly in the monastery of Sant'Orsola on the island of Gargano, off the coast of Barletta, with Ginevra's handmaid, the Saracen Zoraide, as their accomplice; she is shown here busy with embroidery. Appiani created an atmosphere of profound emotion with Ginevra's breathless anticipation, having just spotted Ettore's ship on its way toward the island; the warm light of sunset creates the background to the young woman's gaze, which blends chastity and passion, her heart struggling to choose between conjugal fidelity and true love.

Giuseppe Bezzuoli
The Murder of Lorenzino de' Medici
1840, oil on canvas
225 x 296 cm
Museo Civico, Pistoia

When the Pistoian Niccolò Puccini commissioned this work from Bezzuoli in 1838 he suggested that the painter use the stage costume of *Lucrezia Borgia* presented in the Teatro Alfieri as his source for the clothing of the woman kneeling to the left. The episode of Florentine history provided the background for several theatrical productions during the nineteenth century, including *Lorenzaccio* by Alfred de Musset. Bezzuoli conceived the painting as a stage scene, set in the small square of Santi Giovanni e Paolo in Venice, where Lorenzino, in flight after killing Alessandro de' Medici, has been stabbed by the killers hired by Duke Cosimo I and sent to avenge the crime. Supported by a gondolier, the wounded tyrannicide lies stretched out on the ground in the dramatic pose of a dead Christ, a reference completed by the figure of his weeping mother leaning over him. Even the direct light, which heightens the white tones, creates a theatrical effect, as do the dramatic gestures of the other figures.

Augustus Jules Bouvier
Carlotta Grisi in the Role of Giselle
1841,
colored lithograph
Victoria and Albert Museum, London

Together with Marie Taglioni, Carlotta Grisi (1819–1899) was a leading protagonist on the Romantic scene in the world of ballet. After studies at La Scala in Milan, she made her debut at age thirteen as a ballerina and singer; her encounter with the choreographer Jules Perrot in 1834 proved determinant for her rapid career, and she achieved true triumph in 1841 when she performed at the Paris Opéra in *Giselle, ou Les Willis*, a role created expressly for her. *Giselle*, the prototype of the Romantic ballet—and still a centerpiece of the classical repertory—involved contributions from the choreographers Perrot and Corsalli with a libretto written by Théophile Gautier and Vernoy de St.-George set to music by Adolphe Adam. It is a tragic story of love and wandering spirits, reworking a legend from the *Germania* by Heinrich Heine. Acclaimed for years in the major European theaters, Grisi passed into history for her extraordinary technique and for having introduced the use of ballet slippers with steel points.

LOUIS-LÉOPOLD BOILLY
The Melodrama Effect
1830, oil on canvas
32 x 41 cm
Musée Lambinet, Versailles

A melodramatic comment on feminine sensibilities. Unable to bear any longer the emotional drama she has been watching, a spectator faints: a true *coup de théâtre* reserved for the elegant public in a Parisian orchestra box.

LOUIS-LÉOPOLD BOILLY
A Front Seat during a Free Performance
1830, oil on canvas
33 x 41 cm
Musée Lambinet, Versailles

Created in pendant to the above work, this canvas offers a view of Boilly's skills as a portraitist, here presenting in playful details the gestures and rough features of ordinary people crowded into a box to take advantage of free admission.

In 1859 Charles Baudelaire noted, "From day to day art is losing respect for itself and is prostrating itself before exterior reality. The artist is more and more inclined to paint not what he dreams, but what he sees." Baudelaire was a poet with a Romantic soul; he was also a great admirer of Delacroix, but on the threshold of the 1860s he could not bring himself to accept the freedom with which artists were turning to the real world. The opposite of his restrictive judgment shows up in Delacroix's impression of the works of Gustave Courbet that he had occasion to see on August 3, 1855, when he visited the Pavillion du Réalisme that Courbet had set up a few meters from the main hall of the Paris Universal Exposition, which had rejected his paintings, including *The Painter's Studio* (see page 312). As he noted in his journal: "I went to see the Courbet exhibition. . . . I stayed there for nearly an hour and discovered a masterpiece in the very picture they had rejected [*The Painter's Studio*]. . . . They have rejected one of the most remarkable works of our time . . . but Mr. Courbet is not the man to be put off by a little thing like that." Delacroix was right: in the end Courbet achieved success, and in the 1860s he rose to triumph. The contrasting opinions of realism expressed by two Romantics underline the complexity of a phenomenon that had been taking shape in the very heart of Romantic culture for several years. Realism was opposed to very little of Romanticism's principal beliefs; indeed it further developed certain aspects of Romanticism. The artist's right to present truth can be seen as the determination to portray the ugly side of reality—the neoclassical aesthetic that gave primacy to beauty had long since been discarded—and this position had been formulated by such leading artists as Victor Hugo in the preface to his drama *Cromwell* (1827) and Théodore Géricault who, in paintings like the *Raft of the "Medusa"* (see page 128) and in portraits of the mentally ill, introduced images of disconcerting realism. Romanticism had instilled in artists the belief that it was their right to open themselves to new horizons, and over the years that belief had grown stronger; what had changed was the inner attitude, so that subjectivity and sentiment were gradually replaced by the observation of reality. So it was that in 1849 Ernest Meissonier presented a scene of graphic reality in his view of a Parisian street transformed into a battleground during the uprising of 1848. In France, this orientation toward the precise representation of reality, anticipated by Géricault, reappeared in the 1830s in the Middle Eastern paintings of Horace Vernet. It shows up in the strong chromatics adopted by Paul Delaroche as well as in the landscapes that Camille Corot began to paint from life using a revolutionary technique involving large masses of color. He kept those paintings more or less secret, exhibiting at the Salon idyllic canvases that were more in keeping with official taste, works that made him famous. Beginning in 1825 he made several trips to Italy, and his presence there was determinant both for his own formation and for the influence he had on artists who saw him at work. Unlike those who looked at the Italian landscape and saw only echoes of the past, Corot was struck by the light, by the way the sun lit up the colors, making them the direct instruments in his pictorial creations, and he began to paint according to his own sensibilities, no longer making use of traditional design procedures. His contacts with the painters of the Barbizon School were not accidental; Théodore Rousseau and the friends who joined him near that small town by Fontainebleau forest chose to paint landscapes free of artifices or rhetorical idealizations, animated by the desire to experience a total immersion in nature, far from the city. Between 1830 and 1850 the population of Paris had doubled, and the large-scale transformations of the city carried out under the direction of Baron Haussmann, which involved knocking down entire sections of the medieval city and the construction of the great boulevards, had made Paris a true metropolis. The suburbs and the life of the countryside were increasingly seen as places of lost peace and, like the landscapists of Fontainebleau, many painters developed an attachment to the rural world and to painting *en plein air*. There were those, such as Auguste-Barthélemy Glaize, who turned to scenes of the

Auguste-Barthélemy Glaize, *The Picnic*, 1850, oil on canvas, 115.5 x 45.7 cm; Musée Fabre, Montpellier

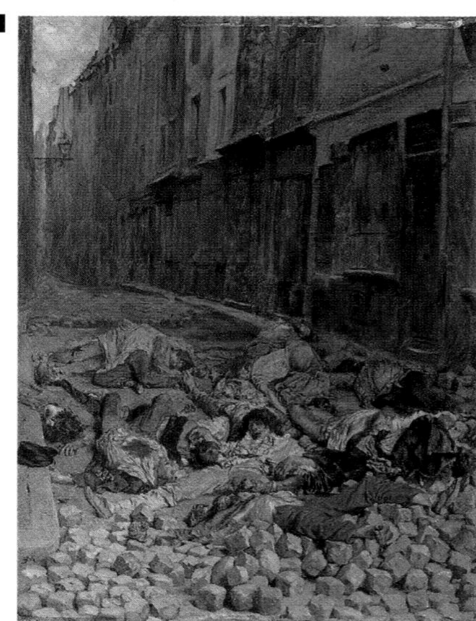

Ernest Meissonier, *Barricades in Rue de la Mortellerie, June 1848*, 1849, oil on canvas, 29.2 x 22.2 cm; Musée du Louvre, Paris

Jules Breton, *The Blessing of the Wheat at Artois,* 1857, oil on canvas, 129.5 x 320 cm; Musée d'Orsay, Paris

amusements of city dwellers in the country, with paintings like *The Picnic* of 1850, which anticipated a subject made famous by the Impressionists (*Le déjeneur sur l'herbe* by Edouard Manet, exhibited in 1863, or the *Luncheon on the Grass* by Claude Monet of 1865, both in the Musée d'Orsay, Paris). Glaize's *Picnic* is a lively composition, but the figures are not yet completely free and seem to be striking poses, most of all the man at the center, the wealthy Alfred Bruyas, who a little later was to become Courbet's patron. Courbet presented a somewhat similar subject in a canvas that again, in 1857, provoked a scandal at the Paris Salon: *The Young Ladies on the Banks of the Seine.* The scene of young women resting on grass in attitudes not in keeping with the behavior expected of "good society" girls was judged vulgar and immoral, offering a rude and graceless version of a scheme until then reserved to the presentation of nymphs and mythological figures. But Courbet was used to such altercations: his *After Dinner at Ornans* (1849) had met with approval, but the introduction of contemporary figures in scenes until then reserved for the more "idyllic" repertory continued to irritate both critics and the more morality-minded public. In 1853 Napoleon III, indignant at what he considered the excessive realism in the nudes of *Bathers* (Musée Fabre), struck the canvas with his riding crop; in 1855 the jury rejected the canvases Courbet had sent to the Salon, still unprepared to see paintings include "people who have not changed their underclothes and have the pretense to impose themselves on good society," as thundered the count of Nieuwerkerke, France's imperial superintendent of fine arts. A very different fate awaited another side of realism, one that was far more agreeable to the more timid spectators. The canvases of Rosa Bonheur and Jean-François Millet pleased everyone, since they presented the reality of peasants and the less-well-to-do classes without impinging on the emotional involvement so dear to the Romantic sensibility. *The Blessing of the Wheat at Artois* by Jules Breton, among the leading French naturalists, met with great success at the Salon of 1857, for he had created an image of reassuring beauty, with a procession of peasants crossing a golden field immersed in an atmosphere of serene harmony and devotion, touched by wonderful light effects.

Toward realism

Gustave Courbet, *The Young Ladies on the Banks of the Seine,* 1856, oil on canvas, 174 x 206 cm; Musée du Petit Palais, Paris

Jean-Baptiste-Camille Corot
Chartres Cathedral
1830, oil on canvas
65 x 50 cm
Musée du Louvre, Paris

Corot shared the Romantics' conviction that nature can be understood by the artist only by way of the emotions, but his technique was highly innovative, as can be seen in this canvas of 1830, composed of brushstrokes soaked in light and with volumes assembled like masses of color, a style of painting that was completely revolutionary for the period.

Louis-Auguste Lapito
Landscape of Fontainebleau
circa 1830,
oil on canvas
32 x 45 cm
Musée de la Picardie, Amiens

Lapito was a prolific landscapist, turning out more than two thousand paintings. This canvas shows the appealing rendering of light and the descriptive spontaneity that made him stand out as one of the first *en plein air* painters to anticipate the criteria of realism.

Giovanni Carnevali
Countess Anastasia Spini
circa 1840,
oil on canvas
136 x 89 cm
Accademia Carrara, Bergamo

Carnevali was quite familiar with the countess, having visited the Spini family since he was eight; his father had begun working for them, and he had played in the garden of the villa at Albino. Countess Anastasia, the unmarried sister of Count Pietro Andrea, was not completely sane, but the painter tempers her unhappy condition with touches of lively good humor. Without altering the reality of her features, he captures her serene and childlike spirit, which goes well with the tone of certain details that stand out from the painting. There are the writing accessories on the table behind the woman, the shiny gold snuffbox she holds in one hand and the ruby ring on the index finger of that hand, the colorful red and green ribbons of her bonnet, which frame her face, and even the magpie that stands at her feet with calm familiarity.

PAUL DELAROCHE
Pilgrims in Rome
1842, oil on canvas
164 x 205 cm
Muzeum Narodowe, Poznan

Delaroche had spent time in Rome in 1834, making many studies of sites and figures; eight years later he drew on those works to make this picture of a family of pilgrims during a moment's rest in Rome. The subject of pilgrims, part of the repertory of genre painting very much in vogue on the market, was associated with images of ordinary people, and Delaroche, attracted by the picturesque aspects of regional clothes and costumes, took to the subject with interest. The resulting work is surprising, since the attention to the details of reality is exalted by the high definition of the pictorial rendering. The figure of the woman, true protagonist of the painting in her elegant pose, stands out forcefully, both because of her penetrating expression and the brilliant clarity of her clothing. It was precisely in such violent contrasts of tonalities that Delaroche was a precursor of the coming experiments of realist painting.

Domenico Morelli
The Iconoclasts
1855, oil on canvas
257 x 212 cm
Museo Nazionale di Capodimonte, Naples

Morelli was a great admirer of Delaroche and studied his paintings closely while working on this canvas. He took the subject from an ancient chronicle narrating the persecution of Lazarus, a painter monk who lived in the eighth century during the period in which the Byzantine emperor announced the decrees against icons. The brushes on the stones to the left and the mural painting indicate the monk's icon-making activity, while in the foreground an emissary breaks an icon underfoot; all the figures are portraits of actual people. The work attests to Morelli's up-to-date awareness and his lively exchange of ideas with other artists, such as the Tuscan Macchiaioli group, who were actively moving painting toward greater realism. During these years he was working on the relationships between impression and chromatic values, on the expressive power of color as a means of revealing and making perceptible sensations and emotions.

Filippo Palizzi
View of Valletta from Fort Emmanuel, Malta
1843, oil on canvas
31.5 x 48 cm
Galleria Nazionale d'Arte Moderna, Rome

Founder of the new Neapolitan painting, as he was called by his fellow countryman D'Annunzio, Filippo Palizzi interpreted the landscape with an adherence to reality tied to the conviction that nature itself was an artist's best teacher; studying nature with simple emotions free of all preconceptions would lead the painter directly to the expression of feelings. On his way home from a trip to Moldavia that had begun in 1842, Palizzi visited Constantinople and Malta, making several highly evocative views, including this one. Despite the small format, the promontory of Valletta takes on a sense of solemn vastness. The almost dazzling treatment of light creates an effect of direct immersion in the landscape, which is supported by the minute reproduction of details in the right foreground, which reveals a marked inclination for the realistic citation of objects regardless of their importance.

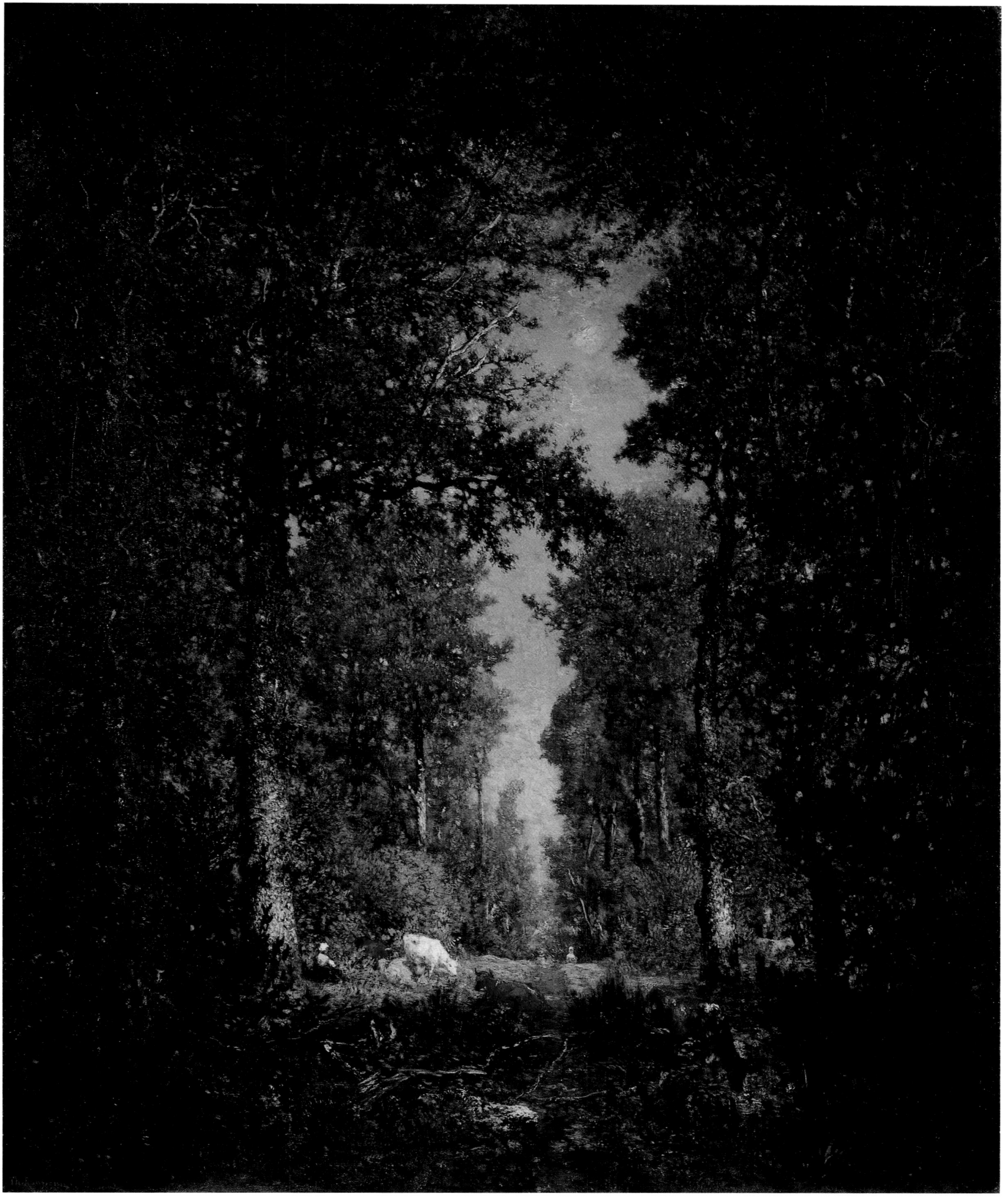

Théodore Rousseau
Avenue of Trees, Forest of l'Isle-Adam
1849, oil on canvas
101 x 82 cm
Musée d'Orsay, Paris

Principal exponent of the Barbizon School, Rousseau saw the forest of Fontainebleau as a kind of Arcadia and imagined that Virgil and Homer would have enjoyed composing verses in the shade of its enchanted settings. Like his Barbizon School colleagues, he found in the still uncontaminated landscape the values of a lost serenity and a simpler past that were being gradually destroyed by the progress of industrial civilization. His works were a transposition of those sentiments to canvas through a strongly naturalistic imprint capable of creating a sense of reality. By the end of the fourth decade of the nineteenth century, Rousseau's landscapes, although still full of Romantic reveries, were moving toward a change in technique capable of presenting the fascinating imprint of modern painting. This is visible most of all in the effects of light, as in the summer sunlight filtering its way into the heart of the woods in this canvas.

Rosa Bonheur
Plowing in the Nivernais
1849, oil on canvas
134 x 260 cm
Musée d'Orsay, Paris

Internationally famous exponent of French realism, Rosa Bonheur was the first female artist to be awarded the Legion of Honor. She began distinguishing herself at the Salon in the 1840s with paintings of animals, but not the tigers, lions, and jaguars of Romantics like Delacroix. Bonheur was drawn instead to domestic and farm animals, most of all those used in rural labors. Although she had grown up in Paris she did not like the city, far preferring life in the fields. In addition to this there was her strong passion for books on zoology and her studies of livestock; such was her passion that she managed to obtain police permission to dress as a man in order to visit libraries, since women were not then allowed to do so. In

all this Bonheur was supported by a family that firmly believed in social equality. In 1848 the government commissioned her to make this monumental canvas, in which she portrays her favorite animals, oxen. The work was a clamorous success. The scene of great harmony unfolds along parallel horizontal lines, with the slight curve of the hill following the team of oxen, realistic and stately at the same time; the clods of earth, like all the details of the landscape, are rendered with meticulous accuracy and are exalted by the extraordinary atmospheric transparency. Bonheur's paintings were often compared to the contemporary novels of George Sand; this canvas in particular seems to reflect the atmosphere that pervades the pages of *The Devil's Pond* (1846).

JEAN-BAPTISTE-CAMILLE COROT
Morning, the Dance of the Nymphs
1850, oil on canvas
98 x 131 cm
Musée d'Orsay, Paris

Along with his experiments in painting based on volumetric synthesis and contrasting arrangements of color, Corot carried on, together with his Barbizon friends, the dreamy vision of the landscape, evocative of mythology but rendered realistic by vibrant atmospheric effects achieved using a sophisticated technique.

JEAN-BAPTISTE-CAMILLE COROT
First Leaves, near Nantes
1855, oil on canvas
34 x 46 cm
Carnegie Museum of Art, Pittsburgh

In this beautiful painting the dreamy, Romantic atmosphere of the landscape is transferred to the real world, with peasants at work in the woods; their figures remain marginal, however, since Corot has dedicated the canvas to the tenderness of the grass and leaves that put touches of green in the trees, all of it cast in the wonderful light of spring.

Charles-François Jalabert
Nymphs Listening to the Songs of Orpheus
1853, oil on canvas
103.5 x 93.3 cm
Walters Art Gallery, Baltimore

Born like Courbet in 1819, Jalabert exhibited this painting at the Salon of 1853, revealing his complete artistic divergence from his colleague. The direct opposites of the female figures with which Courbet declared war on the academics and with which he had scandalized the public several times, Jalabert's nymphs recline languidly in a sort of enchanted wood. The flowing drapery of their clothing accentuates the tones of dreamy abandon with which they listen to Orpheus entertain them with the lyre. The scene resounds with echoes of the themes and vaporous images of such ballets as *La Sylphide* and *Giselle*, which had been thrilling Parisian audiences for several years. Although anchored to a classical-style mode of painting, this work is already moving toward a modern sensibility, interpreting a scene from mythology with a new plasticity and a magical spirit veined with sensuality.

GUSTAVE COURBET
After Dinner at Ornans
1848, oil on canvas
195 x 297 cm
Musée des Beaux-Arts, Lille

Exhibited at the Paris Salon of 1849, this canvas was Courbet's first great success; Delacroix saw it as an exceptional sign of innovation, and Ingres admired its pictorial quality, although he did think its choice of subject matter was "dangerous." In effect Courbet used the large format of history paintings or paintings on grand noble themes for a simple genre scene set in the home of Urbain Cuenot in Ornans. On a day like any other, as the painter's friend Marlet, having returned from hunting, lights his pipe and his dog rests under his chair, Adolphe Promayet plays the violin as Régis, the painter's father, seated to the left, and the bearded owner of the house listen with a tired air. The entire scene is rendered with its full rusticity, without any lively or pretty colors, and in low light that does not, however, keep the viewer from noting the disorder of the room's furnishings and tableware. It is a scene that, in the wake of the revolutionary movements of 1848, marks a major change in French painting.

Gustave Courbet
The Meeting, or "Bonjour, Monsieur Courbet"
1854, oil on canvas
129 x 149 cm
Musée Fabre, Montpellier

The canvas represents the artist meeting his patron Alfred Bruyas, accompanied by a servant and his dog. The two had met the year before in Paris, when the rich Bruyas had bought two of Courbet's paintings at the Salon, the *Bathers* and *The Sleeping Spinner,* asking him to make his portrait. The result was a close friendship based on shared political, artistic, and social ideals and a spiritual tie to which this painting makes symbolic allusion, with the meeting taking place at the convergence of two roads. The setting is in fact near Montpellier, where the artist had been Bruyas's guest in the summer of 1854. The careful reproduction of the countryside stands out, with the flowers and most of all the clear light of southern France, all of it presented with the nearly photographic effects of the perfect adherence to reality that Courbet gave the scene.

JOHN FREDERICK LEWIS
A Frank Encampment in the Desert of Mt. Sinai
1856, watercolor and pencil on paper
64.8 x 143.3 cm
Yale Center for British Art, New Haven

The taste for Oriental subjects also followed the evolution of painting over the arc of the century. Far from the inviting atmosphere of a harem or an action scene with powerful impact, this watercolor presents the almost scientific registration of reality. Frederick Lewis spent much time traveling through the countries of southern Europe, spending time in Spain around 1845 and visiting the Holy Land and Egypt. This view is set in a desert zone near Mount Sinai. Aided by the use of a watercolor technique, Lewis describes every element of the scene with an almost lenticular precision in the details, delineating millimeter by millimeter the colors and thicknesses of fabrics, beards, camels, utensils, and tableware of the camp, skimping, if at all, on the human elements in the scene, which are summarized primarily in the almost absent expression of the figure resting to the right.

Auguste Clésinger
Woman Bitten by a Snake
1847, marble
56.5 x 180 cm
Musée d'Orsay, Paris

Exhibited at the Paris Salon of 1847, this sculpture aroused a scandal because of the blatant sensuality of the life-size female figure. In order for such realism to fall within the parameters of morality it had to be justified by an ennobling iconographic theme: had Clésinger given the work a title based on the name of a heroine or goddess he might have got by, but he abstained, thereby challenging public opinion. The work's embarrassing realism had critics divided, but what truly caused scandal—and also greatly increased the artist's fame—was the recognition that the writhing female was Madame Apollonie Sabatier, until recently the artist's lover and most famous, perhaps, for inspiring the poetry of Charles Baudelaire. Several years later, in 1863, the painter Alexandre Cabanel used this sculpture as the inspiration for his painting of *The Birth of Venus* (Musée d'Orsay, Paris), which won him the highest honors.

Pierre Numa Bassaget
Monsieur Budget and Mademoiselle Cassette Strolling in the Tuileries
1832, colored lithograph from *La Caricature* of February 2, 1832

La Caricature, a newspaper of political satire against the government of Louis Philippe, was founded in Paris in 1831. Among its contributors was Honoré Daumier, arrested in 1832 for making a cartoon of the king with the features of Gargantua. This work by Bassaget, another cartoonist member of the group, took aim at the management of the finance ministry, creating eloquent personifications in "Mr. Budget" and "Miss Strongbox," who stroll arm in arm through the Tuileries Gardens. A centuries-old genre, the caricature was an important chapter in the figurative arts of the 1830s, presenting a lively prelude to realism, the language and themes of which it openly manipulated as it transformed itself into an effective tool of political comment and social protest.

Edgar Degas
The Old Italian Woman
1857, oil on canvas
73.7 x 61 cm
Metropolitan Museum of Art, New York

From July 1856 to the spring of 1859 Edgar De Gas—to use his original last name—was in Italy. In Naples he stayed with his paternal parents and in Florence with his Aunt Laura, who had married Baron Bellelli; he also spent much time in Rome, visiting the students at the French Academy. In Paris he had begun to dedicate himself to painting, taking private lessons, showing enthusiasm both for the works of Ingres and for those, with an opposite orientation, of Delacroix. A little before his departure for Italy he had visited the Pavillon du Réalisme, where he was greatly impressed by the paintings by Courbet. It should not be surprising, then, that this study, made about two years later, reveals the strong imprint of realism, which was at the base of the extraordinary naturalness of his portraits.

1780	**1780** Henry Fuseli, *The Artist in Despair over the Magnitude of Antique Fragments.* Joseph Vernet, *Storm.* Birth of Jean-Auguste-Dominique Ingres.	**1781** Henry Fuseli, first version of *The Nightmare*		**1783** End of the American War of Independence. First balloon flight over Paris. Birth of Stendhal (pseudonym of Henri Beyle).	
1790		**1791** Birth of Théodore Géricault. Death of Wolfgang Amadeus Mozart.	**1792** The republic is proclaimed in France. Construction and use of the guillotine.	**1793** Execution in Paris of King Louis XVI; Robespierre begins the Reign of Terror. Jacques-Louis David, *Death of Marat.* Anne-Louis Girodet-Trioson, *Sleep of Endymion.* The Musée Royal des Arts opens.	
1800	**1800** Napoleon's second campaign in Italy; defeats Austrians at Marengo. Jacques-Louis David, *Napoleon Crossing the St. Bernard Pass.* Congress holds its first session in Washington, D.C.		**1802** Napoleon is made consul for life in France and president of the Italian republic. François Richard, *Valentina of Milan Mourning the Death of Her Husband.* Anne-Louis Girodet-Trioson, *Ossian Receiving the Generals of the Republic.*		**1804** Napoleon is crowned emperor of the French; Beethoven composes the Third Symphony, the Eroica, in his honor. Antoine-Jean Gros, *Napoleon Visits the Plague Victims of Jaffa.*
1810	**1810** Pforr and Overbeck's group moves to Rome, becoming the Nazarenes. Napoleon marries Marie Louise, daughter of Francis I of Austria. Philipp Otto Runge, *Morning.* Caspar David Friedrich, *Monk by the Sea* and *Abbey in the Oaks.*		**1812** Napoleon invades Russia, occupies Moscow, and is forced to retreat. Joseph Mallord William Turner, *Snow Storm: Hannibal and His Army Crossing the Alps.* Pierre Révoil, *A Tournament in the 14th Century.*	**1813** Napoleon is defeated at Leipzig. Birth of Giuseppe Verdi. Francesco Hayez, *Rinaldo and Armida.*	**1814** Napoleon is exiled to Elba. Théodore Géricault, *The Wounded Cuirassier.* Francisco Goya, *The Second of May 1808* and *The Third of May 1808.* Dominique Ingres, *Grande Odalisque.*

1780–1859 Events,

1820	**1820** First Carbonari movement in Italy; arrest of Silvio Pellico. George IV ascends the throne of the United Kingdom. Joseph Mallord William Turner exhibits *Rome from the Vatican* on the centenary of the death of Raphael.	**1821** Napoleon dies on Saint Helena. Births of Charles Baudelaire and Gustave Flaubert. John Constable, *The Hay Wain.*	**1822** Greeks begin war of liberation against the Turks; massacre of rebels on the island of Chios.		**1824** Triumph of Romantic painting at the Paris Salon. Caspar David Friedrich, *The Sea of Ice.* France: Charles X succeeds Louis XVIII. Deaths of Théodore Géricault and George Byron.
1830	**1830** July Revolution in France; Louis Philippe, duc d'Orléans, is made king. Eugène Delacroix, *Liberty Leading the People.* France conquers Algeria. Death of George IV.	**1831** John Constable, *Salisbury Cathedral from the Meadows.* Victory Hugo, *Notre-Dame de Paris.* Birth of the newspaper "La Caricature." Giuseppe Mazzini founds the secret society Giovine Italia ("Young Italy").	**1832** Romantic ballet comes into being with *La Sylphide,* performed by Marie Taglioni. Death of Johann Wolfgang von Goethe. Eugène Delacroix travels to Morocco. Birth of Édouard Manet.	**1833** Karl Pavlovich Briullov, *The Last Day of Pompeii.* Horace Vernet travels to Algeria. Francesco Hayez, *The Penitent Magdalene.*	**1834** Eugène Delacroix, *Women of Algiers.* James Pradier, *Satyr and Bacchante.* Birth of Edgar Degas.
1840	**1840** The ashes of Napoleon are transferred from Saint Helena to Paris. Victoria marries Albert of Saxe-Coburg-Gotha. Alessandro Manzoni, definitive edition of *The Betrothed.*	**1841** The ballerina Carlotta Grisi triumphs in *Giselle.* Jean-Auguste-Dominique Ingres returns to Paris. Théodore Chassériau, *The Toilet of Esther.*	**1842** Giovanni Dupré, *Dying Abel.* Performance in Milan of *Nabucco* by Giuseppe Verdi. Purismo manifesto in Italy.		**1844** Joseph Mallord William Turner, *Rain, Steam, and Speed.*
1850		**1851** Great Exhibition in London. John Ruskin defends the Pre-Raphaelites.	**1852** End of the Second Republic in France; Louis Napoleon becomes emperor as Napoleon III. John Everett Millais, *Ophelia.* Gustave Moreau, *The Suitors.*	**1853** Holman Hunt, *The Light of the World.*	

1785 Joseph Wright of Derby, *The Indian Widow*. Joshua Reynolds, *Mrs. Siddons as the Tragic Muse*. Birth of Alessandro Manzoni.	**1786** Grand Duke of Tuscany Peter Leopold of Lorraine abolishes the death penalty. John Trumbull, *The Death of General Warren at the Battle of Bunker's Hill*.	**1787** Representatives of the thirteen colonies sign the Constitution.		**1789** The French Revolution begins in Paris on July 14 with the storming of the Bastille. George Washington is elected first president of the United States.	**1780**
1795 In Paris the Convention is disbanded and the Directory is installed. The Musée des Antiquités et Monuments Français opens.	**1796** First Napoleonic campaign in Italy; Napoleon marries Josephine de Beauharnais. William Beckford builds Fonthill Abbey. Antonio Canova, *The Penitent Magdalene*. Francisco Goya, *The Sleep of Reason Produces Monsters*.	**1797** Treaty of Campo Formio: France cedes Venice to Austria. Bertel Thorvaldsen arrives in Rome. Ludwig Tieck writes *Puss in Boots*. Births of Franz Schubert and Gaetano Donizetti.	**1798** The French enter Rome. Horatio Nelson destroys the French fleet at Aboukir. August and Friedrich Schlegel found the *Athenaeum*. Births of Eugène Delacroix and Giacomo Leopardi.		**1790**
1805 Napoleon is crowned king of Italy in Milan. Battle of Trafalgar: Horatio Nelson destroys the French and Spanish fleets. Pierre-Paul Prud'hon, portrait of the Empress Josephine. Birth of Giuseppe Mazzini.	**1806** French troops occupy Berlin. Joseph Bonaparte is made king of Naples. Ingres moves to Rome. Anne-Louis Girodet-Trioson, *Scene of the Deluge*.	**1807** French victories in Russia; treaties of Tilsit; Jérôme Bonaparte is made king of Westphalia. Jacques-Louis David, *Coronation of Napoleon*. Ugo Foscolo, *Sepulchres*.	**1808** Rebellion in Madrid against Joseph Bonaparte, king of Spain. Antoine-Jean Gros, *Napoleon on the Battlefield at Eylau*. Dominique Ingres, *Valpinçon Bather* and *Oedipus and the Sphinx*. Caspar David Friedrich, Tetschen Altar.	**1809** Franz Pforr and Friedrich Overbeck found the Brotherhood of St. Luke in Vienna. Napoleon divorces Josephine de Beauharnais. Johann Wolfgang von Goethe, *Elective Affinities*.	**1800**
1815 Napoleon escapes from Elba, returns to France, is defeated at Waterloo. The Congress of Vienna ends. Friedrich Schinkel, *Medieval City on a River*.		**1817** In Rome, the Nazarenes begin decoration of the Casino Massimo. Joseph Mallord William Turner, *The Decline of the Carthaginian Empire*. William Blake, *Dante's "Divine Comedy": Hell, Canto 5*. John Martin, *The Bard*.	**1818** Caspar David Friedrich, *Wanderer on the Sea of Fog*. In Milan publication of "Il Conciliatore," a newspaper of Romantic literature and politics. Birth of Gustave Courbet.	**1819** Théodore Géricault, *The Raft of the "Medusa."* Dominique Ingres, *Angelica and Ruggero*. Caspar David Friedrich, *A Man and Woman Contemplating the Moon*. "Il Conciliatore" is suppressed.	**1810**

artists, works

1825 Corot's first trip to Italy. Massimo D'Azeglio, *The Death of Montmorency*. New York: Thomas Cole lays basis for the Hudson River School. Deaths of Henry Fuseli and Jacques-Louis David.	**1826** James Fenimore Cooper publishes *The Last of the Mohicans*.	**1827** Turks defeated at Navarino. Victor Hugo, *Cromwell*. Alessandro Manzoni, *The Betrothed*. Deaths of Ugo Foscolo and Ludwig van Beethoven. Eugène Delacroix, *Death of Sardanapalus*.		**1829** Joseph Mallord William Turner, *Ulysses Deriding Polyphemus*.	**1820**
1835 Lorenzo Bartolini, *Trust in God*. Eugène Delacroix, *Combat of the Giaour and the Pasha*. Édouard Cibot, *Anne Boleyn in the Tower of London*. Dominique Ingres returns to Rome.	**1836** Death of Giacomo Leopardi.	**1837** Queen Victoria takes the throne in Britain. George Catlin opens his Indian Gallery.		**1839** Louis-Jacques-Mandé Daguerre perfects the daguerreotype.	**1830**
1845 George Catlin brings his Native American exhibition to Paris.	**1846** Jean-Léon Gérôme, *Cockfight*.	**1847** Thomas Couture, *Romans in the Decadence*. Auguste Clésinger, *Woman Bitten by a Snake*. Vincenzo Vela, *Spartacus*.	**1848** Revolutions across Europe; first war of independence in Italy; Second Republic in France, Louis Napoleon Bonaparte president. Pre-Raphaelite Brotherhood is formed in London. Gustave Courbet, *After Dinner at Ornans*.	**1849** First Pre-Raphaelite exhibitions in London.	**1840**
1855 Universal Exposition in Paris. Jean-Léon Gérôme, *The Age of Augustus: The Birth of Christ*. Gustave Courbet, *The Painter's Studio*, exhibited in the Pavillon du Réalisme.	**1856** Edgar Degas travels to Italy. Edmond Duranty founds the newspaper "Réalisme." Dominique Ingres, portrait of *Ines Moitessier*. First works of the Macchiaioli group in Tuscany.	**1857** Gustave Courbet, *The Young Ladies on the Banks of the Seine*, causes scandal at the Salon. Champfleury (Jules Husson) publishes *Le Réalisme*. Charles Baudelaire, *The Flowers of Evil*.	**1858** Accord between Camillo Cavour and Napoleon III against Austria. The Virgin Mary appears to Marie Bernarde Soubirous at Lourdes. Jean-François Millet, *The Angelus*. Arthur Hughes, *April Love*.	**1859** Second war of independence in Italy; Lombardy, ceded to France by Austria, goes to the kingdom of Sardinia. Charles Darwin, *Origin of Species*. Francesco Hayez, *The Kiss*.	**1850**

References

Biographies
•
Bibliography
•
Index of names and places
•
Photographic references

Biographies

EDITED BY
Veronica Buzzano,
Alessandra Licheri,
Sergio Scardoni

NICOLAI ABRAHAM ABILDGAARD
(Copenhagen, 1743 – Frederiksdal, Copenhagen, 1809)

Danish painter, designer, and architect. He spent the years 1772 to 1777 in Italy, studying classical art and the great masters of the sixteenth century; upon his return to his homeland, he contributed to the spread of the neoclassical style through his paintings (including the large frescoes for the banquet hall of the Christiansborg Slot, 1778–91), his teaching, and his direction of the Danish Academy (1789).

JACQUES LAURENT AGASSE
(Geneva, 1767 – London, 1849)

English painter of Swiss birth. After studies in Paris in the atelier of J.-L. David he moved to London, where he exhibited at the Royal Academy for almost fifty years. He is best known for his activities as an animal painter, and his works had great influence on English artists.

EUGENIO AGNENI
(Sutri, 1819 – Rome, 1888)

Italian painter. He was a student of Francesco Coghetti. In 1847 Pope Pius IX entrusted him with the execution of the decoration of the throne room of the Quirinal Palace. His reputation was such that in Paris in 1852 he was included in the group of artists charged with decoration of the Louvre. He then moved to London, where Queen Victoria commissioned him to paint one of the rooms of Covent Garden.

FILIPPO AGRICOLA
(Rome, 1795–1857)

Italian painter. He studied with his father, perfecting his classical training with Gaspare Landi and Vincenzo Camuccini. In 1836 he was given the chair in painting at the Academy of St. Luke in Rome, later serving as president (1854–55). He became one of the most typical exponents of Raphaelesque portraiture, and his paintings, such as the portrait of *Constance Monti Perticari* (page 164), were often made on commission from Italian and foreign nobles.

AUGUST-WILHELM-JULIUS AHLBORN
(Hannover, 1796 – Rome, 1857)

German allegorical and landscape painter and copyist. In 1827, after studies in Berlin, he left for Italy and set himself up there, attracted by the artistic setting and the beauty of the landscape, which led him to adopt Italian forms. He was elected a member of the Berlin Academy. Most of his landscapes present Italian views, but he also painted sites in the Tyrol and northern Germany.

JEAN ALAUX
(Bordeaux, 1786 – Paris, 1864)

French painter. He studied with Pierre Narcisse Guérin and won the Prix de Rome in 1815, spending the next six years in Italy. Thanks to support from King Louis Philippe he was among the artists commissioned to decorate rooms in the Louvre; he also worked on the dome of the Senate in Paris and the historical gallery of Versailles. He was director of the French Academy in Rome from 1847 to 1852. The Musée Ingres in Montauban has his *Atelier of Ingres in Rome* (page 142).

FRIEDRICH VON AMERLING
(Vienna, 1803–1887)

Austrian painter. After courses at the Vienna Academy, which he entered in 1816, as well as that of Prague (1824–26), he visited both London and Paris, returning to Vienna in 1828. In 1832 he was made court painter. Attentive to the details and taste of the middle class he became the most sought-after portraitist in Vienna during the Biedermeier period.

ANDREA APPIANI
(Milan, 1754–1817)

Italian painter and designer. He studied with Martin Knoller, increasing his knowledge of the technique of oil painting. Napoleon's high opinion of his talent resulted in a series of portraits of the emperor and his circle. Invited to Paris in 1804 he met J.-L. David; the next year he was named *premier peintre* to Napoleon. Among his works is *Napoleon, King of Italy* (page 44).

ANDREA APPIANI JUNIOR
(Milan, 1817–1865)

Italian painter, grandson of the more famous Andrea Appiani (above). He attended the Academy of St. Luke in Rome; on his return to Milan he made paintings in a style similar to that of Francesco Hayez. He received prestigious commissions for work in the Biblioteca Braidense in Milan and took part almost annually in the

Brera exhibitions with portraits and history paintings. He also made fresco decorations, as in the parish church of Bolbeno (Trent), for which he painted four large medallions together with Giovanni Consonni.

ARCHIBALD ARCHER
(Nineteenth century)

English portrait painter. He was active in London and Liverpool early in the nineteenth century; between 1810 and 1845 he exhibited at the Royal Academy in London. Among his works is *The Temporary Elgin Room* (page 304).

GIUSEPPE PIETRO BAGETTI
(Turin, 1764–1831)

Italian painter. He first studied music at the conservatory in Turin, then turned to architecture. He attended the studio of the Bolognese designer P.G. Palmieri, from whom he learned to paint watercolor landscapes; he was then given prestigious commissions. In 1800 he was made a captain of topographical engineers and over the next eight years he painted scenes of the engagements of Napoleon's army and made topographical surveys and copies of maps. With the fall of Napoleon he returned to Turin and painted landscapes with a picturesque style.

LORENZO BARTOLINI
(Prato, 1777 – Florence, 1850)

Italian sculptor. He studied in the Paris atelier of J.-L. David, where he met Jean-Auguste-Dominique Ingres, with whom he shared admiration for fifteenth-century Italian art. He returned to Italy and was made a professor at the Florence Academy in 1839, opening the way to new teaching methods based on the observation and imitation of reality.

WILHELM BENDZ
(Odense, 1804 – Vicenza, 1832)

Danish painter. He was a student of C. W. Eckersberg at the Copenhagen Academy. In 1831 he set out for Italy, stopping along the way and spending nearly a year in Bavaria. He reached Italy in 1832 and died there shortly after his arrival. Primarily a portrait painter—isolated figures and family groups—he showed originality in the cropping of his works, which are often set in interiors, with complex effects of artificial lighting.

MARIE-GUILLEMINE BENOIST
(Paris, 1768–1826)

French painter. She studied with Elisabeth Vigée-Lebrun in 1781 and worked in the studio of J.-L. David in 1786, learning a neoclassical orientation. The recognition of her talent led to many official commissions, and she made many religious works. Her *Portrait of a Negress* (page 196) reveals the harmonious combination of the skillful use of color and plastic rigor.

PIETRO BENVENUTI
(Arezzo, 1769 – Florence, 1844)

Italian painter. At twelve he entered the Florence Academy of Fine Arts. From 1792 to 1804 he was in Rome, studying with Vincenzo Camuccini, the Danish painter Asmus Jakob Carstens, and the sculptor Bertel Thorvaldsen; in 1804 he was made director of the Florence Academy. He received numerous commissions for portraits from nobles and the middle class during the Napoleonic regency of Elisa Baciocchi, Bonaparte's sister, such that he was considered her official court painter; to this period dates *Elisa Baciocchi and Her Court* (page 53).

GIUSEPPE BEZZUOLI
(Florence, 1784–1855)

Italian painter and teacher. He attended the Florence Academy and became a student of Pietro Benvenuti in 1803. In 1812 he went to Rome and studied the works of Raphael and between 1815 and 1817 went to Bologna several times to study the works of seventeenth-century painters. During this period he was active in Rome, Naples, and Pistoia. In 1827 Grande Duke Leopold II commissioned him to make the large painting of *Charles VIII Entering Florence* (page 110).

FRANÇOIS-AUGUSTE BIARD
(Lyons, 1798 – Les Plâtreries, 1882)

French painter of historic and military subjects. He studied with Pierre Révoil and in 1827 began a long series of trips. He led an adventurous life that influenced his art, which is characterized by the scrupulous attention to reality, powerful lyricism, and profound sentiment—he became one of the most popular artists of his period. Outstanding among his compositions are those based on his trip to the North Pole, such as *Magdalene Bay* (page 283).

GEORGE CALEB BINGHAM
(Augusta County, Virginia, 1811 – Kansas City, Missouri, 1879)

American painter, one of the leaders of nineteenth-century genre painting. A sharp interpreter of daily life, he painted subjects located in the Midwest, along the Mississippi and Missouri rivers. He went to Europe in 1856 and stayed three years. His *Fur Traders Descending the Missouri* (page 227) marks the beginning of the most prolific period of his career.

WILLIAM BLAKE
(London, 1757–1827)

English printmaker, painter, and poet. Of modest origins, Blake trained at the Royal Academy of London. He earned his living illustrating books and selling his volumes of "illuminated printing." His works blend a taste for the fantastic and the visionary with medieval and biblical references, hallucinations, mysticism, and the ferments of early Romanticism. Notable among his works are the illustrations he made for stories and poems, including twenty-two engravings of the Book of Job (1826) and the monumental, unfinished series of watercolors for the *Divine Comedy* of Dante.

KARL BLECHEN
(Cottbus, 1798 – Berlin, 1840)

German painter. After studies at the Berlin Academy he studied with Johan Christian Dahl and Caspar David Friedrich (1823) in Dresden. Nominated professor at the Berlin Academy in 1831, in 1836 he was struck by a serious mental illness. Like Friedrich, he considered the landscape a vehicle for the expression of the most profound spiritual emotions. In some paintings he reveals himself an important precursor of realism.

MERRY-JOSEPH BLONDEL
(Paris, 1781–1853)

French painter. A prolific artist, he trained in the atelier of Jean-Baptiste Regnault. After three years (1809–11) at the Villa Medici, he dedicated himself primarily to history painting and obtained numerous commissions, not only for churches of Paris but also the Louvre, Versailles, and the Luxembourg Palace. He was elected professor at the École des Beaux-Arts in 1832.

DETLEF CONRAD BLUNK
(Breintenburg (Holstein), 1799 – Hamburg, 1853)

Danish history, genre, and landscape painter. He attended the Copenhagen Academy and studied with J.L. Lund. On receiving a grant he left for Italy and during the trip stayed in Berlin and Dresden. On his return to Denmark he was elected member of the academy thanks to his painting *Noah Welcomes the Dove in the Ark* (Thorvaldsens Museum, Copenhagen).

GIUSEPPE BOCCACCIO
(Colorno, 1790 – Parma, 1852)

Italian history and landscape painter. The National Gallery of Parma has two of his paintings, *A Wood* and *The Piazza Grande of Parma*.

LOUIS-LÉOPOLD BOILLY
(La Bassée, 1761 – Paris, 1845)

French painter and printmaker. He learned the technique of *trompe l'oeil* from Dominique Doncre at Arras and then set himself up in Paris, working for private patrons. The works dating to the 1790s are primarily of amorous or sentimental subjects, with sensual settings and costumes. After 1800 his compositions became more complex and deal most of all with street scenes, presented with spontaneity and refinement. He made an important collection of portraits and facial features, all in a caricatural style.

ANTOINE-FÉLIX BOISSELIER
(Paris, 1790 – Versailles, 1857)

French painter. He attended the atelier of J.V. Bertin, from whom he learned the art of landscape painting. He exhibited regularly at the Salon and participated in large projects, such as the Galerie de Diane at Fontainebleau and the Salles des Croisades at Versailles. He was awarded the Legion of Honor in 1842. His landscapes, initially characterized by purity of line and vast panoramic perspectives, gradually became more personal and realistic.

ROSA BONHEUR
(Bordeaux, 1822 – Thomery, 1899)

French painter and sculptor, daughter of the painter Raymond Bonheur. She specialized in Dutch-style rural scenes with animals that enjoyed great success in France, England, and the United States. Her studio in Thomery is open to the public.

AUGUSTUS JULES BOUVIER
(London, 1837–1881)

English watercolorist. He studied at the Royal Academy of London, completing his studies in France and Italy. He became a member of the New Water Colour Society in 1865 and made genre scenes and a series of idealized female portraits.

KARL PAVLOVICH BRIULLOV
(St. Petersburg, 1799 – Manziana, 1852)

Russian painter of history, genre, and religious subjects as well as a portraitist, with an international and eclectic background. He trained at the St. Petersburg Academy and visited Italy in 1822. He returned to St. Petersburg in 1835 and became professor of painting at the academy and made many portraits.

FYODOR BRUNI
(Milan, 1802 – St. Petersburg, 1875)

Russian painter and etcher born in Italy. He began studies at the St. Petersburg Academy in 1808 and in 1819 went to Rome, where in 1828 he made the *Bacchante Giving Cupid a Drink* (page 87); the model who posed for the painting became his wife in 1835. In 1836 he returned to St. Petersburg and was nominated professor at the academy.

ALEXANDRE CABANEL
(Montpellier, 1823 – Paris, 1889)

French painter known for high-quality portraits and masterful mythological scenes. His history paintings are famous for their fine detail and iconographic richness. He had an important role in the official Salons during the Second Empire and was firmly against Impressionism.

IPPOLITO CAFFI
(Belluno, 1809 – at sea, Lissa, 1866)

Italian painter. Following studies at the Venice Academy from 1827 to 1829 he went to Rome in 1842 and dedicated himself to landscape painting. He traveled a great deal, including trips to the Middle East. He met with great success with his Venetian-style *vedute* ("views") and nocturnes, sketched from life and completed in his studio. A fervent patriot he participated in the third war of independence and died in the sinking of the *Re d'Italia* while attempting to record the naval battle against the Austrians off Lissa, on July 20, 1866.

GIUSEPPE CANELLA
(Verona, 1788 – Florence, 1847)

Italian painter, one of the leading landscapists in Verona in the first half of the century, creator of new Romantic and atmospheric effects in paintings of Venetian-style *vedute* ("views"). After taking part in the exhibitions at the Brera in Milan in 1818, 1819, and 1822, he took a trip to Spain, visiting Madrid, Valencia, and Barcelona; between 1822 and 1828 he lived in Paris. He returned to Milan, where his northern *vedute* met with notable success.

ANTONIO CANOVA
(Possagno, 1757 – Venice, 1822)

Italian sculptor, painter, and architect. After training in Venice he moved to Rome in 1781, eventually becoming the most acclaimed sculptor of neoclassicism. The works he made during the last years of the century show the clear evocation of classical art in the ideals of balance and harmony in keeping with the theories of Winckelmann, but at the same time some of his sculpture was already showing pre-Romantic sensibilities. Summoned to Paris by Napoleon I in 1802, he sculpted portraits for him and his family that are emblematic of the neoclassical style. He spent the last years of his life in his birthplace, Possagno, in the area of Treviso.

GIOVANNI CARNEVALI
(Montegrino, Varese, 1804 – Cremona, 1874)

Italian painter. Son of a bricklayer, he was admitted to the Carrara Academy of Bergamo at eleven. From his first works he demonstrated adherence to the Lombard tradition of Renaissance painting. In 1831 he arrived in Rome to study Raphael, having walked there (he made several such long journeys on foot, to Paris, Rome, and Naples). He worked in nearly every genre of painting, from landscape to portraits to biblical stories and mythological themes to those based on fantasy. He died by drowning in the Po River near Cremona in 1874.

CARL GUSTAV CARUS
(Leipzig, 1789 – Dresden, 1869)

German painter and draftsman. He studied the natural sciences, philosophy, and medicine at the university of Leipzig, moving to Dresden in 1814 to teach obstetrics; in 1827 he became medical adviser to Prince Frederick Augustus of Saxony. In 1816 he met Caspar David Friedrich, who encouraged him to paint. Carus's work is composed almost entirely of stormy landscapes that, unlike those of Friedrich, tend to render an atmosphere without allegorical or symbolic references.

GEORGE CATLIN
(Wilkes-Barre, Pennsylvania, 1796 – Jersey City, New Jersey, 1872)

American painter and writer. He began his career as a portraitist in Philadelphia, but decided to document every aspect of the life of the Native American populations. Beginning in 1830 he undertook numerous expeditions to the West, assembling a collection of portraits and watercolors that he exhibited in 1833 and brought to Europe. He died forgotten, but many of his works are in Washington, D.C., and thanks to their detail constitute a precious source for historians and ethnologists.

CONSTANCE MARIE CHARPENTIER
(Paris, 1767–1849)

French painter. She studied with J.-L. David and François Gérard. From 1795 to 1819 she exhibited portraits at the Paris Salon, few of which can be traced today. Her most famous work, which has strongly pre-Romantic intonations, is *Melancholy* (page 254).

THÉODORE CHASSÉRIAU
(Santa Barbara de Samaná, 1819 – Paris, 1856)

French painter. Student of Ingres and of Delacroix, he debuted at the Salon of 1836 with portraits and paintings of religious subjects. From 1840 to 1841 he was in Rome studying Renaissance frescoes; on his return to Paris he made a name for himself as a portraitist. He was also involved in history painting and in 1846 traveled to Algeria, where he acquired an extraordinary taste for color. He was quite prolific during the last ten years of his life, turning out works of very high quality.

NIKANOR CHERNETSOV
(Luch, 1805 – St. Petersburg, 1879)

Russian painter. He studied at the St. Petersburg Academy, becoming a member of the staff in 1832. From 1820 to 1831 he traveled in the Caucasus, Georgia, and Black Sea regions, painting nature from life. In 1838 he traveled on the Volga, living on a houseboat-studio; he also visited Italy, Egypt, and Palestine. His production is composed primarily of landscapes and views in which he sought to present nature "as it is."

FREDERIC EDWIN CHURCH
(Hartford, 1826 – New York, 1900)

American landscape painter, leader of the second generation of the Hudson River School. He studied with Cole and settled in New York in 1849; in search of new landscapes he traveled to the western United States, then to South America, becoming famous for his large-scale panoramic views, known for the accuracy of the scenery portrayed.

ÉDOUARD CIBOT
(Paris, 1799–1877)

French painter. A student of Pierre Narcisse Guérin, he debuted at the Salon of 1827 and by 1833 was enjoying success. Thanks to his interest in historical subjects, he was commissioned to make paintings for Versailles. During his stay in Italy he became passionate about Raphael and dedicated himself primarily to religious and spiritual paintings, abandoning the balanced compositions of earlier years for works saturated with color.

AUGUSTE CLÉSINGER
(Jean-Baptiste Clésinger)
(Besançon, 1814 – Paris, 1883)

French painter and sculptor. He got his artistic education from his father, Georges Philippe; he also attended the atelier of Bertel Thorvaldsen in Rome. He debuted at the Paris Salon of 1843 and obtained his first great success at that of 1847. In 1849 he was awarded the Legion of Honor. He married the daughter of George Sand in 1870.

LÉON COGNIET
(Paris, 1794–1880)

French painter. A student of Pierre Narcisse Guérin, he was an excellent portraitist, one of the leading French landscapists and genre painters, as well as a skilled interpreter of exoticism. Until 1822 he was at the Villa Medici, returning to Paris to exhibit at the Salons of 1822 and 1824. He received numerous commissions: for the church of Saint-Nicolas-des-Champs, for the Council of State, for the new halls of the Louvre, for the history museum of Versailles, and for the church of the Madeleine in Paris.

THOMAS COLE
(Bolton-le-Moors, Lancashire, 1801 – Catskill, New York, 1848)

American landscape painter and poet, born in England. He moved to the United States in 1818, living first in Ohio and then Philadelphia, where he attended the Philadelphia Academy of Fine Arts. His paintings met with success and thanks to an important collector he was able to travel to Europe, visiting France, England, and Italy. In 1825 he moved to New York and dedicated himself to landscape painting, eventually forming the Hudson River School, so-named for the excursions he made in the company of other artists along the valley of the Hudson River.

JOHN CONSTABLE
(East Bergholt, 1776 – Hampstead, 1837)

English landscape painter. The son of a miller, he moved to London in 1799 to take courses at the Royal Academy. His paintings combined the direct observation of nature with vibrant luministic and chromatic effects; in anticipation of Monet and Cézanne, he made repeated views of the same subjects (usually in Suffolk, where he was born). With a spirit similar to that of early English Romantic poetry, he sought and found harmony in nature. He was appreciated late in his homeland, being admitted to the Royal Academy only in 1829, but was greatly admired in France.

PETER CORNELIUS
(Düsseldorf, 1783 – Berlin, 1867)

German painter. He studied at the Düsseldorf Academy, moving to Frankfurt in 1809 and Rome in 1811, where he was drawn to the Brotherhood of St. Luke formed around Friedrich Overbeck, becoming one of its principal members. In 1819 he was commissioned by Crown Prince Ludwig of Bavaria to paint the fresco decorations with mythological scenes (lost) in the Glyptothek, Munich. In 1819 he was made director of the Düsseldorf Academy and in 1825 of that of Munich.

CHERUBINO CORNIENTI
(Pavia, 1816 – Milan, 1860)

Italian painter. In 1828 he moved to Milan to join his brother Giuseppe, an engraver and lithographer, and enrolled in the Brera. Obtaining a scholarship for painting he went to Rome in 1844 but returned to Milan in 1848 during the Five Days battle and made several drawings on patriotic themes. He met the painter Karl Pavlovich Briullov, and that painter's influence is clearest in Cornienti's paintings on religious subjects.

JEAN-BAPTISTE-CAMILLE COROT
(Paris, 1796–1875)

French landscape painter. He turned late to painting, which he began studying in 1822. Between 1825 and 1828 he was in Rome, where he created his first masterpieces. His landscapes and images of ordinary people reveal his desire to present natural realities, thus opening the way for painting *en plein air*. On his return to France he found inspiration in the forest of Fontainebleau. Another two long stays in Italy reinforced his style, in which the sense of light and the recognizability of the settings never declined into mere "touristy" illustrations but remained full of lyric emotion.

AUGUSTE COUDER
(Paris, 1790–1873)

French painter. He was a student of Jean-Baptiste Regnault and J.-L. David at the Paris Academy, which he entered in 1813. He debuted at the Salon of 1814, receiving the Legion of Honor in 1841 and the Gold Medal in 1848. Among his works is *Notre-Dame de Paris* (page 339), a celebration of the historical novel by Victor Hugo designed as a medieval polyptych.

GUSTAVE COURBET
(Ornans, 1819 – Vevey, 1877)

French painter. In 1840 he was in Paris, studying the great painters of the past, most of all Rembrandt, at the Louvre; a later trip to Holland reinforced this experience. He displayed his works at the Salon (1844 and 1846), took part in the uprising of 1848, and won recognition in 1849 with *After Dinner at Ornans* (page 370). His large-size scenes of ordinary life opened the way to realism. In 1855 he presented a summary of his life and art in a vast composition, *The Painter's Studio* (pages 312–13). In 1870 he took part in the uprising of the commune of Paris; arrested, he was imprisoned for six months.

JOSEPH-DÉSIRÉ COURT
(Rouen, 1797–1865)

French history painter and portraitist. He studied with Antoine-Jean Gros. From 1824 until his death he exhibited regularly at the Salon, earning attention most of all in 1827. His activity as a portraitist was vast and heterogeneous, blending historical portraits for the galleries of Versailles with portraits of high officials, dignitaries, and generals.

THOMAS COUTURE
(Senlis, 1815 – Villiers-le-Bel, 1879)

French painter. He trained in the ateliers of Antoine-Jean Gros and Paul Delaroche. Hoping to attract attention in the field of history painting he exhibited *Romans in the Decadence of the Empire* (page 99) at the Salon of 1847. He obtained prestigious commissions during the reign of Napoleon III, but because of his difficult character his relationship with the imperial family deteriorated. In 1859 he retired to Senlis, working only for private patrons.

RICHARD DADD
(Chatham, 1819 – Broadmoor Hospital, Berkshire, 1886)

English painter. Following studies at the Royal Academy he began making a name for himself as a genre painter. In the summer of 1842 he traveled to Egypt; perhaps the strong African sun delivered the *coup de grace* to his already precarious psychological balance: by the fall he had lost his reason and had to be closely watched by his father. In a fit of violence Dadd killed his father and fled to France. Arrested and certified insane, he ended his days in psychiatric hospitals, all the while continuing to paint.

JOHAN CHRISTIAN DAHL
(Bergen, 1788 – Dresden, 1857)

Norwegian painter active in Germany. After training in Bergen he moved to Copenhagen in 1811, where he attended the academy. In 1818 he moved to Dresden, where he remained for the rest of his life except for a stay in Naples and Rome in 1820–21 and occasional visits to Norway. Becoming friends with Caspar David Friedrich he earned recognition with Romantic landscapes; his paintings present nature in its most grandiose and dramatic aspects (including many shipwrecks), but also reveal a singular sensibility to atmospheric rendering.

FRANCIS DANBY
(Wexford, 1793 – Exmouth, 1861)

English historical and landscape painter born in Ireland. He made his debut very young, exhibiting his first landscapes in Dublin. He moved to London, where he gave watercolor lessons and became a member of the Royal Academy in 1825. He lived in Switzerland between 1831 and 1836, producing small paintings of little value for private patrons. He returned to London in 1840 and moved to Exmouth in Devonshire in 1847.

CHARLES-FRANÇOIS DAUBIGNY
(Paris, 1817–1878)

French landscape painter and engraver. At seventeen he went to Rome; on his return to Paris he earned recognition as an engraver and participated in the Salon. Thanks to his success as well as an inheritance he was able to build a houseboat on which he explored the Seine and its canals, painting beautiful and original river landscapes. He was awarded the Legion of Honor in 1874. He was already weak when he began his last trip, in the summer of 1877, and his heart did not survive the effort.

JACQUES-LOUIS DAVID
(Paris, 1748 – Brussels, 1825)

French painter. In 1775, following studies in Paris, he won the Prix de Rome and spent five years in Italy, where he studied the models of seventeenth-century classicism and ancient sculpture. He used his sense of classicism to create a series of monumental works presenting individual and collective virtues. He became one of the greatest illustrators of the French Revolution and then the foremost recorder of Napoleonic events. With the Restoration he went into exile in Brussels.

MASSIMO D'AZEGLIO
(Turin, 1798–1866)

Italian painter, writer, and statesman. In Rome in 1814 he took up landscape painting. In 1831 he moved to Milan and was active in Romantic circles; he was a friend of Alessandro Manzoni, whose daughter Giulia he married. He wrote the novel *Ettore Fieramosca; or, The Duel of Barletta* (1833) and earned constant success with his landscape and historical-novelistic paintings. In 1849 he was nominated prime minister of Savoy-Sardinia; he resigned in 1852 and returned to painting.

ALEXANDRE-GABRIEL DECAMPS
(Paris, 1803 – Fontainebleau, 1860)

French painter. He made his first trip to the East in 1828, staying at Smyrna nearly a year. He gained attention at the Salon of 1831 and became one of the foremost Orientalist painters. *A Turkish Patrol on the Route to Smyrna* (page 195) is typical of his style. He also made history paintings and works on biblical subjects. An exhibition of his works was presented at the 1855 Universal Exposition.

EDGAR DEGAS
(Paris, 1834–1917)

French painter and sculptor. Between 1856 and 1859 he took long trips to Italy, and on his return to Paris created classical subjects, far removed from the artistic clichés imposed by the Salon; he experimented with other techniques, from etchings to aquatints, lithographs to sculpture. After his father's death he no longer participated in official exhibitions and became involved with the Impressionist shows, although he never adopted the Impressionist technique.

GIOVANNI BATTISTA DE GUBERNATIS
(Turin, 1774–1837)

Italian landscape painter. His positions as diplomat and minister of finance involved him in a great deal of travel, which had a determinant effect on his art, which consisted primarily of watercolor views and landscapes. He also made studies and sketches of ancient Roman and Gothic monuments, most of all in Piedmont. He rarely exhibited his works; the four works he sent to the 1812 Salon of Paris won him a Gold Medal.

EUGÈNE DELACROIX
(Charenton-Saint-Maurice, 1798 – Paris, 1863)

French painter, one of the foremost French Romanticists. Son of a state official he trained in the studio of Pierre Narcisse Guérin in Paris and became friends with Théodore Géricault and Antoine-Jean Gros. His debut at the Paris Salon in 1822 made him famous and soon he was considered the leader of the opposition to the neoclassicism of David. His *Liberty Leads the People* (page 132) was a manifesto of revolutionary spirit. After a trip to Algeria and Morocco in 1832 his painting acquired dramatic intensity and greater dynamism. He worked on many public commissions in France and painted fine portraits.

PAUL DELAROCHE
(Hippolyte Delaroche)
(Paris, 1797–1856)

French history and portrait painter. He entered the atelier of

Antoine-Jean Gros in 1818. Drawn to English history he spent time in London in 1827; *The Sons of Edward* (page 114) and *Cromwell Opening the Coffin of Charles I* (Musée des Beaux-Arts, Nîmes), presented at the Salon of 1831, confirmed his fame. He also visited Italy. His later production is dominated by religious themes.

ALEXANDRE DESGOFFE
(Paris, 1805–1882)

French genre and classical landscape painter. He studied in the atelier of Jean-Auguste-Dominque Ingres in 1828 and began exhibiting at the Salon in 1834. Between 1834 and 1837 and between 1839 and 1842 he visited Switzerland, Auvergne, and Italy. He participated in the decoration of important churches and public buildings in Paris.

MARTIN DRÖLLING
(Oberhergheim, Colmar, 1752 – Paris, 1817)

French painter. He got most of his training in Paris, copying the works of great masters displayed in the Louvre and from 1802 to 1813 worked for the Sèvres porcelain manufactory. He painted genre scenes and vigorous portraits.

GIOVANNI DUPRÉ
(Siena, 1817 – Florence, 1882)

Italian sculptor and writer. He studied at the Siena Academy, his style approaching the naturalism of Lorenzo Bartolini. Prolific but sporadic, he made groups in a severe style and monumental works of a typical celebratory historicism. His most famous works include the *Dying Abel* in marble (page 190), of which he also made a bronze cast.

LOUIS DUPRÉ
(Versailles, 1789 – Paris, 1837)

French history painter. He was nominated official painter to Jérôme Bonaparte, king of Westphalia, in 1811; he participated in the Salons between 1817 and 1837 with drawings and watercolors. Following a trip from Athens to Constantinople he painted numerous views from life.

ASHER B. DURAND
(Springfield Township, New Jersey, 1796 – Maplewood, New Jersey, 1886)

American painter and engraver; friend of Thomas Cole, member of the Hudson River School, he was among the founders of landscape painting in the United States. He began his career as an engraver and spent the year 1840 traveling in Europe. His early works show the influence of seventeenth-century Dutch and Flemish artists as well as the Barbizon School, but by 1850 he was moving toward realism. He is best known for his celebrations of the American landscape.

JEHAN DUSEIGNEUR
(Jean-Bernard Duseigneur)
(Paris, 1808–1866)

French sculptor. After studies with Bosio, Dupaty, and Cortot, he participated in the Salon between 1831 and 1866, obtaining a second-class medal in 1834. Among his works is *Orlando Furioso* (page 341), which was cast in bronze after his death. He was the friend of several Romantic writers, such as Gérard de Nerval and Pierre-Joseph Borel.

WILLIAM DYCE
(Aberdeen, 1806 – Streatham, 1864)

Scottish painter. Influenced by the art of the Nazarenes, he gained fame in his homeland as a portraitist after 1829. He followed the style of the Pre-Raphaelites in 1850 in highly detailed, intense landscapes. He participated in the fresco decoration of the British Parliament with subjects drawn from Arthurian legend.

CHARLES LOCK EASTLAKE
(Plymouth, 1793 – Pisa, 1865)

English painter, museum director, and writer. He achieved fame with a scene of contemporary history he had witnessed: *Napoleon Aboard the Bellerophon in Plymouth Sound* (1815), the sale of which permitted him to visit Paris and then Rome, where he remained from 1816 to 1830. His primary successes include views of Italian and Greek landscapes painted in the 1820s. He continued to make Mediterranean subjects after his return to London. He became an art historian, was a member and then president of the Royal Academy, and directed the National Gallery.

C. W. ECKERSBERG
(Christoffer Wilhelm Eckersberg)
(Jutland, 1783 – Copenhagen, 1853)

Danish painter. He studied with Nicolai Abraham Abildgaard at the Copenhagen Academy and in the Paris studio of J.-L. David. He lived in Rome between 1813 and 1816. His best works are portraits and seascapes. He also made architectural views.

SALVATORE FERGOLA
(Naples, 1799–1874)

Italian painter. He was taught painting by his father, Luigi. In 1819 he drew the attention of Ferdinand I, king of the Two Sicilies, who commissioned various Neapolitan views from him and allowed him to travel in his retinue. In 1830 he was named court painter and made a series of celebratory historical views. His later production includes landscapes and Romantic historical subjects.

HIPPOLYTE FLANDRIN
(Lyons, 1809 – Rome, 1864)

French painter, a favorite student of Jean-Auguste-Dominique Ingres. He won the Prix de Rome in 1832. He is best known for his church decorations, including those of Saint-Séverin, Saint-Germain-de-Prés, and Saint-Vincent-de-Paul in Paris. He was also a fine portraitist, highly esteemed for his harmonious manner and skillful use of color.

JEAN-PIERRE FRANQUE
(Buis-les-Baronnies, 1774 – Paris, 1860)

French painter. A student of J.-L. David, he exhibited at the Salon from 1806 to 1853. In 1836 he received the Legion of Honor. He is best known for his historical portraits, of which Versailles has an important series; he also made several large official paintings.

CASPAR DAVID FRIEDRICH
(Greisfswald, 1774 – Dresden, 1840)

German landscape painter. After studies at the Copenhagen Academy, he moved in 1798 to Dresden, with its cultural mixture of the poetry of Goethe and developments in Romantic idealism. His 1808 *Cross in the Mountains* (page 178) presents a mountain landscape on which a cross stands out. A supporter of patriotic sentiments, Friedrich was the principal exponent of the Romantic concept of the sublime in landscape paintings, emphasizing the symbolic values of nature.

HENRY FUSELI
(Johann Heinrich Füssli)
(Zurich, 1741 – London, 1825)

Swiss-born English painter. He moved to London in 1763 and visited Italy between 1769 and 1778, most of all Rome, where he studied the works of classical antiquity and those of Michelangelo. Together with William Blake, he anticipated many themes of English Romanticism, such as visionary scenes, the unleashing of the world of dreams, and the blending of heroes from Greco-Roman myths with scenes of medieval sagas, which he presented with a subtle but penetrating eroticism.

JOSEPH MICHAEL GANDY
(London, 1771–1843)

English architect, writer, and illustrator. He studied at the Royal Academy and traveled to Italy. He worked as a draftsman for John Soane, also exhibiting drawings and paintings at the Royal Academy.

JEAN-BRUNO GASSIES
(Bordeaux, 1786 – Paris, 1832)

French painter. He traveled to England and Scotland and was profoundly impressed by the beauty of the misty landscapes, which he the reproduced with great skill in his paintings. He is best remembered, however, for views and scenes of interiors, in which he made skillful use of light.

AUGUSTIN-ALPHONSE GAUDAR DE LA VERDINE
(Bourges, 1780 – Siena, 1804)

French painter of historical subjects. In 1799 he won the Grand Prix in painting and went to Rome. He died of malaria in 1804 during a trip to Florence undertaken in an attempt to get away from the unhealthy air of Rome. An outstanding example of his work is the *Orlando Furioso* of 1804 (page 330).

FRANÇOIS GÉRARD
(Rome, 1770 – Paris, 1837)

French portrait and history painter. A student of J.-L. David, he painted historical and mythological subjects that are distinguished by chromatic delicacy and compositional harmony, but is best known for his talents in portraiture, for which he was highly esteemed by the public of the time. Louis XVIII appointed him court painter in 1814.

THÉODORE GÉRICAULT
(Rouen, 1791 – Paris, 1824)

French painter. He trained in Paris, studying masterpieces in the Louvre and attending the atelier of Pierre Narcisse Guérin, where he met Jacobins and veterans of the Napoleonic campaigns. He was full of the fervent desire for liberty, not only political but also artistic. During a trip to Italy in 1816–17 he met Jean-Auguste-Dominique Ingres and admired the works of Michelangelo and Caravaggio. Stimulated by friendship with the young Eugène Delacroix he made his masterpiece, *The Raft of the "Medusa"* (pages 128–29). His untimely death was caused by the fall from a horse.

JEAN-LÉON GÉRÔME
(Vesoul, 1824 – Paris, 1904)

French history and genre painter. He was a student of Paul Delaroche, with whom he traveled to Italy, where he was greatly impressed by classical antiquity, which influenced his style. With his *Cockfight* (page 93) he became the leader of the Néo-Grec movement. In 1855 his *Age of Augustus* (pages 192–93) aroused great sensation and was one of the most important events of the Universal Exposition. The various trips he made to Egypt, Turkey, and Algeria inspired him to make Orientalist works.

ANNE-LOUIS GIRODET-TRIOSON
(Anne-Louis Girodet de Roucy-Trioson)
(Montagris, 1767–Paris, 1824)

French painter. A student of J.-L. David, he won the Prix de Rome in 1789 and spent five years in Italy. He dedicated himself to subjects of ancient history, Napoleonic events, and themes drawn from contemporary and ancient literature, which he illustrated with a decidedly pre-Romantic sensibility, detaching himself from the severe neoclassical lines typical of his master. Outstanding examples are his *Sleep of Endymion* (page 32) and *Burial of Atala* (page 217).

CHARLES GLEYRE
(Chevilly, near Lausanne, 1808 – Paris, 1874)

Swiss painter and teacher active in France. A student of Hersent in Paris, he took several trips to Italy and the Middle East, during which he painted *Evening: Lost Illusions* (page 263), which won a prize at the Salon of 1843. He set himself up in Paris, taught at the École des Beaux-Arts, and directed the former studio of Paul Delaroche, where such artists as Renoir, Monet, and Sisley got their training.

FRANCISCO GOYA Y LUCIENTES
(Fucendetodos, 1746 – Bordeaux, 1828)

Spanish painter and graphic artist. Following studies in Spain and Rome, he first came to attention, in 1774, for a series of tapestry designs for the Madrid court. In 1786 he was made official painter to the king. Suffering a terrible illness he was nearly deaf by 1792; he threw himself into prodigious activity: the frescoes in the church of San Antonio de la Florida (1798) and the etchings of *Los Caprichos*. He made enduring documents of the Napoleonic invasion in his series *Disasters of War* and the two paintings dedicated to the uprising in Madrid. In 1824 he left Spain for Bordeaux.

FRANÇOIS-MARIUS GRANET
(Aix-en-Provence, 1775 – Malvalat, 1849)

French history painter, watercolorist, and designer. Following training in his birthplace, he attended the Paris atelier of J.-L. David for a short time. From 1802 to 1819 he lived in Rome, where he made enthusiastic sketches of ancient ruins and painted views and interiors of churches and monasteries, along with splendid landscapes inspired by the Roman countryside. He was named conservator of the Louvre in 1826, and in 1830 Louis Philippe made him director of the Musée Historique de Versailles. His works include beautiful sketches of Paris and the outskirts of Aix-en-Provence.

ANTOINE-JEAN GROS
(Paris, 1771 – Meudon, 1835)

French painter. He was one of the outstanding students of J.-L. David, although he soon distanced himself from the models of classical antiquity. He spent much time in northern Italy, earning a reputation as a fine portraitist. He became one of the leading French painters of the Napoleonic period, celebrating the events of Napoleon's campaigns (he also made frescoes in the dome of the Pantheon in Paris). His career declined following the Restoration, probably one of the reasons for his suicide.

ALESSANDRO GUARDASSONI
(Bologna, 1819–1888)

Italian painter of historical and religious subjects. Following a trip to England and France he approached the style of Paul Delaroche and Thomas Couture. From 1859 on he dedicated himself to the study of photography and stereoscopes and their application to painting, using them to work out a special painting technique.

THÉODORE GUDIN
(Paris, 1802 – Boulogne-sur-Mer, 1879)

French painter. A student of A.-J. Gros, he began exhibiting at the Salon in 1822, obtaining the first-place medal in 1824 and the Legion of Honor in 1827. He was an official artist in the Algerian expedition of 1830 and became one of the most famous marine painters. A prolific artist, he was criticized by his contemporaries for abandoning the care and reflection that characterized his early works in order to accept a great quantity of official commissions.

PIERRE NARCISSE GUÉRIN
(Paris, 1774 – Rome, 1833)

French painter and defender of classicism. He drew much inspiration from the classical antiquity he studied during trips to Rome and Naples. He won the Prix de Rome in 1797. He painted primarily historical and mythological subjects, drawing inspiration from the plays of Aeschylus and Racine. His choice of subjects reveals his attraction to the more violent events of the ancient world, the horror and drama of which he rendered with great mastery. His pupils included Delacroix, Géricault, and Ary Scheffer.

CONSTANTIN HANSEN
(Copenhagen, 1804–1880)

Danish painter. After early training from his father, Hans, a portraitist, he studied with C.W. Eckersberg, dedicating himself primarily to portraiture. In Italy from 1835 to 1844, he painted views of ancient monuments, areas of the city, and landscapes. Returning to Copenhagen in 1853 he made works notable for their harmonious fusion of elements of the Danish tradition with references to the ideals of Italian Renaissance painting.

BENJAMIN ROBERT HAYDON
(Plymouth, 1786 – London, 1846)

English painter of historical subjects and writer. His dedication to large-size works involving much time and resources led him into financial difficulties: he was jailed for bankruptcy several times. He was admired by such writers as Wordsworth and Keats, whose portraits he painted, but his artificial style, overly dramatic and rhetorical, was not highly appreciated. He died a suicide.

FRANCESCO HAYEZ
(Venice, 1791 – Milan, 1882)

Italian painter active in Rome, Venice, and Milan, where he became one of the leaders of Romanticism at the Brera Academy. He was made director of the academy in 1855 and in 1860 its president. He participated in the Universal Exposition in Paris in 1855 and in the International Exhibitions in Munich in 1851 and 1873.

FRANÇOIS-JOSEPH HEIM
(Belfort, 1787 – Paris, 1865)

French painter, son of a professor of design. He had a brilliant career, winning the Prix de Rome in 1808 at age twenty. He painted historical, religious, and mythological subjects with great originality, in broad strokes with a particular eye for composition, often constructing his scenes on a diagonal. His works reveal a spirit and tension that are rare among his contemporaries.

ARTHUR HUGHES
(London, 1832–1915)

English painter. He was associated with the Pre-Raphaelite group and drew inspiration from the style of John Everett Millais for his subjects. His works include medieval themes; he made illustrations for children's books.

WILLIAM HOLMAN HUNT
(London, 1827–1910)

English painter and friend of Dante Gabriel Rossetti, with whom he founded the Pre-Raphaelite Brotherhood in 1848. In 1854 he left England, moved by great Christian fervor, and went to the Near East. He painted landscapes and religious paintings, including the famous *The Light of the World* (page 174), sometimes referred to as the most famous Protestant painting of the nineteenth century.

JEAN-AUGUSTE-DOMINIQUE INGRES
(Montauban, 1780 – Paris, 1867)

French painter. A pupil of J.-L. David, he won the Prix de Rome in 1801 and moved to Italy in 1806, where he spent eighteen years. His *Vow of Louis XIII* (page 182) met with great success at the Salon of 1824. His production includes portraits, historical paintings, paintings on literary subjects, large-scale celebratory works, and drawings.

EUGÈNE ISABEY
(Paris, 1801 – Montévrain, 1886)

French marine and genre painter, son of the painter Jean-Baptiste and ranked among the great innovators in the landscape genre and one of the minor masters of Romanticism. He is best known for marine scenes, beaches, episodes of port life, storms, and shipwrecks.

GEORG FRIEDRICH KERSTING
(Güstrow, 1785 – Meissen, 1847)

German painter. After studies in Copenhagen he moved to Dresden. He belongs to the first generation of German Romantic painters, those who sought to develop a national art capable of inspiring patriotic spirit. His best-known works are presentations of the daily life of the German middle class.

CHRISTEN KØBKE
(Copenhagen, 1810–1848)

Danish painter. A student of C.W. Eckersberg, he painted portraits and landscapes, notable for the delicacy of the line and his striking sense of color, making him one of the most interesting representatives of Danish Romantic painting.

JOSEPH ANTON KOCH
(Obergibeln, Tyrol, 1768 – Rome, 1839)

Austrian painter and writer. He is considered one of the leading nineteenth-century landscapists and, together with his friend Johann Christian Reinhart, is credited with beginning the genre of the "heroic" landscape. Among his masterpieces is *Heroic Landscape with Rainbow* (1805; Staatliche Kunsthalle, Karlsruhe). He also painted landscapes with biblical and mythological scenes.

GASPARE LANDI
(Piacenza, 1756–1830)

Italian painter. After early studies in Piacenza he moved to Rome, where he lived most of his life. He was commissioned to make works glorifying Napoleon but painted principally mythological themes (his paintings of Homeric subjects were accompanied by sonnets by Ippolito Pindemonte) and portraits.

EDWIN HENRY LANDSEER
(London, 1802–1873)

English painter, famous as an animal painter. He is best known for humanized, sentimental pictures of dogs, sometimes made into symbolic representations of human virtues and vices. Very popular in the reign of Victoria, he was also a famous high-society portraitist.

JÉRÔME-MARTIN LANGLOIS
(Paris, 1779–1838)

French painter. He attended the atelier of J.-L. David, but soon distanced himself from David's teaching in favor of a mannerist style with extravagant forms and colors. In 1809 he won the Grand Prix and spent much time in Rome. He painted historical and religious subjects, along with numerous portraits.

LOUIS-AUGUSTE LAPITO
(Joinville-le-Pont, 1803 – Boulogne-sur-Mer, 1874)

French painter. He attended the atelier of François-Joseph Heim and made numerous trips to the south of France, Corsica, Italy, Germany, and Holland. He exhibited regularly at the Salon until 1870. His prolific production numbers more than two thousand paintings, only about fifteen of which can be traced.

THOMAS LAWRENCE
(Bristol, 1769 – London, 1830)

English portrait painter. When very young he made portraits of the guests in his father's hotel and eventually was considered the greatest portrait painter of his generation in Europe. In 1792 he became painter to King George III; he made many portraits of the royal family and public figures. In 1820 he was made president of the Royal Academy.

AUGUSTE-XAVIER LEPRINCE
(Paris, 1799 – Nice, 1826)

French painter, son of the painter Pierre. When he participated in the Salon at the age of twenty he seemed to be at the beginning of a brilliant career, but his life was cut short by a heart ailment. Despite his premature death, he left a notable production composed primarily of landscapes and genre scenes, examples of the "Dutch" taste in vogue during the Restoration period.

JOHN FREDERICK LEWIS
(London, 1805 – Walton-on-Thames, 1876)

English painter, most famous for his watercolors. In 1856 he was made president of the Society of Painters in Watercolour. He made several trips to Spain and Egypt, drawing inspiration for his paintings and contributing to the diffusion of the taste for Oriental subjects, which enjoyed great success in England.

LUDOVICO LIPPARINI
(Bologna, 1800 – Venice, 1856)

Italian painter. He showed signs of his great talent when young and began teaching at the Venice Academy in 1831. He painted portraits, mythological subjects, and subjects drawn from contemporary history, the last-named most of all in the 1840s, when he sought to join the aesthetic needs of painting to patriotic sentiments and the representation of reality.

PHILIPPE JACQUES DE LOUTHERBOURG
(Philip James de Loutherbourg)
(Strasbourg, 1740 – London, 1812)

Alsatian painter and stage designer active in France and England. He moved to London in

1771. He painted genre scenes, landscapes, battles, and religious subjects and was among the first artists to document aspects of the industrial revolution in paintings.

JEAN-BAPTISTE MALLET
(Grasse, 1759 – Paris, 1835)

French painter. A pupil of P.-P. Prud'hon, he is best known for small-size watercolors in which he presented scenes of daily French life during the periods of the Directory and the Empire. These interiors and boudoir scenes are sometimes similar in style to the works of the Troubadours.

HANS DITLEV CHRISTIAN MARTENS
(Kiel, 1795–1864)

German architecture painter. He studied at the Copenhagen Academy and lived in Rome from 1826 to 1855. During that period he made *Pope Leo XII Visiting Thorvaldsen's Atelier in Rome in 1826* (page 310).

JOHN MARTIN
(Haydon Bridge, Northumberland, 1789 – Isle of Man, 1854)

English painter and engraver. He painted landscapes, views, and classical and biblical subjects. He made successful use of a glass-painting technique. He moved to London and exhibited at the Royal Academy and came to the attention of the public with large canvases presenting natural catastrophes and biblical episodes, such as *Great Day of His Wrath* (page 191). He was especially popular among French Romantics.

ADOLF VON MENZEL
(Breslau, 1815 – Berlin, 1905)

German painter and illustrator, considered one of the leading exponents of German realism. He painted historical subjects, also drawing inspiration from contemporary themes, especially daily scenes of the Prussian court but also episodes of daily life and domestic scenes. He was highly honored in life and various European cities dedicated retrospective shows of his works.

GIOVANNI MIGLIARA
(Alessandria, 1785 – Milan, 1837)

Italian painter and scenographer. He painted views and landscapes and excelled at interiors of medieval churches and monasteries. In 1833 he was made painter to the court of Charles Albert, king of Sardinia, and received many royal commissions for paintings of Savoy history.

JOHN EVERETT MILLAIS
(Southampton, 1829 – London, 1896)

English painter. With Dante Gabriel Rossetti and William Holman Hunt he was a founder of the Pre-Raphaelite Brotherhood and made his best works within that sphere, including the famous *Ophelia* (page 345) and *Christ in the House of His Parents* (pages 170–71). In 1896 he became president of the Royal Academy.

TOMMASO MINARDI
(Faenza, 1787 – Rome, 1871)

Italian painter. He studied in Rome at the Academy of St. Luke, where he became professor of design. He came into contact with the German Nazarenes in the convent of Sant'Isidoro and in 1842 signed the Purismo manifesto along with Friedrich Overbeck. He painted mythological and religious subjects.

GIUSEPPE MOLTENI
(Affori, Milan, 1800 – Milan, 1867)

Italian painter, active as restorer and consultant to such museums as the Louvre and the British Museum. A rival of Hayez in Lombardy, he painted portraits of aristocrats, artists, and other important persons that were highly praised for their resemblance and attention to detail. His genre scenes were also well received.

GUSTAVE MOREAU
(Paris, 1826–1898)

French painter. He was profoundly influenced by the study of classical painting in Rome, Florence, and Venice, which he used to create an original style that was highly criticized by contemporaries. He moved toward a more baroque manner in elaborate compositions that by the middle of the century made him one of the leading exponents of symbolism. The surrealists esteemed him for the visionary character of his works.

DOMENICO MORELLI
(Naples, 1823–1901)

Italian painter. He studied at the Naples Institute of Fine Arts, winning the first prize in painting in 1844. He moved to Rome and then Florence, where he came in contact with the artists at Caffé Michelangelo. He painted works of Romantic-historical and religious subjects characterized by unusually violent expressions.

LUIGI MUSSINI
(Berlin, 1813 – Florence, 1888)

Italian painter and administrator. He began to draw when very young and in 1830 enrolled in the Florence Academy. He joined the Tuscan Purismo movement and with the painter Adolph von Sturler opened a private school spreading its ideas. He spent time in Paris, where he met Ingres, Théodore Chassériau, and Hippolyte Flandrin, drawing lessons for greater stylistic rigor. In 1851 he was made director of the Siena Academy.

FRIEDRICH OVERBECK
(Lübeck, 1789 – Rome, 1869)

German painter. Together with Franz Pforr he founded the Brotherhood of St. Luke in 1819. That group of German artists moved to Rome, where they became known as the Nazarenes. The community sought the renewal of art in accordance with patriotic and religious ideals. Overbeck's work is marked by deep religious sentiment and by the effort to create aesthetic beauty without sensuality.

GIOVANNI PAGLIARINI
(Ferrara, 1808–1878)

Italian painter. He attended the Venice Academy and was active in Udine, Trieste, and Istria, returning to Ferrara only in 1870 to teach. His works are distinguished by a firm light that creates enamellike colors and gives solid form to materials, as in the portraits he made in the 1850s that are today in the Musei Civici of Udine.

PELAGIO PALAGI
(Bologna, 1775 – Turin, 1860)

Italian painter. He attended the Clementina Academy of Bologna, where he painted his first Venetian-style *vedute* ("views"); he went to Rome in 1806 and participated in the Paris Salon of 1810. His style approached the pre-Romanticism of William Blake and Henry Fuseli. Because of his reputation he was named inspector of the Italian Academy in Palazzo Venezia. Around 1815 he moved to Milan as an exponent of historical Romanticism. In 1832 he was summoned to Turin by the house of Savoy to oversee the furnishing and renovation of Castello di Racconigi.

FILIPPO PALIZZI
(Vasto, 1818 – Naples, 1899)

Italian painter. He attended the Naples Academy and was drawn to landscape painting. He took part in the uprising of 1848 and drew inspiration from it in several portraits and battle scenes. In 1854 he moved to France, where he came into contact with the Barbizon School. He then toured Europe. After 1864 he dedicated himself to the study of light in the open and from 1870 on was involved in engravings. He was awarded many honors and was a member of several art academies in Italy and other European countries.

FRANZ PFORR
(Frankfurt am Main, 1788 – Albano, 1812)

German painter. He attended the Vienna Academy and founded the Brotherhood of St. Luke with Friedrich Overbeck. He moved to Rome in 1810 and became one of the most original artists in the Nazarene group.

THOMAS PHILLIPS
(Dudley, 1770 – London, 1845)

English painter. Around 1790, after working as a painter on glass in Birmingham, he moved to London and made a name for himself with historical paintings, later becoming known as a portraitist.

ANTON SMINCK PITLOO
(Arnhem, 1791 – Naples, 1837)

German artist. He studied at Arnhem, Paris, and Rome, setting himself up in Naples in 1815. Pitloo joined the Neapolitan tradition of *vedute* but renewed it. He preferred to paint from life and was drawn to natural images, making reference to northern landscapists (such as Dahl), those English (Turner and Constable), and to painters of the Barbizon School.

FRANCESCO PODESTI
(Ancona, 1800 – Rome, 1895)

Italian painter. He studied in Rome at the Academy of St. Luke and attended the atelier of Antonio Canova. In 1826 he traveled across Italy, visiting Milan, Venice, Florence, and other cities before going to London, Paris, and Brussels; he then set himself up in Rome, where he was highly active. He was commissioned by Ancona to make his most important painting, *Oath of the Anconians under Siege by Barbarossa* (1853), and made fresco decorations in one of the Vatican Stanze.

JAMES PRADIER
(Jean-Jacques Pradier)
(Geneva, 1792 – Bougival, 1852)

French sculptor. He was born into a family of sculptors, and after studies in Geneva and Paris lived in Rome from 1813 to 1819. He became the best-known sculptor during the period of Louis Philippe and was the leading sculptor in Paris, since his classical style pleased the middle-class taste of the period. Among his best-known works is the *Satyr and Bacchante* (page 91), which caused a scandal at the Salon of 1834.

PIERRE-PAUL PRUD'HON
(Cluny, 1758 – Paris, 1823)

French painter. He spent four years in Italy (1784–88), studying the works of Michelangelo, Raphael, and most of all Leonardo, from whom he learned perfection and thoughtful execution. In Paris he painted portraits characterized by natural poses and settings. He abandoned mythological themes to dedicate himself to allegory. His fame reached its peak during the Napoleonic period, and he received many commissions for the decoration of public and private buildings.

PIERRE RÉVOIL
(Lyons, 1776 – Paris, 1842)

French painter. He joined the atelier of J.-L. David in 1795. In 1810 he became a member of the Troubadour group and made works of historical anecdote, a genre in which he became one of the outstanding exponents, abandoning the miniaturist style only in his last works. He was so attracted to the Middle Ages that he studied the *langue d'oc* and collected period objects. Considered the founder of the Lyons School, he was professor of painting at the École des Beaux-Arts in that city.

JOSHUA REYNOLDS
(Plympton, Devonshire, 1723 – London, 1792)

English portrait painter, long considered the most important of England's painters. After three years of study abroad, most of it spent in Rome studying Michelangelo and Raphael, he opened a studio in London, where his portraits enjoyed great success. He was gifted with a strong pre-Romantic sensibility. In 1768 he was made the first president of the Royal Academy; the following year he was knighted. During his maturity he also made history paintings as well as works of fantasy, genre, and religious scenes and landscapes. He is credited with raising the artist to a position of respect in England.

FLEURY RICHARD
(Lyons, 1777–1852)

French painter. He studied with Grognard and worked in the

atelier of J.-L. David; together with other young painters he formed the Troubadour group, so-called for their dedication to medieval themes. Until 1824 he created primarily delicate small-format paintings distinguished by the use of light.

HUBERT ROBERT
(Paris, 1733–1808)

French painter and landscape architect. A student at the French Academy in Rome, he studied with Jean-Honoré Fragonard and, becoming a follower of Giovanni Battista Piranesi, specialized in idealized views of ancient monuments and fantastic scenes of ruins (earning the nickname Robert des Ruines). On his return to Paris in 1765 he was given a post at the Royal Academy. In his paintings of the Roman remains of Languedoc (1787) he blended the greatness of the creations of man with the majesty of the natural landscape in a truly pre-Romantic style.

DAVID ROBERTS
(Edinburgh, 1796 – London, 1864)

Scottish painter and watercolorist. He was admitted to the Society of British Artists in 1824; in 1839 he became a member of the Royal Academy. He was a great traveler: in 1824 he visited Normandy, drawing numerous medieval buildings; he traveled elsewhere in Europe and then visited Syria and Egypt, expressing himself with painting in oil and watercolor. During the last years of his life he painted only English subjects.

DANTE GABRIEL ROSSETTI
(London, 1828 – Birchington-on-Sea, 1882)

English poet and painter. Son of an exiled Italian poet he was a founder in 1848 with William Holman Hunt and John Everett Millais of the Pre-Raphaelite Brotherhood, drawing inspiration primarily from fifteenth-century Florentine painters. After 1860 he turned his attention to the art of the High Renaissance. His painting finds its most important expression in figures of women, whether angelic or perverse, always gifted with an inaccessible fascination.

THÉODORE ROUSSEAU
(Paris, 1812 – Barbizon, 1867)

French landscape painter, leader of the Barbizon School. His interest in landscape led him when young to make trips, making sketches and designs to later make into paintings. Rejected by critics, he chose to live and work in solitude at Barbizon in the forest of Fontainebleau, soon joined by other painters. He earned recognition at the Salon of 1848 and the 1855 Universal Exposition, but preferred to continue his tranquil life at Barbizon.

PHILIPP OTTO RUNGE
(Wolgast, 1777 – Hamburg, 1810)

German painter. He studied at Hamburg, Copenhagen, and Dresden, where, between 1801 and 1803, he became friends with Romantic intellectuals and artists, being drawn to the cult of nature. In 1804 he moved to Hamburg, where he divided his time between painting, book illustration, and literary activity. Aside from portraiture he worked in complex allegories that blended mysticism and naturalistic elements.

FRANCESCO SABATELLI
(Florence, 1803 – Milan, 1830)

Italian painter, the son, student, and collaborator of Luigi (see below). He worked primarily on religious, mythological, and history paintings, often working in fresco.

GIUSEPPE SABATELLI
(Florence, 1813–1843)

Italian painter, son of Luigi (see below) and younger brother of Francesco (see above). In November 1833 the grand duke of Tuscany offered him a monthly pension and many prestigious commissions. In 1839 he was elected professor at the Florence and Milan academies and was commissioned by Niccolò Puccini of Pistoia to make *Farinata degli Uberti at the Battle of the Serchio* (page 111). Like his brother, he died of tuberculosis.

LUIGI SABATELLI
(Florence, 1772 – Milan, 1850)

Italian painter. After studies at the Florence Academy he went to Rome (1788–94), where he made engravings based on the *Divine Comedy* and scenes from Roman history. In 1808 he was given the chair of painting at the Brera Academy and in 1820 was commissioned by the grand duke of Tuscany to decorate the Sala dell'Iliade in the Pitti Palace with subjects from the *Iliad*. He made numerous frescoes. His works include *Radimistus Killing Zenobia* (page 37).

SIMON SAINT-JEAN
(Millery, 1808 – Écully, 1860)

French painter. He first exhibited at Lyons in 1828, beginning to exhibit at the Paris Salon in 1834 and becoming known for his paintings of flowers, which enjoyed success in France and elsewhere, especially in Brussels and Amsterdam. He had powerful patrons, including field marshals of King Louis Philippe and Baron Charles de Corvisart, grandson of Napoleon I's doctor, and was highly praised by the critics in Lyons.

ARY SCHEFFER
(Dordrecht, 1795 – Argenteuil, 1858)

Dutch painter and sculptor active in France. He moved to France in 1809, entered the atelier of Pierre Narcisse Guérin in 1811, participated in the Salon from 1812 to 1846. Painter of historical subjects, he obtained numerous official commissions for churches in Paris and Versailles and rivaled Eugène Delacroix during the "Romantic dispute" of 1824–27. In 1822 he was made drawing master to the children of King Louis Philippe, to whom he remained faithful, refusing every contact with the future Napoleon III.

GOTTLIEB SCHICK
(Stuttgart, 1776–1812)

German painter. A student of J.-L. David in Paris between 1798 and

1802, he painted fine portraits with classical inspiration but a certain Romantic sensibility. He visited Rome. His works include the *Hereditary Prince of Saxe-Gotha-Altenburg* (page 28).

KARL FRIEDRICH SCHINKEL
(Neuruppin, 1782 – Berlin, 1841)

German architect and painter, one of the leading German architects of the nineteenth century. In Italy between 1803 and 1805, he made sketches of classical and medieval buildings; upon his return he made his living as a stage designer and painter of Romantic landscapes, using architectural features in his paintings. Following the popular English style, he made dioramas and panoramas, producing forty-five. In 1811 he became a member of the Berlin Academy and was made a professor in 1820. His paintings are located in the sphere of Romantic classicism.

CARL SPITZWEG
(Munich, 1808–1885)

German genre painter and draftsman. After studying to be a pharmacist he turned to painting in 1833, having received a large inheritance. Self-taught, he began making humorous scenes in 1839. He also took regular trips, and in 1855 he visited the Universal Exposition in Paris and was so fascinated by the landscapes of the Barbizon School and the oil sketches of Eugène Delacroix that he changed his style of painting, turning from the humorous to the fabulous in scenes usually set in small German cities.

PIETRO TENERANI
(Torano, Rieti, 1789 – Rome, 1869)

Italian sculptor. He studied at the Carrara Academy and collaborated with Bertel Thorvaldsen in making several monuments and mythological subjects in the Romantic taste. He signed the Purismo manifesto with Tommaso Minardi and Friedrich Overbeck. His works include *Abandoned Psyche* (page 166), the tomb of Pius VIII in St. Peter's, and many statues of famous people, including Simón Bolívar.

ANTOINE-JEAN-BAPTISTE THOMAS
(Paris, 1791–1834)

French painter. He attended the atelier of Vincent and won the Prix de Rome for history painting in 1816. During his brief career he made both religious paintings and dramatic scenes of national history, participating in all the vicissitudes of Romanticism. He was also a successful lithographer, which he used to express his satirical vein. His works include *The Procession of San Gennaro at Naples* (page 133).

GIUSEPPE TOMINZ
(Gorizia, 1790 – Gradiscutta, 1866)

Italian painter. He studied in Rome with Domenico Conti Bazzani and was in contact with Antonio Canova, Bertel Thorvaldsen, and Peter Cornelius. Upon his return to Gorizia he earned recognition as a portraitist, including his *Self-Portrait with Brother Francesco* (page 66), and by the end of the 1820s he was making multiple portraits set in Biedermeier interiors and against landscape backgrounds; those works enjoyed great success, unlike his production of religious paintings and genre scenes.

GIACOMO TRÉCOURT
(Bergamo, 1812–Pavia, 1882)

Italian painter. He made historical and religious subjects following the academic tradition, along with fine portraits, including his highly original *Self-Portrait in Oriental Costume* (page 208). He taught at Pavia, where his students included Carnevali and Tranquillo Cremona.

JOHN TRUMBULL
(Lebanon, Connecticut, 1756 – New York, 1843)

American painter. He earned a diploma from Harvard and served as an aide-de-camp to Washington during the Revolution. Going to London in 1780 he studied under Benjamin West, then dedicated himself to painting scenes of the national history of the United States. In New York in 1817 he was elected a director of the American Academy of Fine Arts and served as its president (1817–35). His many commissions included decorations for the U.S. Capitol rotunda.

JOSEPH MALLORD WILLIAM TURNER
(London, 1775–1851)

English landscape painter. He trained at the Royal Academy of London. He sought a middle ground between the past (seventeenth-century Dutch landscapists) and his yearning for experimentation, leading to visionary interpretations of the landscape. Always attentive to light and atmospheric transparencies, in his mature period he experimented with effects of dampness and vapor, painting one of the first images of a train in motion: *Rain, Steam, and Speed* (page 319).

PIERRE-AUGUSTE VAFFLARD
(Paris, 1777–1840)

French painter. A student of Jean-Baptiste Regnault, he participated regularly in the Salon with history paintings made in a style acceptable to the academic norms then in place. Outstanding among his works are *Young Holding His Dead Daughter in His Arms* (Musée des Beaux-Arts, Angoulême), based on Edward Young's *Night Thoughts*, and *Emma and Eginhard; or, The Stratagems of Love* (page 240).

VINCENZO VELA
(Ligornetto, Canton Ticino, 1820–1891)

Italian sculptor. He attended the Brera Academy and was influenced by the Romantic painting of Francesco Hayez. Moving to Turin in 1853, he taught at the Albertina Academy. Most of his works are of an official, celebratory nature; after the unification of Italy he turned to humanitarian works. He is known for his *Spartacus* (page 97).

HORACE VERNET
(Emil-Jean-Horace Vernet)
(Paris, 1789–1863)

French painter. He participated in the Salon for the first time in 1812 and in 1820 spent a short period in Rome. Because of his liberal sympathies many of his paintings were rejected by the Salon of 1822 and only two years later was he able to display two works, which met with success. From 1828 to 1833 he directed the French Academy in Rome and later made trips to North Africa, developing a strong interest in the faithful reproduction of reality.

CARL CHRISTIAN VOGEL VON VOGELSTEIN
(Wildenfels, 1788 – Munich, 1868)

German portraitist. He enrolled in the Dresden Academy in 1804; after four years spent in St. Petersburg he went to Rome, where he met other northern artists and the Nazarenes. He went to Dresden in 1820, received numerous honors, and taught at the academy until 1853. He made many trips in Europe. He was the author of various religious works and was active as an engraver and lithographer.

PIERRE-JACQUES VOLAIRE
(Toulon, 1729 – Italy, ca. 1790–1800)

French painter. Born into a family of painters, he worked with Claude-Joseph Vernet, whose influence appears in his landscape views. After a stay in Rome, during which he was admitted to the Academy of St. Luke, he moved to Naples, where he made nocturnal views of Mount Vesuvius in eruption, producing many popular variations.

HENDRIK VOOGD
(Amsterdam, 1766 – Rome, 1839)

Dutch painter. After attending the Amsterdam Communal Academy of Design he went to Rome on a grant and met landscapists and history painters. In 1808 he opened a sort of painting school and was one of the landscapists from the Low Countries most in demand in Rome, where his style showed signs of early Romanticism. He was also involved in lithography and received numerous official recognitions.

ROBERT WALTER WEIR
(New Rochelle, 1803 – New York, 1889)

American landscape painter. He studied with J.W. Jarvis and Pietro Benvenuti in Florence; upon his return to New York he became a member of the National Academy and taught at the U.S. Military Academy at West Point for forty-two years. His works include *The Landing of Henry Hudson* (page 219).

KARL FREDERICH HEINRICH WERNER
(Weimar, 1808 – Leipzig, 1894)

German painter of architecture and landscapes, lithographer and watercolorist. After attending the Leipzig Academy (of which he later became professor) he continued his studies in Munich and Italy, where he spent twenty years. He often traveled to England and visited Spain and the East. He exhibited in London, once at the Royal Academy and often at the Water Colour Society, of which he became a member.

BENJAMIN WEST
(Springfield, Pennsylvania, 1738 – London, 1820)

American historical painter active in England. In 1760 he went to Rome, where he took lessons from Anton Raphael Mengs; he became a member of the academies of Bologna, Florence, and Parma. Considered one of the leading history painters in England, he was nominated painter to the court of George III. In 1792, following the death of Sir Joshua Reynolds, he was elected second president of the Royal Academy in London.

ANTOINE JOSEPH WIERTZ
(Dinant, 1806 – Brussels, 1865)

Belgian painter and sculptor. He attended the Antwerp Academy and studied classical painting in Rome. He became famous for his enormous historical and religious canvases, most of all for paintings full of violent and bloody scenes, with precise details and luministic effects creating a surreal atmosphere. He moved to Brussels in 1848, where he set up a large atelier.

CHARLES WILD
(London, 1781–1835)

English painter and architectural designer. He was active most of all in churches in England, Belgium, Germany, and France. Some of his watercolors are preserved in the National Gallery of Dublin, the British Museum, and the Victoria and Albert Museum in London, the latter including *Fonthill Abbey* (see page 26).

FRANZ XAVER WINTERHALTER
(Menzenschwand, 1805 – Frankfurt, 1873)

German portrait painter. He began working in Munich as a lithographer in 1823; he then made portraits at the court of Karlsruhe and, in 1834, in Paris. He moved to London where he became the favorite painter of the upper middle class.

JOSEPH WRIGHT OF DERBY
(Derby, 1734–1797)

English painter. He trained in London and did almost all of his work in Derby, one of the first centers of the industrial revolution, where he found space for his passion for scientific research. He created a highly distinctive style of painting in which a violent chiaroscuro, usually the result of artificial lighting, illuminates a scientific undertaking, such as *An Experiment on a Bird in the Air Pump* (page 316). He also made landscapes, portraits, and mythological scenes.

Bibliography

Romanticism has been the subject of a vast number of books. The works listed here include artist biographies, exhibition catalogs, general overviews, and specialized studies that should be relatively easy to find in libraries or bookstores.

Andrews, Keith. *The Nazarenes; a Brotherhood of German Painters in Rome*. Oxford: Clarendon Press, 1964.

Boime, Albert. *Art in an Age of Bonapartism, 1800–1815*. Chicago: University of Chicago Press, 1990.

Brookner, Anita. *Romanticism and Its Discontents*. New York: Farrar, Straus and Giroux, 2000.

Brown, David Blayney. *Romanticism*. London, New York: Phaidon, 2001.

Butlin, Martin, and Evelyn Joll. *The Paintings of J.M.W. Turner*. New Haven: Yale University Press, 1984.

Conisbee, Philip. *Painting in Eighteenth-century France*. Ithaca, NY: Cornell University Press, 1981.

Craske, Matthew. *Art in Europe, 1700–1830*. Oxford, New York: Oxford University Press, 1997.

Deuchar, Stephen. *Noble Exercise: The Sporting Ideal in Eighteenth-century British Art*. New Haven: Yale Center for British Art, 1982.

Driscoll, John Paul. *All That Is Glorious Around Us: Paintings from the Hudson River School*. Ithaca: Cornell University Press, 1997.

Frank, Mitchell Benjamin. *German Romantic Painting Redefined: Nazarene Tradition and the Narratives of Romanticism*. Burlington, VT: Ashgate, 2001.

Gaunt, William. *Bandits in a Landscape: A Study of Romantic Painting from Caravaggio to Delacroix*. New York: Studio Publications, 1937.

Guégan, Stéphane; Pomarède, Vincent; Prat, Louis-Antoine. *Théodore Chassériau, 1819–1856: The Unknown Romantic*. New York: Metropolitan Museum of Art; New Haven: Yale University Press, 2002.

Honour, Hugh. *Romanticism*. London: Allen Lane, 1979.

Lister, Raymond. *British Romantic Painting*. Cambridge, New York: Cambridge University Press, 1989.

Marchetti, Francesca Castria, ed. *American Painting*. New York: Watson-Guptill, 2002.

Nicholson, Kathleen. *Turner's Classical Landscapes: Myth and Meaning*. Princeton: Princeton University Press, 1990.

Noon, Patrick. *Crossing the Channel: British and French Painting in the Age of Romanticism*. New York: Harry N. Abrams, 2003.

Norman, Geraldine. *Biedermeier Painting, 1815–1848: Reality Observed in Genre, Portrait, and Landscape*. New York: Thames and Hudson, 1987.

Porterfield, Todd. *The Allure of Empire: Art in the Service of French Imperialism, 1798–1836*. Princeton: Princeton University Press, 1998.

Rosenblum, Robert. *Transformations in Late Eighteenth Century Art*. Princeton: Princeton University Press, 1967.

Sabine, Rewald. *Caspar David Friedrich: Moonwatchers*. New York: Metropolitan Museum of Art; New Haven: Yale University Press, 2001.

Vaughan, William. *Romanticism and Art*. London, New York: Thames and Hudson, 1994.

---, et al. *Caspar David Friedrich, 1774–1840: Romantic Landscape Painting in Dresden*. London: Tate Gallery, 1972

Wood, Gillen D'Arcy. *The Shock of the Real: Romanticism and Visual Culture, 1760–1860*. New York: Palgrave, 2001.

Index of names and places

Numbers in *italics* refer to illustrations (names of artists and locations of museums).

Abildgaard, Nicolai Abraham 14, 37, 246, *249*, 379
Adam Adolphe 356
Agasse, Jacques Laurent 19, *212*, 379
Agliè *112*
Agneni, Eugenio *137*, 379
Agricola, Filippo 59, *164*, 379
Ahlborn, Auguste-Wilhelm-Julius 81, *94*, 379
Aix-en-Provence *109*
Ajaccio 40
Alaux, Jean 139, *142*, 379
Albert of Saxe-Coburg 74, 75, 77, 117, 308
Alexander, grand duke of Russia 285
Alfieri, Vittorio 346
Algiers 199
Ali-Ben Hamet, Caliph 207
Amercoeur 46
Amerling, Friedrich von 139, *149*, 379
Amiens *254, 360*
Ammirato, Scipione 111
Amsterdam *286*
Anacreon 96
Appiani, Andrea *44, 61*, 379
Appiani, Andrea, Junior *354*, 379
Archer, Archibald *304*, 380
Arcole, 40, 43
Ariosto, Ludovico 326, 332, 341
Arnim, Achim von 228
Arthaber, Rudolf von 149
Audubon, John James 214
Augustus 192, 193
Aunet, Léonie d' 265, 283
Autun *80, 115, 183, 279*

Baculard d'Arnaud, François-Thomas 327
Bagetti, Giuseppe Pietro *276*, 285, *289*, 380
Baltimore *136, 369*
Balzac, Honoré de 326
Banks, Sir Joseph 314
Barberi, Michelangelo 285
Barbizon 20, 285, 299, 358, 365
Barras, Paul 40
Barrias, Félix-Joseph *80*, 81
Bartolini, Lorenzo 157, *167*, 190, 380
Basel 159
Basoli, Antonio *314*
Baudelaire, Charles 12, 59, 207, 247, 263, 312, 326, 358
Bayeux *82, 86*
Beatrice di Tenda 240
Beauharnais, Hortense de 305
Beckford, William 13, 26
Belley, Jean-Baptiste 60
Bellini, Gentile 194
Bellini, Vincenzo 346, 347
Belluno *210*
Bendz, Wilhelm *145, 301*, 380
Benoist, Marie-Guillemine *196*, 380
Benvenuti, Pietro *50, 53*, 380
Béranger, A. *40*, 41
Béranger, Pierre-Jean de 311
Berchet, Giovanni 119, 135
Bergamo *347, 361*
Berlin *13, 94, 103, 106, 146, 156, 158, 160, 231, 232, 235, 258, 264, 268, 284, 346*
Berlioz, Hector 247
Bertin, Louis François 19
Bezzuoli, Giuseppe *110, 355*, 380
Bianchini, Antonio 156, 157
Biard, François-Auguste *226*, 265, *283*, *310*, 380
Bindesbøll, Gottlieb 153
Bingham, George Caleb *227*, 380
Birmingham *108, 157, 252*
Blake, William 15, *246, 252*, 327, *329*, 380
Blanchard, Jean-Pierre 322
Blechen, Karl *211*, 380
Blondel, Merry-Joseph 83, 381
Blunk, Detlef Conrad 139, *152*, 381
Boccaccio, Giovanni 137
Boccaccio, Giuseppe *179*, 381
Boilly, Louis-Léopold 16, *120, 302, 357*, 381
Boisselier, Antoine-Félix *288*, 381
Boleyn, Anne 115, 351
Bologna *88, 240, 314, 315*, 346, 350, *351*
Bommer, Caroline 146, 233, 267
Bonaparte, Caroline (Murat) 17, 49, 195, 197
Bonaparte, Elisa (Baciocchi) 49, 53
Bonaparte, Joseph 300
Bonaparte, Louis 305
Bonaparte, Pauline (Borghese) 45, 49, 349
Bonheur, Rosa 20, 359, *366*, 367, 381
Bonn *103*
Bonpland, Aimé 214
Bordeaux *131*
Bossoli, Carlo *119*
Bossuet, Jacques-Bénigne 192
Botzaris, Marco 195
Bouvier, Augustus Jules *356*, 381
Bowood 73
Boydell, John 327
Bradford *265*
Brentano, Bettina (von Arnim) 95
Brentano, Clemens Maria 156
Brescia *135, 187, 293, 320*
Breton, Jules 20, *359*
Bristol 237, 241, *264*
Briullov, Karl Pavlovich 71, 81, *98*, 346, 381
Brown, Ford Madox *157*
Browning, Robert 157
Bruni, Fyodor *87*, 381
Brussels *31, 176, 262*
Bruyas, Alfred 312, 359, 371
Bryant, William Cullen 236
Buondelmonti, Cece dei 111
Bürger, Gottfried August 327, 333
Burke, Edmund 13, 22, 24, 264
Buxton, Thomas 226
Byron, George Gordon 18, 19, 73, 80, 119, 125, 131, 194, 195, 198, 208, 327, 336, 352

Cabanel, Alexandre *345*, 373, 381
Caffi, Ippolito 19, 194, *210*, 285, *297*, 381
Cairo 52, 121
Cambridge *172*
Canella, Carlo 285
Canella, Giuseppe 285, *293*, 381
Canova, Antonio 18, *23*, 41, *45*, *53*, 67, 148, *176*, 185, 331, 382
Capponi, Pier 110
Caravaggio, Michelangelo Merisi da 180
Carnevali, Giovanni 16, *361*, 382
Caroline of Brunswick 67, 68
Cartellier, Pierre 306
Carus, Karl Gustav 228, *235*, 265, 274, 382
Caserta *323*
Catlin, George 214, *221*, 223, 382
Chabert, Carlotta 76, 88
Chambéry 82
Champfleury (Jules Fleury-Husson) 312
Chantilly *195, 203*
Chapelle, Madeleine 142
Charlemagne 41, 42, 47, 102, 202, 240, 341
Charles VIII of France 110
Charles X of France 80, 103, 109, 119, 132, 176, 177, 182, 306
Charpentier, Constance Marie 247, *254*, 382
Chartres *247*
Chassériau, Théodore *78*, *100*, 101, 194, 195, *206*, *207*, 242, 382
Chateaubriand, François-René de 19, 81, 176, 194, 214, 217, 220, 322, 327
Chateauroux *330*
Chatelinau, Jacques 65
Chernetsov, Nikanor *290*, 382
Chingford 175
Chios 16, 130
Cholet *65*, *118*
Chopin, Frédérich 15, 18, 311
Church, Frederic Edwin *215*, 284
Cianfanelli, Nicola *315*, *340*
Cibot, Édouard 115, 382
Cicognara, Leopoldo 67
Ciseri, Antonio 347
Clarke, Alphonse 156
Clésinger, Auguste *373*, 382
Cleveland *18*, *284*
Coalbrookdale 25, 318
Coburg *28*
Cogniet, Léon 16, *18*, *181*, 382
Cole, Thomas 19, 81, 103, *116*, 215, *224*, *225*, 236, 265, *282*, 284, *294*, 326, *338*, 383
Compiègne *188*
Constable, John 16, 284, *295*, *296*, 383
Cooper, James Fenimore 215, 224, *326*
Cope, Charles West *228*
Copenhagen *41*, *72*, *141*, *144*, 145, 152, *153*, 228, 287, *301*, *310*

Corday, Charlotte 31
Cornelius, Peter 156, *160*, *162*, 383
Cornienti, Cherubino 19, *209*, 383
Corot, Jean-Baptiste-Camille 20, 242, 298, 358, *360*, *368*, 383
Constantinople 194, 364
Cottin, Marie-Sophie 334
Couder, Auguste 339, 383
Courbet, Gustave *20*, 301, *312*, 313, 358, *359*, 369, *370*, *371*, 375, 383
Court, Joseph-Désiré *344*, 383
Couture, Thomas 81, *99*, 101, 383
Cuenot, Urbain 370

Dadd, Richard 229, *245*, 383
D'Agincourt, Seroux 67
Daguerre, Louis-Jacques-Mandé 315
Dahl, Johan Christian 265, *281*, 384
Danby, Francis *222*, *228*, 229, *237*, *241*, *264*, 265, 384
D'Annunzio, Gabriele 364
Dante Alighieri 15, 80, 137, 157, 161, 252, 326, 327, 342
Darwin, Erasmus 222, 237
Daubigny, Charles-François 20, 285, *299*, 384
Daumier, Honoré 16, 315, 374
David, Giovanni 349
David, Jacques-Louis 14, 17, 18, 23, 29, *31*, 32, *34*, *42*, *48*, 53, 534, 57, 58, *69*, 102, 141, 167, 196, 212, 254, 264, 339, 384
D'Azeglio, Massimo 16, 103, *110*, 285, *291*, *334*, 354, 384
Decamps, Alexandre-Gabriel 19, 194, *195*, *242*, 285, 384
Degas, Edgar *375*, 384
De Gubernatis, Giovanni Battista *269*, 384
Delacroix, Eugène 15, 16, *18*, 19, 58, 78, 80, *81*, 99, 100, 101, 119, *130*, *131*, *132*, 195, *198*, *199*, *205*, 206, 207, 214, 215, *220*, 242, 247, *253*, 326, 327, *343*, 358, 366, 370, 375, 384
Delamare, Delphine 344
Delaroche, Paul (Hippolyte Delaroche) 16, 41, *57*, 93, 96, *102*, *114*, 177, *189*, 306, 307, 327, 358, *362*, 363, 384
Delavigne, Casimir 114, 327
Denon, Dominique Vivant 103, 194, 202
Derby *216*, 316
Deroy, Émile 59
Desaix, Louis-Charles-Antoine 33, 61
Desgoffe, Alexandre *298*, 385
Dickens, Charles 171, 311
Dieppe *105*
Dijon *277*
Domenichini, Girolamo *352*
Donizetti, Gaetano 115, 346, 347, 351, 352
Doppelmayr, Friedrich Wilhelm *138*
Dortmund *289*
Dresden 146, *178*, 228, 232, 265, 272, 274, 281
Drölling, Martin *140*, 385
Drouet, Juliette 91
Dublin *35*, 129
Dupré, Giovanni *190*, 347, 385
Dupré, Louis *322*, 385
Durand, Asher B. 215, 228, *236*, 385
Dürer, Albrecht 156
Duseigneur, Jehan (Jean-Bernard Duseigneur) *341*, 385
Düsseldorf *162*, *229*
Dyce, William *163*, 177, 385

Eastlake, Charles Lock *108*, *336*, 385
Eckersberg, C.W. 139, *141*, *287*, 385
Edinburgh 58
Edward III of England 117, 280
Edward IV of England 114
Edward V of England 114
Eichrodt, Ludwig 139
Elgin, Thomas Bruce, earl of 300, 304
Erizzo, Paolo 209
Evreux *240*
Eylau 51

Fabre, François-Xavier-Pascal 53
Favelli, Stefania 349
Ferdinand I of Austria 70
Ferdinand I of Naples 324
Ferdinand II of Naples 315, 323
Ferdinand VII of Spain 251
Fergola, Salvatore *309*, *323*, *324*, 385
Ferrara 352
Field, John 15
Fieramosca, Ettore 354
Flandrin, Hippolyte 80, *90*, 247, *257*, 385
Flandrin, Paul 201, 298
Flaubert, Gustave 344
Florence 16, *36*, *50*, *89*, *110*, *111*, 137, 157, 161, *165*, *166*, 182, *190*, 301, *315*, *326*, *340*, *342*, *346*, 347, 375
Fontainebleau 20, 285, 358, 365
Fonthill 13, 26, 103
Foscolo, Ugo 119, 135
Fouqué, Friedrich de La Motte 146
Francesca da Rimini 252, 327, 346
Francis I of Naples 309
Francis I of France 109
Francis II of France 109
Frankfurt *159*, *248*
Franklin, Benjamin 317
Franque, Jean-Pierre *54*, 385
Frederick Barbarossa 110
Frederick of Saxony-Gotha-Altenburg 28
Frederick of Holland 94
Frederick William III of Prussia 211, 259
Friedrich, Caspar David *13*, 15, 20, 103, *107*, 139, *146*, 147, 176, *178*, 179, 228, 230, *232*, *233*, *234*, 235, 247, *258*, 259, *264*, 265, *266*, *267*, *268*, *270*, 271, *272*, *274*, 275, 281, *284*, *289*, 386
Fromentin, Eugène 19, 326
Fuseli, Henry 14, *15*, 23, *27*, 37, 229, *246*, 247, *248*, 327, *328*, 385
Füssli, Johann Heinrich. *See* Fuseli, Henry

Gandy, Joseph Michael *303*, 386
Garneray, Louis 194
Garrick, David 22
Gassies, Jean-Bruno *279*, 386
Gaudar de La Verdinne, Augustin-Alphonse *330*, 386
Gauss, Karl Friedrich 315
Gautier, Théophile 81, 93, 247, 326, 341, 356
Genoa *176*
George IV of Great Britain 19, 68, 212
Georget, Étienne 247, 253
Gérard, François *63*, *86*, *176*, 254, *327*, 386
Geremei, Bonifacio de' 350
Géricault, Théodore 15, 16, 18, 58, 118, *123*, 126, *128*, 132, 247, *253*, *255*, 358, 386
Gérôme, Jean-Léon 81, *93*, *96*, *192*, 386
Giambologna (Giovanni Bologna) 307
Giotto 156, 157
Giovanni delle Bande Nere (Giovanni de' Medici) 108
Girodet-Trioson, Anne-Louis 18, 19, *23*, *32*, *33*, 41, *60*, *64*, *65*, 119, *121*, 214, *217*, 265, *277*, 327, 386
Glaize, Auguste-Barthélémy 358, 359
Glasgow *279*
Gleyre, Charles 247, *263*, 386
Glover, John *223*
Goethe, Johann Wolfgang von 12, 22, 95, 103, 228, 235, 246, 327
Gogol, Nikolai Vasilyevich 98
Gorizia *66*
Gosse, Nicolas *305*
Gounod, Charles 311
Goya y Lucientes, Francisco *15*, 16, 58, *59*, 118, *122*, 246, *247*, *250*, *251*, 386
Granet, François-Marius *29*, 102, 387
Graziano d'Asti 354
Greuze, Jean-Baptiste 46
Grimm, Jakob 228
Grimm, Wilhelm 228
Grisi, Carlotta 347, 356
Gros, Antoine-Jean 17, 18, 40, 41, *43*, *50*, *51*, *82*, 118, 120, 126, 387
Guardassoni, Alessandro *315*, 346, *351*, 387
Gudin, Théodore 118, *127*, 387
Guérin, Pierre Narcisse 17, 18, 41, 52, *118*, 119, 387
Guillemardet, Ferdinand 59

Halévy, Fromental 347
Hamann, Johann Georg 12
Hamburg *230*, *239*, *266*, *270*, *274*, *327*
Hamilton, Sir William 300
Handel, George Frideric 37
Hannibal 41, 42, 265, 278
Hansen, Constantin 139, *153*, 387
Hartford *224*
Harun el-Rashid 202
Hasenclever, Johann Peter *229*
Hauley, William 214, 216
Haussmann, Georges Eugène, Baron 358
Haydon, Benjamin Robert 139, *150*, 387
Hayez, Francesco 14, 16, 19, *20*, *40*, 41, *59*, 67, *70*, *76*, 81, 88, *102*, 119, *135*, *185*, *187*, 194, 208, 247, *260*, *331*, *335*, *347*, *349*, *353*, 387
Heidelberg 228
Heim, François-Joseph *306*, 387
Heine, Heinrich 356
Heirich, August 232
Hélène of Russia 322
Hemans, Felicia 338
Henry II of France 109, 112
Henry IV of France 49, 305
Henry VIII of England 115
Herder, Johann Gottfried 12, 103
Hervey Foster, Elizabeth 35
Hillerød *152*
Hoffmann, E. T. A. 229, 346
Homer 55, 80, 157, 327, 365
Howe, Elias 315
Hudson, Henry 215, 219
Hughes, Arthur *175*, 229, *239*, 387
Hugo, Victor 16, 194, 198, 326, 327, 339, 345, 358
Hull 226
Humboldt, Alexander von 211, 214
Hunt, William Holman 157, *174*, 387
Hutten, Ulrich von 107

Ingres, Jean-Auguste-Dominique 16, 17, *19*, 41, *46*, *47*, *55*, *58*, 59, 78, *79*, *80*, 96, 100, 139, 142, 156, 157, 165, 167, 177, *182*, *183*, 194, 195, *197*, *200*, 201, 207, 247, *256*, 257, 298, 306, 307, 326, 327, *332*, 370, 375, 388
Isabey, Jean-Baptiste *300*, 302
Isabey, Eugène *56*, 265, 283, 388

Jacquand, Claudius *326*, 327
Jaffa 50
Jal, Auguste 119
Jalabert, Charles-François 81, *369*
Jena 12, 50
Josephine 33, 40, 48, 62, 102, 104
Juvenal 99

Kant, Immanuel 22, 264
Karpenisi 195
Kersting, Georg Friedrich 139, *147*, *231*, 388
Kiel *147*
Kleist, Heinrich von 258
Klinger, Maximilian 12
Klopstock, Friedrich Gottlieb 12, 239
Knox, John *279*
Købke, Christen 139, *144*, 388
Koch, Joseph Anton 156, *161*, 388
Küchler, Albert 152
Kuhn, Karl Gottlob 178
Kussmaul, Adolf 139

Lamartine, Alphonse de 311
Lamertazzi, Imelda de' 350
Lami, Eugène 347
Lamme, Arie Johannes *311*

Landi, Gaspare *202*, 388
Landolt von Rech, Anna 246
Landseer, Edwin Henry *74*, *117*, *138*, *213*, 388
Langlois, Jérôme-Martin *82*, 388
Lapito, Louis-Auguste *360*, 388
Laurent, Jean-Antoine 102
Lavater, Johann Kaspar 246
Lawrence, Thomas *12*, *35*, 59, *68*, 388
Lefuel, Hector-Martin 305
Legnano 110
Lehmann, Henry 59
Leipzig 123, 246
Lenoir, Alexandre 14, 102, 300
Leo X 109
Leo XII 310
Leonardo da Vinci 137, 186, 343
Leopardi, Giacomo 166
Leopold II of Lorraine 190, 326, 340
Leprince, Auguste-Xavier *291*, 388
Leslie, Charles Robert 138, *139*
Lessing, Gottlieb Ephraim 12
Lessing, Karl Friedrich *103*
Lewis, John Frederick 194, *195*, *372*, 388
Liège 81, *370*
Lincoln, Abraham 215
Lindstroem, Carl Jakob 16
Linnell, John 327
Lipparini, Ludovico 67, *194*, 195, 388
Liszt, Franz 311
Liverpool *156*, 315
Lodi 40
London 14, *17*, 19, 22, 23, *25*, *26*, *41*, *45*, *73*, 74, *79*, *84*, *85*, *92*, *102*, *124*, *125*, *126*, 129, *138*, *139*, *150*, *157*, *168*, *169*, *170*, *173*, 174, *191*, *194*, *195*, 203, *204*, 214, 218, *222*, 226, *237*, *238*, *241*, *242*, *244*, *245*, 246, 247, *265*, *278*, 284, *295*, *296*, 301, *303*, *304*, 308, *314*, 315, *316*, *319*, *327*, *329*, *336*, *345*, *348*, *356*
Longhi, Giuseppe 40
Longinus 13
Longwood 40
Lorrain, Claude 84, 286
Louis XIII of France 182
Louis XV of France 300
Louis XVIII of France 103, 118, 215, 332
Louis d'Orleans 104
Louis Philippe of France 56, 99, 103, 132, 195, 199, 204, 205, 374
Louise of Prussia, Princess 94
Loutherbourg, Philippe Jacques de 22, 23, 25, 314, 318, 388
Loveno (Como) *59*
Lucca 111
Lucchini, Vincenzo *351*
Luther, Martin 107
Lyons *13*, 14, 188

Macchiavelli, Niccolò 110, 137
Macpherson, James 13, 55, 327
Madrid *122*, *215*, *250*, *251*, *282*, 300
Maffei, Andrea 353
Malfatti, Girolamo 76, 88
Mallet, Jean-Baptiste *105*, 389
Manchester *246*, 315
Manet, Édouard 359
Mantua 325
Manzoni, Alessandro 291, 326, 340
Marat, Jean-Paul 31
Marcotte, Charles 195, 200
Marengo 40, 61
Marguerite of Valois 109, 112
Maria, duchess of Leuchtenberg 190
Marie Louise, archduchess of Austria 40, 45, 139, 148, 179
Marilhat, Prosper 194
Marsigli, Filippo 80, *81*
Martens, Hans Ditlev Christian *310*, 389
Martin, John 15, *177*, *191*, 265, *280*, 389
Massimo, Carlo 161
Mayer, Constance 180
Mazzini, Giuseppe 14, 135
Medici, Alessandro de 355
Medici, Caterina de' 109
Medici, Cosimo I de' 355
Medici, Lorenzino de' 355
Medici Lenzoni, Carlotta 166
Mehmed II 209
Meissonier, Ernest *358*
Menzel, Adolf von 247, *261*, 389
Mérimée, Prosper 307
Messina 324
Metternich, Prince 70, 166
Metz 177, 180
Michelangelo Buonarroti 137, 183
Migliara, Giovanni *134*, 389
Milan 14, *20*, 40, 43, 44, *67*, *70*, 71, 97, 106, *119*, *134*, *167*, *185*, 240, *247*, *347*, *349*, 356
Millais, John Everett *156*, 157, *170*, *172*, *173*, 189, *244*, *345*, 389
Millet, Jean-François *20*, 359
Milton, John 15, 327
Minardi, Tommaso *36*, 139, 156, 157, *186*, 389
Minneapolis *15*, *64*
Missolonghi 119, 131, 195
Moitessier, Ines (Marie-Clotilde-Ines de Foucauld) 58, 79
Moistessier, Sigisbert 79
Molteni, Giuseppe 67, *148*, 349, 389
Monet, Claude 359
Montauban 55, *142*, 177, *182*
Montenotte 40
Montepulciano *351*
Montgolfier, Jacques Étienne 322
Montgolfier, Joseph Michel 322
Monti, Vincenzo 164
Monti Perticari, Costanza 164
Montpellier *345*, *358*, *371*
Moreau, Gustave 81, *101*, 389
Morelli, Domenico *363*, 389
Moriani, Napoleone 351
Mornay, Charles de 205
Morrocchesi, Antonio 346
Morse, Samuel F.B. 315
Moscow *71*, *143*
Mozart, Wolfgang Amadeus 346
Mulready, William 138, *139*
Munich *145*, *157*, *160*, 163, *228*, *261*, *281*
Murat, Joachim 50, 122, 197
Murray, John 73
Musaeus 92
Musset, Alfred de 40, 355
Mussini, Luigi 17, 157, *165*, 389

Nadar (Félix Tournachon) 315
Nantes 65, *184*
Naples 24, 34, 71, 76, *81*, 133, *202*, 244, *285*, 292, 300, *309*, 315, 323, *324*, *363*, 375
Napoleon Bonaparte 16, 17, 18, 19, 22, 33, 40, 41, 42, 43, 44, 45, 46, 47, 48, 49, 50, 51, 52, 53, 54, 55, 56, 57, 59, 81, 102, 103, 118, 121, 122, 123, 124, 125, 143, 148, 194, 202, 228, 278, 300, 314, 327
Napoleon III 192, 195, 305, 315, 359
Nathan, Mendel Levin 141
Nathanson, Bella 141
Nathanson, Hanna 141
Navarino 194
Navez, François-Joseph *176*
Nelson, Horatio 40, 124, 300
Nerval, Gérard de (Gérard Labrunie) 327
Neuchatel *118*
New Haven *12*, *38*, *177*, *280*, *318*, *372*
Newton, Isaac 320
New York *58*, 215, *220*, *225*, *227*, *236*, 285, 294, 326, *375*
Nicholas I of Russia 285
Nicholas II of Russia 190
Nodier, Charles 347
Noel, Alexis *265*
Norbin, Sébastien-Louis *322*
Nottingham *163*
Nourrit, Adolphe 347
Novalis (Friedrich Leopold von Hardenberg) 12, 13, 15, 103, 228
Nuremberg *138*

Odorici, Federico 293
Oldham *228*
Orléans *253*
Orombello, Michele 240
Ossian 18, 33, 55, 80, 327
Ostra, reserve of 272
Ottawa *218*
Overbeck, Friedrich 14, 59, 156, 157, *158*, *160*, 177, 389
Ovid 83
Oxford 170, *174*, *175*, 244

Pacini, Amacilia 71
Pacini, Giovanni 347, 349
Pacini, Giovannina 71
Pagliarini, Giovanni *350*, 389
Palagi, Pelagio 81, *88*, *240*, *320*, 321, 390
Palermo 324
Palizzi, Filippo *364*, 390
Papety, Dominique *119*
Parga 135
Paris 14, 17, *18*, *19*, *20*, *23*, *24*, *30*, *32*, *33*, 41, *42*, *47*, *48*, *50*, *51*, 56, *57*, *59*, *62*, *63*, *69*, *78*, *80*, *91*, *93*, *99*, *100*, *101*, 102, 104, *114*, *119*, *120*, *123*, *127*, *128*, *130*, *132*, 137, *140*, 167, *177*, *180*, 181, *189*, *192*, 193, *196*, *197*, *198*, *199*, 201, 204, *206*, 211, 212, 214, 215, *217*, *223*, *243*, *255*, *256*, *257*, *263*, *283*, *291*, *298*, *299*, *300*, 301, *302*, *305*, *306*, *307*, *310*, *311*, *312*, 315, 326, 327, 330, 331, *332*, *333*, *338*, *339*, *341*, *343*, 347, 356, *358*, *359*, *360*, *365*, *366*, *368*, 371, *373*, 374, 375
Parma *148*, *179*
Parry, Edward William 270
Pasini, Alberto 194
Paton, Joseph Noel 229
Pavia *208*, *325*, *353*
Paxton, Joseph Noel 229
Penn, William 214
Perrault, Charles 243
Perrot, Jules 356
Perticari, Giulio 164
Perugia 186
Petipa, Lucien 347
Petipa, Marius 347
Petrarch 137
Pforr, Franz 14, 156, 158, *159*, 177, 390
Philadelphia *214*, *219*, 221, 294, *317*
Phillips, Thomas *73*, 390
Pia de' Tolomei 346
Picou, Henri-Pierre 81
Piranesi, Giovanni Battista 23, 27
Pistoia 37, *355*
Pitloo, Anton Sminck *292*, 390
Pittsburgh *368*
Pius VII 40, 48, 310
Planché, James Robinson 117
Plautus 64
Podesti, Francesco *112*, 390
Poe, Edgar Allan 157, 247
Pollard, James *314*, 315
Pollastrini, Enrico *346*
Pompeii 98, 100
Portici 315, 323
Possagno *23*
Potocki, Count Stanislaw 34
Pourtalès-Gorgier, James-Alexandre de 307
Poussin, Nicolas 99, 101
Poznan *362*
Pradier, James (Jean-Jacques Pradier) *91*, 390
Préault, Auguste *247*
Price, Uvedale 22
Proudhon, Pierre-Joseph 313
Proud'hon, Pierre-Paul 58, *62*, 177, *180*, 390
Provins 298
Puccini, Niccolò 355
Puccini, Tommaso 37

Raeburn, Henry *58*
Raphael Santi 17, 19, 34, 47, 59, 109, 156, 157, 160, 163, 164, 177, 182, 186, 197
Raynal, Guillaume 60
Regulus, Marcus Atilius 17
Rennes *181*, *326*
Révoil, Pierre *13*, 14, 102, *109*, 390
Reynolds, Sir Joshua 23, 59, *348*, 390
Ribe *287*
Richard, Fleury 14, 102, *104*, 109, 229, 243, 390
Richard III of England 114
Rivoli 40
Robert, Hubert *30*, *300*, *302*, 391
Robert, Léopold *118*
Roberts, David *194*, *308*, 391
Robespierre, Maximilien Marie Isidore de 40
Romani, Felice 351, 352
Rome 14, 16, 17, 23, 27, 28, 29, 34, 66, 71, 72, 87, 909, 98, 99, 100, *102*, 108, 136, 139, 141, 142, 152, 153, *154*, 156, 157, 161, *164*, 165, *186*, 195, 200, 203, 204, 246, 285, 286, 287, 288, *292*, 310, *322*, 330, 342, 362, *364*, 375
Romney, George 327
Rossetti, Dante Gabriel 157, *168*, *169*, 170, 391
Rossetti, Michael 157
Rossini, Giachino 311, 347
Rotterdam *161*
Rouen *344*
Rousseau, Jean-Jacques 12, 18, 300
Rousseau, Théodore 20, 285, 358, *365*, 391
Roustam 50
Rubens, Peter Paul 34, 198
Rudolf I of Hapsburg 159
Rügen 267
Runge, Philipp Otto 228, *230*, *239*, 391
Ruskin, Effie 173
Ruskin, John 157, 168, 173, 174, 238, 326

Sabatelli, Francesco *89*, 391
Sabatelli, Giuseppe *111*, 391
Sabatelli, Luigi *37*, 391
Sabatier, Madame 373
Sacchi, Defendente 350
Sacchi, Gaetano 325
Saint-Étienne *90*
St.-George, Vernoy de 356
Saint Helena 40, 41, 56
Saint-Jean, Simon *188*, 391
Saint Louis 221
St. Petersburg *87*, *98*, *104*, *190*, *233*, *234*, *285*, *290*
Salisbury 296
Samoilova, Yulia 71, 349
Sand, George 18, 215, 367
Santarelli, Emilio 53
Sappho 80, 82
Sardanapalus 198
Savonarola, Girolamo 110
Savoy, Emmanuel Philibert of 112
Savoy, house of 112, 113
Savoy, Maria Adelaide of 113
Schadow, Friedrich von 156, *157*, 177
Scheffer, Ary 242, 311, *327*, *333*, 391
Schelling, Friedrich Wilhelm 12, 235, 346
Schick, Gottlieb 28, 391
Schiller, Friedrich von 12, 284
Schinkel, Karl Friedrich *14*, 81, 94, 95, *103*, *106*, 211, *346*, 392
Schlegel, August 12
Schlegel, Friedrich 12, 17, 156, 177, 228, 255
Schneitzhoeffer, Jean 347
Schnorr von Carolsfeld, Julius *156*, *228*
Schnorr von Carolsfeld, Ludwig 156
Schubert, Franz 327
Schweinfurt *211*
Scott, Sir Walter 115, 173, 279
Scribe, Eugène 347
Serni, Angelica 87
Sèvres 19, *40*
Shakespeare, William 14, 15, 80, 157, 228, 244, 326, 327, 328, 329, 335, 345
Siddons, Sarah 348
Sloane, Sir Hans 300
Smargiassi, Gabriele *285*
Smith, William 214
Soane, Sir John 303
Sødring, Frederik 144
Sommariva, Angelo 176
Spartacus 97
Spenser, Edmund 229
Spini, Anastasia 361
Spini, Pietro Andrea 361
Spitzweg, Carl 139, *145*, 392
Staël, Germaine de 194, 307, 333
Stapleton 237, 241
Stendhal (Marie Henri Beyle) 58, 176, 284, 326
Stephenson, George 315
Stockholm *16*, *249*
Strasbourg 103
Sue, Eugène 344

Tacitus 37
Taglioni, Marie 347, 356
Talleyrand, Charles Maurice de 49
Tasso, Torquato 331
Tenerani, Pietro 156, *166*, 392
Tennyson, Alfred 238
Tetschen 178
Thomas, Antoine-Jean-Baptiste *133*, 392
Thomas, Joseph 329
Thorvaldsen, Bertel *41*, 72, 152, 310
Thun-Honenstein, Franz Anton 178
Tieck, Ludwig 12, 13
Tischbein, Wilhelm 22
Titian 76, 331
Tominz, Giuseppe *66*, 392
Tominz, Francesco 66
Tosio, Paolo 320
Toulouse *96*, *205*
Trafalgar, battle of 40, 124
Trécourt, Francesco *325*
Trécourt, Giacomo *208*, 325, 392
Tremezzo *335*
Trent *76*
Trieste *194*, *350*
Trollope, Frances 214
Troyes *22*
Troyon, Constant 20, 285
Trumbull, John 23, *38*, *39*, 392
Turin 112, 137, 269, 276, 289, 301, 334, 354
Turner, Joseph Mallord William *17*, 81, *84*, *85*, *92*, 119, *124*, *125*, *265*, *278*, 284, 314, 315, *318*, *319*, 392
Tuscaloosa *294*

Uberti, Asino degli 111
Uberti, Farinata degli 111

Vafflard, Pierre Antoine Augustin 229, *240*, 392
Valenciennes, Pierre-Henri de 22
Valentina of Milan (Valentina Visconti) 102, 104
Vanderlyn, John *214*, 215
Van Dyck, Anton 34
Van Hamburgh, Isaac 213
Vassalli, Carlo 67
Veit, Philip 156
Vela, Vincenzo 80, *97*, 392
Venetsianov, Aleksey 143
Venice *67*, 194, *297*, 325, *331*, 353, 355
Verdi, Giuseppe 347
Vernet, Claude-Joseph 20, *22*
Vernet, Horace (Emil-Jean-Horace Vernet) 19, *72*, *126*, *136*, 176, *184*, 195, *203*, *204*, 322, 327, 358, 392
Vernet, Louise 189
Veronese, Paolo 99
Versailles *43*, *52*, *53*, *54*, *56*, *60*, *61*, 103, *121*, *133*, *207*, 332, *357*
Vesuvius, Mount 22, 24, 98, 133
Victor Emmanuel II 14, 113
Victoria, Queen 59, 74, 77, 117, 171, 213, 308
Vienna *44*, *149*, 156, 158, 301
Viganò, Salvatore 347
Vigée-Lebrun, Elisabeth-Louise 196
Villa, Andrea *326*
Villeneuve, Juliette de 69
Visconti, Ermes 346
Visconti, Filippo Maria 240
Visconti, Louis 305
Vogel, Ludwig 156
Vogel von Vogelstein, Carl Christian *342*, 393
Volaire, Pierre-Jacques 22, *24*, 393
Volta, Alessandro 314, 315
Volterra 347
Voogd, Hendrik *286*, 393

Wackenroder, Wilhelm Heinrich 12, 13
Walpole, Sir Horace 13, 103
Warren, Joseph 38
Warsaw *34*
Washington, D.C. *116*, *214*, *215*, *221*, *288*
Washington, George 38
Waterloo, battle of 40, 41, 84, 125, 126
Watt, James 314, 315
Weber, Karl Maria von 229, 346
Weber, Wilhelm Eduard 315
Wedgwood, Josiah 314
Weimar *14*, *107*
Weir, Robert Walter 215, *219*, 393
Wellington, Arthur Wellesley, duke of 41
Werner, Karl Frederich Heinrich *154*, 393
West, Benjamin 23, *214*, *218*, *317*, 327, 393
White Cloud 221
Wiertz, Antoine Joseph *262*, 393
Wild, Charles *26*, 393
Wilkie, David *41*
William I of Württemberg 201
Wimar, Carl *215*
Winckelmann, Johann Joachim 13, 27, 67
Windsor *68*, *74*, 75, *77*, *117*, *212*, *213*, *308*
Winterhalter, Franz Xaver 59, *77*, 393
Winterthur *253*, *267*
Wolfe, General James 218
Wordsworth, William 265
Wright of Derby (Joseph Wright) 214, *216*, 314, *316*, 393
Wüest, Johann Heinrich *22*

Young, Edward 15

Zelentsov, Kapiton *143*
Zurich *15*, *22*, *27*, *246*, *328*

Photographic references

Accademia Carrara, Bergamo
Archivio d'Arte Pedicini, Naples
Archivio Electa/Mondadori, Milan
Art Gallery and Museum, Kelvingrove, Glasgow
Artothek, Weilheim
Fiorenzo Cantalupi, Pavia
Cassa di Risparmio di Bologna, Bologna
Civico Museo Revoltella—Galleria d'Arte Moderna, Trieste
Dulwich Picture Gallery, London
Ursula Edelmann, Frankfurt
Galleria Civica d'Arte Moderna, Turin
Mario Gatti, Bologna
Harvard University Art Museum, Cambridge
© Hermitage 2003, St. Petersburg
John Soane's Museum, London
Kunsthalle, Hamburg
Kunsthistorisches Museum, Vienna
Kunstmuseum, Ribe
Musée Baron Gérard, Bayeux
Musée d'Art et Histoire/Studio Golder, Cholet
Musée des Beaux-Arts, Orléans
Musée des Beaux-Arts de Lyon/Studio Basset, Lyons
Musée des Beaux-Arts de Rennes/Adélaide Beaudoin, Rennes
Musée d'Evreux Ancien Evêché, Evreux
Musée Fabre/Frédéric Jaulmes, Montpellier
Musée Granet/Bernard Terlay, Aix-en-Provence
Musée Rolin, Autun
Musées Royaux des Beaux-Arts de Belgique/Cussac, Brussels
Musei Civici, Pavia
Museo del Teatro alla Scala, Milan
Museo Poldi Pezzoli, Milan
© Museo Thyssen-Bornemisza, Madrid
Museum and Art Gallery, Birmingham
Nationalmuseum med Prins Eugens Waldemarsudde, Stockholm
Ernani Orcorte, Turin
Oskar Reinhart Sammlung/Museum, Winterthur
Photothèque des musées de la ville de Paris/Habouzit, Paris
Rabatti e Domingie, Florence
Réunion des Musées Nationaux/A. Danvers/Le Mage/D. Arnaudet/J. Schor/Bulloz/H. Lewandowski/G. Blot/R.G. Ojeda/C. Jean/L'hoir/J.G. Berizzi/D. Chenot Florence, Paris
Saporetti, Milan
Scala, Florence
Giuseppe Schiavinotto, Rome
Staatliche Kunstammlungen Dresden, Dresden
Staatliche Museen zu Berlin-Preussischer Kulturbesitz Nationalgalerie/J.P. Anders/Petersen/E.Walford/K. Göken, Berlin
Statens Museum for Kunst, Copenhagen
© Tate Gallery 2003, London
The Bridgeman Art Library/Archivi Alinari, Florence
The British Museum, London
The Fitzwilliam Museum, Cambridge
The National Gallery, London
The Philadelphia Museum of Art, Philadelphia
The Science Museum, London
The Wallace Collection, London
The Walters Art Museum, Baltimore
The Whitworth Art Gallery, Manchester
Victoria and Albert Museum, London
Wadsworth Atheneum Museum, Bequest of Alfred Smith, Hartford
Windsor, Royal Collection © 2003, Her Majesty Queen Elizabeth II

With gratitude to the following for permission to reproduce images:
Soprintendenza Speciale per il Polo Museale Fiorentino/Galleria degli Uffizi/Palazzo Pitti-Galleria dell'Accademia
Soprintendenza per il patrimonio storico artistico e demoetnoantropologico for the provinces of Milan, Bergamo, Como, Lecco, Lodi, Pavia, Sondrio, Varese/Pinacoteca di Brera, Milan
Soprintendenza per il patrimonio storico artistico e demoetnoantropologico of Parma and Piacenza/Galleria Nazionale
Soprintendenza per i Beni Artistici e Storici of Naples and its province/Museo di Capodimonte, Naples
Soprintendenza Speciale Arte Contemporanea: Rome, Galleria Nazionale di Arte Moderna

The editor regrets any errors or omissions.